DISPUTING THE FLY QUESTION

(*See History of the Moose, Plate 4*)

# FAVORITE FLIES
# AND THEIR HISTORIES

BY

MARY ORVIS MARBURY

WITH MANY REPLIES FROM PRACTICAL
ANGLERS TO INQUIRIES CONCERNING
HOW, WHEN, AND WHERE TO USE THEM

*ILLUSTRATED BY THIRTY-TWO COLORED PLATES OF FLIES*
*SIX ENGRAVINGS OF NATURAL INSECTS, AND EIGHT*
*REPRODUCTIONS OF PHOTOGRAPHS*

*FOREWORD BY SILVIO CALABI*

Manufactured in Hong Kong.
Color origination by Regent Publishing Services, Ltd.
Printed by Leefung-Asco Printers, Ltd.

ISBN: 1-55521-241-7

TO MY FATHER

## CHARLES FREDERICK ORVIS

I LOVINGLY AND GRATEFULLY PROFFER THIS RECORD OF
HIS INSTRUCTIONS TO ME REGARDING HIS FAVORITE
RECREATION, WITH THE HOPE THAT THE SAME
MAY BE USEFUL TO ALL WHO ARE FOND
OF THIS PLEASANT PASTIME, AND ESPE-
CIALLY TO THE MANY WHO HAVE
PROVED THEMSELVES HIS
FRIENDS, AND THERE-
FORE MINE

1892

# CONTENTS.

## PART I.

## PART II.

# LIST OF ILLUSTRATIONS.

## LIST OF ILLUSTRATIONS.

# "The most famous but one female angling author..."

That was how the *Fishing Gazette* headlined Mary Orvis Marbury's obituary when she died in 1914. As much as anything said or written about her in her lifetime, it signaled the place she occupied in sportfishing, for the "*most* famous" female author would be none other than the mysterious Dame Juliana Berners, who reputedly produced, in 1492, the first book on fishing. Since this beginning, women have played a small—in numbers—but important role in fly-fishing, and Mary Orvis likely ushered modern womanhood into not only the sport but also the business behind the sport. Today the path she blazed is being followed by luminaries like Joan Salvato Wulff and Maggie Merriman.

Mary was the first (of four—the others were boys) child of Charles F. Orvis and Laura Walker Orvis, of Manchester, Vermont. She was born in 1856, the year that marked the founding of The Orvis Company, which has survived and prospered mightily in Manchester to the present day. This is due in part to daughter Mary's direct efforts as a fly tier, businesswoman, author and editor. Mary wed a John Marbury in 1877, but the marriage didn't "take"; they separated and their only child died young.

The Orvises were apparently one of Manchester's "first families" in the second half of the 19th Century. Charles and his brother Franklin became notable entrepreneurs and hoteliers, and helped put their tiny home town on the map as a prime summer watering-hole for the well-to-do of New York, Philadephia and Boston. (The grand old Equinox House, which Franklin opened in 1853, and which later took over Charles's Orvis Hotel, next door, was totally refurbished and reopened to the public in 1984.)

Charles Orvis was one of those practical Yankee tinkerer-businessmen who helped make the New England reputation for mechanical innovation combined with high standards of quality. He invented the modern lightweight fly reel, and while he didn't come up with any similar breakthroughs in fly rods he and his company did much to make first-class rods widely available. In the Victorian Era fly-fishing became popular as a "refined" way to fish, and the modern merchandising triangle of manufacturer, publisher and consumer was established. It functioned just as it does today—small companies make tackle, the sporting press writes about it, and anglers buy it. Curiously, then—as now also—fishing flies were in short supply; or at least the sort of flies that were first, effective on trout and other gamefish, and second, recognized as such by anglers in general. Exotic materials for tying flies—ranging from polar bear hair to macaw plumes—were available, and in a great flurry of activity every region of America was busy developing its own fly patterns and its own names for flies that anglers in another watershed might know as something entirely different.

Into the breach stepped Mary Orvis. To assure her dad of a reliable source of flies tied to consistent standards, in 1876 she took over the company's commercial fly production. She had earlier shown considerable interest in fly-tying, so much that Charles, nobody's fool, had hired an expert "fly dresser" to come to Vermont from New York City to teach her all he knew. Mary's half-dozen tiers, all young women, worked upstairs in a white clapboard building on Union Street that still belongs to Orvis. At the time there were larger fly factories in America, but from this small one would come not only very fine flies but also the beginnings of the standardization that brought order to fly-pattern chaos.

This book, the first of many to be published about flies in America, began to take shape around 1890. Orvis wrote to anglers around the country ("in the localities affording the finest fishing") soliciting information on their favorite flies and how they were to be made and used. The result was this book, published in 1892. It was so well received that, according to Schullery & Hogan's *The Orvis Story*, it went through at least nine printings by 1896—a fishing best-seller even by today's standards. Until this edition, *Favorite Flies* had been reprinted only once since then, in 1955, by the Charles T. Branford Company, Boston.

Mary was not truly the author of this book; think of her instead as the compiler and editor, a formidable task itself. Her inquiries resulted in publishable responses from more than two hundred fly fishermen in thirty-eight states, detailing almost three hundred flies. At last there was a definitive encyclopedia of American (as opposed to British) patterns, accompanied by fascinating—and expert—advice on their use. Much of it sounds startlingly current.

*Silvio Calabi*

The sun was setting and Vespers done, from Chapel the monks came one by one, And

down they went thro' the garden trim in cassock and cowl to the river's brim; Ev'ry brother his

rod he took, ev'ry rod had a line and hook, Ev'ry hook had a bait so fine, and

*rit.* thus they sang in the e-ven-shine: "Oh! to morrow will be Fri-day so we

*rit.* fish the stream to-day, oh! to-morrow will be Fri-day so we fish the stream, Be-no

di- .ci .te."

MOLLOY.

# FAVORITE FLIES.

## PART I.

### INSECTS, NATURAL AND ARTIFICIAL.

I'm wrapped up in my plaid, and lyin' a' my length on a bit green platform, fit for the fairies' feet, wi' a craig hangin' ower me a thousand feet high, yet bright and balmy a' the way up wi' flowers and briars, and broom and birks, and mosses maist beautiful to behold wi' half-shut ee, and through aneath ane's arm guardin' the face frae the cloudless sunshine; and perhaps a bit bonny butterfly is resting wi' faulded wings on a gowan, no a yard frae your cheek; and noo waukening out o' a simmer dream, floats awa' in its wavering beauty, but, as if unwilling to leave its place of mid-day sleep, comin' back and back, and roun' and roun' on this side and that side, and ettlin in its capricious happiness to fasten again on some brighter floweret, till the same breath o' wund that lifts up your hair sae refreshingly catches the airy voyager and wafts her away into some other nook of her ephemeral paradise. — CHRISTOPHER NORTH.

To create history one should be a great general, an inventor, or an explorer, but to those of us who are not so fortunate as to be creators is permitted the more humble mission of recording what is accomplished by others.

We confess, though, that we are not quite content in this latter capacity, but are ambitious to submit some day to the angling fraternity a series of imitations of natural insects peculiarly our own. Those now known, it seems to us, are not as perfect representations of nature as they might be, and therefore not wholly satisfactory; but before offering to displace them we desire to extend our study of entomology, and prove, by repeated experiments, other imitations of greater value. At present, fishermen are chiefly indebted to the fly-makers of Great Britain for copies of the insects alluring to game fish. Their experience extends back for centuries before our time or country even, and until we have studied more thoroughly our own stream-life we do well to abide by many of their conclusions; but there can be no question that in the years to come the differences between the insects of the two countries will be better understood and defined, and that a collection of the water-insects interesting to the fishermen of America, with directions for accurate imitations, arranged after the manner of Alfred Ronald's "Fly-Fisher's Entomology," would be of value.

Until this can be successfully accomplished, it has seemed well to preserve carefully our present form of adopted and adapted patterns, fancy flies, and theories and associations connected therewith; or, before venturing too far in untrodden fields, to mark well the paths we have thus far taken, and establish beyond a possibility of removal or forgetfulness the landmarks of the past.

The associations connected with artificial flies are so many and so pleasant that they should neither be lost nor ignored, since they constitute one of the charms of angling. To us, beyond the value of service, past or prospective, a fly is often of more real interest in being the reminder of more than its actual worth. In accord with this, one angler writes: "When I take one of my fly-books out of an evening or at any time during my waking hours in winter, I generally seek out some tattered fly that is wrapped carefully in a paper and placed in one of its pockets. The book may be full of flies, sombre or gorgeous in all the freshness of untried silk, mohair, or tinsel; but take, for instance, this one with the legend on its wrapper;" then follows a loving and enthusiastic reminiscence of other days and happy scenes. That these " veterans of many a fight " are not forgotten and thrown aside, but are carefully treasured, inspires the belief that their histories, so far as may be repeated, will be gladly welcomed. The field is so extensive that we are led in many and diverse ways. We desire so earnestly to indicate the identity and personality of each one who is associated with the flies spoken of in these pages that, even at the risk of seeming prolix, we shall take the liberty of quoting, as far as possible, his own words relative to anything in their connection, and thus to enter the camp-fire circle of anglers, and with them contribute our share of interest and information ; our primary motive being to bring forward the many valuable suggestions given in the letters from fishermen, which form Part II. of this book. These introduce many new flies that are their personal favorites, but must, of course, come into general popularity when their merits are known ; and our special mission, with the exception of the few patterns of our own invention and introduction during the last ten or twelve years, will be to preserve the history and associations, or, as a noted society leader would say, to write of these three hundred flies " as I have found them."

Except to a studious few, dissertations upon the intricacies of entomology and of artificial-fly nomenclature are wearisome and to be avoided. The object of this treatise is to aid those who fish and observe for pleasure, — who seek fresh vigor and strength in a pursuit which occupies mind and body in the open air, and yields excitement without worriment.

The Creator has endowed the majority of mankind with an ambitious spirit, presumably for the advancement of the human race, undoubtedly promoting by it a restlessness, strife, and contention that can be satisfied only by the evasive will-o'-the-wisp success. Success blindly accomplished is difficult to sustain, but success achieved by study and care and delight in the same develops a power to hold its own, be the affairs mighty or trifling. Who of all that go a-fishing will deny the feeling of calm content and the glow of satisfaction consequent upon a creel a little heavier or a fish a little larger than that of his fellow-fisherman?

There seemed to us no better way in which to assure success than to learn from the experience of those who had succeeded; hence this collection of notes from anglers in all parts of our country.

To give this testimony it has been necessary greatly to condense, but it has been done with reluctance, for it was much more satisfactory to let each one tell his story in his own way, as if it were a firelight chat in a summer camp, or a winter's retrospect in a snug library. The voices are many, and we trust they will meet old friends and make new ones in this assemblage of their experiences.

Artificial flies have been made and recorded since the third century; until, now, protests are frequently heard against the " accumulation of ages." Wonder is expressed that they are so many in form and name. Indignation is hardly suppressed at the thought of more being added to increase the perplexity of those whose minds are already dismayed by the problem wherein the unknown quantity is represented by the interrogative Which? We do not always stop to consider that the many imitations are, in the main, the work of eyes and fingers that see and execute differently, each with the worthy aim of greater perfection in representing some insect. But strive as they may, use what they will, they cannot create the buoyancy, glitter, and glow of life. All are failures in a measure, yet other attempts will be made again and again, and with ever-varying effects. We can best be guided to a choice among these by known results from their use in all places, seasons, and methods. No one man could determine this for us, but surely from the expressions of hundreds one can find hints that may be firm stepping-stones to cross the stream of doubt.

In the naming of flies, there has been an attempt in many instances to follow the classifications of insects. Sometimes this has been done correctly, and is most helpful; but often it has been done carelessly or ignorantly, and then it is bewildering. Again, flies have been tied hastily, with whatever materials might happen to be at hand; or a liking for certain combinations of color has resulted in what we now term "fancy flies," as distinguished from imitation flies.

In America, "fancy flies" are more numerous than the imitations, especially since their introduction as a lure for black bass.

In Great Britain, the entomology of the stream-life has been carefully studied, and subjects have been copied; but, alas, the latter has been done in such varying ways and endowed with such varying names that one finds himself in a labyrinth of minute diversities. You wander round and round among these delightfully accurate (?) perplexities, thankful enough if, at last, you find yourself back again remembering the point whence you started. The path is a narrow one to be taken this time; and frequently there are big stones of contradictions, lost records, and conflicting claims to confront us. We have tried to roll aside as many as possible; but now and then one will be found one too heavy, too deeply fixed, or too insignificant to be moved : such we must pass as best we may.

As before stated, in America the majority of flies are the creation of fancy, without an attempt to imitate any known insect, and are named according to circumstances. Yet some that are imitations of insects have not been named after the originals, but after the person who first made or used them. As an instance, the Reuben Wood is a well-known artificial fly. One day Mr. Wood, while fishing in the Adirondacks, saw the fish feeding upon a fly that he imitated as nearly as possible. Fishing with this, he had great success. He then sent a sample to a professional fly-dresser, and had a number tied, which he afterward distributed among his friends, who called them, after him, the Reuben Wood. The fly became popular, and the name will now never be changed.

Another fly, the Morrison, is a small dark fly noticed by Colonel Morrison upon the waters of a little lake in the Northern woods, and before observed in many other places, always eagerly seized by the trout. He preserved no specimen, but described it as a tiny black fly, having a dark red body ringed with black. The color in the body he thought was due to the blood, which in the light shone through the delicate dark skin; the wings and feet were black. The fly was made after this description. He tried it, and found it all he had hoped, and, not knowing the name of the insect which it represented, allowed it to be called the Morrison.

The Dorset is a trout fly, described by a fisherman who was expert in catching fish, noticing their ways and all that concerned them, but having no scientific knowledge. In the little town of Dorset, Vermont, he fished frequently on a small pond. In the month of June he observed that when a certain fly was upon the water the fish refused anything he might offer them, even though his assortment was varied. He therefore concluded that his only chance of success lay in offering them a fly similar to that which engrossed their attention. From his description a fly was made which, he said, was very like the one he had seen. The copy was given a trial, proved successful, and has since been found effective in other waters. As the original was never obtained and identified, the new fly was called the Dorset.

Many other familiar flies, with a like history, might be mentioned, with regret that the knowledge of entomology is not more general, as they might have been given names that would convey more clearly their characteristics.

Modern entomologists have divided insects into sixteen orders, as follows:

| Order I. | Thysanura. | Sprig-tails, Bristle-tails. |
|---|---|---|
| II. | Ephemeroptera. | May-flies, Day-flies. |
| III. | Odonata. | Dragon-flies. |
| IV. | Plecoptera. | Stone-flies. |
| V. | Platyptera. | White ants, Book-lice. |
| VI. | Dermaptera. | Ear-wigs. |
| VII. | Orthoptera. | Locusts, Cockroaches, Crickets. |
| VIII. | Thysanoptera. | Thrips. |
| IX. | Hemiptera. | Squash-bugs, Water-bugs, Parasites. |
| X. | Coleoptera. | Beetles, Weevils. |
| XI. | Neuroptera. | Corydalas, Lace-winged flies, Ant-lions. |
| XII. | Mecoptera. | Scorpion-fly. |
| XIII. | Trichoptera. | Caddis-flies. |
| XIV. | Lepidoptera. | Moths, Butterflies. |
| XV. | Hymenoptera. | Honey-bee, Saw-flies, Ants. |
| XVI. | Diptera. | Flies, Gnats, Mosquitoes. |

Of these sixteen orders, five only are of special interest to the angler: the Ephemeroptera, or short lived day-flies; the Plecoptera (πλέκος, plaited; πτερόν, a wing), from the peculiar folded

way in which the wings rest upon the long flat body, concealing
and extending beyond it ; the Neuroptera (νεῦρον, a nerve), or lace-
winged fly, as the beautiful "golden-eyed gauze-wing ;" the Trichoptera (hairy-winged flies), sometimes called caddis-flies or case-
worms ; and the Diptera, or two-winged flies.

The orders Hemiptera, Coleoptera, Lepidoptera, and Hymenop-
tera furnish occasional specimens for imitation, but the five just
named yield those of more frequent service.  All of these orders are
divided again and again into groups, divisions, families, until the
whole is too complex for any but those who have unlimited time
and the gift of great continuity of thought.  To those so blessed,
what can be more fascinating than the study of entomology, giving,
as it does always, new thoughts, new forms, the opportunity for
out-of-door searchings, and study that need not cease when winter
forces one within ; for then is the time to arrange specimens and
verify opinions.

To the one who shall simplify the branch relating to the insects
of interest to anglers great gratitude will be due, for it will be a
worthy work, and it will add an almost unlimited pleasure to fishing with the fly ; but as yet this seems a difficult and bewildering
task.

One who has made a life-study of insects, and perhaps has written more clearly of them than any one else, in describing the Libu-
lidæ, or family of dragon-flies, and the Ephemeridæ, or May-flies,
writes of the latter, —

"This group is the most characteristic of those heretofore classed
with the Neuroptera, or veiny-winged insects, and most interesting
to the systematist, as it is composed of so many heterogeneous forms
which it is almost impossible to classify in our rigid and at present

necessarily artificial systems. We divide them into families and sub-families, genera and sub-genera, species and varieties, but there is an endless shifting of characters in these groups. The different groups would seem well limited after studying certain forms, when, to the systematist's sorrow, here comes a creature, perhaps mimicking an ant, or aphis, or other sort of bug, or even a butterfly, and for which they would readily be mistaken by the uninitiated.

" Bibliographers have gone mad over books that could not be classified. Imagine the despair of the insect-hunter and entomophile, as he sits down to his box of dried neuroptera. He seeks for a true neuropter in the white ant before him, but its very form and habits summon up a swarm of true ants ; and then the little wingless book-louse (*Atropos*), scampering irreverently over the musty pages of his 'Systema Naturæ,' reminds him of that closest friend of man, *Pediculus vestimenti*. Again, his studies lead him to that gorgeous inhabitant of the South, the butterfly-like Ascalaphus, with its resplendent wings, and slender, knobbed antennæ so much like those of butterflies, and visions of those beautiful insects fill his mind's eye ; or sundry dun-colored caddis-flies, modest and delicate, with finely fringed wings and slender feelers, create doubts as to whether they are not really allies of the clothes-moth, so close is the resemblance.

" Thus the student is constantly led astray by the wanton freaks Nature plays, and becomes skeptical as regards the truth of a natural system, though there is one to be discovered, and at last is disgusted with the stiff and arbitrary systems of our books, — a disgust we confess most wholesome, if it only leads him into a close communion with nature.

" The sooner one leaves those maternal apron-strings, — books,

—and learns to identify himself with nature, and thus goes out of himself to affiliate with the spirit of the scene or object before him, or, in other words, cultivates habits of the closest observation and most patient reflection, — be he painter or poet, philosopher or insect-hunter of low degree, he will gain an intellectual strength and power of interpreting nature that is the gift of true genius."

If, after years of investigation and thought, such conclusions as these are admitted, we who can give but limited attention to the study naturally approach it with hesitation and doubt, realizing, —

> " Truth dwells in gulphs, whose deeps hide shades so rich
>   That Night sits muffled there in clouds of pitch,
>   More darke than nature made her : and requires
>   (To cleare her tough mists) heaven's great fire of fires
>   To wrestle with heaven-strong mysteries."

No attempt will be made in these histories closely to trace the similarity between the natural insects and their artificial representations. That would be ample for a work by itself, and would absorb too much time and space, when the present motive is to show the flies best known, most used, and where, when, and how. Until recently, but few fishermen felt that they could designate artificial flies by names; it was only now and then that you would meet one who spoke with confidence in his knowledge. You would hear him describe his favorites, and such descriptions! He would declare, "For an all-round fly, give me a Professor with a green body!" meaning a Grizzly King. The next might say, "Now I tell you, the best fly for black bass, every time, is a large-sized Ferguson with a green body and a speckled wing;" again a Grizzly King was intended. One who wrote the above to us pitifully added, "But I can no more get the right Ferguson; I have ordered of many dealers, and they always send the wrong fly." A specimen of the Grizzly King was sent to help him out of his dilemma, and he wrote back gratefully, saying, "You are the first I have met in a long time who knew the real Ferguson."

It is surprising to find how many men call blue green, or *vice versa*. Experience shows us that most of them also call chestnut-brown a red; drab, a gray; purple, a blue; with no distinction at all for the various shades of olive, claret, maroon, and yellows.

The colored plates in "Fishing with the Fly" have seemed to remedy this in a marked degree, and it is cheering to notice how many can now give by name, readily and correctly, a long list of flies. We feel sure that this is due in a great measure to the plates mentioned, as the naming adopted in them is the one generally known and used. In adding to these plates, we have endeavored to give, as far as could be learned, the patterns best known and most liked; also their origin and history, briefly, so that in the future these records may be consulted when claims conflict. We urge that when a new pattern is adopted it be given a distinctive name; and we also urge all to avoid giving old flies new names, or old names to new flies.

Mention has been made of the need of a better knowledge of entomology, and this, when attained, will assist in the whole system of fly making and naming; but, until it is acquired, let us take good care to keep the present knowledge as clear as possible. We have many valuable periodicals in which to announce and preserve our discoveries and inventions. In time we may establish some simple and perfect system for classification and nomenclature.

Michael Theakston, an English fisherman, has adopted a practical method of classifying natural insects, which, although imperfect, is helpful in identifying and suggestive for naming. He divides the insects most imitated into seven classes, naming them as follows : —

| | |
|---|---|
| First Class . . . . . . . | Browns. |
| Second Class . . . . . . | Drakes. |
| Third Class . . . . . . | Duns. |
| Fourth Class . . . . . . | Spinners. |
| Fifth Class . . . . . . . | House-flies, |
| Sixth Class . . . . . . | Beetles. |
| Seventh Class . . . . . . | Ants. |

Each of these classes embraces many varieties ; but the class confers the surnames, to which is prefixed the additional name distinguishing each member of the class. This prefixed name may indicate size, color, season, or circumstance, but the class name suggests the shape. Many of the variations in a class consist only of a slight difference in size or shade of coloring. These variations are immensely increased by the metamorphoses of insects.

In the varying stages of development, it is often difficult to say where the larva ends and the pupa begins; also where the pupal state ends and the imago begins. In one genus, the Chloëon, of the order Ephemeroptera, Sir John Lubbock has described twenty-one stages of existence.

With the caddis-flies, belonging to the order Trichoptera, the developments are comparatively abrupt and well defined, but among the many families of the Ephemeroptera and Neuroptera may be seen minute and imperceptible gradations, until ample excuse is offered any imitator for a variation in copy ; for who can be sure the subject was in the same stage as that chosen by another worker as a model ?

LARVA

IMAGO

*I CLASS*

*BROWNS, STONE-FLIES*

This may easily be a chief source of confusion and dispute regarding the differing imitations. It is not so much that each man may be wrong, but that each man may be right from his own standpoint. So, with the endless variety of insects and the never-ending variations of the same, there is multiplied the diverse patterns, until who can determine if each imitation of the Red Spinner was not true at the time of capture; but, if possible, let a spinner be called a spinner, be it red, brown, or black; a drake, a drake; an ant, an ant; and a beetle, a beetle.

We do not urge the adoption of Mr. Theakston's classification, but will explain it as we understand it from his notes, compiled by Mr. Francis M. Walbran, and published in a little book entitled "British Angling Flies." In that book there is no attempt to connect or show a relation between his own classification and that of the scientific entomologist, so, for the service of those who may not be informed regarding either method, a typical specimen is given of each of Theakston's seven classes, and its place in the sixteen orders of Hexapoda, or six-footed insects. From these types, if any one desires to do so, it will be possible to identify forms, and trace connections to the greater information to be found in available scientific books.

Theakston's first class, or Browns, includes a number of flies familiar in name: the Needle Brown, Early Brown, Orange Brown, Yellow Brown or Yellow Sally, and others; also, the valuable Stone-fly.

Of the last-named fly Charles Cotton wrote: " The Stone-fly has not the patience to continue in his crust, or husk, until his wings be full grown; but so soon as ever they begin to put out, that he feels himself strong, — at which time we call him a Jack, — squeezes himself out of prison, and crawls to the top of some stone, when, if he can find a chink that will receive him, or can creep betwixt two stones, the one lying hollow upon the other, which by the way we lay so purposely to find them, he there lurks till his wings be full grown, and there is your only place to find him, and from thence doubtless he derives his name; though, for want of such convenience, he will make shift with the hollow of a bank, or any other place where the wind cannot come to fetch him off."

The Stone-fly is the largest of the class, and prefers to come out in the dusk or dark days; but all the other flies are seen in the daytime. The females of this class may sometimes be noticed on the tops of posts and rails, or on the beams of bridges, whence they drop their eggs into the water; from these eggs are hatched the larvæ, or, as they are called in Great Britain, the " creepers."

The eggs and creepers vary in size according to genus, the latter resembling in shape and construction of body the parent flies. In the larval or "creeper" state they are extremely active, running about on the bed of the stream or hiding under stones. When ready to change into flies they seek the edge of the streams, sometimes leaving the water and running up the stems of plants; but the greater number fasten themselves by a glue-like substance to the under sides of stones just at the water's edge, and there the creeper skin splits open, permitting the imago, or perfect fly, to escape.

The Browns belong to the order Plecoptera, family Perlidæ. They are also known as Perlids.

The second class, Drakes, are perhaps the favorites in the fishermen's list. They are most interesting, and were formerly classed by scientists in the order Neuroptera. Though they have the delicately veined wings of that class, it has been decided that, owing

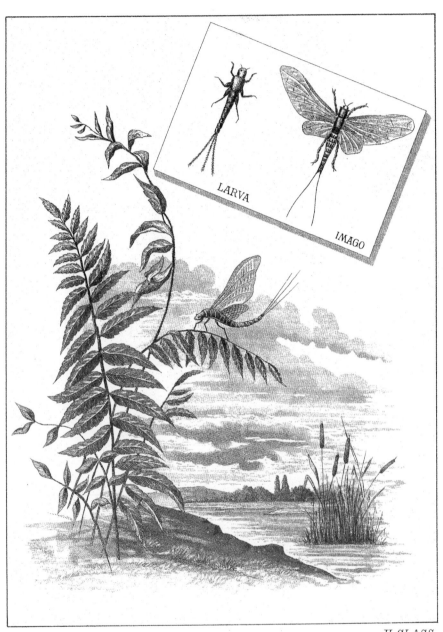

LARVA

IMAGO

DRAKES

II CLASS

to their many peculiarities, they do not rightly belong to any of the older established orders, but must be noted as distinct in specialization, and are difficult to locate. They are named by some writers the Plectoptera, but this is so similar in orthography to Plecoptera that, to avoid confusion, the latest authorities place them in the second order, Ephemeroptera. As Day-flies, or Drakes, they exist for a brief time in two distinct stages, the sub-imago (called by Theakston the pseudo-imago) and the imago; in these forms they possess only the most rudimentary mouth-parts, and take no food. The thorax is peculiar in being globular; the prothorax, mesothorax, and metathorax are each very small. The abdomen is very long and slender, terminating in two or three long delicate stylets. The wings are net-veined. The mature insects exist but a short time, and for the purpose of reproduction only; but as larvæ and pupæ they live one, two, or three years, burrowing in the mud, hiding under stones and among grass and weeds. During this time they pass through many changes and a gradual development until the time arrives for them to assume the imago. In different localities they are known under various names, as " May-flies," or " day-flies," but generally " drakes," because of the peculiar reversed and elevated position of the stylets; owing to this they are also known as " cocktails," and in Ireland as " caughlans," meaning cocktails. After leaving the pupa-skins, they may be seen assembled in groups or swarms about the waters on summer evenings. In some places they appear in immense numbers, so that they seem to fall in showers. By many persons they are thought to emerge from the caddis cases; but this is an error, the larva being hatched from the egg laid by the parent drake or cocktail. This larva changes to the pupa, progressing toward the perfect insect;

but during this entire time, be it one, two, or three years, it is an aquatic insect and is preyed upon by the fish, its only protection being its ability to "run and hide." As the larva and pupa it is a voracious creature, feeding upon other insects; but in its final and great change it assumes the most delicate shapes and colors, in a seemingly endless variety. Among the species best known are the Green Drake, Brown Drake (March Brown), Iron Blue, Amber Drake, Gray Drake, Black Drake, Yellow Drake, and many more.

Theakston's third class, the Duns, is a very numerous one, varying in shades from a light copper hue to the deep dun of the thunder-cloud, from which he gives them this name. Of the Hexapods, they are the thirteenth order, designated Trichoptera ($\theta\rho\iota\xi$, a hair; $\pi\tau\epsilon\rho\acute{o}\nu$, a wing) from the hairy aspect of their wings and body. The structure of the wings and general development of the caddis-flies in some respects bear resemblance to those of the moths; indeed, they are commonly but erroneously called "water-moths." Like the insects of the two classes previously mentioned, the flies of this class lay their eggs upon the water, or attach them to stones and cover them with a jelly-like substance. From these eggs are hatched the larvæ, or "creepers," but, unlike other larvæ, all of this family, that is, the Phryganidæ, as soon as they hatch begin to construct a covering of tiny sticks, stones, bits of sand, gravel, or shells. These they cause to adhere by means of a glue-like thread, until they have formed about themselves a case, the outside showing the substance of which it is composed, while the interior of the structure is perfectly smooth and round, apparently lined by the thinnest possible coating of the glutinous substance that assisted in its construction. While abiding in this they are known as case-worms or caddis-worms. Of them Izaak Walton

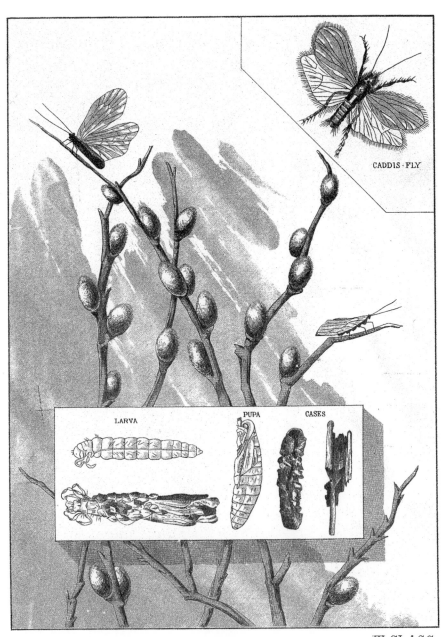

CADDIS-FLY

LARVA    PUPA    CASES

*DUNS*    *III CLASS*

wrote in the long ago : " You are also to know, that there be divers kinds of *cadis*, or *case-worms*, that are to be found in this nation in several distinct counties, and in several little brooks that relate to bigger rivers, as namely one *cadis* called a *piper*, whose husk or case is a piece of reed about one inch long or longer, and as big about as the compass of a two-pence ; these worms being kept three or four days in a woolen bag with sand at the bottom of it, and the bag wet once a day, will in three or four days turn to be a yellow ; and these be choice bait for *chub* or *chevender*, or indeed any great fish, for it is a large bait.

" There is also a lesser *cadis-worm*, called a *cock-spur*, being in fashion like the spur of a cock, sharp at one end, and the case or house in which this dwells is made of small *husks* and *gravel* and *slime*, most curiously made of these, even so as to be wondered at, but not made by man (no more than the nest of a bird is :) this is a choice bait for any flote fish ; it is much less than the *piper-cadis*, and to be so ordered ; and these may be so preserved ten, fifteen or twenty days.

" There is also another *cadis* called by some a *straw-worm*, and by some a *ruffe-coate*, whose house or case is made of little pieces of bents, and rushes, and straws, and water-weeds, and I know not what, which are so knit together with condens'd slime, that they stick up about her husk or case, not unlike the bristles of a *hedge-hog ;* these three *cadis* are commonly taken in the beginning of summer, and are good indeed to take any kind of fish with flote or otherwise. I might tell you of many more, which as these doe early, so those have their time of turning to be flies later in summer ; but I might lose myself and tire you by such a discourse. I shall therefore but remember you, that to know these, and their several kinds, and to what flies every particular *cadis* turns, and then how to use them, first as they be *cadis*, and then as they be flies, is an art, and an art that every one that professes angling is not capable of."

In most species, the caddis-worm, or larva, is able to walk or move about on the bed of the stream by thrusting forth from its tubular case its head and forefeet ; it then travels along dragging its case with it. In many species the lower end of the case is partially closed, having only a small air-hole, and it is in the power of the larva to raise itself and habitation by secreting a sufficient portion of air with which to buoy itself up, and they may often be seen in groups apparently hanging in the water " heads down." A sudden alarm or touch will cause them to descend instantly by expelling the air through the round holes " at the end of the cases." When ready to assume the pupal form, the larva closes up the opening of the case with a grating or thick silken mesh ; while so inclosed the insect undergoes the changes peculiar to the pupa, the wings form and the body alters its shape. When finally mature, the pupa pushes through the network at the end by means of its two front hooks (which meet each other like a beak) ; and, though previously immovable, it can then walk or move again with agility by means of the four fringed forelegs, now free. The pupæ of the larger species crawl up the stems of water-plants, there throw off thin pupa-skins, expand their wings, and betake themselves to the new element, leaving the old caddis cases to be washed away by the current.

In the plate the caddis-flies are represented with wings extended, poised, and folded, the larva, pupa, a case with the larva protruding its head, and two varieties of the closed cases.

CRANE FLY

SPINNERS

In Great Britain over two hundred species have been identified, but in North America they have not been as fully studied, though they are numerous, and have been named to a considerable extent.

It is said of the family Phryganidæ that they are of greatest value as fish-food, the fish devouring eagerly the flies, larvæ, and even the cases. They are also valuable as indicating the chemical composition of the water, and its adaptability to fish-culture, no ponds being considered suited to pisciculture unless the Phryganidæ or caddis-flies are abundant in them. Efforts are being made to determine if they can be readily propagated, in order to increase them, and so add to the supply of fish-food.

The Spinners are numerous upon the water and frequent upon the land. Familiar types are the crane-flies, daddy-long-legs, and mosquitoes. There are vast numbers in this fourth class of these slender, long-legged insects belonging to the family Tipulidæ, of the order Diptera ; the mosquitoes are of the same order, but another family. These delicate water insects exist in endless variety.

Spiders are classed also by Theakston with the Spinners, although they do not belong to the division of insects, but are of the Arachnida.

Among the well - known imitations of the fourth class are the Jenny Spinner, Early Spinner, Black Spider, Black Hackle, etc.

In the fifth plate examples are given of both the fifth and seventh classes, viz. : the fifth class represented by the House - fly, which has so many allies in the order Diptera, as the blue-bottle, cow dung fly, gnat, etc., and the Ants, or seventh class, are equally familiar to all of us.

The Beetles, forming the sixth class, properly belong to the order Coleoptera, and are easily distinguished by their shell-like wing-covers. They are most interesting, and of untold variety in shape, color, and habits. Theakston makes the sixth class also embrace the insects of the order Hemiptera, or bugs, owing probably to the fact that many of these, to the casual observer, appear of the same structure. Belonging to the latter order are the back-swimming water-boatmen, so common on our ponds, and the giant water-bugs that are so terribly destructive to young fish; also the squash-bug and the soldier-bug, often erroneously called the "soldier-beetle."

Theakston seemed to allow no place in his classes for the insect known to fishermen as the "golden-eyed gauze-wing," and to naturalists as the Hemerobius. We have therefore added it to the drawing showing the beetles, for it is of value to anglers and a most interesting little creature; beginning with the peculiar form of the eggs; then during its good service in the larval stage, when one species is known as the "aphis lion," because it destroys on the rose-bushes and hop-vines myriads of these tiny pests; and finally when it develops into the pale green lace-winged fly, with its bright golden eyes, and is a treasure to the fisherman, but so delicate that it is difficult to use the natural fly and the imitation is generally preferred. (See Plate P, No. 138.)

Although we have mentioned only a few types, it will be seen how, with a little more study, a much better understanding and intelligent observation can be acquired. Christopher North found his greatest pleasure in the noonday rests, when, lying on the green grass, he could watch with half-closed eyes the dream-like motions of the airy creatures flitting in and out through the sunlight. We may also see in the waters the earlier stages of these ephemeral forms, and so can find added interest in the ripples and wave-washed shores. Each stone shall suggest to us a possible home for some

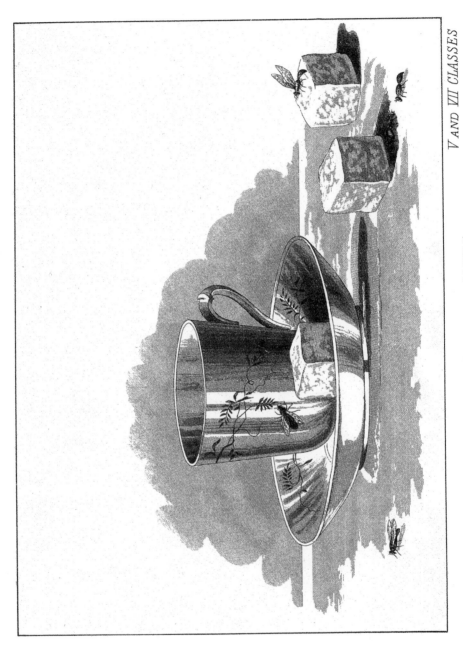

FLIES AND ANTS

shy life, to be noticed carefully, that we may better copy its features and offer a more true enticement to the elusive, fickle-minded trout ; a fish whose chief charm, perhaps, lies in its varying moods, — moods that demand incessant change, a demand born of a life of change, owing to the ever-varying seasons and gradations of insect life. In our studies we should bear in mind that we are to endeavor to judge from the standpoint or instincts of the fish rather than from our own impressions. Too little thought is given to this, although Ronalds and Henry P. Wells have made some interesting experiments by the aid of glass tanks and other apparatus; but there is yet an almost unlimited field for study and discovery beyond their attempts. Sir John Lubbock, in his thoughtful work on " Animal Intelligence," is very suggestive in the following : —

" The general aspect of nature must present to animals a very different impression from what it does to us. These considerations cannot but raise the reflection how different the world may — I was going to say must — appear to other animals from what it does to us. Sound is the sensation produced on us when the vibrations of the air strike upon the drum of our ear. When they are few the sound is deep ; as they increase in number, it becomes shriller and shriller ; but when they reach forty thousand in a second they cease to be audible. Light is the effect produced on us when waves of light strike on the eye. When four hundred millions of vibrations of ether strike the retina in a second, they produce red, and as the number increases the color passes into orange, then yellow, green, blue, and violet. But between forty thousand vibrations in a second and four hundred millions of millions we have no organ of sense capable of receiving the impression. Yet between these limits any number of sensations may exist. We have five senses,

and sometimes fancy no others are possible.   But it is obvious that
we cannot measure the infinite by our own narrow limitations.

"Moreover, looking at the question from the other side, we find
in animals complex organs of sense richly supplied with nerves, but
the function of which we are yet powerless to explain.   There
may be fifty other senses, as different from ours as sound is from
light; and, even within the boundaries of our own senses, there
may be endless sounds which we cannot hear, and colors as different
as red from green, of which we have no conception.   These and a
thousand other questions remain for solution.   The familiar world
which surrounds us may be a totally different place to other animals.
To them it may be full of music which we cannot hear, of color
which we cannot see, of sensations which we cannot conceive.   To
place stuffed birds and beasts in glass cages, to arrange insects in
cabinets, and dried plants in drawers, is merely the drudgery and
preliminary of study; to watch their habits, to understand their
relations to one another, to study their instincts and intelligence, to
ascertain their adaptations and their relations to the forces of nature, to realize what the world appears to them, — these constitute,
as it seems to me at least, the true interest of natural history, and
may even give us the clue to senses and perceptions of which at
present we have no conception."

To know and understand only a little of all this will give a wider
reach to skill and fancy and our interest in this wonderful universe.

Legends there are, too, associated with many of these tiny creatures.   They have a folk-lore all their own, brought down to us by
wondering tradition.   Who can see the quaint old daddy-long-legs
without an echo of the childlike rhyme relied upon in the day we
were sent to "call the cattle home"?   We well remember our

IMAGO

EGGS    LARVA

VI CLASS

BEETLES AND CHRYSOPA

searchings for the little prophet that would point one foot to tell us whither they had gone ; again the air is fresh with the sweet smell of the damp earth, for the dew has fallen ; again we see the pussy-willows, and then the stray white blossoms of the wild strawberries, promises of the tiny tempting red berries that will later cause many delays in the home-coming. We remember, too, the other delights following one after another all through the long, happy summer days, till finally the beechnuts under the big tree by the brook-side, and the blue gentians on the knolls, told us it was nearly time for wanderers to desert the pasture lands.

Perhaps even yet the old childish fear clings to us as the dragon-fly, or "darning-needle," darts by, and we instinctively pull our hats down closer, that it may not "sew our ears up," as we once so firmly believed it could. And do we not yet stop to listen, and perhaps shiver a little, when we hear the dreaded "death-tick"?

A few years ago we attempted raising the American silkworms, that is, the silkworms native to this country, and so much larger than the foreign worms; hoping, if successful, to procure from them strands of gut of greater length and strength than that obtained from the Chinese worms. We had much difficulty at first in collecting the cocoons of the kinds we desired to experiment with, but finally succeeded in gathering quite a number of both the Cecropia and the Polyphemus moths. We raised from these thousands of worms. Space will not permit us to describe in detail how interesting we found it to watch and wait for the transformations, the marvel it was to note the development from the cocoon to the beautiful moth, the hundreds of tiny eggs, then the little furry black specks that were hatched and grew and grew into the huge clumsy worms of an exquisite green. These yielded strands of silk of astonishing length, but insufficient in strength. This we thought probably owing to the larvæ not having been fed on the proper food; but though that experiment was in one sense a failure, it quickened our observation regarding the great interest there is in the transformation of insect life.

A few books, a few visits to the good collections of insects in the museums, a few searchings and watchings, and you have unceasing entertainment to fill in the time when the fishing is poor, or you have gathered knowledge to help make it better.

Theakston's classification must be considered only as suggestive to fishermen. Other writers on angling have endeavored to simplify it all by adhering to two classes only; but that hardly permits sufficient examples, and confuses by its generalities and wideness.

Explanation must also be made here regarding the reproduction of some of the flies depicted in the colored plates in " Fishing with the Fly." It was at first intended not to do this, but as letters came from different anglers, they so often mentioned as their favorites those already pictured in that book that it was found necessary to include some of the old standard varieties among the many new favorites. As an instance, the Coachman could not be omitted, even though, in the new collection, the Parmacheene Belle was a strong rival for favor.

Moreover, in writing what we know of the histories of these flies, it seemed clearer to show the flies than to refer to them by descriptions. But one duplicate is given in varying sizes, although many are often so used, and the greatest care has been taken to ascertain the best authorized dressings.

The kind interest manifested by so many fishermen will be shown by the letters here gathered together. They are an all-sufficient reason for the existence of this book. We have been surprised at and most grateful for the same, and hope their arrangement may please the writers and their many friends. Our desire has been to produce in this way a reliable amount of practical information to assist fishermen when going to new waters. Each will be able to find something relating to the section of special interest to him, and from the suggestions build up his own theories.

One is slow to part with friends. These letters, and the writers of them, have been in our thoughts constantly ever since our first request for their experiences and opinions. We shall feel lonely when turning from them to other affairs, for as we have read the letters we have imagined the faces of the writers, and have been with them by the river-side, in the dewy mornings and the noonday rest, and in the gloaming.

As the fishing days grow fewer, the heart grows more wistful. We miss the old friends that will never be forgotten, and because they are gone hold the more steadfastly to those yet within reach. Old scenes are dear to memory, and new ones are doubly pleasant as they revive the recollections of other days. Thus our lives grow richer, notwithstanding we are so often called upon to lay down what it seems to us we cannot go on without.

There is so much more we would say in these pages, but we can only trust that many of us may some day meet face to face, and together cast our favorite flies upon waters " where memories and fancies and facts rise."

Though I love civility, I hate severe censures.

Izaak Walton.

## PLATE A.

1. Red Hackle.
2. Soldier **Palmer**.
3. Ashy.
4. Zulu.
5. Yellow Hackle.
6. Scarlet Hackle.
7. Brown Hackle.
8. Grouse Hackle.
9. Coch-y-Bonddu Hackle.
10. Yellow Pennell Hackle.
11. Brown Pennell Hackle.
12. Green Pennell Hackle.
13. Deer-hair Hackle.
14. Deer-hair Hackle.
15. Crane-fly.
16. Epting Hackle.
17. Black Spider (W. C. Prime's pattern).

## THE HISTORY OF THE RED HACKLE.

Fly-fishing is a most ancient, and, as the ever-moderate Walton claims for it, "a most virtuous pastime." We find suggestions of its pursuance by men of all stations in all times, and it may be interesting to some to know how one little fly has held its name and form from century to century. An old "North Country Fisher's Garland" contains in the following verses a pretty tribute to

### THE BONNY RED HECKLE.

Away frae the smoke an' the smother!
  Away frae the crush o' the thrang!
Away frae the labour an' pother
  That has fettered our freedom sae lang!
For the May 's i' full bloom i' the hedges
  And the laverock 's aloft i' the blue,
An' the south wind sings low i' the sedges,
  By haughs that are silvery wi' dew.
Up angler, off wi' each shackle!
  Up, gad an' gaff, an' awa'!
Cry 'Hurrah for the canny red heckle,
  The heckle that tackled them a'!'

We 'll see if the Shaperton lasses
  Are winsome, as in our young days —
If they 'll rin to the ringin' o' glasses,
  Or the lilt o' the auld merry lays.
Oh, we 'll shake off the years wi' our laughter,
  We 'll wash out our wrinkles wi' dew, —
An' reckless o' what may come after,
  We 'll revel in boyhood anew!

Up, angler, off wi' each shackle !
    Up, gadd an' gaff, an' awa' !
Cry 'Hurrah for the canny red heckle,
    The heckle that tackled them a' ! '

.   .   .   .   .   .   .

Then back to the smoke and the smother,
    The uproar an' crush o' the thrang ;
An' back to the labour and pother,
    But happy and hearty and strong.
Wi' a braw light o' mountain and muirland,
    Out-flashing frae forehead and e'e,
Wi' a blessing flung back to the norland,
    An' a thousand, dear Coquet, to thee !
As again we resume the auld shackle,
    Our gad an' gaff stowed awa',
An' — goodbye to the canny 'red heckle,'
    The heckle that tackled them a' !

Empires have risen and fallen ; cities been built, lived in, and crumbled to dust ; continents discovered, populated, and grown old in wealth and culture ; human ingenuity has conquered space, and the knowledge of new inventions has sped round the world to the aid of all men ; unknown forces have been made familiar, and now light our ways, warm, feed, speak for us, and convey us where we will ; but in all these strides we who fish have carried with us, and handed on and on down through the ages, the tiny " bonny red heckle."

Over two hundred years before Christ, Theocritus wrote of fishing with " the bait *fallacious* suspended from the rod," but failed to tell of its color or method of construction. Who first thought to substitute feathers for the delicate gauze-like wings of insects, and bind them to hooks, outlining in shape the ephemera of the

streams, we do not know; but in the third century after Christ
Ælian writes as follows: —

"I have heard of a Macedonian way of catching fish, and it is
this: Between Boroca and Thessalonica runs a river called the
Astracus, and in it there are fish with spotted (or speckled) skins;
what the natives of the country call them you had better ask the
Macedonians. These fish feed on a fly which is peculiar to the
country, and which hovers over the river. It is not like the flies
found elsewhere, nor does it resemble a wasp in appearance, nor in
shape would one justly describe it a midge or bee, yet it has something of each of these. In boldness it is like a fly, in size you
might call it a bee; it imitates the color of a wasp, and it hums like
a bee. The natives call it a Hippourus. As these flies seek their
food over the river, they do not escape the observation of the fish
swimming below. When, then, a fish observes a fly hovering above,
it swims quietly up, fearing to agitate the water lest it should scare
away its prey; then, coming up by its own shadow, it opens its jaws
and gulps down the fly, like a wolf carrying off sheep from the
farmyard: having done this, it withdraws under the rippling water.
Now, though the fishermen know of this, they do not use these flies
at all for bait for the fish; for, if a man's hand touch them, they
lose their color, their wings decay, and they become unfit for food
for the fish. For this reason they have nothing to do with them,
hating them for their bad character; but they have planned a snare
for the fish, and get the better of them by their fisherman's craft.
They fasten red (crimson red) wool round a hook, and fit on to
the wool two feathers which grew under a cock's wattles, and which
in color are like wax. Their rod is six feet long, and the line is
of the same length. Then they throw their snare, and the fish,

attracted and maddened by the color, comes up, thinking to get a dainty mouthful; when, however, it opens its jaws, it is caught by the hook and enjoys a bitter repast, a captive." [1]

This is our first recorded description of the "canny red heckle" so often after to be tossed with eager watchfulness into "the current's quick ripple."

Time rolled on, carrying with it the fallen Roman Empire, and creating history for us to ponder over with a fascinated wonder. The Dark Ages, full of mysticism, poverty, romance, and bigotry, came and passed. After forcing many a knee to bend in submission to the "Koran, tribute, or sword," Mahomet and his caliphs drifted into the stream of events. Then the mighty Charlemagne, whose strong arm had reached north, south, east, and west, wielding its force alike on the powerful and the weak, appeared and disappeared, the earnest brain and active hand overwhelmed by the flood, and remaining unstirred by the thunders of the Crusaders as they went singing and praying on their holy quest; chivalry turned into the tide story and song, and on the waters was thrown the bread of sweet courtesy and the care of true love, to be found "after many days" in elements that create and bind our loyalty and homes.

England shared in all this turbulent, restless time, and from the days of the good King Alfred to Richard II. wars and bitter contentions had held the thoughts of nearly all; yet "far from the madding crowd" there were those who found time to meditate upon and write of the follies, pleasures, and pursuits of the day. In the Benedictine nunnery of Topwell, near St. Albans, its wise, pious, and stately prioress dictated graciously and well of "hawkynge,

---

[1] Translation from Ælian's Περὶ Ζώων ἰδιότητος (more generally known as *De Animalium Natura*), Book xv. cap. i.

huntynge and fysshynge." Her precepts first went out into the
world in quaint old black-letter English on sheets of vellum; afterwards they were printed on paper by Caxton, and later by his work-
man, Wynkyn de Worde of Lorraine. These are among the dear-
est treasures of the bibliophile. In the course of the good dame's
kindly discourse, she advises the angler " how to make his harnays
and tackle." After giving minute directions for the same, and the
use of various baits, in writing of their use for trout she concludes
thus: " From April tyll September ye troughte lepyth. Then angle
to hym with a dubbyd hoke accordinge to the moneth, whytche
dubbyd hokys ye shall fynde in thende of this treatyse and the
moneythys wyth theym." This is followed by descriptions of the
many fish she considers of value, with directions how to take them,
at the end of which we read: —

" Thyse ben xij. flyes wyth whytch ye shall angle to ye trought
and grayllying and dubbe lyke as ye shall now hear me tell."

Then come rules for dressing the flies, and the names of the
months in which to use them. To quote the whole would be to
repeat what perhaps many are familiar with, but it is interesting to
find the following: " In the begynning of Maye a good flye, the
body of roddyd wull and lappid abowte wyth blacke silke; the
wynges of the drake of the redde capons hakyll."

So again we find record of the Red Hackle of the Macedonian
fishermen. The knowledge of the old, peaceful pastime drifts on
for two centuries more, and then Izaak Walton, biographer and
philosopher, gave to the world his " Compleat Angler." This " little tome, brown-jerkined, friendly-faced," came to be worth more
than its weight in gold; and it would be impossible to estimate the
number of fishermen who have read its precepts. It has reached

its hundredth edition ; no one knows the number of copies in each
edition, or the number of readers to each book, in the generations
after generations.   These have been carefully treasured, for to-day
may be seen and read the little book of which Westwood has written : —

<blockquote>
" Ah ! if thou couldst tell<br>
Thy story — how, in sixteen fifty-three [1]<br>
Good Master Marriott standing at his door,<br>
Saw anglers hurrying — fifty — yea three score,<br>
To buy thee, ere noon pealed from Dunstan's bell : —<br>
And how he stared and — shook his sides with glee ;<br>
One story, this, which fact or wisdom weaves."
</blockquote>

And of which Charles Lamb wrote to his friend Coleridge :
" Amongst all your quaint readings did you ever light upon Walton's Compleat Angler ?   I asked you the question once before.
It breathes the very spirit of innocence, purity, and simplicity of
heart ; there are choice old verses interspersed in it ; it would
soften a man's temper at any time to read it ; it would christianize
every discordant, angry passion.   Pray make yourself acquainted
with it."

Who can analyze the atmosphere of Walton's writings ?   Whoever reads must fall under the charm of the simple, direct language,
kindly in all its turnings, and full of gentle graciousness and yet a
wise reserve.   Walton instructs his pupil Viator in the use of twelve
special flies.   The fourth, or the " ruddy fly," is to be used " in the
beginning of May."   " The body made of red wool wrapt about
with black silk, and the feathers are the wings of the drake ; with
the feathers of the red capon also, which hang dangling on its sides
next to the tail."

---

[1] 1653, the date of publication of the *Compleat Angler* in St. Dunstan's Churchyard.

Twenty-two years later, Charles Cotton wrote his treatise on "The Art of Fly-fishing," submitted it to his "Father" Izaak Walton, who affectionately approved the discourse of his adopted son; and you may now find in many copies of the "Compleat Angler" this second part by Charles Cotton, and in it more minute explanations regarding the making of artificial flies. Among them he mentions three for February, which are varied reproductions of the bonny red hackle, but called by Cotton the "Plain or Palmer Hackle" and the "Great Hackle," — and so still we find the first favorite surviving time and change.

Times were more peaceful now, and books more frequent. The little fly held its own until two hundred years more had rolled by, and then we are given beautiful engravings of it, many of them colored by hand, and later exquisitely lithographed. In one book — "A Quaint Treatyse on Flies and the Art of Artificiale Flee Making" — we may see the fly itself on medallions inserted in the pages, with the materials for its construction, so that to-day we need not fear losing the formula. The original materials, "redde wulle and a capon's hackle," are yet used. Sometimes all the hackle is wound in at the head of the fly, when it is called simply a Red Hackle; but when the hackle is wound the entire length of the body it is "a palmer." The red coat or body of the fly suggested the distinction of "*soldier* palmer," but either fly, the "bonny red hackle" or the "soldier palmer," can boast the oldest record of any fly known and used to-day.

The White Hackle, Yellow Hackle, Black Hackle, and a number of others are named simply after their color; the Grouse Hackle, by the feather of which it is made, as is the Deer-hair hackle from its material. The Cock-y-Bonddu Hackle is made in imitation of a small beetle, sometimes called the Bracken-clock. There are several species, some of them found upon poplar-trees, and others are numerous upon ferns by the water-side. Fly-makers vary the size of the fly and its color slightly, and name it according to locality, as the Marlow Buzz, Shorn-fly, Hazel-fly, Brown Beetle, etc.

We quote the following from Mr. Pennell's book, " The Modern Practical Angler," in explanation of the " Pennell Hackles : " —

" I propose to substitute six typical flies, three for salmon and grilse, and three for trout, grayling, etc., for the whole of the artificial flies now used. . . . I will not go so far as to say that there may not be exceptional occasions, or even exceptional rivers, though that I should much doubt, on which some local patterns of fly may not prove more killing than the three typical flies I recommend; but I am quite satisfied that, taking the average of waters and weathers, and the great saving of time in the avoidance of experimental changing of flies, my patterns will kill more fish in the course of the year than any others at present generally known."

The Spider Hackle is a favorite pattern with Mr. W. C. Prime, who considers its action upon the water extremely lifelike.

The Ashy is intended to represent one of the many species of caterpillars. It is made with an orange or red body, its entire length wound with a dun or ash-colored hackle feather. These feathers are worth more than their weight in gold, being exceedingly rare and desirable for many of the gray dun flies. The Ashy is what would be termed among fly-makers a " palmer " or " palmer hackle," and some one may have wondered why they do not use the more familiar term caterpillar.

We find early mention of the palmer-worm, or caterpillar, in the

Bible. The good Izaak Walton set the fashion of using this name, and gave his reason, saying, "It is needless to tell you what the curious searchers into nature's productions have observed of these worms and flies; but yet I shall tell you what one *Topsel* says of the canker or palmer-worm or caterpillar : that whereas others content themselves to feed on particular herbs or leaves (for the most think, those very leaves that gave them life and shape, gave them a particular feeding and nourishment, and that upon them they usually abide;) yet, he observes, that this is called a pilgrim or palmerworm for his very wandering life and various food; not contenting himself (as others do) with any certain place for his abode and any certain kind of herb or flower for his feeding; but will boldly and disorderly wander up and down, and not endure to be kept to a diet, or fixt to a particular place."

The term "palmer" has, from this, come to be applied to all bodies of artificial flies made to resemble the hairy caterpillar.

Mr. T. E. Pritt, in his book on "Yorkshire Trout Flies," makes the following claims in the support of the use of hackles: "In one important matter the fancy of Yorkshire anglers, and indeed of anglers all over the north of England, has undergone a change during the past twenty-five years. It is now conceded that a fly dressed hacklewise is generally to be preferred to a winged imitation. The reasons for this are not far to seek and are satisfactory. It is far more difficult to imitate a perfect insect, and to afterwards impart to it a semblance of life in or on the water, than it is to produce something which is sufficiently near a resemblance of an imperfectly developed insect, struggling to attain the surface of the stream. Trout undoubtedly take a hackled fly for the insect just rising from the pupa in a half-drowned state; and the opening and closing of the fibres of the feathers give it an appearance of vitality which even the most dexterous fly-fisher will fail to impart to the winged imitation. Moreover, trout are not accustomed to see perfect winged flies underneath the surface of the water; a drowned fly always looks drowned, and although hungry trout will sometimes take a winged fly very well, it will generally be found that the hackled flies account for the largest number of fish. Perhaps too much attention is commonly given to the wings of artificial flies, and too little to the bodies.

"These remarks, it must be understood, are written mainly of our Yorkshire and other north country rivers, which abound in rippling streams and rough, broken water. In the clear, smooth-gliding waters of the chalk streams of Hampshire and a few other counties, the case is different. There, fly-fishing as an art is perhaps at its greatest perfection, and to deceive the wary two or three or four pound trout which abound, say, in the Test, all the skill which the angler can bring to bear is required, and to accomplish this it is often necessary to fish what is called the 'dry' fly. In this the angler pins his faith on a single fly, a winged one, which he throws up stream over a rising fish, and so manipulates it as to bring it floating down the river with upright wings like a living fly. The hackled fly fished on such rivers would, of course, be out of place; and whilst strongly leaning to hackles for our own rivers, there are times in big, bold waters, and when fishing imitations of large flies, when winged flies will sometimes kill quite as well as hackled or spider flies. One other point. Within reasonable limits, the flies for Yorkshire rivers, and for most other rivers of equal size, —for, as the size of your river increases, so, to an extent, must your flies, — cannot well be dressed too sparingly in the matter of feather.

It stands to sense that, to a creature with such wonderful vision as a trout, it is better to err in offering a deception rather too small than too large. Do not make the mistake, though, of fishing hooks which are too small, or you will fail to strike your fish. You will find it worth while to examine your hooks every time you touch a fish and miss him. The point of a fish-hook is probably more liable to go than any other kind of steel, because the hooks are all pointed before they are hardened. You may remedy an accident of this kind with a bit of Arkansas whetstone, which you can get from any watchmaker and carry in your waistcoat pocket."

Although the foregoing suggestions were applied to Yorkshire trout streams, they may not be inappropriate in theory to all trout streams, subject, of course, to different conditions; but, whatever theories may be advanced in approval of hackles, there is no disputing their very general and successful use. In those two most delightful books, "The Rod and Line in Colorado Waters," and "Mountain Trails and Parks in Colorado," written by Mr. L. B. France ("Bourgeois"), he speaks frequently of the usefulness of hackles above other artificial flies. In one place Mr. France gives an amusing account of assisting a fellow-fisherman out of discouragements, in the course of which he "gave him a Gray Hackle, and told him that was to the trout what bread was to civilized man, a staple article of which he seldom grew tired, or, if he did, to try the Brown Hackle, which still, like the bread, was a wholesome change;" and he further adds: "In the matter of lures, the taste of the trout must be considered; as to all else you may consider your own. It is well to have in your fly-book a *little* of everything, but of Gray and Brown Hackles, as already mentioned, Coachman and Professors, an abundance."

## PLATE B.

| | | |
|---|---|---|
| No. 18. Silver Doctor. | | No. 21. Mitchell. |
| No. 19. Kennedy. | | No. 22. Inver Green. |
| No. 20. Harlequin. | | No. 23. Blue Doctor. |

**No. 18. The Silver Doctor.** Many salmon fishers would place the Jock Scott before the Silver Doctor, were they naming the most successful flies for salmon; but in this country the Silver Doctor salmon fly has been proved effectual under so many circumstances, and for such a variety of fish, that it is probably valued by American anglers more than any other salmon fly. If we were speaking of salmon flies alone, the Jock Scott and other patterns would be considered equally good, if not better, but the universality of the Silver Doctor for all game fish would be undisputed.

The fly did not originate in this country, though it has been so heartily adopted, and adapted to all waters by making it on all sizes of hooks, from very large to very small. English salmon fishers have a theory that if you " raise " a salmon with a Silver Doctor, and fail to secure him, you must change your fly for one of a smaller size, or some other and darker pattern; but it seems especially relied upon by them for "raising" or exciting the fish.

**No. 19.** The Kennedy may be called an American salmon fly, although it was first tied by Forest & Sons, of Kelso, Scotland. Mr. John S. Kennedy, of New York city, having secured some very perfect wild turkey feathers, sent them as a gift to the celebrated fly-dressers; they in return made a fly of them which they called the Kennedy. Mr. Kennedy tried it and found it to be successful for Canadian salmon.

As the fly is becoming known to other anglers, they announce its success in Maine and Lake Superior waters. When correctly made it is very pleasing, the wings being of the beautiful burnished feathers growing just above the long tail-feathers of the wild turkey. None of the domestic turkeys furnish feathers of exactly the same shade of brown, or with the same gleaming, metallic lustre. They are few in number on the wild turkey, even, and the more brilliant are found on the large fine birds. The body and hackle of the fly are subdued in color, but harmonize perfectly with the wing; altogether, the fly, from an artistic point of view, as well as the more practical, is very gratifying. It has a good name, too, this American salmon fly, a name that brings to mind generous gifts for the aid of the poor and suffering.

Walton liked to tell of "the good Doctor Nowel," who, he writes, "was chosen in the time of the Reformation of Queen Elizabeth (1550), not that of Henry VIII., because of his meek spirit, deep learning, prudence and piety, to make the catechism for public use, such a one as should stand as a rule for faith and manners to their posteritie. And the good man (though he was very learned, yet knowing that God leads us not to Heaven by hard questions) made that good plain, unperplext catechism, that is printed with the old service book. I say this man was as dear a lover and constant practicer of angling, as any age can produce; and his custom was to spend (besides his fixed hours of prayer, those hours which by command of the Church were enjoined the old clergy, and voluntarily dedicated to devotion by many primitive Christians:) besides those hours, this good man was observed to spend, or, if you will, to bestow, a tenth part of his time in angling; and also (for I have conversed with those which have conversed with him) to bestow a tenth part of his revenue and usually all of his fish, amongst the poor that inhabited near to those rivers in which it was caught, saying often that *charity gave life to religion;* and at his return would praise God he had spent that day free from worldly trouble, both harmlessly and in a recreation that became a churchman."

The last words in Walton's book, written so long, long ago, were to implore a blessing "upon all that hate contentions and love quietness and vertue and Angling;" and one cannot but think how he would rejoice at the noble charities of one of those who, withal, "Hath no scorn of common things," but

> "Doeth little kindnesses
> Which most leave undone or despise
> For naught that sets one heart at ease,
> And giveth happiness or peace
> Is low-esteemed in his eyes."

**No. 20.** The Harlequin. It frequently occurs that there is need of a bright, strong fly. All the salmon flies are tied with an aim to the utmost strength and durability possible; but in some patterns the construction of the body or the material of the wings is too delicate for all rivers and seasons. The Harlequin is a firm, well-protected fly, and as its name suggests a power of adaptability as well as a gay and varied dress, it may, like those other Harlequins in the well-remembered pantomime of Christmas time, be able to accomplish wonders.

We are indebted to the salmon fishers across the Atlantic for this pattern.

**No. 21.** The Mitchell. In Part II. of this book will be found a letter from Mr. Mitchell giving an account of this fly and its record. Its success has since been further proved, and we feel it is destined to be one of the standard salmon flies of America. Its symmetry and judicious combination of colors certainly entitle it to first rank.

Mr. Mitchell is a most accomplished fisherman, and at the Fly Caster's Tournament, held in New York city in 1889, was greatly envied by all who witnessed his casting. His grace and accuracy aroused unlimited enthusiasm.

**No. 22.** The Inver Green is a Scotch salmon fly originated by Mr. Charles Austen Leigh, who named the fly after the river which identifies also quite a class of flies as the "Inver flies."

This fly is heartily indorsed by the anglers of Scotland, but it is not as well known in this country. We include it in the plate because of the good reports of the fly, and to give variety to the patterns depicted.

**No. 23.** The Blue Doctor is heartily recommended by nearly all salmon fishers. Special mention of it will be found in some of the letters in Part II. relating to salmon fishing in Canada. It is also used for the large trout in the Maine lakes. The fly is one of the best known and best liked. It is called by some writers the Doctor, merely, while the other flies of the same type are distinguished as the Silver Doctor, Black Doctor, etc.

# PART II.

So may it be : that so dead yesterday,
No sad-eyed ghost, but generous and gay,
May serve you memories like almighty wine,
            When you are old.
                                    HENLEY.

Charles F. Orvis.

# PREFATORY.

THE letters which form Part II. of this book were written to Mr. Orvis in response to letters of inquiry which he sent to anglers in all parts of this country. Two or three years were spent in collecting information in this way. The kind interest shown by fellow-fishermen in cordial replies giving their knowledge and opinions was both surprising and delightful, and awakened warmest gratitude. These letters are records of actual experiences, and conclusions deducted from the same. We feel, therefore, that they cannot fail to be of great assistance to any one who may wish suggestions regarding new waters. That these suggestions may be the more available the letters have been geographically classified.

The inquiries made had reference to the following subjects : —

Favorite fly or flies among those well known.

Testimony regarding the same, in connection with locality, time of day, and season.

Facts relating to the origin of any fly ; either those well known or new creations.

Incidents proving efficacy of above.

New Flies. — Origin, time, name, place.

Theories regarding shape, size, and kind of hooks.

Theories regarding snells, whether stained or clear, light or heavy, twisted or single, short loops or long strands.

# CANADA.

C. B. BURNHAM . . . . . . .
{ Black Hackle.
Red Hackle.
Scarlet Ibis.
Royal Coachman.

GEORGE L. WETMORE.

DR. J. H. BAXTER . . . . . .
{ Jock Scott.
Silver Gray.
Silver Doctor.
Black Dose.

ARCHIBALD MITCHELL . . . . .
{ Mitchell.
Silver Doctor.
Jock Scott.

N. C. SMILLIE, M. D . . . . .
{ Silver Doctor.
Jock Scott.
Curtis.
Fairy, etc.

WALTER GREAVES . . . . . .
{ Massassaga.
Lake Edward.
Hofland's Fancy, etc.

C. W. YOUNG . . . . . . . .
{ Jock Scott.
Silver Doctor.
Blue Doctor.
Durham Ranger.

JOHN E. EDEN, GUIDE . . . . .
{ Jock Scott.
Black Dose.
Silver Doctor.
Dawson, etc.

FRANK G. SIMPSON . . . . . .
{ Silver Doctor.
Alder.
Red Spinner.
Jenny Spinner.

C. M. PALMER . . . . . . .
{ Jock Scott.
Parmacheene Belle.
Brown Hackle.

CHARLES HUNTER . . . . . .
{ Jock Scott.
Silver Doctor.
Parmacheene Belle.
Montreal, etc.

J. M. Dill . . . . . . . .
{ Jenny Lind.
Silver Doctor.
Toodle-bug.
Yellow May, etc.

W. W. Hall . . . . . . . .
{ Queen of the Water.
Parmacheene Belle.

C. W. Bunn . . . . . . . .
{ Blue Jay.
Professor.
Raven.
Blue Bottle.

F. Halloway . . . . . . .
{ Parmacheene Belle.
Grizzly King.

C. W. Hinman . . . . . . .
{ Silver Doctor.
Montreal.
Grizzly King, etc.

Julius P. Bucke . . . . . .
{ Fiery Brown.
Lord Baltimore.
Munro.

Claude D. Black . . . . . .
{ Zulu.
Soldier.
Ibis.
Queen of the Water.

Edward E. Flint . . . . . .
{ Brown Hackle.
Coachman.
Grizzly King, etc.

C. E. Martel . . . . . . .
{ Oak Fly.

Erastus Corning, Jr.

Francis C. Green . . . . . .
{ New Fly.
Red Ibis.
Coachman, etc.

E. S. Merrill . . . . . . .
{ Brown Hackle.
Silver Doctor.
Jenny Lind.
Parmacheene Belle.

E. T. Whitmore . . . . . .
{ Toodle-bug.

O. D. M. Baker . . . . . . .
{ Strawberry.
Josephine.

James Barnes Baker . . . .
{ Jock Scott.
Silver Doctor.
Durham Ranger.

| | |
|---|---|
| *Canada.* | { Black Hackle.<br>Red Hackle.<br>Scarlet Ibis.<br>Royal Coachman. |

C. B. Burnham,                       St. Louis,                       Missouri.

The first trout I ever captured with a fly was a half-pound fish, seduced from his hiding-place by a fly with scarlet wings and body, the latter embellished with gilt spirals. If that fly had then been christened (it was in 1836), I did not know its name; but I now think it to have been a Scarlet Ibis. I wore out that fly subsequently in the waters of a Vermont stream, and made frequent unsuccessful attempts to tie others resembling it, until I finally abandoned all idea of becoming an adept at fly-tying. In 1842 I became a resident of Canada, in a section where trout were abundant. I procured improved tackle from Montreal, with which I worried the fish to a degree and extent reflecting seriously upon my reliability as an employee; but I went a-fishing all the same, and found the trout in those waters to be partial to a caddis with pale green wings. On one occasion, while fishing with a companion from a boat, my chum struck a three-pound trout, a fine fellow, which gave fine sport. We had broken the staff of our landing-net, and the problem was how to land the fish. A shot-gun, which was a component of our outfit, was loaded and in the boat; at the proper moment, while my companion handled the fish, I saluted the trout by discharging a load of shot at his head, and by that means saved the fish.

The flies we found the most killing in the section to which I refer were Caddis, Black and Red Hackle on No. 4 hooks. In 1847 I went West to grow up, and located in a Western city where Salvelinus was unknown, and not until 1883 did I have any intercourse with the trout family. But in August of that year, while sojourning at a town in California near the Merced River, I made a friend of Tom, a Digger chief who purveyed for the hotel where I was stopping. Tom was a dandy; by contributing to his wardrobe I gained his confidence to a degree that eventuated in his promise to conduct me to "where the trout hide." Tom's outfit consisted of stout brogans, no stockings, a ventilated pair of overalls, a calico shirt, a mat of hair cut straight across his forehead, and a wide-brimmed straw hat in its third or fourth summer. His fishing-rod was a twelve-foot sapling covered with the skin of a rattlesnake, no reel, a black silk line of equal length of rod, no leader, line attached to a small Black Hackle tied on a No. 4 Sproat hook.

My wardrobe did not permit me to appear in a like costume. I purchased a Japanese jointed hollow cane rod, line and flies à la Tom, and, borrowing a reel, we sallied forth. Arriving at the stream, I discovered Tom had me at a disadvantage; he could wade, while I was unprepared to follow his lead in that respect, and must jump from rock to rock to fish the pools. I outcounted Tom, taking six trout to his two; he, however, had his revenge, for, plunging into the stream among the rocks, he made for the most inviting pools. I essayed to follow by jumping from rock to rock, and alighted upon a sloping water-worn boulder, from which I slipped to my waist into the icy water, my glasses shot from my face into a pool beyond, and, falling face downward on the boulder I fell upon, I smashed my rod and broke my arm. I fished no more that day, nor have I since cast a fly on California waters.

I made a discovery, however, viz., that a black line is substantially invisible in air and water.

In 1884 I first indulged in salmon fishing in New Brunswick

waters.  Trout under such circumstances are a nuisance, and, when moderately abundant, are continually fooling with and spoiling one's flies; they take anything, have no discretion, and with their sharp teeth will destroy a Jock Scott at seven dollars per dozen with no more compunction than they pull to pieces a Fairy costing half that money; while a salmon, toothless, does very little injury to a fly.

In 1888 I fished in Moose River waters, contiguous to Moose village and Jackmantown, in streams emptying into Long Pond, where trout were plenty, but small.  Black and Red Hackles on No. 4 hooks seemed to best please them in these streams, but removing to Big Wood and Little Big Wood ponds a different lure was requisite; the fish were larger, and Ibis, Montreal, Royal Coachman, and Lady of the Lake on No. 2 Sproat were more alluring.  At the outlet of Long Pond I caught, with a Royal Coachman on a No. 2 Sproat, a three-pound male trout.  Opening his stomach to ascertain upon what he fed, I found wing feathers from the common wood sparrow lying upon one another, and in perfect condition; otherwise the stomach was empty.  How they got there I did not ascertain, but I washed, dried, and wrapped those feathers, intending to preserve them, and placed the parcel in my fly-book, from which it escaped without my knowledge.

In August of this year (1889) I found myself sixty miles, or thereabout, from settlements on one of the rivers of New Brunswick.  I went there purposely to try for trout, and found them abundant, and of good size and weight.  They apparently had appropriated pools apportioned in extent to the size of the fish; that is, $2\frac{1}{2}$ to $3\frac{1}{2}$ pound fish occupied a larger and deeper pool than fish of 1 to 2 pounds.  The favorite fly there was one with red in it, either all of that sanguine color or combined with white.  I cast with two flies, Scarlet Ibis or Scarlet Hackle for a tail, changing the dropper frequently as an experiment, all tied on No. 2 Sproat hooks, with two red flies on my cast. I on these occasions struck doublets, saving two pairs and losing one of the third; the scamps ran against the canoe and broke one of the hooks; they were fine fish.

My limited experience in trout fishing does not qualify me to respond in full to your several questions; but I conclude that red with red and white, and black with red, have been the combinations with which I have been most successful.

I prefer the Sproat in shape, size dependent upon the weight of fish angled for. One can impale a small trout upon a large hook and save him, but a heavy fish on a small hook one is liable to lose. My favorite sizes are No. 4 or smaller for fish of eight ounces or less, and No. 2 for larger. I prefer stained snells, the darker the better, — if black, best of all, — light or heavy in proportion to size of hook; for light fish single, for heavy twisted; short loops for large hooks, say from No. 3 up; long strands for No. 4 and smaller; twisted if the gut is thin, otherwise single.

Time of day and season " do not count." If a trout will, he will; if he won't, he won't, and that 's all about it, except he may or will take this when he won't take that. So have a fair variety of hackles and colors, ditto of wing-flies; tempt him with everything, even to a bit of red flannel; and possibly, should your patience and perseverance endure, you may secure your reward.

GEORGE L. WETMORE,　　　　　　Schreiber,　　　　　　Canada.

I fill the position of Resident Engineer on the Canadian Pacific Railway between Port Arthur and White River. I do a great deal of traveling, and fish more or less almost every day; consequently during the season kill a large number of fish. My favorite points are Nipigon and Steel rivers, and along the shore of Lake Superior, where the fishing is excellent. I do not catch a great number, six to eight being an average catch for an afternoon and evening; but the fish are all large and very strong; will weigh from $1\frac{1}{2}$ to 5 pounds.

Those who are fond of fishing and can spare the time could not do better than spend a few weeks along the north shore of Lake Superior. They would have to take a camping outfit, but would not require guides or canoes, so that, outside of railroad fare, expenses would be light. The fishing is done from the shore, which is rock, and free from trees and underbrush.

The Canadian Pacific Railway runs along the shore of the lake, so there is no trouble in moving from point to point. The weather is always cool, scenery delightful, and there are *no flies.* Good river fishing can also be had without difficulty. The most desirable points are Jack Fisk, Peninsula, Middleton, and Gravel River, all stations on the Canadian Pacific Railway.

Canada.     $\left\{\begin{array}{l} \text{Jock Scott.} \\ \text{Silver Gray.} \\ \text{Silver Doctor.} \\ \text{Black Dose.} \end{array}\right.$

DR. J. H. BAXTER,                    Washington,                    D. C.

I am sorry to say that I am not a good authority on trout flies, for I have fished only for salmon for the past six years.

The best trout fly, according to my experience, is the Coachman. The best salmon flies are in the following order: 1st. Jock Scott; 2d. Silver Gray [1] or Silver Doctor; 3d. Black Dose.

----

Canada.     $\left\{\begin{array}{l} \text{Mitchell.} \\ \text{Silver Doctor.} \\ \text{Jock Scott.} \end{array}\right.$     $\left\{\text{Salmon.}\right.$

ARCHIBALD MITCHELL,                    Norwich,                    Conn.

I take pleasure in sending you the Mitchell salmon fly, as requested. Its history is short and easily told. I conceived the idea that a very dark fly would be a success on the Penobscot River, for salmon, and tied a few of them for the first time during the winter of 1887–88. It is my own invention, and was not copied from any other fly. It was first tried on the Penobscot during the following spring.

A gentleman from Boston put one on his leader, when fishing one day after dinner, and, to my surprise and his delight, he hooked and brought to gaff two salmon on this fly during the afternoon. I gave another to a well-known Bangor fisherman. A few days later, while using it he hooked a salmon, but the fish broke away. Still later he struck another; this time his leader parted, and the

----

[1] See Silver Gray in *Fishing with the Fly*, salmon fly plate.

salmon, as well as the fly, was lost. Last spring, well on toward the end of the season, Mr. F. W. Ayer, of Bangor, killed a 27 pound salmon on one of these flies.

The writer, while on his way to Canada, during the last week in May, last year, spent one day at Bangor, and hooked a salmon, also on this fly; it made two leaps in the air and broke away, being lightly hooked. This happened at a time when the fishing was very poor, and it was the only fish that had been struck during the past ten days.

I therefore consider this fly, for a new one, has made a fair showing. It should be varied in size according to the season, condition of water, etc. It has not yet been named, but Mr. Ayer suggested that it be called the "Mitchell." The one I sent to you is not as good a specimen as I would like to have, it being a last year's fly and the best I have on hand now; but it is good enough to show you its formula of construction.

I have not tied any of these flies this winter yet, as I find considerable difficulty in procuring natural black feathers long enough in the fibre to make wings for large flies. Can you inform me where I could get some?

In replying further to your letter, I would say that for salmon fishing the Silver Doctor is my favorite, having killed more salmon on this fly than any other. However, I am of the opinion that the Jock Scott would have been almost, if not equally, successful had I used it as often; but I killed my first salmon on the former, which gave me confidence to persist in fishing with it. Having confidence in a fly goes a long way toward making it a success. A fisherman will almost invariably kill the greatest number of fish with the fly he uses the most.

As to my opinion regarding hooks, I would say that for salmon, trout, and black bass flies I consider the O'Shaughnessy the best, unless for very small trout flies tied on very fine and drawn gut, such as are used on the streams of Scotland. For these I believe there is no hook equal to the Carlisle Round Bend as manufactured by Samuel Alcock & Co., and Addlington & Hutchinson, of Redditch, England. I prefer to have the gut slightly stained, just enough to take the " white glare " off. (If gut were made translucent, as it should be, if possible, instead of opaque, there would be no need of staining it.) The object to be attained is to have it as nearly invisible to the fish as possible, and I think nothing comes nearer to that, after the gut is softened by the water, than a light mist color (so called). The first receipt given in the " American Angler," by Norris, is a good one for dyeing gut.

I never use anything but single leaders, and those always as fine as the size of the fish and condition of the water, etc., will admit of. In other words, I believe in always fishing as fine as possible, and by so doing long ago found by experience that, to use an expression of Izaak Walton's, " if you can attain to angle with a single hair, you will get more rises and catch more fish." That was written a long time ago ; and if it was necessary to use fine tackle in those days, it is much more so to-day. I have known many occasions when fine tackle skillfully handled filled a basket, and coarse tackle under the same conditions was almost a complete failure ; the difference between the fine and the coarse tackle was simply the difference between the thickness of the leaders and the size of the flies used.

| | | |
|---|---|---|
| *Canada.* | ⎧ Silver Doctor.<br>⎪ Jock Scott.<br>⎨ Black Dose.<br>⎪ Fairy.<br>⎪ Curtis.<br>⎩ Fiery Brown. | ⎰ Salmon.<br>⎱ |

N. C. SMILLIE, M. D.,                    Gaspé,                    Canada.

There are three rivers in the immediate vicinity of Gaspé, and all contain salmon and trout; there are also many small streams containing the latter fish. Our lakes are both large and small. There are some five or six within a day's journey of this place; though I can assert that they all contain trout, not much is known about them, as the salmon fishing absorbs the interest of most of us, so that the fishing of the lakes is neglected. In the same way, we do not make much distinction with regard to flies for trout, as they will take almost any kind of fly; this is a fact. In fishing the rivers we are seeking salmon, and if we do try a cast or two at the lower end of the pool for trout, we generally use an old salmon fly, a Jock Scott, Fairy, Fiery Brown, etc.

Regarding salmon flies, on the St. John River, early in the season, with high water, the Silver Doctor, Jock Scott, Black Dose, and flies of that sort are best. Later in the season the fish are more difficult to deceive, and smaller flies are required; the Fairy, Curtis, etc., are the most taking. On York River the same will hold good, as well as on the Dartmouth, where I have found a Popham or Prince William of Orange good flies early in the season.

Of flies for the small streams and lakes I have nothing to relate, but should think that any well-stocked fly-book would get a good score. My experience with double hooks is that they are a delusion. Casting lines must be chosen according to the water, high or low, heavy or light casts, and should be able to stand a dead pull of respectively four and two pounds. Snells or loops on the fly should be roomy, as well as the loops on the casting line; whether stained or clear gut is used I have no preference, finding one as good as the other, provided it is sound.

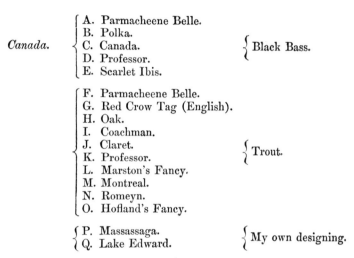

Canada.
- A. Parmacheene Belle.
- B. Polka.
- C. Canada.
- D. Professor.
- E. Scarlet Ibis.

} Black Bass.

- F. Parmacheene Belle.
- G. Red Crow Tag (English).
- H. Oak.
- I. Coachman.
- J. Claret.
- K. Professor.
- L. Marston's Fancy.
- M. Montreal.
- N. Romeyn.
- O. Hofland's Fancy.

} Trout.

- P. Massassaga.
- Q. Lake Edward.

} My own designing.

WALTER GREAVES,      Ottawa,      Canada.

A. I feel that I cannot speak too highly of this fly, both for trout and bass. I am of the same opinion in regard to it as Mr. H. P. Wells. (See p. 90 in " Fishing with the Fly.") I generally use one in my cast, and find that in all kinds of weather and at all times of the day, where fish are rising at all, the Parmacheene Belle holds its own against all others; that is, on an average.

B. This is a capital fly (thanks to Dr. Henshall). From my own experience, and from what other people have told me, I think it may safely be ranked as one of the best; in fact the best on many occasions. During the months of August and September I have had excellent sport with it on the Bay of Quintè, county of Hastings, and at Sharbot Lake, county of Addlington, Ontario.

C. Body scarlet, ribbed with gold tinsel ; wings gray mallard ; red cock's hackle ; tail scarlet ibis. For bright days, same as above, with exception of the body being claret ribbed with silver tinsel. I give the formula of this fly because it is made differently by some people. I have not, however, used it sufficiently myself to be able to express a definite opinion as to its merits ; but from the experience I have had, and from what I have heard from a thoroughly practical angler (Mr. R. Hilton, of Trenton, Ontario), I am convinced that it is an excellent fly.

D. A very taking fly on a dull day.

E. At times I have found this fly to prove successful when many others failed. I have found it useful on rather rough, dull days.

F. The Parmacheene Belle heads the list on an average, so far as my experience goes.

G. First-class fly. Have used it with success in several localities.

H. I have used this fly with considerable success in streams during June and later in the season.

I. I have found this to be a very good fly for dull days or during the evening.

J. This is an excellent fly, particularly for lake fishing. Took many trout with it in Lake Edward, P. Q., last season.

K. Used with much success in various localities.

L. Capital fly on No. 12 hook for streams. Used with success on Quyon River, P. Q., and at Springbrook, Ontario.

M. Good fly for a bright day.

N. Judging from the few times I have tried this fly, I should think it a good one.

O. This is a splendid fly for stream fishing. It is made thus: body bright green peacock side feathers, ribbed with gold tinsel; small red tag; red cock's hackle; hook No. 10.[1]

P. Designed by myself in 1885, merely as an experiment. Body green, with gold tinsel; wings guinea-fowl dyed yellow; hackle yellow; tail scarlet ibis. In fishing for bass on the Bay of Quintè, county of Hastings, I have found this fly to take better than any fly I have used, and several of my friends say the same thing. It takes particularly well during the evening, say between six o'clock and sundown, in the months of July and August.

Q. I made this fly in July, 1888, when at Lake Edward (on the Quebec and Lake St. John Railway, where the trout fishing is first-class), and found that it generally proved the most taking fly I used whilst there. Body reddish-brown mohair; silver twist; tail golden pheasant; hackle claret; wings dark bronze or brown turkey, with thin strips of dyed bright yellow and purple feathers on each side.

Regarding hooks and snells, I prefer the Pennell Limerick eyed, the Sproat, and the Kendal sneck bend hooks. For bass fishing I generally use flies (I am not a bait fisherman) dressed on hooks between No. 7 and No. 0, and for lake fishing for trout, No. 7 to No. 1. For stream fishing for trout I prefer small flies, say from No. 7 to No. 15. At Lake Edward I caught most of my trout on flies dressed on No. 1 hooks.

I do not think that with stained leaders or snells one is liable to take more fish than with those of the natural color. I do, however, think that the finer the gut is the better, particularly for trout fishing; provided, of course, that it is of the desired strength. As to

[1] This, although doubtless an excellent fly, is not the usual formula for Hofland's Fancy. — M. E. O. M.

leaders, I prefer them with loops on which to attach the flies, as I find it much easier and quicker to change flies when your leaders are thus made, and they are not nearly so liable to break where the fly joins the leader.

I strongly recommend the best of everything for fly-fishing purposes, no matter what the cost may be; and I advocate light rods and tackle.

---

|            |  |  |
|---|---|---|
| *Canada.* | Jock Scott. <br> Silver Doctor. <br> Blue Doctor. <br> Durham Ranger. <br> Fairy. | Salmon and Sea Trout. |

C. W. YOUNG,　　　　　　　　Cornwall, Ont.,　　　　　　　　Canada.

My fishing is confined principally to the Gaspé rivers. I have found there that, for salmon, the Jock Scott, Silver Doctor, Blue Doctor, Durham Ranger, and a few Fairies will generally do the business. We are using double hooks, Sproat, exclusively, and find them much more satisfactory than the single hooks.

I fancy that a good deal of the blue is needed in every fly for these waters; the guides, who watch things pretty closely, seem to think so. Hooks with loops only are best. As to leaders, they must be strong; that is the chief consideration under ordinary circumstances. I do not think it makes much difference whether they are stained or bright.

A friend of mine, who fished one of the north shore rivers, saw fishermen using all kinds of flies; he impaled a live green frog on his fly hook, and floating it down over the salmon it was taken with a rush. This would seem to conflict with the generally received opinion that salmon don't feed in fresh water.

As for sea trout, they will take anything a salmon will; old salmon flies are good enough. The trout will ruin any fly in short order. I caught a great many trout with a large Coch-y-Bonddu Hackle dressed on a sneck bend hook.

One day I used a Brown Hackle, Pennell, and a Parmacheene Belle, and landed from a pound to two pounds or over of trout in two parcels every time. They were thick that day! Two of us caught about one hundred and fifty in a few hours, all large, half a pound and upward to two or three pounds.

---

|  |  |  |
|---|---|---|
| *Canada.* | Jock Scott.<br>Black Dose.<br>The Butcher.<br>The Dawson.<br>The Fairy.<br>Silver Grey, etc. | Salmon. |

JOHN A. EDEN, Guide, Gaspé Basin, Canada.

I can give you a little information about fly-fishing, as I have been with gentlemen for twenty seasons in the Gaspé River and north shore rivers.

The Black Dose is a good fly for a bright day. The Butcher, the Dawson, the Fairy, Silver Grey, Fiery Brown, Parson, and Prince William of Orange. The two best flies, I find, are the Silver Doctor and Jock Scott for any kind of waters. When salmon won't take these two flies it is no use to try any others.

These flies should be tied with a short loop of twisted gut, and no other. For heavy waters should be double hook, flies about the size of No. 2, 3, 4, of the O'Shaughnessy hooks. Trout flies are not worth speaking about, as they will take any kind of flies in our rivers. It is very nice for a man to have a book of flies, but those that are mentioned are all that are required, excepting a few others.

The Blue Doctor is a very nice fly. If any gentlemen want to know anything about our rivers, or north shore rivers, I will be happy to let them know, and if they want to go fishing, I will go with them and hire men for them, and have good safe canoes on hand. The canoes are four feet long and thirty inches wide, made out of aspen wood; will carry from sixteen to eighteen hundred pounds.

The St. John River, Gaspé, is a very fine river, a good river for four rods for salmon, and plenty of trout. Anything else you want to know I will tell you.

---

| *Canada.* | Montreal.<br>Yellow Professor.<br>Cinnamon.<br>Coachman.<br>Tinseled Ibis.<br>Blue Professor. | Land-locked Salmon. |

The foregoing list of flies gives those advised for land-locked salmon by Mr. Genio Scott, on page 259 of his most instructive book.

## PLATE C.

No. 24. The Notion.      No. 27. Dun Wing.
No. 25. Childers.        No. 28. Dusty Miller.
No. 26. Baker.           No. 29. Thunder and Lightning.

No. 24.  The Notion was first made and named by John Shields, the veteran fly-maker of Brookline, Mass.  It was intended for land-locked salmon, but we hear of it as also successful for salmon, trout, and black bass.  Dressed on a large hook it is very beautiful, the gilt and golden brown harmonizing perfectly ; it can also be adapted to a small hook.  It is a fly that many anglers "take a notion to," and value for the good it does as well as for its beauty.

No. 25.  Childers.  A year or two ago "The English Fishing Gazette" wrote to a number of dealers in fishing tackle asking the following question :  "What six flies do you use most, consider best to have for the widest range, or sell the greatest number of for Scotch salmon angling ? "

In answer to this inquiry the paper received lists of the salmon flies that were most largely sold, and in these lists the Childers was frequently included.  It is well known to American fishermen, and is said to be an excellent general fly for salmon anywhere on this continent, being good in either bright or dull weather, its yellow body being effective in the latter.  In 1869 there was an especial furore over this fly, and it was almost impossible for the dealers to supply the demand ; and although, since then, new favorites have appeared to claim attention, the Childers has not lost its prestige.  It is usually considered better dressed rather small than large.

No. 26.  The Baker is one of three celebrated salmon flies, viz., "the Butcher, Baker, and Candlestickmaker."  The Butcher is better known and more used than the other two ; but as it had already been depicted in "Fishing with the Fly," it seemed better to give in this collection its companion, the Baker.  The Candlestick-maker is the least popular of the three, but is recommended by Mr. Francis as "a fly to light the salmon to bed with."  He writes of it : "I dressed one as a whim, several years since, and sent it to a friend, who reported favorably of it to me; since then it has done useful service. The body, for the lower half, is black silk; the upper, black pig's wool, very bushy towards the shoulder, and picked out at the breast; hackle, golden-olive, with claret at the shoulder; tinsel, broad silver; tail, scarlet ibis and wood-duck; wing, five or six toppings with double jungle-cock on either side. At dusk this fly will often show the salmon the way upstairs, when others will fail." The Butcher has the greatest reputation of any of the three, and by the man who first brought it into popularity it was called " the finest fly in creation." He was a tradesman and skillful angler by the name of Moon, and because he sometimes traded in meat for the table the fly known to be his favorite was called " the Butcher." The pattern was invented by Mr. Jewhurst, of Tunbridge, Kent, England, and was but little known until 1838, and before then as Moon's fly merely; a number of years after that it was tied and sold by Blacker, and then began to be known as " the Butcher," because, it is supposed, of its advocate's connection with this trade. It has been a remarkable killer on nearly all waters frequented by salmon, especially when the waters were clearing, and the Baker is said to be "always the best change" and invaluable to use in conjunction with the Butcher.

The Parson is usually mentioned whenever this trio is spoken of, as it seems to belong with them, perhaps, because of the old rhyme that is current regarding the worthy divine after whom this last fly was named : —

> " Butchers and Bakers, Wheelwrights and Watchmakers,
> A Clark smooth and Parson 'to boot,'
> Whose orthodox views filled his church-pews,
> Though he took a day off to fish or to shoot."

No. 27. The Dun Wing is mentioned in Mr. Francis's " Book on Angling " as one of the Tweed flies, and well known on that river. It has also been adopted in this country as a favorite, first on the salmon rivers of Canada, and later for large trout in the Maine lakes. A year or two ago, a party of gentlemen from Waterbury, Conn., were going up into Maine to camp and fish; just before they started we sent to them, among other flies, a large-sized Dun Wing. They had great success on that trip, and the next year wrote to us saying: " We want to get some more flies like the one you sent us called the 'Sure Thing,' for it was a sure thing every time ; we caught some of our largest fish on it." We could not imagine what fly they meant, and wrote saying that we knew of no fly of that name, and would like to see the one they mentioned. They wrote back that they were sorry, but the fly was all used up ; that they had only the card to which it was fastened. This they returned, and on it was written the name of the fly, Dun Wing, but so carelessly that it could easily be translated Sure Thing. We then explained that the true name of the fly was Dun Wing, an old and well-known salmon fly ; but they replied : " Well, we call it the Sure Thing ; that name suits it better, and we all know it by that name now." So it is probable that in time the similarity between the Dun Wing advocated by one angler and the fly known as the Sure Thing by another will puzzle those who do not know the history of these names.

No. 28. The Dusty Miller is sometimes, but not often, called " the Beryl." As the season advances and the fish begin to seek deeper water, the gayly dressed flies with bright silver bodies are found desirable to take the place of the ever-reliable Jock Scott and other favorites. Where the water is rough and rapid, or deep, a large fly should be used, and the Dusty Miller, Silver Doctor, and Wilkinson are admirable for this purpose.

No. 29. The Thunder and Lightning was once known as the " Great Storm fly," deriving its name from the fact that in its early days it was universally used when the water was rising after a storm. At this time the appetite of the salmon or grilse is thought to be more keen, and with the proper fly success more probable. But of late other patterns have become more valued for this state of the water, and the Thunder and Lightning is considered best to raise fish in low clear water, or for autumn fishing.

Mr. George Kelson writes : " It has been proved that the fly can also be advantageously used on other occasions than in clear water. Under trees in bright water, or in water that is slightly discolored, the fly certainly shows well, and therefore should kill well. I cannot call to mind any other standard pattern that is equally effectual, regardless of changeable weather, state of the water, either clear or dirty, or the humor of the fish. There is no river that I have ever visited where it has not succeeded at one time or another."

|  | | |
|---|---|---|
| *Lake Superior Region and Rocky Mountains.* | Silver Doctor. | { For Nipigon fishing. |
| | Alder. | |
| | Red Spinner. | { For the trout in smaller streams. |
| | Olive Gnat. | |
| | Jenny Spinner. | |
| | Iron Blue. | |

FRANK G. SIMPSON,                 Winnipeg,                 Manitoba.

It is the aim of all fly fishermen to obtain a certain amount of knowledge of entomology, which beyond doubt places the possessor in an advantageous position in the rank of anglers, and more particularly those who possess the ability to construct their own flies.

I may as well be candid at once, and state that I have so often fished with skilled work, and my ideas of neatness in flies are such, that my conscience would not permit me to offer my productions at the shrine of *Salmo fontinalis*, for fear that if I should be able to see him he might appear to me as pointing his tail to the corner of his eye, in a manner that might suggest to me the question of there being "any green there."

As to entomology, I have a smattering of it, which I find very valuable, and which was gathered at the stream-side and by careful attention to the flies on the water, and am often rewarded with success which I can attribute to the little information I possess of this science.

My fishing has been done on streams where fish were shy; also on those where they would rise to almost anything that resembles a fly.  On streams of the former kind is where knowledge comes to one's aid, and where the novice would be sore pressed to make a basket, when success depends upon skill and close observation. I am inclined to think that one of the chief elements of success lies in avoiding flies of too large a size, whether they be close imitations of the natural fly or conventionalized.

On all small streams flowing into and out of Lake Superior, whose waters are for the most part clear, I find that the moderately dark-colored flies are the most killing, and for that class of fishing I carry an assortment of such flies as Alder, Red Spinner, Olive Gnat, Jenny Spinner, and Iron Blue Dun, dressed on No. 8 and 10 hooks, and some as small as No. 12; also Ginger and Brown Hackles. These will be found quite good enough for the small streams, and the angler will be safe in selecting these, or similar ones.

To demonstrate what I say, last year I met by accident, as I landed from the steamer at the Sault Ste. Marie, a brother I had not seen for thirteen years, and having in our younger days taken many a basket of trout from the beautiful rapids there, we decided to remain over a few days and enjoy a reminiscence of old times. I had rod, reels, and flies with me, but we were told it was absolutely useless to go, as the waters were fished to death, and a catch of two brace of trout was considered good. However, we went, and on reaching the rapids we intended to fish we counted six canoes containing anglers and their guides, and the shore seemed to be lined with fishermen, — surely a poor outlook. We commenced to fish and to kill, using a cast of Flight's Fancy, Olive Dun, and Coachman-leadwing, changing to Marryat, Iron Blue, and Jenny Spinner, all dressed on No. 10 hooks, and on reaching the foot of the rapids our baskets contained respectively forty-three and thirty-six trout, the largest being about one pound. Our friends soon arrived, and the best catch among them was seven fish to one canoe of two rods, and well I remember the looks of astonishment at seeing our catch, and more so at seeing the flies we used. I looked at their casting line, and perhaps my look astonished them as much, for they were using flies, such as Parmacheene Belle, Scarlet Ibis, and Coachman, dressed on No. 4 hooks, and large and gaudy enough to frighten a trout to death. We consoled them by giving them our entire catch to divide, and they good-naturedly took about all the flies I had, just as samples.

The finest fish as regards size are those in the Nipigon River, and there you are safe with almost any fly so long as you are careful as regards size. I am satisfied that anglers go to the extreme in the way of large flies on this river. It must, of course, be remembered that three-pound fish are common, and I have known them to be killed as large as seven pounds and a quarter; for these fish, flies dressed on No. 2 and 4 hooks are plenty large enough; still it is a common thing to see men use No. 2/0 hooks, and they certainly should not blame the fish if they refuse to take them. In my opinion, success on this river depends, not so much in color of the flies as in the size of hooks used.

My favorite fly on the Nipigon is that in your list of Lake Flies called Silver Doctor, and were I limited to the use of any single fly it would be this; it certainly is a grand fly, and will kill every day of the season. I consider it the best, and so do many of my friends to whom I have sent it to try. This fly, with Coachman, Coachman-leadwing, Green Drake, Portland, Canada, and Parmacheene Belle, will carry any angler successfully through a season on the Nipigon. By the way, an improvement in dressing the Silver Doctor is the substitution of silk in place of wool, usually used for the head.

On mountain streams, should an angler's fancy carry him to such a place (I speak of the rivers flowing through the Rockies), he will find that from the extreme clearness of the water it is necessary to use very small flies, and there the Black Gnat and Iron Blue are great favorites. I have done a great deal of fly-fishing on the rivers, but would not advise any one to go there if he is able to select any other locality. The trout are poor as compared to those of Eastern rivers, and are not capable of giving the same sport. These rivers are supplied with water from the melting snow and glaciers, and the fish are soft, and give in easily; still, what the angler misses in gameness is to an extent made up in number of fish to be killed; but too soon it becomes tiresome, and I would sooner kill a five-pound fish on the Nipigon than one hundred fish in a mountain river such as the Bow.

To sum up the whole question of flies, my theory is, that as a rule favorite flies are dangerous. I remember once having a theory that I could select say six varieties that would carry me through safely, but how often was I disappointed! And on occasions of that kind, some flies considered of very little value would, upon being used, turn the current of events so much in my favor that I have said to myself, " All kinds are good in their proper time, and I shall in future depend no more on favorites." This sentiment is my present " theory," and I carry it to success by keeping a book of flies well assorted both as to size and color, of close imitations of nature as well as conventional, and this without unnecessarily duplicating colors.

To the beginner, this idea of variety suggests an endless changing of flies on the water to suit the sometimes fickle fancies of the trout. It looks difficult to decide properly, and so it is; and just there is where the pleasure is felt by the angler of experience at being able, by the judicious selection of a fly, to make a trout that has been sulking come with such a rush as if his whole existence depended upon his securing that particular fly. All that the beginner has to learn; but by careful notations, as he goes on from day to day, he will shortly acquire knowledge obtainable in no other way, — no, not by all the books ever written on the subject; then, and then only, will he be able to appreciate fly-fishing as it should be. I would again strongly urge a goodly selection of flies outside of favorites; you never know at what moment you may be sorely in need of them.

As to the shape of hook upon which flies are usually dressed, viz., Sproat or O'Shaughnessy, Limerick, etc., it is my opinion that it would be difficult for any one to decide which is the best. Circumstances will prejudice us against a certain bend of hook, and in favor of another. Should fish on some day be dilatory in rising, or some peculiar circumstance connected with the color of the fly cause a fly to strike short and become so lightly hooked that the hold gives way, the hook is generally blamed; and on the circumstances being the reverse the hook is praised. In the selection of one or the other of the hooks mentioned, I should be influenced only by the appearance of the fly when dressed, and from this standpoint I would choose Limerick, or, better still, Pennell Limerick. This hook, aside from its neat appearance, has the shape to a marked degree that gives the hook-point the full benefit of the direct draft of the line, causing it to enter the more readily; and if I were restricted to the use of any particular hook it should be this one. Still I would be happy at any time on a good river with any of the others, and some of my best days have been with Sproat and O'Shaughnessy.

Regarding snells and loops, I prefer snells, and more particularly on small flies; they have a neater appearance, and for this reason I

M. Bradley Co. Lith.

Made by **C.F. ORVIS**, Manchester, Vt.

PLATE A: DESCRIPTION PAGE 27

M. Bradley Co. Lith.

Made by **C.F. ORVIS**, Manchester, Vt.

PLATE B: DESCRIPTION PAGE 39

Made by C.F. ORVIS, Manchester, Vt.

PLATE C: DESCRIPTION PAGE 63

M. Bradley Co. Lith.

Made by C.F.ORVIS, Manchester,Vt.

PLATE D: DESCRIPTION PAGE 81

am now using Pennell Limerick turned-down-eyed hooks. With the proper attachment, you get the full strength of a loop, with the idea of the snell carried out as closely as if you originally tied it with the fly at construction, and I think I can plainly see the universal adoption of this hook in the near future, for most certainly its advantages are great.

---

|  |  |
|---|---|
| *Canada.* | { Jock Scott.<br>Parmacheene Belle.<br>Brown Hackle. |

C. M. PALMER,        Minneapolis,        Minn.

My experience this summer was in the Lake St. John country in Quebec, and I can give you little new information as to flies, as I found the trout there willing to take almost anything. For winninisch, in the River Mistassini, I used the Jock Scott mostly, but found nearly all brown, red, gray, and bright flies taken as readily, when the fish were rising at all.

Just as an experiment I used a dozen or more abortions, some of them big enough for shark fishing, made by a Western amateur, who evidently tried to work off a surplus stock of millinery goods in fly manufacture, and found them just as good as the best English and American flies for trout ranging from one to four pounds, on the upper Metabetchouan, Metesquac, Ecorce, and other streams in the wilderness.

The result was to confirm my already strong belief, that when trout are biting one fly is about as good as another. I was two months in the woods out of sight of man, and if I were to repeat the trip I would take a few dozen Jock Scotts of different sizes, some Parmacheene Belles, and a good lot of Brown Hackles.

With this outfit I can keep up with the angler who has a trunk full of flies, and I would be willing to take any two of the varieties I name, and try to do so.

For the waters I have named, by all means use single gut stained brown, with long strands for snells. The long snells are better than the loops, because they can be used anywhere on the leader, which should also be of single gut stained brown.

---

*Canada and the Nipigon.*
{
Jock Scott.
Silver Doctor.
Professor.
Parmacheene Belle.
Montreal, etc.
}
{
Salmon and Lake fishing.
}

{
Coachman.
Parmacheene Belle.
Montreal.
Hackles.
}
{
Trout.
}

CHARLES HUNTER,                    Toronto,                    Canada.

My favorite flies are : for brook trout, *Salmo fontinalis,* in Ontario, Red Hackle, Coachman, Parmacheene Belle, Brown Hackle, Dark Montreal, Ginger Hackle, Black Hackle. These are all I find necessary to ring the changes. I use Sproat hooks only, and tie on No. 4 to 7 stretchers ; 8, 9, and 10 for droppers.

A good evening cast is White Coachman for stretchers, Ginger Hackle for droppers. In Muskoka, have found the Parmacheene Belle and Dark Montreal most effective.

In Province of Quebec, I have found the most taking flies to be Red Ibis, Parmacheene Belle, Dark and Light Montreal, Professor ; these may be tied on larger hooks than used in Ontario, as the fish run larger and the waters are less fished. I tie the Montreal and Parmacheene Belle as follows. Montreal : body, crimson silk or wool, ribbed with gold tinsel; wings, feather from turkey wing; hackle, red or scarlet; tail, three fibres red ibis; tag, gold tinsel. Parmacheene Belle: body, lemon-yellow mohair, ribbed with scarlet silk, gold or silver tinsel; wings, equal parts white goose and red ibis; hackle, red; tail, goose and ibis; tag, gold tinsel. The latter is also a very killing bass fly.

On the north shore of Lake Superior I have fished the Puckaso, Steele, Magpie, Nipigon, and a number of smaller rivers, and have invariably found the usual trout flies to be of no use to catch the large fish. On most of the rivers small salmon flies were the most taking. On the Nipigon the large salmon flies we had were not too large. The largest fish I caught ($5\frac{1}{4}$ pounds) and the best sport I had on the river was with a fly made for me by Major Scott, a commissioner of fisheries in Ireland. It was tied on a very large hook; body was made from black hair from an Indian dog, wound with yellow wool, making largely marked alternate bars of black and yellow, ribbed with thin gold tinsel; yellow hackle; wings of dark turkey feather and red ibis; tail, three fibres of red ibis. This fly proved so successful that our whole party used it, and found it very killing. Black silk chenille may be used to replace the Indian dog hair.

As to salmon flies, I found the Silver Doctor to be by long odds the most taking; next to that, Jock Scott and Professor.

A word about the Nipigon fishing. I have met a number of fishermen in the last year or two who insist upon it that the Nipigon fishing is overrated; but this has not been my experience, or that of the parties with whom I have been fishing; and I believe the fish are as plenty to-day and run as large as they did five years ago; but they are certainly better educated, consequently more wary, and not to be caught by tyros who throw their flies any how into the water. But the skilled fisherman, the man who can place his flies like thistledown on the water fifty to seventy feet away, and can handle them when hooked, will always find grand sport in this noble river, and very large fish.

At the same time it would not be surprising if the river was depreciating, when we consider it is the ambition of all North American trout fishers, good, bad, or indifferent, to get to the Nipigon, and that at one time in August of last year there were nearly one hundred on this short river of fifty-six miles.

I use nothing but the Sproat hook; I prefer it to the Pennell eyed hook. For leaders and snoods, I use the finest and best gut I can find, and use only single gut. If care were taken always to well moisten and to test the gut before making up and before using, there would be little necessity for doubling.

---

| | | |
|---|---|---|
| *Canada, Nova Scotia, and Maine.* | Jenny Lind.<br>Silver Doctor.<br>Professor.<br>Toodle-bug.<br>Black Gnat.<br>Parmacheene Belle.<br>Yellow May. | Trout, Grilse, and Bass. |

J. M. Dill,                    Dorchester,                    Mass.

One summer, a friend and I, with guides, went into the woods north of the St. Lawrence, on the headwaters of the Rivière du Loup. We carried the usual assortment of flies, but a small Jenny Lind was about the only fly that seemed to give any sport; this was in July and August.

Another season, on the Liverpool River in Nova Scotia, all other flies, including the Red Ibis, Jenny Lind, Professor, Silver Doctor, Toodle-bug, the various Hackles, etc., were all useless, and a small, very small Black Gnat was the only thing grilse would touch. My studies of bright flies for dull days, bright ones for twilight, have never brought that success which the books warrant. In northern Maine, and the vicinity of the Tim and Seven Ponds, the Parmacheene Belle seemed the best, judging from my own and others' experience; this was in July. Over on the waters of the West Branch of the Penobscot, I found the Professor the best August fly in my book.

In my somewhat limited bass fishing, I remember that on some of the ponds in Maine the Yellow May was a taking fly. These are my especial experiences, as I recall them; possibly another man on the same waters will testify quite differently. I am, as I said at the beginning, no fisherman; like Abou Ben Adhem, I fear my name is not in the book, but I write as one who loves the woods and streams, and who has passed many happy hours in and near them.

---

| *Canada.* | { Parmacheene Belle. <br> { Queen of the Lake. | |
|---|---|---|
| W. W. HALL, | Quebec, | Canada. |

I consider the Parmacheene Belle the best fly all round for trout, and no more can be said for the same than the recommendations given in " Fishing with the Fly."

We find that a fly closely resembling the Abbey, with a small jungle-cock feather laid over the wing, is a very taking fly indeed, especially in the evening, and on dull days; we call it the " Queen of the Lake." The jungle-cock feathers I consider a great improvement to a number of flies; some flies, of course, it would not suit.

---

|                                   |                                                          |              |
|-----------------------------------|----------------------------------------------------------|--------------|
| *Nipigon River and Wisconsin.* | { Blue Jay. Professor. Royal Coachman. Grizzly King. Silver Doctor. |              |
|                                   | { Raven. Blue Bottle.                                   | { For Bass. |

C. W. Bunn,                          St. Paul,                              Minn.

As regards trout fishing in Wisconsin and about Lake Superior, I have found the Silver Doctor perhaps the most taking fly under all circumstances. The Professor, Royal Coachman, and Grizzly King, in the territory mentioned, are among the most reliable flies, and any fisherman equipped with the flies above mentioned can certainly take trout where trout are to be found.

In April, 1889, fishing for trout in northern Wisconsin, which you will observe was very early in the season for fly-fishing, I found the Silver Doctor, Professor, and Seth Green, in the order named, to be the most taking flies; the remainder of the party fishing with bait, I caught with those flies a larger number of fish than was taken by any other of the party, and of quite a good average size.

In the Nipigon River, the Silver Doctor and Royal Coachman I have found on the whole to be very effective. The largest trout I have ever taken, or seen taken there, weighing up to six pounds, were taken after five o'clock in the evening, on one or the other of these flies. However, last summer I had remarkable success upon the Nipigon with the Blue Jay; so much so that with a Blue Jay fly on the leader I seldom caught trout on any other. These flies were tied usually on No. 1 hooks.

One more word in regard to flies for black bass fishing, which may be of interest. I have no hesitation in placing the Raven at the head of the list, and the Blue Bottle next. Without exception, where I have seen these flies used they have taken two to one as many fish as any others, and I have frequently found black bass rising freely to these flies when it was almost impossible to allure them with anything else.

---

| *Canada.* | { Parmacheene Belle<br>{ Grizzly King. |

F. HALLOWAY,                    Quebec,                    Canada.

My best takes have been on the Parmacheene Belle and Grizzly King flies, which are strongly recommended for the lakes of the north of Quebec.

---

| *Nova Scotia.* | { Silver Doctor.<br>Montreal.<br>Queen of the Water.<br>Professor.<br>Brown Hackle.<br>Grizzly King.<br>Parmacheene Belle. |

C. W. HINMAN,                    Boston,                    Mass.

My fly-fishing has been principally for trout in Nova Scotia, where the water is somewhat colored; and it has been confined to the month of May (in Nova Scotia).

The best trout run from $\frac{1}{4}$ to $2\frac{1}{2}$ pounds in weight, and I find No. 4 to No. 6 a good size for hooks. I have had good success as a general thing with the Montreal, but have found the Silver Doctor nearly if not quite as good. With these two flies and the Queen of the Water and Professor, I think I could catch just as many trout where I am accustomed to fish as with any number of flies.

The Brown Hackle and Grizzly King are also good flies, and I have found the Coachman good at dusk, while the Parmacheene Belle proved good during the last of the fishing. For the last three years I have had all my flies tied on Pennell eyed hooks. I consider these hooks the best shaped of any on the market. The eye enables one to use a fly until it is worn out, does away with the fly-book, and allows the flies to be kept in a box without being pressed flat; also, the change of flies can be made quicker than with ordinary snell.

---

| *Canada.* | { Fiery Brown.<br>Lord Baltimore.<br>Munro. |
| --- | --- |

JULIUS P. BUCKE,                    Sarnia, Ontario,                    Canada.

The cast I prefer for trout is the Fiery Brown, made by Trout & Son. Body, bright reddish mohair, ribbed with tinsel; hackle, bright dark red; tail, strands of golden - pheasant crest feather; wings, dark mallard.

I send you samples of the two others. They are tied by myself. One has been called the Munro; the original of it was found in a bush, on a stream emptying into Lake Superior, by a friend, who found it to work well, had it repeated at Toronto, and gave me one for a pattern. I have called it after him. Tail, red ibis and mallard, dyed yellow; hackle, yellow; body, bright green, ribbed with gold tinsel; wings, red ibis, covered with wild turkey. The other fly is the Lord Baltimore modified. These flies will catch trout, and so will others, but I always have had success with them, and feel confident and like going in to win when they are on the cast. Of course, I always like to have a general assortment of winged flies and hackles along, for, as a Spiritualist once observed during his lecture in this town, "sometimes the spirits will work, and sometimes they won't; it depends upon the conditions." Trout are fickle also. This cast has been found to work well on Loon Lake and the Nipigon, north shore of Lake Superior, and in the water near Murray Bay, Quebec.

---

*Nova Scotia.*

- Zulu.
- Soldier.
- Gray Drake.
- Ibis.
- Queen of the Water.
- Grizzly King.
- Cow Dung.

CLAUDE D. BLACK, Amherst, N. S.

The Gray Drake and Grizzly King are fished with successfully on bright days, but the best satisfaction I ever get is with the Red Ibis, or the Soldier, in a sluggish stream or on a cloudy day. In relation to size, I do not think the Ibis as successful as the Queen of the Water in taking large fish, though it is a very sure fly for all around fishing.

I have had great success at times with a fly called the Zulu, having several times taken trout with it when I could do nothing with any other. It is of English origin, and is black, with a short red tail, and is tied on a No. 12 hook, being very small. Most of our flies are tied on No. 6 or 8 hooks, No. 8 being the popular size.

The most of my fishing has been for trout on lakes and streams. We seldom take one larger than 3 pounds, but fish from 1 to 1¾ pounds are not scarce.

| *Canada.* | { Professor.<br>Wickham's Fancy.<br>Duns. | { Trout. |

WILLIAM WOODRUFF,         London, Ontario,         Canada.

In the month of May, I use the Professor, Wickham's Fancy, almost all the standard brown flies, such as the March Brown, Turkey Brown, Brown Hen or Chantrey, Governor, Brown Palmer, Red Cock Palmer, Cow Dung, when the water is lumpy; Coachman on dark days; and the Alder when the weather is warm, — all upon No. 9 hooks; the Blue and Olive Duns, of dark to light and lighter shades, upon Nos. 10 and 12 hooks. With regard to the Duns, I believe in the theory that their shades vary; that on cool days they become darker, whilst on warm, sunshiny days they assume lighter shades. After a flood, during the latter part of May or early in June, when the water is yet high, the fish all over the stream, and the water not over clear, the Coch-y-Bonddu, the Soldier Palmer, and a bright Red Cock Palmer will do great execution. In fact, the Coch-y-Bonddu, the Red Cock Palmer of suitable sizes, as well as the Wickham's Fancy and Governor, may be relied upon all through the season. As the season advances, the weather becoming warmer and the water low and clear, I use flies on No. 12 hooks; the colors of subdued shades, with the hackle quite plentiful, that they may float more or less. When any gray flies are upon the water, the Gray Palmer and Gray Drake are effective. During hot weather, when the midges are on and the fish are skirmishing around, I rely chiefly upon the Furnace Hackle; later on, and in the fall, the King of the Water, the Light and Dark Montreal, and the Grizzly King; on cloudy days, as well as in the evening, the Coachman, Gray Stone, and Gray Palmer.

## PLATE D.

| | |
|---|---|
| No. 30. Jock Scott. | No. 33. Popham. |
| No. 31. Durham Ranger. | No. 34. Wilkinson. |
| No. 32. Black Dose. | No. 35. Black Doctor. |

No. 30.  The Jock Scott seems to arouse the enthusiasm of every one who writes or speaks of it.  In the nineteen lists of flies, spoken of in connection with the Childers, received in response to the questions sent out by the " English Fishing Gazette," and published in that paper, the Jock Scott is included in every list except two, and the other seventeen lists are led by either the Jock Scott or the Silver Doctor, these two flies being without doubt the prime favorites with salmon anglers the world over.  Major Treherne indorses the Jock Scott in these words : " During my long experience, I have found it to be the best fly ever invented.  I have used it from the largest size, in spring fishing, down to the small one inclosed, with which I killed a twenty-three pound fish in the Dee, where the water was so low that every one else had given up trying."  Perhaps Mr. George Kelson's praise is the most powerful of any we find, because he clearly explains his reasons and conclusions in the following : —

" Remembering the simple method of judging, at the river-side, which kind of fly is best for the moment, thus adapting what has been said with regard to light and shade, color of water, and so on, we shall find that no fly illustrates my theories so perfectly and so satisfactorily as does Jock Scott.  Fitted with all the most ingenious appliances of color devised by angling science, no other pattern puts forward such pretensions to be perpetually in season.  It is equally of service when the light is gathering strength, in the grayness of morning, as in even the brightest of noonday sunshine.  Or when we welcome peaceful evening in, implicit confidence may also be placed in it, many instances having occurred of its successes at this time of day.  Against the sombre background of summer woods Jock Scott is equally effective, while all sorts and conditions of men sing its praises in high or low water, in gales of wind or in dead calms.  Whether used in rushing torrents or in more tranquil waters, where its appearance is enhanced according to geological formations or the varieties of substance in the bed of the river, the attractiveness of this special treasure is ever the same. Other origin than that of its intrinsic worth, of its legendary influence, equally observable in the brightest or dullest weather or water, there is none. No other fly fishes so well in ordinary pools, streams, flats, and rapids, taking them altogether, eddies and still waters alone excepted. Coming to the details necessary to show how the universal fitness of Jock Scott comes about, I am naturally forced to the conclusion that, before constructing this fly, its inventor, the late Lord John Scott's water bailiff, had come to hold similar opinions to my own with regard to the effect of certain colors. It stands to reason that this experienced and ingenious individual asked himself the question, What colors assembled together would play the important part of invariably accommodating themselves to the ever-varying elements of weather and water, on which salmon anglers are so dependent? That he succeeded in his choice goes without the saying, since every one readily admits that, if perchance one were peremptorily restricted to the use of one fly only all the year round, that fly would be none other than Jock Scott. The majority prefer it because they find it successful, doubtless without knowing that the success is the natural outcome of its wonderful combinations.

"There is ample show and attraction in the tail and first portion of the body, backed up by the gaudy fibres in the wings, the cheeks, and the sides, to lead one to select the pattern for employment in clear water. It is when the water is bright that one and all of those items appear at their best, and therefore most advantageously.

"On the other hand, in dark water nothing shows so well as black; and here we have the natural black hackles, doing duty over floss silk of the same color, besides the white-tipped turkey in the under wing, together with the gallina throat. To complete the gathering, the strands of the sword feather of the peacock have the power of active operation in dark, deep dells and nooks and corners. The inventor of Jock Scott incontestably took his cues from nature herself, who seldom leads her earnest students astray."

Our own reliable authority in this country, Mr. Henry P. Wells, who never makes a statement until he has carefully thought upon and tested its truth, suggests in his book, "The American Salmon Fisherman," the following as a limited assortment for salmon fishing in Canada: "Jock Scott, Silver Doctor, Black Dose, Brown Fairy, Durham Ranger, Fiery Brown, Butcher or Popham, and Black Fairy. But always have plenty of Jock Scotts. It holds the rank among salmon flies of the Brown Hackle among trout flies, in that it is universally applicable to any and every water with good effect."

Mr. Wells has invented a salmon fly, which will be seen in Plate H, that has proved valuable in American waters. It is to be used in conjunction with Jock Scott. He calls it the Moisic-Grub, and writes of its success, as will be seen in the note accompanying the fly. We feel an eagerness that it shall prove a worthy squire to the older and ever-valiant knight.

No. 31. The Durham Ranger was invented nearly thirty years ago by James Wright, of Sprouston, Kelso, and has continued popular ever since its first appearance. It is especially recommended for three qualities, — proportions, transparent brilliancy owing to the abundance of golden-pheasant feathers, and a power of attracting from a distance. Mr. H. P. Wells has described some interesting experiments made by means of a glass tank, looking up through which he could view the effect of the flies as seen by the fish. The depth of the water was not sufficient to convey all the impressions of the stream or lake, but it was, to an extent, satisfactory and conclusive. When our magnificent aquarium is completed for the Columbian Exposition, there may be opportunity for experiment, and an astonishing amount of light be thrown upon the mysteries of effectiveness of artificial flies. It is to be hoped that this chance for investigation will not pass unimproved.

We quote from Mr. Wells's account of his experiments several paragraphs that will explain somewhat the advantages of the combination called the Durham Ranger, a combination containing nearly all the materials most powerful in luminous qualities.

" The tank was five feet long and fourteen and a half inches deep, measured on the inside. Where the bottom met the ends apertures were formed three inches high and the width of the tank, which were inclosed with plate glass. When the tank was in use, the head of the observer and the end of the tank, as well as the glass at the opposite end, were so wrapped in black rubber-cloth as to exclude all light except such as entered through the surface of the water.

" To the end of a salmon-rod tip a piece of copper wire, in shape like an inverted T, was secured by a freely movable joint. To the cross-piece of the T the flies to be examined were secured by pieces of very soft iron wire, about the thickness of fine sewing thread. The joints at the points where the iron wires were secured to the copper wire, as well as where they were attached to the loop at the heads of the flies, admitted of perfect freedom of movement. Six flies could thus be simultaneously compared.

" It was thought best to choose well-known flies of uniform size, and by a well-known maker, for experiment.

" Flies tied by Forest, of Kelso, Scotland, on No. 1 O'Shaughnessy hooks were therefore selected, of the following varieties: Jock Scott, Durham Ranger, Silver Doctor, Silver Gray, Butcher, Black Dose, and Black Fairy. Subsequently a Fiery Brown was added. My first effort was addressed to determine whether the salmon did mistake the fly for a minnow or shrimp, as by many supposed. My belief that salmon take the fly as and for food, and for no other purpose, has been elsewhere stated, together with the reasons upon which that belief is based. . . .

" The sky was entirely overcast and leaden in color, with rain  The water in the tank was in what would generally be considered first-class fishing condition ; that is, very slightly turbid, the tank having just been filled. A whitebait was selected of the same length as the wings of the flies, and suspended in a like manner from the copper wire with two flies on each side. Throughout these experiments the flies were manipulated two or three inches below the surface of the water, as is customary in salmon fishing.

" A marked increase in the size of both fish and flies when submerged, over that in air, was first noticed, — an apparent increase of one half, if not somewhat more.

" At the extreme farther end of the tank the whitebait was unmistakably a fish, and nothing else. As long as the flies were sufficiently near the observer to enable him to distinguish their details of construction, they bore not the faintest resemblance to the fish. But when moved to the farther end of the tank, the bodies of all, except those of the Silver Gray and Silver Doctor, disappeared altogether. Then, when those flies were moved which were provided with mixed wings, of which the crest of the golden pheasant formed part, the wings seemed to flash with reflected light in a manner and with an appearance not unlike that of the fish. The effect was extremely beautiful to my eye. It was like the intermittent flash of a firefly, lighting up the closely contiguous water with a mellow glow, yellower in color, and by no means so pronounced and incisive as the flash of the minnow. Mere inspection would, I believe, fail to enable any one to determine the nature or form of the object ; but something was there softly luminous, and endowed with motion and apparent life. Had it been possible to view the fish through a thicker stratum of water than that of the five feet which the tank contained, I could not question that as its form became more obscure  its resemblance to such flies became more and more marked. . . .

" Whether the full blaze of an unclouded sun fell on the water, or whether the sky was like lead and the hour late, at all times and under all circumstances light colors were far more conspicuous than dark. This was to be expected. All non-luminous opaque bodies are visible solely by reflected light, and the more perfect the reflecting surfaces, the more light will reach the eye and the more visible they will be. The silver bodies of the Silver Doctor and Silver Gray were the most obtrusive; then yellow, including golden-pheasant crests, jungle-cock neck feathers, the darker color of golden-pheasant tippets, reds, browns, and blacks, in the order given. With the rain-sky, only the butt of the brown mallard wing of the Black Fairy where it merged into the gray could be seen at their feet, while all but the wing of the Black Dose disappeared as well. The Fiery Brown could be seen a little farther, and a little beyond this the Butcher disappeared. Those flies having a mixed wing with a golden-pheasant crest topping, or light colors in the body, were at the same time quite visible the entire length of the tank.

" Swan's feather and goat's beard, both dyed yellow, were added to the wing of the Black Fairy, to test their respective values as substitutes for the expensive golden-pheasant crests. Both lacked the peculiar sheen of the crest, and were thought to be decidedly inferior. The jungle-cock neck feather, employed so frequently upon the cheeks of flies, was a very conspicuous feature at all times, when anything beyond the flash of the crest feather of the wing or the sheen of the silver bodies could be seen. When a dark-colored body was visible the hook was invariably at least equally conspicuous. Silver tinsel appeared to be more efficient than gold, as might be expected from its higher reflecting power, though both held their own well."

Therefore, according to these experiments of Mr. Wells's, confirming well-established theories, that furnish suggestions for the construction of any fly, we find fulfilled in the Durham Ranger the requisites for a brilliant and well-nigh irresistible fly.

No. 32. Black Dose. We find that we are taking too much space for theories and facts regarding the growth of favorite flies into popular favor, and we must curtail accounts of the same, although it would be interesting to quote the thoughtful opinions of various fishermen; for we desire these notes to express, as far as possible, prevailing views regarding flies, and the individuality of the anglers who have used them, rather than our own personal opinion and knowledge merely

But to give all we should like in relation to them would too greatly enlarge a book already grown far beyond our original intentions. We shall, therefore, strive to limit where we can, and will only say of the Black Dose that it has become especially noted for fishing in Norway and Canada, and is generally to be found in the fly-books of the salmon anglers frequenting those localities.

No. 33. Anglers contend for the honor of having invented the Popham. A variety of it is said to have been introduced over thirty years ago by Mr. John George Children, living at that time at Halstead-place, Kent, England; but the pattern that is most familiar to us is that named after Mr. F. L. Popham, another British angler. This Popham is, I fancy, more popular on this side of the Atlantic than in the land of its birth. It is in particular favor for the salmon of the Pacific slope; it has also been found excellent for trout fishing in the lakes of Maine.

The Prince William of Orange salmon fly, represented in "Fishing with the Fly," bears a strong resemblance to the Popham, and seems to be used under similar circumstances with equal success.

No. 34. The Wilkinson is another fly that has been adopted by American anglers as an especial favorite. Its silver body and bright feathers cause it to be liked for late fishing. Mr. P. D. Malloch recommends it highly for autumn fishing, to follow the Jock Scott, and be used where such flies as the Silver Doctor or Dusty Miller would be chosen.

No. 35. Black Doctor. The energy with which men and women will each uphold their own especial favorites among the medical fraternity against the claims of others is a well-established fact, and amusing if you do not happen to be in the controversy; if you are drawn into it, your own powers of defense are apt to be as vigorous as those you inclined to ridicule when not involved. Of artificial flies, the Doctor, Silver Doctor, Blue Doctor, and Black Doctor each have their adherents, but like the doctors of the medical profession they have their specialties, and each upon occasion is more successful than the others; so it is well to acknowledge their merits as a whole, and judge by their successes, which may be most relied upon under different circumstances; for the circumstances of time, place, wind, weather, dan state of the water determine the case, and dictate a choice among them. Where one would fail, another may rescue from despair.

Made by C.F. ORVIS, Manchester, Vt.

PLATE E: DESCRIPTION PAGE 95

Made by C.F. ORVIS, Manchester, Vt.

PLATE F: DESCRIPTION PAGE 113

Made by **C. F. ORVIS**, Manchester, Vt.

PLATE G: DESCRIPTION PAGE 125

Made by C.F. ORVIS, Manchester, Vt.

PLATE H: DESCRIPTION PAGE 139

| | | |
|---|---|---|
| *Nova Scotia.* | Brown Hackle.<br>Coachman.<br>Cow Dung.<br>Royal Coachman.<br>Grizzly King.<br>Parmacheene Belle. | Trout and<br>Grayling. |

EDWARD E. FLINT, Chicago, Ill.

My favorite fly is the Brown Hackle, but I have been almost as successful with the Coch-y-Bonddu, which it so closely resembles. I have found it a killing fly at all hours and seasons, and in many waters.

The Cow Dung, Coachman, Royal Coachman, and Grizzly King have at times been equally good. When all these have failed, a Parmacheene Belle, Reuben Wood, and a large silver-bodied fly with a black head, and red and yellow wings, name unknown to me, have occasionally proved successful.

While fishing in Nova Scotia for brook trout, last May and early in June, a red-bodied Brown Hackle and the Parmacheene Belle were my most taking flies, the latter at evening. In September, in the same streams, I found the Cow Dung much superior to the other flies. I think seven out of every ten trout I caught on this fly. Of twenty-four taken on successive days, and weighing a fraction over twenty-four pounds, all but three were taken on the Cow Dung. The preference for it was so marked that I repeatedly changed its position on my cast, sometimes using it for a stretcher, and again as a dropper, in connection with perhaps twenty different flies, and always with but two on every cast ; there was no change ; it was invariably the favorite.

I have often heard of such instances, when trout showed a decided preference for one particular fly, but it stands alone in my personal experience. My flies are tied on a sneck Kendall hook No. 7 and

8, except the Parmacheene Belle, when a No. 3 is used. I believe the peculiar bend of this hook strikes a happy medium between ease of penetration and holding powers. I am convinced the snells should be stained and of a dark mist-color, and should be as fine as possible, and yet strong enough to serve the purpose, say capable of standing a strain of 1 to 1½ pounds for ordinary trout fishing. The loops seem to be more convenient when short.

Getting a fly upon the water carefully and making its motions resemble those of the insect have always appeared to me far more important than the use of any particular fly.

----

*Canada.*                    Oak Fly.

C. E. MARTEL,                    Quebec,                    Canada.

Having heard very often that trout do not rise to the fly on Lake Edward, I take the liberty of inclosing one that I have used on that lake with fair success.

The best season to fish on this lake is, to my knowledge, from the 1st to the 15th of June.

NOTE. — The fly sent was a large Oak fly on No. 2 O'Shaughnessy hook.

----

*Canada.*                    Salmon Fly.

ERASTUS CORNING, JR.,                    Albany,                    N. Y.

My fishing is all done in Canada. I use up there, on a stormy day, *i. e.* windy and dark, a light brown fuzzy fly tied on a No. 6 hook, and very large. I have had good success with it, but the fly is condemned by my fishing friends in this vicinity for trout fishing. I believe the best flies are the White Miller, Professor, Green Drake, and Hackles, tied on No. 12 sneck bend hooks.

| | | |
|---|---|---|
| *Canada.* | New Fly.<br>Red Ibis.<br>Professor.<br>Coachman.<br>Brown Hackle. | Trout. |

FRANCIS C. GREEN, Boston, Mass.

The only fish that I have killed that are not in the common way were some trout on Prince Edward's Island.

In Charlottetown, I made the acquaintance of the "Old Fisherman" of the town, and he made a fly for me like the one I inclose, which is killing in those parts in early summer. You may know this fly, but as I never saw one anywhere else, I am under the impression that it is original with my friend in Charlottetown.

I have had only good sport at the head of the Brudnell River, P. E. I., when I used with varying success the Red Ibis, Professor, Coachman, and Brown Hackle.

NOTE. — See fly called Prince Edward in plate of Lake Flies.

---

| | |
|---|---|
| *Canada, Maine,*<br>*and*<br>*New Hampshire.* | Brown Hackle.<br>Silver Doctor.<br>Professor.<br>Grizzly King.<br>Scarlet Ibis.<br>Coachman.<br>Parmacheene Belle.<br>Jenny Lind. |

E. S. MERRILL, Winchendon, Mass.

It is doubtful if I can give you anything new or of much interest, as I have never given much thought or attention to a large variety of gaudy flies, but have made the acquaintance of the more modest. After casting awhile and getting no rise, I exchange for another kind.

When I first fished the Rangeley Lakes, forty years ago, we thought there was no fly like the Montreal, and it proved very good, too; for thirty years I used that, and the Brown, Ginger, White, and Gray Hackles, and the English Blue Jay; later on, I depended more on Brown Hackles with tinsel and green bodies, and the newer flies that were then coming on. The first nine-pound trout I caught below Morrell Rocks I took with a Brown Hackle; the one a few years later with a large Montreal.

Fishing one day below the dam, at Rangeley, a gentleman who had fished near me for some time, and without success, asked what kind of fly I was using. I told him that I had taken the last fish on a Brown Hackle. He wanted one, and I gave him two or three, putting one of them on his leader. He had not cast ten minutes before he hooked a five-pound trout. But they will not always take Brown Hackles at this same dam: the year following, I fished with a good fisherman, and tried in one day, nearly three dozen large gaudy flies without getting a rise.

In Canada waters, I have had good success with the Silver Doctor, Professor, Grizzly King, Scarlet Ibis, Coachman, Jenny Lind, Hackles, and Grey Miller. For King and Bartlett lakes, and Tim Pond, near Eustis, Maine, the Parmacheene Belle is quite taking and the Silver Doctor good. Of course I use many other flies not named, and take fish with them. For water that I do not know, and for a "blind cast," or as a reserve cast, I generally use a Brown Hackle, Scarlet Ibis, or Parmacheene Belle, and, third, some other fancy fly.

Different waters and latitudes have their influence, also. As an instance, a hundred and fifty miles northeast from Montreal, I noticed the flies and insects upon and around the water, and upon which the trout feed, differed somewhat from those of a more southern latitude. I find that if the artificial fly is assimilated to their food they take it apparently more readily, but at times they will take the opposite from pure wantonness, seemingly. I have a small trout pond of eight or ten acres where the common black house-fly seems to be the favorite, and a small Jenny Lind: these two also are good at Monadnock Lake in Dublin, N. H.

---

| *Maine.* | Toodle-bug. | Trout. |
|---|---|---|
| E. T. WHITMORE, | Putnam, | Conn. |

The Toodle-bug is greatly used by the fishermen at Rangeley, and with much success.

---

| *St. Lawrence River and The Catskills.* | Strawberry. Josephine. |
|---|---|
| O. D. M. BAKER, | Poughkeepsie, N. Y. |

For a number of years I have used flies quite extensively each season, and, upon the whole, with satisfactory success.

As to bass flies, I have had the best results in the use of red, white, and the combination in various forms of the two colors.

Six or seven years ago, in tying some bass flies for my own use, in a random way I made a few with scarlet chenille bodies, white hackles, and grass-green wings; also some with bodies of the same shade of green chenille, with scarlet wings, — both kinds tied upon 1/0 Sproat hooks.

The appearance of these colors so much resembled the strawberry and leaves that I dubbed the flies the Strawberry.

Except on the St. Lawrence River, I have had no special success in their use, but there, on several occasions, I have been exceptionally favored in being able to take larger fish, in greater numbers, than did my associates using other flies.

In the waters of that river I have also had excellent sport through the use of hackles of the Pennell style, with bodies, about the diameter of an ordinary lead pencil and as long as possible to tie upon a 1/0 Sproat hook, wound with large white hackles and a silver or gilt cord made of a number of small gilt threads twisted, and with heavy white hackles at each end of the body.

At other times a hackle of the same pattern, made with yellow gilt cord instead of silver, has proved very useful.

Flies of this style can be used in a strong wind, when it would be almost impossible to cast those having wings, while the grub-like shape and appearance in the water at times seem attractive to the fish.

For trout fishing I have ordinarily used the standard varieties of flies.

The only exception in my experience came in this way. Several years ago, my daughter, then about thirteen years of age, was so seriously injured as to be confined to the house for a long time, and, to amuse herself, very successfully made trout flies in imitation of those found in my fly-book; then the spirit of variations possessed her, as it does all amateurs, I believe, and she made, among others, some like the ordinary Coachman, except in the substitution of scarlet wings for white.

I have used these flies in the Catskills for three successive seasons, and have taken more and larger fish with them than with any other fly.

We have called them the Josephine, after the name of the maker.

It may be that there is nothing new in any of these flies, but I have never seen or heard of them elsewhere.

The clear, light single snell has always been the most satisfactory to me, and I have never observed any indication that the fish were in any way alarmed by the white appearance of the unstained silk.

---

| *Restigouche and Matapediac Rivers.* | Jock Scott.<br>Black Dose.<br>Silver Doctor.<br>Durham Ranger. | Salmon. |
| --- | --- | --- |

JAMES BARNES BAKER,              New York,              N. Y.

In writing of the Restigouche and Matapediac rivers one necessarily writes of the Restigouche Club, because that club now controls the larger portion of the fishing on both rivers.

I should advise any novice who is fortunate enough to have an invitation to fish these waters, or, for that matter, any salmon stream, to read Mr. Henry P. Wells's book, " The American Salmon Fisherman." Mr. Wells wrote this book shortly after he became a master in the art, and had not yet forgotten the trials and failures that beset the beginner. In it he sets forth, in his clear and exhaustive way, everything that can be of assistance, and a careful study of this book will give one more real facts, free from personal theories and " guides' tales," than any other book I know of.

The Jock Scott, Black Dose, Silver Doctor, and Durham Ranger are the regular diet of the Restigouche salmon. The value of these flies ranges as they are written, — the Jock Scott first, and the Durham Ranger last. In size, No. 1/0 and No. 2 single hooks, No. 5 and No. 8 double hooks, I have found sufficient. If flies are made on the Pennell eyed hooks, they will last much longer. The hook itself is a good one, made on scientific principles. A few flies of any variety added to the list given, to make a decided change for a fish that has "come short," I found answered every purpose.

The club keeps a book in which are recorded the weight of fish, when taken, fly used, and general remarks. At the end of last season's fishing, the four flies named had taken about three hundred out of three hundred and seventy fish, actual count from the record. The seventy were scattered through twenty varieties. I prefer a first-class, plain, well-made click-reel, and I don't know of any one who makes a satisfactory one for the market. The best way, perhaps, is to get the best reel to be had, and have it altered to suit. Its mechanism should be as perfect as that of any delicate piece of machinery. I prefer a rod of about fifteen feet. It is too hard work to use one much over that in weight; a rod much under is coming near the line of a single-handed rod, and might be mistaken for such, to one's mortification.

In handling the canoe the main point is to keep below the fish, so that he has both the current and line to take away his strength. It seems to me that the supposed time of killing a fish is much exaggerated unless the actual time is taken. I once killed a twenty-five-pound fish, fresh run, on a medium-weight, fifteen-foot rod, and happened to have my watch lying on the bottom of the canoe before me. When the fish was in the canoe, and had received its quietus, I asked the guide "how long the fight lasted." He said "about twenty minutes." His assistant agreed. The actual time was a few seconds over seven minutes![1]

---

[1] In the photograph entitled "A Pleasant Memory" may be seen the salmon referred to in Mr. Baker's letter as having been killed in a little over seven minutes. — M. E. O. M.

**No. 36.** The Alexandra, named after the Princess Alexandra, may not properly be called an artificial fly, being intended as a vague imitation of a minnow, and was originally recommended to be cast and played minnow fashion just below the surface of the water.

This pattern was invented by Dr. Hobbs a number of years ago, and it came into great favor with English fishermen; indeed, it was believed to be so taking that its use was forbidden on some streams. Their favorite method was to allow the line to run with the current, and then draw it back up stream by short, sudden jerks that opened and closed the hackles, giving glimpses of the bright, silvery body.

In this country the Alexandra is not often dressed on small-sized hooks, but is preferred on large hooks, and is used for trout in deep, dark waters, or for black bass, for either of which it is frequently effective, owing probably to its likeness, when being drawn rapidly through the water, to a tiny minnow. This fly was originally named by General Gerald Goodlake "Lady of the Lake," but this name was afterwards abandoned in favor of Alexandra.

**No. 37.** The Brazilian Blue-Wing, known quite as often as the Beatrice, was named at first from the feather of its wing. It is one of those odd flies that one falls back upon in emergencies, which is not of the uniform value we attribute to other patterns, yet many times proves of exceptional service.

Blue is not a popular color for trout or bass flies, yet it would sometimes seem that it is the best color with which to raise a sulky, obstinate trout. The extraordinary experiences related by many with the Jenny Lind, Puffer, and other flies having blue in their composition go to prove that it is never wise to be without some fly with blue in its make-up, any more than it would be safe to rely wholly upon flies of that color alone, for there are times when these blue flies are successful where all other flies seem to fail. They form an interesting study, fruitful of many theories.

No. 38. The B. Pond is written of in the letters from Mr. Freeland Howe and Mr. R. N. Parish. It was named after one of the Maine lakes near Middle Damand is popular for that region. The fly strongly resembles another called the Brandreth, after Colonel Frank Brandreth, of Sing Sing, N. Y. The latter fly is much used in the lakes of Hamilton County, and is an excellent fly for both trout and bass. We cannot gain positive information as to which fly was first introduced, and which should have the precedence in name and credit.

No. 39. Black Prince. Perhaps no fly, since the ever famous Fiery Brown, was more discussed and written of, for a few years, than the Black Prince. As with the Black Knight of romance, there was a mystery connected with this Black Prince; no one seemed to know, or perhaps to be ready to declare, just whence he sprang, and to assert his true rights; and many were the doubts as to the correctness of his colors, whether the doublet should be of silver or gold. Even the tiny plume of red was declared out of place on this black knight, but finally the Prince with doublet of gold, scarlet plume, and sable mantle held his own, and was accepted as tried and true and admired of all, and has since fought and conquered in many a royal battle.

It should also be mentioned, in connection with the Black Prince of American origin, that there is another and quite different fly known in England under this name. It is a salmon fly, the invention of Major Treherne. The following is the formula for dressing it : —

*Tag.* — Silver twist and very dark yellow silk.

*Tail.* — A topping.

*Butt.* — Black herl.

*Body.* — Three equal divisions of silver tinsel (flat), butted with two black feathers from the nape of the Indian crow at the termination of each section, and peacock herl.

*Wings.* — Five or six golden toppings.

*Korns.* — Blue macaw.

*Head.* — Black herl.

Something in this fly may have suggested the American Black Prince, but his successor is far less richly dressed, though we hope as well arrayed for contests and conquests.

No. 40. The Royal Coachman was first made in 1878 by John Haily, a professional fly-dresser living in New York city. In writing of other matters, he inclosed a sample of this fly for us to see, saying : "A gentleman wanted me to tie some Coachmen for him to take up into the north woods, and to make them extra strong, so I have tied them with a little band of silk in the middle, to prevent the peacock bodies from fraying out. I have also added a tail of the barred feathers of the wood-duck, and I think it makes a very handsome fly." A few evenings later, a circle of us were together "disputing the fly question," one of the party claiming that numbers were "quite as suitable to designate the flies as so many nonsensical names." The others did not agree with him, but he said : "What can you do? Here is a fly intended to be a Coachman, yet it is not the true Coachman ; it is quite unlike it, and what can you call it ? " Mr. L. C. Orvis, brother of Mr. Charles Orvis, who was present, said : "Oh, that is easy enough ; call it the Royal Coachman, it is so finely dressed ! " And this name in time came to be known and used by all who are familiar with the fly.

No. 41. The Cassard was designed in 1886 by Mr. William J. Cassard, of New York city.

Mr. Cassard is the happy owner of undoubtedly the finest collection in the United States of everything in the shape of modern fishing implements. All are arranged and kept with the most perfect system. A beautiful chest or long box of cedar, lined with softest plush, holds his fly-books. Each book is filled with flies, and has a memorandum of contents, so that a glance tells one where to find anything wanted. These books contain flies of every description, for Mr. Cassard aims to make his collection as complete as possible, and no one is better informed than he regarding the endless varieties. His snuggery is a fascinating place to any one loving hunting or fishing. One corner is devoted to pictures of flies and fish, and shelves filled with angling-books ; another is occupied by rods of every description ; a third to a case of reels ; the fourth to guns ; a side of the room to a cabinet holding photographs of the many happy hunting and fishing grounds, for Mr. Cassard is an expert photographer as well as angler. His exquisite taste and intelligence regarding all these possessions make the hours fly by like moments, when in the midst of his treasures. Pipes and easy-chairs there be, too ; and when, at last, we turn from all these we echo " the brave old sign,"

" Hic habitat felicitas ! "

Under the yaller-pines I house,
   When sunshine makes 'em all sweet-scented,
An' hear among their furry boughs
   The baskin' west-wind purr contented,
While 'way o'erhead, ez sweet an' low
   Ez distant bells that ring for meetin,'
The wedged wil' geese their bugles blow,
   Further an' further south retreatin'.

LOWELL.

## MAINE.

GEORGE H. PENDERGAST . . . .
$\begin{cases} \text{Scarlet Ibis.} \\ \text{Silver Doctor.} \\ \text{Parmacheene Belle.} \\ \text{Yellow May.} \end{cases}$

JOSEPH B. TOWNSEND, JR. . . . { Silver Doctor.

WILLIAM GOLDTHWAIT . . . .
$\begin{cases} \text{Red Ibis.} \\ \text{Reuben Wood.} \\ \text{Jenny Lind.} \\ \text{Parmacheene Belle, etc.} \end{cases}$

IRVIN N. FRASSE . . . . . .
$\begin{cases} \text{Bumble Bee.} \\ \text{Parmacheene Belle.} \\ \text{Jungle Cock.} \\ \text{Montreal, etc.} \end{cases}$

GEORGE F. GALE . . . . . .
$\begin{cases} \text{Scarlet Ibis.} \\ \text{Silver Doctor.} \\ \text{Montreal.} \\ \text{Grizzly King, etc.} \end{cases}$

FRANK S. FAY . . . . . . .
$\begin{cases} \text{Montreal.} \\ \text{Tim Pond.} \\ \text{Jenny Lind.} \\ \text{Silver Doctor, etc.} \end{cases}$

A. C. HEFFENGER . . . . . .
$\begin{cases} \text{New Lake.} \\ \text{Professor.} \\ \text{Toodle-bug.} \\ \text{Cabinet, etc.} \end{cases}$

CHARLES H. CHESEBORO . . . .
$\begin{cases} \text{Blue Jay.} \\ \text{Montreal.} \\ \text{Professor.} \\ \text{Katoodle-bug, etc.} \end{cases}$

W. G. BRIERY . . . . . . .
$\begin{cases} \text{Grizzly King.} \\ \text{Silver Doctor.} \\ \text{Montreal.} \\ \text{Hackles.} \end{cases}$

R. E. PICKTHALL . . . . . .
$\begin{cases} \text{Silver Doctor.} \\ \text{Parmacheene Belle.} \\ \text{Montreal.} \end{cases}$

| | |
|---|---|
| D. W. C. FARRINGTON . . . . . | { Professor.<br>Silver Doctor.<br>Plymouth Rock.<br>Juno, etc. |
| FREELAND HOWE . . . . . . | { B. Pond.<br>Montreal.<br>White Miller.<br>Royal Coachman, etc. |
| JOHN W. WEBSTER . . . . . . | { Webster.<br>Montreal.<br>Silver Doctor, etc. |
| EDGAR W. CURTISS . . . . . . | { Hamlin.<br>Montreal.<br>Silver Doctor. |
| J. W. HILL . . . . . . . . | { Hill Fly.<br>Portland.<br>Ibis.<br>Parmacheene Belle, etc. |
| C. W. NEWHALL . . . . . . . | { White Miller.<br>Red Ibis.<br>Cow Dung.<br>Montreal, etc. |
| RAYMOND B. PARISH . . . | { B. Pond.<br>Abbey.<br>Parmacheene Belle.<br>Yellow Sally, etc. |

---

| | | |
|---|---|---|
| *Maine and*<br>*Canada.* | { Scarlet Ibis.<br>Silver Doctor.<br>Parmacheene Belle.<br>Yellow May. | { Trout and<br>Land-locked<br>Salmon. |

GEORGE H. PENDERGAST,            Charlestown,                         Mass.

Although a lover of the sport of fly-fishing, I make no claim to be an expert. My experience has been chiefly in Maine and New Brunswick for trout, and in New Brunswick for land-locked salmon.

For trout, a gaudy fly seems best, and none better than the Scarlet Ibis, although the Silver Doctor and Parmacheene Belle are nearly as good.

For land-locked salmon, Parmacheene Belle, Yellow May, and Silver Doctor are my favorites. I think when fish are rising the kind of fly does not make so much difference as many imagine. In a dark day a brilliant fly can be used, and in a very clear day a darker fly, with something bright on it to glitter; the silver on the Silver Doctor seems to be effectual, and then again, without any apparent reason, the fish will have nothing to do with any fly, conditions as far as seen being the same.

I like a No. 5 Sproat hook for general use, and I hardly think it makes much difference whether the snells are stained or not, but they should be with loops every time, as they are more convenient in changing flies.

---

| *Maine, Canada, and Pennsylvania.* | { Silver Doctor. | { Trout, Black Bass, and Sea Trout. |
|---|---|---|

JOSEPH B. TOWNSEND, JR.,          Philadelphia,          Pa.

I have no hesitation in saying that I have been more successful, year in and year out, with the Silver Doctor than with any other fly. I tie it in sizes ranging from No. 4 to No. 14, and use it on all waters, and with less varying success than any fly I wot of. I have taken salmon on it, when apparently no other fly would stir a fin; in northern Maine and Canada, both for brook and sea trout, it has proved most successful; in our Pennsylvania mountain streams, on hooks ranging from 10 to 14, I find it extremely killing.

For black bass, too, I find it about the best fly I can use. I tie this fly after a pattern given me on the Magalloway River, several years ago, by a gentleman from Boston, and thinking it may interest you to inspect it, as it differs somewhat from the plate given in your book, I beg to inclose a specimen. I use this fly irrespective of the time of day or the season of the year, and, while the inclosed sample happens to be tied on unstained gut, generally tie it upon gut dyed a neutral tint, approximating " mist color."

NOTE. — See Silver Doctor with guinea-fowl hackle, plate of Lake Flies.

---

| | | |
|---|---|---|
| *Maine.* | ⎰ Red Ibis.<br>Montreal.<br>Parmacheene Belle.<br>Brown Hackle.<br>Professor.<br>Reuben Wood.<br>Seth Green.<br>Jenny Lind. ⎱ | ⎰ Trout. ⎱ |

WILLIAM GOLDTHWAIT,              Springfield,              Mass.

Ten years ago, up in Maine, I took my first lesson in the art of fly-fishing from Professor Alfred M. Mayer, of Stevens Institute. Since that time I have spent the two months from the middle of October at the Maine lakes, at Tim Pond, the Seven Ponds, and of late in the Nickatons Lake region.

The most successful fly at Tim Pond was the Red Ibis. At the other named lakes it was good, but not decidedly the best. My favorite cast for the Maine lakes is a Red Ibis or Parmacheene Belle for stretchers, a Montreal fly for first dropper, and a Brown Hackle for second dropper.

At times, other well-known flies, as the Professor, Reuben Wood, Seth Green, or Jenny Lind, and others, are about as good, but seldom, in my experience, better than the other four.

Very many of the flies said to be the best in other localities I believe to be practically useless in Maine waters. I have tied many flies myself different from anything in the catalogues, and have had good luck with some of them ; but none of them have been named. Perhaps the best was a green chenille body, cardinal red hackle, and mallard wings.

I have used very thin gutta percha for wings ; they look well, and are very durable, but they did not seem to suit the taste of the trout.

I prefer for general use a No. 6 forged O'Shaughnessy hook.

The color of the leader, I think, makes but little difference with the Maine trout. I like single gut, rather heavy for leaders, and flies on long strands.

---

|  |  |  |
|---|---|---|
| *Maine.* | Bumble Bee.<br>Jungle Cock.<br>Parmacheene Belle.<br>Brown Hackle.<br>Montreal. | Trout. |

IRVIN N. FRASSE,                    Philadelphia,                    Pa.

Our camps were situated on Lakes King and Bartlett, Franklin County, Maine.

For the lake fishing, myself and friends found, first, the Parmacheene Belle; second, the Jungle Cock; third, the Brown Hackle; and fourth, Montreal, to be the best; and we preferred a hook varying in size from No. 2 to No. 4. All our flies were tied on Sproats.

For stream fishing we preferred the Parmacheene Belle, Jungle Cock, Brown Hackle, Red Ibis, and Montreal ; and at certain times we found the Bumble Bee excellent, but could find no way to tell when it would be best, except by trying it. We used No. 6 hook.

It was very hard to determine the worth of the flies in stream fishing. We fished on the Spencer, and although I have spent three months out of each year for the last twelve years in hunting or trout fishing, I never saw such a number of trout as I saw in that river. On any ordinary day the trout would take the old frayed flies, or a round naked hook, about as well as the best made fly of our assortment.

---

| *Maine.* | Scarlet Ibis. Brown Hackle. Silver Doctor. Montreal. Grizzly King. Black Gnat. | Trout. |

GEORGE F. GALE, Brattleboro, Vermont.

What fishing I have done for the last twenty years has been with "the fly." Fourteen times I have spent all, or nearly all, of the month of June on or about Moosehead Lake, Maine, fishing only for *Salmo fontinalis* as found in the lakes and large streams. My favorite flies are Scarlet Ibis, Brown Hackle, Silver Doctor, Montreal, Grizzly King, and Black Gnat.

I find by my minutes that the Scarlet Ibis, as tied by C. F. Orvis, has killed more trout for me than any other two flies used. I prefer medium sized rather than large flies. The Black Gnat should be very small. I like the Sproat hooks. Smaller and darker flies on a bright day than on a dark one. Stained gut always, but not too dark. Throw an unstained leader on the water of an aquarium and observe it by looking upward through the water, and it becomes as conspicuous as burnished silver. Long smooth strands for the leader; short ones, six inches, for the fly. I have discarded taper lines for lake fishing. I have killed most trout between three and six o'clock P. M., on the lake.

Maine.　{ Montreal.
Lord Baltimore.
Scarlet Ibis.
Jenny Lind.
Parmacheene Belle.　　} Trout.
Tim Pond.
Brown Hackle.
Yellow May.
Silver Doctor.

FRANK S. FAY,　　　　　　　Meriden,　　　　　　Conn.

For fishing in the lakes and ponds in the Maine woods, from August 15th to September 10th, or thereabouts, my favorites are the Montreal, Lord Baltimore, Scarlet Ibis, Jenny Lind, Parmacheene Belle, Tim Pond, Brown Hackle, Yellow May, and Silver Doctor.

I like the Yellow May for evening fishing, though the Lord Baltimore seemed to work well in all weathers and in all lights, and took the larger fish, while the Silver Doctor caught the smaller. If there were dace or chub about, they generally " went for " the Silver Doctor. Some anglers claim to be able to pick out the trout by a quicker, sharper cast when dace, etc., are troublesome, but I do not know how that is. I do not claim to.

I very much prefer leaders with loops for flies, and good sized, single gut, mist-colored, and not over six feet in length. I prefer about a No. 4 hook, for all flies ; a small fly is good, of course, when bright, hot, no breeze, etc., but I generally stay in camp in such weather, and a large fly, in my experience, gets the larger fish.

A little wrinkle by which I used to get rises was to put a " worm " on the end fly, and let it go down to the bottom, draw up slowly and repeat. I would oftentimes get a bite on that, and in slowly working it up get two fish on my flies, and draw to the surface others that would take my next cast.

This is rather a rambling letter. I should have mentioned locality more definitely. Parmacheene Lake, Tim Pond, the Rangeleys, Upper and Lower Wilson, and Mountain ponds, near Greenville, Katahdin Iron Works, and ponds Long and Big and Little and Houston, are the localities to which I referred in regard to my favorite flies.

---

| *Maine and New Hampshire.* | Coachman. New Lake. Professor. Silver Doctor. Montreal. Grizzly King. Yellow May. Toodle-bug. Cabinet. | Trout. |
|---|---|---|

A. C. HEFFENGER,         Portsmouth,         N. H.

Until 1878 I had faithfully practiced bait-fishing, but some graceful and exhilarating fly-fishing I saw in Maine waters in that year decided me to try the fly, and I have persistently adhered to it since.

My experience has been confined to fishing for trout in the New Hampshire and Maine waters, chiefly in the Rangeleys and Moosehead Lake regions. If I were asked which fly was the most killing at all times and under all circumstances, I should unhesitatingly say the Coachman. I have tried the Coachman noon and night, in bright and in dark days, in roiled and in clear waters, and it was taken more persistently than any other fly I have ever seen.

Of course there are many times when other flies do far better, but in the Rangeley and Moosehead Lake waters it is the best all-around fly, in my opinion.

The next taking fly I have found to be the New Lake, gotten up some years ago by the late Mr. Alonzo Prouty, of Boston. This fly has a silver body, yellow hackle, and brown wings, with a red feather sprig for the tail. After the Coachman and the New Lake, a number of flies have proved equally killing, according to weather and localities. The Professor, Silver Doctor, Grizzly King, Montreal, Yellow May, Toodle-bug, and Cabinet are those I should recommend.

At the west outlet from Moosehead Lake the water is covered with little, brown, large-winged gnats during the latter part of June; but I never got a rise on a Brown Gnat, though the jumping trout would take a fly with red in it while snapping at the natural gnats.

Of course it is well known that a large fly takes in Maine waters, but I think the Rangeley fishermen have overdone it; for many use flies as large as salmon flies, and whip unsuccessfully for hours and days in September, when they would catch double the number of fish on a fly half the size.

The Sproat is unquestionably the best hook to tie flies upon, and it cannot be of too good quality, for I have seen many fine trout lost through the breaking of a hook. The snell should be clear, single, and light or heavy according to the size of the fly, and consequently the fish to be taken.

I prefer long strands of gut with loops; also loops on the leader.

NOTE. — We venture to suggest here that the objection to the Sproat hooks is their liability to break, even those of the best quality and make; for this reason we fear to use them when likely to hook large or strong fish.

| *Maine.* | { Blue Jay.<br>Montreal.<br>Silver Doctor.<br>Professor.<br>Katoodle-bug. | { Trout. |

CHARLES H. CHESEBORO, Putnam, Conn.

I have tried many flies, but have been more successful with the Montreal, Silver Doctor, Professor, and Katoodle-bug. The Professor is good at evening or on a dark day, but the others are good at any time.

I prefer medium-sized hooks, and clear, long strands of gut. This applies entirely to Rangeley Lakes fishing, as that is where nearly all my experience has been obtained. Had wonderful success once at Cedar Stump, on Rapid River, below Middle Dam, capturing eighteen trout, from 2 pounds to 5½ pounds, all taken with a Blue Jay; but the fish were there and ready for business, and perhaps some other fly would have done as well.

---

| *Maine.* | { Grizzly King.<br>Professor.<br>Silver Doctor.<br>Montreal.<br>The Hackles. | { Trout. |

W. G. BRIERY, Dexter, Maine.

During the fishing seasons of 1888 and 1889 I made four or five trips to Moosehead Lake, the date ranging from June 15th to July 15th, and in 1888 one trip as early as June 9th. I found the Grizzly King to be the best fly I could use at any hour of the day. I have used it at all hours, from early morning until evening.

Next to this fly I find the Professor, Silver Doctor, Montreal, and the Hackles are all good, in about the order here named. I like No. 6 Sproat hooks, but at times find No. 1 or No. 2 Sproat hooks good in this vicinity.

---

|            | { Silver Doctor.      |            |
| *Maine.*   | { Parmacheene Belle.  | { Trout.   |
|            | { Montreal.           |            |

R. E. PICKTHALL,                    Boston,                    Mass.

Five years ago I first used a fly-rod, and since then I have availed myself of all opportunities to become better acquainted with the sport of fly-fishing. I am the happy possessor of "Fishing with the Fly," and value it highly.

My fly-fishing has all been at Seven Ponds, Tim Pond, and the Dead River region of Maine, for three years during the latter part of May and the first of June; and in 1887 and 1888, in the month of September. Last year was the first that I kept a regular score-book with notes and account of results from different flies and methods, but my recollections of previous years are good, and of some value to me, at least.

I remember distinctly that in 1884, '85, '86, in which years I visited Tim Pond and Seven Ponds early in June, my cast was made from Scarlet Ibis, Professor, Grizzly King, White Miller, and Brown Hackle; a favorite cast of three flies being Scarlet Ibis, Professor, and Brown Hackle. Last year my order was for eleven varieties, viz., Parmacheene Belle, Silver Doctor, Montreal, Scarlet Ibis, Grizzly King, Professor, Cow Dung, King of the Water, Stone Fly, Seth Green, and Brown Hackle. Of these, my record mentions as favorite casts, Silver Doctor, Parmacheene Belle, Montreal, the Doctor being the most killing fly, while in 1887, the same time of year, September, the Parmacheene Belle seemed to be the best.

While I tried faithfully all the flies named, the cast of three flies given was the best, and it made little or no difference as to position of the flies, or time of day, except, of course, the evening fishing was always the best by far. I do not expect this will be of any particular use to you, as it is a too limited experience, but it is pleasant to recall and relate. I have always used flies tied on Sproat hooks, and have always considered them good; have failed many times to hook my fish when I have had a good rise, but always took all the blame to myself. Last year I fished for bass some, using hellgamites on hooks like sample inclosed, with great success; and one week ago (Fast Day) I took my first trouting trip on a stream not more than ten miles from Boston, and, with a companion, brought home fourteen trout weighing, six hours after caught, $6\frac{3}{4}$ pounds. Both of us used hooks same size and style of inclosed; we hooked every trout that "bit" at our worm; never lost one while "playing" him. Would such a hook be a proper one to use for fly-fishing?[1]

---

|  |  |  |
|---|---|---|
| *Maine.* | Queen of the Water.<br>Montreal.<br>Blue Jay.<br>Red Hackle.<br>Brown Hackle.<br>Red Ibis.<br>Professor.<br>Quack Doctor. | Trout. |

WILLIAM J. EPTING, Philadelphia, Pa.

Just a few lines to let you know how we spent last summer (1891). We stayed at Maquam Bay but seventeen days. The fishing was

[1] The hook inclosed was a "Kendall sneck bend;" and it is a fact worthy of notice, that while it frequently happens that anglers use this hook doubtfully, they testify to their unusual success in hooking their fish with it. — M. E. O. M.

miserable; the largest catch of bass made there in a single day was but eight, and that was made by father and myself. We next went to Round Mountain Lake, in Maine. It is forty miles from Kingfield, the last railroad station, after which you go by stage twenty-eight miles to Eustis, over elegant roads, and make the drive in six hours or better. From Eustis to the camp is twelve miles over a corduroy road. Round Mountain Lake is in the Dead River region. It is about one mile long. The camps are located about one hundred and fifty yards from the lake, and command a fine view of the five round mountains directly opposite on the other side of the lake, which lake abounds with myriads of trout running from $\frac{1}{4}$ to $1\frac{3}{4}$ lbs. Near the camp are two fine trout streams, called the Big and Little Alder. The Little Alder runs into the Big Alder, and that empties into the Dead River. These creeks are full of gamy fish. Father and I caught in Big Alder, in five hours, about five hundred trout with the fly.

Smith's camps are composed of twelve large and separate spruce log cabins. The bark is peeled to keep away the vermin, and the spaces between the logs are filled up with moss to keep out the air. The table is excellent, and the camps are kept in perfect condition; the attendance, also, is very good.

I inclose you a piece of the line I used in England. It is for your daughter, and is intended for a curiosity. They use these lines around Lincolnshire altogether, and catch fifteen-pound lake trout and twenty and thirty pound pike with them.[1]

We stayed eight weeks at Round Mountain Lake.

[1] The piece of line sent was of closely-twisted white silk, soft finish, and not larger than No. 40 white cotton thread. — M. E. O. M.

## PLATE F.

No. 42. Green Weaver.

No. 43. Golden Pheasant.

No. 44. Gray Duke.

No. 45. Fiery Brown.

No. 46. Grackle.

No. 47. Grasshopper.

No. 42. Green Weaver. This fly, so far as we can learn, is one of those that "sprang up in a night," but of sturdy growth in the favor of fishermen. Its delicate coloring is in pleasing contrast to many of the deeper-hued flies; and it seems to be found useful as a change from them in fishing in the large lakes.

No. 43. Golden Pheasant. In our quotation from Mr. Wells's book regarding his experiments with artificial flies viewed through the water in a glass tank is explained the peculiar power possessed by the feathers of the golden pheasant of reflecting the light, making them visible beyond all other materials used in fly-making. While airy and graceful, they are also of hard surface, and do not become matted, nor readily absorb the water. Mr. George Herne, of Hertfordshire, England, has made a specialty of breeding golden pheasants to furnish feathers for fly-making, and the feathers from his birds are far superior to those of any other that we know; the crest feathers deepening to the dark, beautiful orange, almost blood-red tips that so greatly enhance the perfection of the salmon flies; the markings on the neck feathers or frills are also deeper and more distinct. Different makers vary in their dressing of the bodies of the Golden Pheasant flies, but that shown seems to us to be in the best harmony, and is, we think, the best known, and most used for salmon, large trout, bass, and sea trout.

No. 44. The Gray Duke, Golden Duke, and several similar flies have lately become popular patterns for lake fishing, more especially since the yearly migration of camping parties up into the now famous fishing-grounds of the Nipigon and Maine regions, where large, strong flies are a necessity.

No. 45. Fiery Brown. Charles Cotton, in speaking of the proper flies to use in the month of March, describes a fly which is probably the original of the Fiery Brown, but he calls it the Bright Brown, "the dubbing for which is to be had out of the skinner's lime-pits, and of the hair of an abortive calf, of which the lime will turn to be so bright as to shine like gold; for the wings of this fly the feather of the brown hen is best." Later he writes of December, saying: "Few men angle with the fly this month, no more than they do in January: but yet, if the weather be warm, — as I have known it sometime in my life to be, even in this cold country, where it is least expected, — then a brown that looks red in the hand, and yellowish betwixt your eye and the sun, will both raise and kill in clear water." This sentence, "red in the hand, and yellowish betwixt your eye and the sun," has become famous almost, and an enigma. It is used to describe the body of the true Fiery Brown fly; "but it is one of those things no man can find out." Such frequent reference is made to the difficulty in obtaining the "real Fiery Brown" that it may be interesting to reprint the letters regarding the same which appeared in 1864 in "The Fisherman's Magazine," the story having become almost history connected with the "real Fiery Brown."

SIR, — In Mr. Ffennell's very interesting and entertaining article, which appeared in "The Fisherman's Magazine" a few months ago, that gentleman refers to the "real Fiery Brown" in connection with salmon flies. As it is possible that the allusion may not be quite so well known to all your readers as Mr. Ffennell would appear to think, I inclose, for the chance of its being acceptable, an extract from Colonel Sir James Alexander's "Salmon Fishing in Canada," which gives a very humorous account of the origin of the term in question; and am, etc.,          WILDRAKE.

To the Editor of The Fisherman's Magazine.

When I lived [says the colonel] in the county of Clare, and fished Rosroe Lake, a son of Captain Bridgeman, who resided in the neighborhood, used frequently to accompany me in my excursions, and whenever the trout were sulky and the sport was dull my young friend used to heave a heavy sigh, and utter an ardent wish that we had "*one fly made of his father's real fiery brown.*" As this was often the case, and we could not by any manœuvring get hold of the old gentleman's book of colors, I wrote to Martin Kelly to send me a dozen of "fiery browns." In a few days I received the flies, which appeared to me everything that a man or trout could wish for, in an extremely civil letter from old Martin, in which he expressed an ardent hope that they would be found according to order, and an earnest expectation of further commands. I hastened to notice my friend Bridgeman to meet me at Roger Hickey's, the usual rendezvous, early on the following morning, convinced that I had got the real thing, and that we should have a boat full of trout before the shades of evening fell upon us. When at length we had got under weigh, I handed my tail fly to my companion, with the question, "Well, Bridgeman, what do you think of that?"

"Well," said he, "that's a neat fly, and ought to do."

"That's the 'fiery brown,'" said I.

"Oh, no," said he. "It's a good *brown*, but it's not the real fiery brown."

Our sport on this occasion was indifferent, so on the following day I addressed another epistle to old Martin Kelly, telling him I was pleased with the flies he had sent me, and convinced that earlier in the season they would have done good work, and requesting him to send me a dozen of the real *fiery* browns of the same size. In due time Martin transmitted to me the flies, stating that extreme pains had been taken to meet my wishes, and expressing a confident hope that they would give satisfaction.

Again I summoned my friend Bridgeman; again we failed to realize the sport which he had always promised me from the possession and exhibition of the real *fiery brown*. Rather impatient at the bad sport, and disgusted at the imputation cast upon the credit of my ancient friend Martin, I held a fly between Bridgeman's eyes and the light, and rather testily asked him, while I pointed to the glistening fibres in the body, "If that is not fiery brown, will you be good enough to tell me what it is?"

"Oh," said he, "the fly is well enough, and as neatly tied as one could wish; but still it's *not* the *real* fiery brown." Strong in my faith in old Martin, I again addressed him, emphazising in my order for another dozen of flies the word "*real*." Again I had an extremely civil reply, inclosing another dozen of well-tied flies, and assuring me that, in compliance with my former orders, he had done his utmost, as well as in the present instance, to meet my wishes; and venturing very respectfully to suggest that I should send him a pattern of the colored fly I required, in which case he had no doubt but that he could execute the order in such a manner as to give satisfaction. In answer to which, after having failed to have any great success with the flies he inclosed, I wrote to him to say "that a specimen or pattern of the *real fiery* brown was the very thing of which I was in search, and that if he could not furnish it I must only say it was by no means creditable to his establishment." Upon this, I received a short, well-written letter, in which the old man asserted that he had spared no pains, having sent to both Scotland and England for varieties of the fiery brown, specimens of all of which he had sent to me; but he perceived with regret that in the present instance he could not please me, and begged, therefore, very respectfully, to give up the commission. Very shortly after the termination of this correspondence, which was seriously commenced, and towards the conclusion carried on in banter, old Martin Kelly died; and one of my imaginative friends insisted that his inability to discover the *real fiery brown* was the cause of his illness and his death. I should add that the desire for the real fiery brown had spread very widely amongst Irish fishermen at this time, several having read the letters above alluded to, and mentioned the matter to others, so that I believe few days passed over, during that summer, in which there was not some application at Kelly's shop, in Sackville Street, for this mysterious and unobtainable fly.

Several years subsequent to these events, and after I had been four years in Canada, and had ascertained the virtues of the fiery brown in the waters of the Marguerite and Eschemin, having occasion to write to my old friend, college companion, and law agent about some legal matters, I requested him to send me a small parcel of color in his reply, to which request I received the following answer : —

DUBLIN, 41 UPPER M. STREET, 19th *July*, 1845.

MY DEAR FRIEND, — I rejoiced at receiving your epistle, notwithstanding that it was silent as to my last to you.   I essayed to gratify your desire for the " fiery brown " immediately upon learning your wishes, and " I 'll ever remember the day," as the song has it, for " may I never do an ill turn " but I was near suffering for it.

The most natural place for getting the fiery brown was of course the most celebrated and the most convenient, so in I toddled to Martin Kelly's.   It goes by the same name still.

And " Pray," says I, " have you got any fiery brown ? "

" Say that again," says a fellow with an ugly aspect, that put me in acute remembrance of your brother-in-law, Dr. Bell.

" Have you any fiery brown ? " said I again.

" Oh, by the holy," says he, " you 're one of the gang that killed my father.   Fire me if I don't *brown* you ! "

And without doubt he seemed bent on making me *black* and *blue*, for he let fly the butt of a salmon rod at me, which, most fortunately for me, being misdirected by his wrath, went against the glass door of the shop, which it smashed.   I forthwith threw myself on the protection of a policeman who was passing, and who advised me to charge him ; this, however, I declined to do, dreading the publicity of so ridiculous a history as would have come out, and which, as sure as a gun, would have been laid hold of by Lever, and I 'd have been persecuted to the death by the wags.

The next day I went to a decent man of less notoriety, who does a little splicing for me now and then, and sells me flies.   On my proceeding to make the inquiry for you, he grew very red about the gills, and said he was " sorry to find I came to humbug him." I assured him I had no such intention, and that I wanted the article for a gentleman in Canada.   " Oh, now," said he, " I am sure you 're going it, for it was a fellow who went there that killed poor Kelly with his fiery brown ; " and then, altering his tone, he added, " Sir, I 'd rather not have anything to do with the fiery brown at any price ; I am striving to rear a large small family, and for God's sake, sir, leave me to do so in peace."

Now, I 'll tell you what I did next.   I followed Kelly's example and gave up the commission, but I hope it will not cost *me* my life.   Any other kind of brown you want I 'll do my utmost to procure, but just don't ask me to mention fiery brown again in Dublin, or I think it will blow up the city.

*1st August*, 1845.

After I had written the foregoing, and before I could seal and dispatch it, I happened to meet in the street your friend Bomford, and amongst other topics of conversation turned up your commission to me for the fiery brown, and my failures. " Oh, said he, " come with me to Ettingsal, on the quay ; he does a deal of business in Galway, and knows me very well." Of course, as I was most anxious to get you what you wished for, I went with Bomford to the shop. " Pray,'' said I, in the most bland manner possible, " *can* you procure me some fiery brown ? " Whereupon the individual who was behind the counter, after looking steadily at us in silence for a minute or so, drew up his left hand to a level with his mouth, applies his thumb in a very significant manner to the tip of his nose, protrudes a considerable length of tongue, cuts some cabalistic figure or motion with his right hand, and asks me if " my mother is aware that I am out."

I am fearful, my boy, that you have been playing tricks with me, and that either no such thing ever existed as pig's wool, or that a certain black gentleman shaved it all off whin he took to amusing *hisself* in that way ; but I am, as ever,

Your affectionate friend,    T— B—.

I need not take the trouble to explain to my piscatorial readers — and I desire no others — that the fiery brown is now well understood, and may be obtained not only at Martin Kelly's, but at any other respectable fishing-tackle warehouse, without the slightest danger of being smitten with a salmon rod or of disturbing the peace of an industrious tradesman. And, moreover, I would not advise any fisherman to come to Canada without an ample supply of it, though I am confident the *exact* hue of the *real* fiery brown will with difficulty be agreed upon by any two fishermen or manufacturers.

No. 46.  The Grackle flies are named from the birds of that name. The fly shown in the plate is, we think, a greater favorite than the Black and Yellow Grackle, though the latter is often found desirable.

No. 47.  Grasshopper.

> Green little vaulter in the sunny grass,
> Catching your heart up at the feel of June,
> Sole voice that's heard amidst the lazy noon,
> When even the bees lag at the summoning brass ;
> And you, warm little housekeeper, who class
> With those who think the candles come too soon,
> Loving the fire, and with your tricksome tune

Nick the glad, silent moments as they pass ;
O sweet and tiny cousins, that belong,
One to the fields, the other to the hearth !
Both have your sunshine ; both, though small, are strong
At your clear hearts ; and both seem given to Earth
To ring in thoughtful ears this natural song, —
In doors and out, summer and winter, — Mirth.

LEIGH HUNT.

The poetry of earth is never dead :
When all the birds are faint with the hot sun,
And hide in cooling trees, a voice will run
From hedge to hedge about the new-mown mead :
That is the grasshopper's.   He takes the lead
In summer luxury ; he has never done
With his delights ; for, when tired out with fun,
He rests at ease beneath some pleasant weed.
The poetry of earth is ceasing never :
On a lone winter evening, when the frost
Has wrought a silence, from the stove there shrills
The cricket's song, in warmth increasing ever,
And seems, to one in drowsiness half lost,
The grasshopper's among some grassy hills.

JOHN KEATS.

Every one who attempts artificial insects sooner or later undertakes an imitation of the grasshopper.  Some of these imitations bear close resemblance to the originals, and have been made with bodies of wood, cork, or quills, and covered with silk, wool, rubber, and silkworm gut; but they are apt to be clumsy, lacking as they do the spring and softness of the real insect.  Any one who will invent a grasshopper with the natural " kick " in it has a fortune in his hands.  That pictured in the plate can claim semblance only because of colors that in the water may suggest the red-legged grasshopper, so successful as bait.  This pattern came to us ten or twelve years ago from Mr. Harry Pritchard, of New York, who for a time made the only flies sold of this combination; they were in great demand with his customers.  Since then this fly has become generally known, and has proved excellent for large trout and bass, as well as small trout.

| *Maine.* | { Montreal.<br>Royal Coachman.<br>B. Pond.<br>White Miller.<br>Parmacheene Belle. | { Trout. |

FREELAND HOWE,         Norway,         Maine.

I do most of my fishing at the Upper Dam, Oxford County, Maine, where I always go twice, and sometimes three times a year. I go in the spring as soon as the ice is out, when the fish are taken with bait, either still-fishing or trolling with a minnow, by which we take the largest fish. Last spring my largest was six pounds. May, 1888, I took one with an angleworm, weighing eight pounds.

The fall fishing has not been good the past two years. I took one trout with a Montreal fly in the fall of 1888, which weighed five pounds, a beauty, giving me good sport for twenty minutes or more.

The Montreal, B. Pond, and Royal Coachman are good flies, and the White Miller I find the best for evening fishing. For spring fishing I think the Parmacheene Belle the best. It has been used only a few years, but with good success.

Regarding snells, I like the clear heavy gut, long strands. Leader single, without loops, as I use only one fly.

---

Flies recommended for Maine trout by Lorenzo Prouty : —

| | |
|---|---|
| Black Hackle. | Prouty. |
| Scarlet Ibis, with some white. | Nameless. |
| Blue Jay, English Jay. | Tinseled Ibis. |
| Golden Pheasant, tinsel body. | Yellow Moose. |
| Brown Hackle. | Megalloway. |
| Richardson. | Bemis. |

| | | |
|---|---|---|
| *Maine.* | { Webster.<br>Grizzly King.<br>Montreal.<br>Parmacheene Belle.<br>Silver Doctor. | { Trout. |

JOHN W. WEBSTER,                    Waterbury,                    Conn.

I have had much experience in fly-fishing in Maine, having spent several weeks there annually for thirty years.

I have found the Grizzly King, the Montreal, and the "Winged Brown Hackle" standard and always reliable flies. In a dark day the Parmacheene Belle and Silver Doctor are excellent; they are effective in fishing at twilight, also.

There are certain waters, particularly inland ponds, where the Scarlet Ibis is almost the only fly that succeeds. Of course there are numerous other flies which are good, but the varieties named are all that are needed to make a complete outfit. For spring and summer fishing in the Maine waters, flies upon No. 5 Sproat hooks are my preference. In autumn, larger flies are often used successfully. The snell should be medium in weight, reinforced where joined to the hook, but single, and not over six or seven inches in length.

I do not regard the coloring of the snells of much importance, but if stained they should be light blue. The winged Brown Hackle[1] should have a red tail. I will send you a fly that the maker saw fit to name the Webster, which I regard as nearly perfect, and effective on any waters.

---

[1] A Hackle is a hook dressed with the usual materials, but without wings. Mr. Webster probably intended the well known Brown Hackle, with wings added, when it would technically be termed an artificial fly. — M. E. O. M.

*Maine.*　　$\left\{\begin{array}{l}\text{Hill Fly.}\\\text{Portland.}\\\text{Grizzly King.}\\\text{Scarlet Ibis.}\\\text{Parmacheene Belle.}\\\text{Jungle Cock.}\end{array}\right.$

J. W. HILL,　　　　　　　Waterbury,　　　　　　　　Conn.

It would be rather a hard matter to determine which are the best flies at different times, seasons of the year, etc. There are three flies that I think of that I have always had good success with, particularly at the Rangeley Lakes in June, viz., the Portland (or Montreal), Grizzly King, Cinnamon Hackle, and occasionally the Scarlet Ibis. One season I had great sport with the Jungle Cock and Yellow Sally. The Parmacheene Belle is also a good fly for a dark day, or just at sundown. The Katoodle-bug I consider one of the best of flies for all-round fishing, at any season.

I am much in favor of the English tied flies, or I should say of the material they use. The flies furnished Mr. Hunt this spring, tied from the sample of English flies, are as perfect as anything can be, and are just as good as their English prototypes, and cost considerably less. One of the samples I had great luck with last June, in one morning's fishing, taking seventeen fine trout in two hours, from one pound up to two and a half pounds. Mr. Hunt has named it for me, calling it the Hill Fly.

---

*Maine.*　　$\left\{\begin{array}{l}\text{Hamlin.}\\\text{Montreal.}\\\text{Silver Doctor.}\end{array}\right.$　$\left\{\begin{array}{l}\text{Trout and}\\\text{Land-locked Salmon.}\end{array}\right.$

EDGAR W. CURTISS,　　　　　Meriden,　　　　　　　　Conn.

My fly-fishing has been done usually at the Rangeley Lakes, Maine, and in the fall. At times I have had good sport with two flies which are my especial favorites, the Hamlin and the Montreal. My good luck with these particular flies very naturally gives them favor over others, in my mind. Supplementing my experience with the Hamlin in these waters, I can add the testimony of William H. Fullerton, of Windsor, Vermont, with whom I have fished, and whose name gives a weight that will be recognized by all fishermen who have had the pleasure of meeting him.

I have brought more fish to the net with the Hamlin than all others combined. At times the fish would prefer other flies, and as the light began to fade the White Miller would be taking, yet I have seen a five-pound trout captured by moonlight on a Hamlin.

Last year I made a departure from my usual practice and visited the lake in the early part of June, and enjoyed good sport, particularly with the land-locked salmon; for these I used the Silver Doctor. The efficacy of the Silver Doctor with the fish was demonstrated by two other fishermen. Mr. C. P. Stevens, of Boston, caught one weighing 5½ pounds, and Mr. Parish, of Montville, Conn., one of the same weight. This fly, I think, is generally considered the most killing for this fish.

---

| *Maine.* | { White Miller.<br>Red Ibis.<br>Cow Dung.<br>Montreal. | { Stream fishing<br>for Trout. |

C. W. NEWHALL,                    Worcester,                    Mass.

There is such a pleasant and varied picture in following a stream through woodland and meadow that I prefer brook fishing to any other; and on my visits to Maine, with one exception, I have always followed the streams, and with good success. I find that I can catch more fish from five A. M. to ten A. M. than during the remainder of the day.

I have used the White Miller, Red Ibis, Cow Dung, and the Montreal. The first named worked best in a dull day, when the sky was overcast, or toward night. The Red Ibis and Cow Dung have yielded equally good results on the bright parts of pleasant days. I have tried my Montreal flies only once or twice without a rise to reward my efforts. Sometimes you may try every fly made, and the fish will not rise; why, I know not, but have resorted to hooking my fly on an alder-leaf, and with good results.

Prefer medium-sized sneck bend hooks.

---

| *Maine.* | B. Pond. Brown Hackle. Montreal. Abbey. Parmacheene Belle. Yellow Sally. White Miller. | Trout. |

RAYMOND N. PARISH, Hartford, Conn.

Regarding favorite flies, I find each season varies more or less as to the most taking flies. I visit the Rangeleys each year, in June and September usually. Some seasons a fly is unusually good, and perhaps the next year it is not good at all. A most excellent fly with me, nearly every time, is the Brown Hackle; red body, dressed either with the hackle the whole length of the body, or at the head only; not much choice as to that.

The Montreal, dark, or Canada flies have proved very good flies at this season, and I took two of my largest fish with them; there is but little difference in the two flies, but the claret body and hackle suits me the best. The Abbey has also proved a most excellent fly. Some seasons the Professor leads, but this time did not seem to be acceptable.

A local fly at the Rangeleys, called the B. Pond, in most years is the best there. One spring the Yellow Sally was the most taking fly, but I have taken but few fish with it since. The Parmacheene Belle, for two or three seasons past, has been very good in early morning, or just at night, but this year I was not successful with it. The White Miller proved better.

I inclose herein the fly B. Pond. It has been used a little, as you will see; but I have none entirely new. The way it originated is this: a local fly-maker near the Rangeleys made it according to his own fancy several years ago, and used it on a pond near the lakes, called " B " pond, so called from being in the township " B; " he found it to be very successful there, and it has now become one of the standard flies for the large lakes in that vicinity. I do not know that it is made by any other than this local fly-maker. It has proved better for spring than for fall fishing, although sometimes in the fall it is very good. How it will take in other waters I cannot tell, as I have tried it only in the Rangeleys.

NOTE. — The Brown Hackle with a red body, spoken of by Mr. Parish, when made palmer, *i. e.* with hackle wound the length of the body, is known as the Soldier Palmer; when simply made with a red body and hackle tied in at the head, it is known as the Red Hackle. The Red Hackle is the first recorded fly, the oldest known in history. See description in Part I. — M. E. O. M.

# PLATE G.

No. 48. Hart.

No. 49. Hill Fly.

No. 50. Kingfisher.

No. 51. Golden Rod.

No. 52. King of the Woods.

No. 53. Green Glade.

**No. 48.** The Hart is a combination of colors almost unknown among artificial flies, but one that is very beautiful in this fly, which was sent to us by Mr. George Hart, of Waterbury, Conn., after whom it was named. In his letter inclosing this fly he wrote us that it had proved one of their best flies in their late expedition to the Maine woods, where he and a party of friends have recorded some phenomenal catches.

**No. 49. Hill Fly.** This is another pattern used by the same party from Waterbury, Conn., and named after Mr. J. M. Hill, one of its members. The Hill Fly resembles somewhat the Black Doctor, and claims all the merits of that design, with distinguishing qualities of its own.

**No. 50.** Of the Kingfisher, Mr. John B. McHarg, veteran angler and fly-maker of Rome, New York, has written: " If I could have no dinner until I had taken a big trout with the fly, the one particular lure I would select from the multitude would be that which years and years ago I christened the Kingfisher. This is the best of the chosen four with which I have whipped the waters of America for a lifetime, and the only one with which I ever had really good luck casting for shad. For big trout and jumbo bass, I do not believe a more killing fly was ever made. From Skowhegan to Alaska it is always in season. Try it at either end or the middle of the season, anywhere in North America, and my word for it you will find a most killing lure, and worthy a place in the best fly-book on the earth."

Mr. McHarg's enthusiasm is always contagious, and we know his to be one of the generous hearts that enjoy sharing the good things of this world with their fellow-men; we feel a hearty respect for his opinion, as well as for his cordiality and generosity, of which we frequently have had proof.

No. 51. We cannot ascertain who is responsible for the Golden Rod. It is popular for Maine, and whoever named it may have had in mind a pretty little story the scene of which is laid at Mount Desert, in that State, and added to the fame and romance of that picturesque summer resort.

No. 52. King of the Woods. The first fly we ever saw of this name was given to us by Mr. A. N. Cheney, of Glens Falls, N. Y., who had known and used it for some time. As nearly as we remember, he had first seen it used in the woods of northern New York, which he has visited annually since boyhood, and written of most delightfully. He spoke of the fly as of unknown origin, but much esteemed by the guides, and called, therefore, the King of the Woods, as companion to the Queen of the Waters.

No. 53. The Green Glade was originally a Scotch salmon fly, named after a kite, or glade, but it is found more useful in this country for large trout than for salmon.

They were blest beyond compare,
When they held their trysting there,
Amang the greenest hills shone on by the sun.

# VERMONT AND NEW HAMPSHIRE.

JOHN E. HUBBARD . . . .
$\left\{\begin{array}{l}\text{Blue Jay.}\\\text{No Name.}\\\text{Seth Green.}\\\text{Parmacheene Belle, etc.}\end{array}\right.$

FRED E. ATKINS . . . . .
$\left\{\begin{array}{l}\text{Coachman.}\\\text{Alder.}\\\text{Governor.}\\\text{Fin Fly, etc.}\end{array}\right.$

E. B. GRISWOLD . . . . .
$\left\{\begin{array}{l}\text{Gray Hackle.}\\\text{Grizzly King.}\\\text{Seth Green.}\end{array}\right.$

FRANK W. PROCTOR . . .
{ Brown Hen.

C. O. ALLEN . . . . . .
$\left\{\begin{array}{l}\text{Brown Hackle.}\\\text{Professor.}\\\text{Fin Fly.}\end{array}\right.$

SAMUEL WEBBER . . . . .
$\left\{\begin{array}{l}\text{Professor.}\\\text{Grizzly King.}\\\text{Coachman.}\\\text{Scarlet Ibis, etc.}\end{array}\right.$

GEORGE H. COMSTOCK . . .
{ Leadwing Coachman.

E. G. TUTTLE . . . . . .
$\left\{\begin{array}{l}\text{Coachman.}\\\text{Black Gnat.}\\\text{White Miller.}\\\text{Grasshopper.}\end{array}\right.$

| | | | |
|---|---|---|---|
| *Vermont.* | ⎧ Blue Jay.<br>⎪ Alder.<br>⎪ No Name.<br>⎪ Parmacheene Belle.<br>⎨ Seth Green.<br>⎪ Grasshopper.<br>⎪ Grizzly King.<br>⎪ Professor.<br>⎪ Black Gnat.<br>⎩ White Miller. | ⎰<br>⎱ | Trout. |

JOHN E. HUBBARD ("Sylvanus"),  Montpelier,  Vermont.

I consider the following list to be as good as any for such trout fishing as we have in this section, and I have placed them in the order in which I value them : Blue Jay, Alder, No Name, Parmacheene Belle, Seth Green, Grasshopper, Grizzly King, Professor, Coch-y-Bonddu, Black Gnat, White Miller. As to size of hooks, I think they should be suited to the size of fish and the kind of water to be fished, and these two things and the condition of the weather should govern the selection of the cast. On dark days, or with a strong ripple, or in swift streams, or in muddy water, or when fish are in deep water, use colored flies, and hooks as large as No. 5. There is little fishing in Vermont when a large hook is required. On bright days and on clear, still water, use modest and dark colors for flies, and very small hooks, down as small as No. 12. Use only one fly at such times, and let the leader be the very lightest to be obtained. I think that, as a rule, fishermen use leaders that are far too heavy for the game. I prefer leaders made of gut which has not been drawn, and think they should all be dyed a neutral tint, like that obtained by using as a dye equal parts of "Arnold's Writing Fluid" and water.

My first choice for hooks would be the Sproat, and I prefer all flies tied with short loops. The advantages of the loops are many, I think.   A short length of gut, colored to match the leader, can be used to fasten on the dropper; and in place of the loop at the end of these, and on the end of the leader, have just a simple hard knot, and fasten each fly by tying it to the leader with the "angler's knot."   This knot will unfasten so easily that you can change flies much quicker than by drawing them through the old-fashioned loop, and with this arrangement you have a leader that is of one color all the way to the hook, and has none of the objectionable bunches caused by the double loops.   Any close observer will have discovered that the fish often jump at the loops, and at the knots on the leader when they are large.

I will give an incident to prove that it is sometimes advantageous to "change flies."   One day, last season, a friend and myself were fishing a little pond where we felt quite well acquainted with the fish, but as the day was clear and still we were not having much luck.   At last we found a little cove among the bushes where the water was literally alive with trout.   They were small, to be sure, but it would have done your heart good to have seen them jump. We placed our boat carefully where we could reach them with an easy cast, and settled ourselves for sport.   We soon discovered, however, that our flies were not what they wanted, and so got out our fly-books, and did our best to find an assortment of colors that would please them; but though we changed many times, using three flies each, it was of no use.

All the time the trout continued to jump, and though our flies fell among them ever so lightly, and though they were drawn quickly or allowed to rest where they fell, it made no difference and we had not caught a fish.   At last I rested and watched them, and tried to find what it was they were jumping at; and if you have ever tried to do this you know that it is not so easy to find out as one would expect. After a long time, and by watching the different kinds of flies that were over and on the water, instead of watching the fish, I saw a trout take a sort of blue-black fly that settled on the water. I immediately consulted my fly-book, and found a little old-fashioned fly, that, I think, is innocent of a name, but seemed to be a sort of cross between the Black Gnat and the Iron Dun, which resembled very closely the natural fly I had seen taken. I put this on, and the thing was done. I could take fish on that fly anywhere and at every cast; and no matter whether I used it as the hand fly, dropper, or tail fly, the effect was just the same; they were bound to have that fly. I did not have another one like it, and my friend could not find one that much resembled it, and the result was that he did not take a fish while we were in that cove.

I could give many other incidents, but to my mind this one proves the point, and it cannot possibly be explained away. I cannot say very much about bass fishing, as I have had very little experience, but I think it is governed by the same laws as trout fishing. I use hooks several sizes larger, and I find that bright colors are nearly always the best.

So far I have written only of the fishing in this locality, and I think that will be sufficient for one letter. If I were to make a list of flies for such fishing as is to be found in Maine and in Canada, I should put the Parmacheene Belle at the head, and next would come the B. Pond and Katoodle-bug. The two latter are tied by Mr. Whitney, who is one of the famous guides of the Rangeley Lakes. For fishing in these regions the hooks should be, of course, much larger, say No. 1 and 2.

| Vermont. | { Coachman.<br>Alder.<br>Governor.<br>Fin Fly. | { Trout. |

FRED E. ATKINS,           Waterbury,           Vermont.

I have found the Coachman, Alder, Governor, and a red and white fly, something like the one called the Fin Fly, are usually taking ones. The latter was rather a favorite during the middle of the season, and though so light in color seemed good on a bright day and in clear water. I took my largest fish with this fly last season, but sometimes had good success with a small buff or brown-winged fly.

I found the Alder very good on several occasions, and a small-sized Grizzly King was effective for morning fishing or on a cloudy day.

Many persons in this vicinity do not use flies, the usual object being to take fish for food, and they can, as a regular thing, get all they want with bait; but a few of our best fishermen use flies, and I trust to have better opportunities for observation in the future.

---

| Vermont. | { Gray Hackle.<br>Grizzly King.<br>Seth Green. | { Trout. |

E. B. GRISWOLD,           Bennington,           Vermont.

My favorite fly for mountain streams is the Gray Hackle, especially in swift-running waters. Have used it under various circumstances, in clear weather and in dark, cloudy weather, and it is almost invariably a taking fly. For still water and clear weather I use either the Grizzly King or the Seth Green.

No. 10 hooks seem large enough for trout weighing one pound or under, and it appears to make but little difference whether the snells are stained or clear; they should be single strands, and short.

---

|  |  |  |
|---|---|---|
| *Vermont.* | { Brown Hackle. Professor. Fin Fly. | { Trout. |

C. O. ALLEN, Wallingford, Vermont.

I have always been successful with a Brown Hackle and a Professor. I consider these standard for all times of the year. Just at dark I would use a Black Hackle in place of the Brown. I have also had good luck with a fly having white wings and bright red body. Prefer Sproat hooks.

---

*New Hampshire.* Brown Hen. Trout.

FRANK W. PROCTOR, Boston, Mass.

During the past fifteen years my fishing has been mostly done in New Hampshire ponds that have been pretty closely fished, and in which the trout have been well educated. I believe that more than three fourths of my fish have been taken with a whip composed of a Brown Hen for a stretcher fly and a Brown Hackle dropper.

The Brown Hackle I used from the first, upon the advice of brother anglers. The Brown Hen I tried experimentally in common with many other kinds, and found it more taking than any other fly in my book. I have used it more and more, and now I rarely make a whip without it. I think it is best adapted for bright days and clear, smooth waters; but I have found it good under all conditions, excepting at dusk and in discolored waters.

When trout refuse this fly I frequently try other varieties, but in ordinary conditions a change of flies rarely produces better results.  For civilized waters I consider the Brown Hen by far the best fly I am acquainted with.  As to hook and snells, I find no trouble in hooking fish with a Sproat hook, if they seize it.  Without having any special theory on the subject, my acquaintance with trout inclines me to the opinion that hooks and snells should be as light as is consistent with strength, and I prefer stained leaders and snells.

The weak spot in flies I find to be where the snell joins the shank of the hook; with me they usually part there before the fly is otherwise too much worn for use.

| | | |
|---|---|---|
| *New Hampshire.* | Professor. <br> Grizzly King. <br> Coachman. <br> Royal Coachman. <br> Scarlet Ibis. <br> Black Gnat. <br> Coch-y-Bonddu. <br> Hackles. | Trout. |

SAMUEL WEBBER,                         Charleston,                         N. H.

From my past experience I should select for our New Hampshire waters the following, varying the fly with the weather and the time of the day, viz., Professor, Grizzly King, Coachman, Royal Coachman, Scarlet Ibis, Black Gnat, Coch-y-Bonddu, and all the other Hackles, especially the Soldier ; Alder and the Green Drake are also good.

I have to suggest one fly, a hackle or " palmer," which you do not show on your plates in " Fishing with the Fly," viz., a White Hackle with a red body wound with gold tinsel, body rather full or plump.  I have found this fly rather killing after sunset on the celebrated Diamond Ponds, and think it well worthy a place in " Fishing with the Fly " if you propose to get up a new edition. I would suggest as a name for it the Royal White. Generally, I prefer a Limerick hook on a clear, single snell, rather long and stout. Size of hook varies from No. 4 to No. 10.

---

| *New England States.* | Leadwing Coachman. | Trout. |
| GEORGE H. COMSTOCK, | Ivoryton, | Conn. |

The dark-winged Coachman is my favorite fly, after having tried it throughout New England, from Averill Lakes in northern Vermont to the Moosehead Lake in Maine; also all along the southern border of Connecticut in the streams emptying into Long Island Sound. It seems more effective in the evening, but the trout will rise to it at any time of day.

I prefer, for trout not weighing over one pound, No. 8, 10, or 12 O'Shaughnessy or Sproat hooks, using the large hooks early in the season; for trout in the Rangeleys running from one to four pounds, hooks No. 6 and upward are needed.

I prefer stained snells, if for nothing else than neatness of appearance. Snells should be as light as consistent, single, long strands, no short loops, particularly on flies, as I do not care to pick up looking-glasses every time I raise my line to cast.

I make my own leaders, and for use in fine fishing tie the gut together in a single knot. This is perfectly sufficient; never had one come apart in years of so doing. I make no loops whatever, and cut off the loop in the snell of the fly used for the tail fly, and tie both leader and fly together by a single knot. For the upper fly (I never use but two flies at a time) I take a turn in my leader and tie a knot, first cutting off loop on snell of fly, but leaving the knot to secure it. Such a cast as this cannot be improved upon by a man who knows his business; but for the man who changes his flies every few moments, — why, any kind of a leader will do for him !

---

|   |   |   |
|---|---|---|
| *Vermont.* | { Coachman.<br>Black Gnat.<br>White Miller.<br>Grasshopper. | { Trout. |

E. G. Tuttle,                    Manchester,                    Vermont.

Your letter asking for information regarding artificial flies has been received, and in reply will say that your questions are hard to answer, as a fly excellent at one time of the day in any locality or stream, in an hour's time may be good for nothing. One important rule is to observe what kind of flies are upon the water, and use the nearest like them that you may have. The Coachman, representing nothing I have ever seen, is an exception to this rule, and is probably the best of all artificial flies for general use in all localities and waters. A medium-sized black fly is the most useful in a clear day and low water; it should be drawn *up stream.* A Black Gnat or a White Miller is to be used at evening. When it rains, the White Miller, also a Coachman with a slender or partially woven body, are fatal to the fish.

There are several things needful to success in fishing. One must like the sport; must have patience, perseverance, observation, know the locality and the habits of the trout; must have a good rod, reel, line, flies, and hooks; must not get excited; must have an eye for distance; must cause his flies to light gently upon the water; must throw his line so that it will straighten out from his rod, and be sure that it has straightened out behind before making the forward cast, or off will go his flies, snapped off!

If you have a strike, a slight wrist motion hooks the trout, and a taut line holds him; then let your rod do the rest of the work.

It is not often necessary to give much line on our streams, but if you have to do so, make the trout earn every inch he takes; keep him away from all snags, and in the end you will have your fish.

In landing a trout of any size don't try to lift him out with the rod, but use either a landing net or take him with your hand.

I neglected to say that in casting one should always throw up stream and across the current, letting the current carry the fly. No human being ever saw one of the miller species floating *up* stream; in fact, there are but few insects that work up; the majority drift with the current down the stream.

In midsummer comes the grasshopper-fishing, requiring more skill than any other; for this you must first keep the grasshopper on the water with a down-stream motion. Use great care in casting; observe the same rules as when casting a fly, lest you lose your grasshopper. When you have a strike, first give a *downward* wrist motion, and when settled give the upward wrist, or hooking, motion. A slight trembling movement of the rod will cause a natural appearance to the grasshopper as well as the fly.

In " grasshopper time " the trout lie well down stream in the holes; they also gather there towards night during the fly-fishing.

Success in trouting depends greatly upon your having everything to tempt them with; hence bait should always be carried. When not jumping, trout will often take worms or chubs. A trout that is lying close to the bottom will not rise to a fly, and one well up from the bed of the stream will rarely bite when the water is high and roily. At such times bait is the only thing to use. Drop your line in the eddies or near the ripples and near the shores, always letting your bait work around near or on the bottom, with an occasional pull up to the surface, and now and then a jerky motion, always keeping a taut line.

When you have a bite give the upward wrist motion, remembering that a slight wrist motion is all that is necessary to hook a trout.

I have hardly answered any of your questions, except in a general way. Still, I think the advice I have given may be useful to beginners, and perhaps old fishermen may get a new idea. I learn a little every time I go fishing. My final advice to one and all is to provide themselves with a good rod, reel, line, and a large variety of flies, hooks, and bait, and *never* to go a-fishing when the wind is in an easterly direction; a southwest wind is ever the most favorable.

## PLATE H.

No. 54. Moose.

No. 55. Claret Montreal.

No. 56. Moisic-Grub.

No. 57. Mooselucmaguntic.

No. 58. Juno.

No. 59. Plymouth Rock.

No. 54. Mr. John Shields writes to us that the Moose fly was made in imitation of a natural fly of that name. Mr. Shields, on his annual trips to the Maine woods, always carried with him a " box " fitted with a well-assorted stock of materials for fly-making. With these, he was able to create new flies adapted to the different localities. If they proved valuable, he brought them to the notice of his angling friends. It may be interesting to some who read these notes to know the story of the frontispiece in this collection; also how we first learned that the Moose was a good bass fly.

Over fifteen years ago, an uncle, Mr. J. C. Hinchman, while sojourning in the White Mountains, sent to us the original of the picture which forms the frontispiece of this book; but for years the little photograph was fastened with a number of others to the inner side of the door of a bookcase holding angling books. One day, glancing out of the window, I saw sitting on the piazza of the hotel opposite two men, fishing-rods and baskets beside them, and fly-books spread out on a chair between them, as if they were discussing their contents. I was struck by their resemblance to the figures in the photograph from the White Mountains that we had had so many years; attitude, dress, features, all were the same. I watched them a few moments, interested by the similarity, and thought no more of it. Later in the day, my father said, " Mr. W. C. Prime and his friend Mr. Bridge are in town, and this evening I will bring them in to call on you." I was pleased to think of meeting the author of " I Go A-Fishing," and said so; and when evening came found them to be the two fishermen I had noticed and compared with the picture. During the evening I told them of it and showed them the photograph. When Mr. Prime saw it he exclaimed, " Why that was taken of us at Lonesome Lake Cabin as many as fifteen years ago! " So the resemblance was accounted for.

Later, when this book came to be thought of, I wrote to Mr. Prime requesting permission to reproduce the photograph as its frontispiece, thinking the many fishermen who had enjoyed Mr. Prime's delightful writings would be greatly interested in a picture of him.   Mr. Prime kindly consented, and gave permission to mention his name with that of his companion, Mr. William F. Bridge, of New York city, who is " Dupont " of " I Go A-Fishing."

During their call our talk was somewhat of fishing, and I showed Mr. Bridge a fly which he greatly admired.   It was the Moose ; and the next day, as they were about to drive away, I handed a fly like it to my father, asking him to give it to Mr. Bridge with my farewell, and say that I hoped it would bring him a good fish.

The next year Mr. Prime and Mr. Bridge again drove through Manchester, on their annual trip to the White Mountains, and, meeting Mr. Orvis, Mr. Bridge said : " Do you remember that fly your daughter sent to me by you ?   I had the greatest success in the world with it catching black bass ; such success, that after it was all worn out, I kept it on my leader just for luck."   Since then we have frequently heard the testimony in favor of it for black bass repeated, and have rejoiced to think that our good wishes resulted in a discovery of further merit in this pretty fly first intended for Maine trout by its originator, John Shields.

No. 55.   In the note accompanying the Montreal trout fly, No. 179, Plate S, will be found an account from Mr. Leach of the origin of this fly and the correct dressing ; but the Montreal with a claret hackle and body has become so widely known and so generally used that it may perhaps be said to be more of a favorite than the true pattern.   To distinguish between the two we suggest that hereafter this fly be called the Claret Montreal.

No. 56.   The Moisic-Grub should properly be placed among the salmon flies, but we obtained it after those plates had been filled, and we could not make up our mind to displace any of the older favorites for this late comer, and therefore put it among the lake flies.   Because of the marvelous success of the Parmacheene Belle of Mr. Wells's invention, we have great faith in this fly.   Mr. Wells has been good enough to reply to our inquiries concerning this last creation of his in the following letter : —

*January* 9, 1892.

In reply to yours of 7th.   As to all wingless flies provided with two or more hackles, each placed at a different part of the body, I follow the English nomenclature and call them " Grubs." The fly you speak of I therefore call " the Moisic-Grub," using the generic term " grub " since it has one hackle placed in the middle of the body, and another at the head. The wingless flies are, I am informed, quite popular with the more advanced school of transatlantic salmon fishermen. The great rank and file of the fraternity look upon them, it would seem, with less, though perhaps increasing favor.

Naturally fond of reasonable experiment, I have tried these grubs extensively during the past six or seven years, following the printed formulæ of British anglers as well as devising several patterns of my own. They have answered very well, particularly on much-fished waters where they were quite new to the fish. I don't think they will ever supersede the winged flies of best type, such as Jock Scott, Silver Doctor, etc. ; but I do think they supplement them wonderfully well, both under the conditions above named, and as a " change fly " to tempt a fish which has risen short of one of the well-known patterns of winged fly. In the latter case the grub should bear some general resemblance to the primary fly, though much more sober in tint and tone.

Of the various grubs I have tried, both of foreign and domestic design, the Moisic-Grub has been the most used and the most successful. It was originally designed and tied by me in June, 1887, when salmon fishing on the Moisic River, which, as you know, flows into the St. Lawrence on its north shore. Though intended as a change fly for Jock Scott, it was first tried on its own merits, tied on a No. 4 double hook, on a drizzly day with a leaden sky. In a pool from eleven to nine feet deep that grub killed that day four salmon from 21 to $32\frac{1}{2}$ pounds ; besides, two were fastened and lost after a time. Of course it became at once a prime favorite with me, and such it still remains. I have tried it on trout in the Maine lakes with fair but not phenomenal success. I don't know that it has ever been used for black bass. It has, perhaps, been most successful in rainy, dark weather. This is not as conclusive, however, as it may seem. Having made its first success under such conditions, it has naturally had more use under similar circumstances. You know fly-fishermen, the world over, may be divided into two classes, — those who advocate a bright fly on a dark day and a dark fly on a bright day, and those who preach and practice a directly opposite course. The latter are the innovators, and do the most of the talking. For some seven or eight years, now, I have endeavored to decide by experiment and for my own satisfaction which party was right. I have changed from one system to the other, back and forward,

in every alternative I could think of as likely to throw light on the question, and
sometimes fifteen or twenty times in the same day.  Though, perhaps, I have a
slight bias in favor of a dark fly on a dark day, yet to this minute I am quite
uncertain which is the better method.

Yours truly,          Henry P. Wells.

**No. 57.**  The Mooselucmaguntic is another of Mr. John Shields's patterns,
named by him after the lake where he found by trial that it was most successful.

**Nos. 58 and 59.**  Juno and Plymouth Rock are described in the following letter
from Mr. D. W. C. Farrington, of Lowell, Mass : —

My fishing with the fly has been mostly in the Maine lakes and streams, during
the month of June.  My favorite flies are the Professor, Scarlet Ibis, and Plymouth
Rock.  I have been so successful with them in many localities, and at times and
weather so varied, that in making up a cast I generally use one of them.

I consider that the following named flies cover a range of form and color sufficient for the wants of the ordinary fisherman ; but for one who likes to indulge his
fancies a larger assortment may be necessary :  Professor, Silver Doctor, Brown
Palmer or Hackle, Plymouth Rock, and Juno.  The first seven are, as you know,
old and standard flies, and I have found them both killing and durable.

The Plymouth Rock and Juno are of my own creation.  I send you one each of
my own tying.

I have had success with the Plymouth Rock in bright weather in the middle
of the day, when all others failed to cause a rise.  Description : tail, gray from
the mallard duck ; body, silver gilt ; hackle and wings, from the Plymouth Rock
fowl ; head, red.  The Juno, for dark days and in shady places, is a very killing
fly.  Description : tail, red and white ; body, pale green chenille with silver twist ;
hackle, scarlet ; wings, scarlet and jungle fowl.

Fishin' Jimmy had never heard of entomology ; Guénée, Hubner, and Fabricius were unknown names, but he could have told these worthies many new things. Did they know just at what hour the trout ceased leaping at dark fly or moth, and could see only in the dim light the ghostly white miller ? Did they know the comparative merits, as a tempting bait, of grasshopper, cricket, spider, or wasp ; and could they, with bits of wool, tinsel, and feather, copy the real dipterous, hymenopterous, or orthopterous insect ? And the birds : he knew them as do few ornithologists, by sight, by sound, by little ways and tricks of their own, known only to themselves and him. . . . He could tell you, too, of strange, shy creatures, rarely seen except by the early-rising, late-fishing angler, in quiet, lonesome places : the otter, muskrat, and mink of ponds and lakes, — rival fishers, who bore off prey sometimes from under his very eyes, — field-mice in meadow and pasture, blind, burrowing moles, prickly hedgehogs, brown hares, and social, curious squirrels.

Sometimes he saw deer, in the early morning or in the dusk of the evening, as they came to drink at the lake shore, and looked at him with big, soft eyes, not unlike his own. Sometimes a shaggy bear trotted across his path and hid himself in the forest, or a sharp-eared fox ran barking through the bushes. He loved to tell of these things to us who cared to listen, and I still seem to hear his voice saying in hushed tones, after a story of woodland sight or sound : " Nobody don't see 'em but fishermen. Nobody don't hear 'em but fishermen ; " and — " As I was tellin' ye," he said, " I allers loved fishin' and knowed 't was the best thing in the hul airth ; I knowed it larnt ye more about creeters an' yarbs an' stuns an' water than books could tell ye ; I knowed it made folks patienter an' com-monsenser an' weather-wiser, an' cuter gen'ally ; gin 'em more fac'lty than all the school larnin' in creation ; I knowed it was more fillin' than vittles, more rousin' than whiskey, more soothin' than lodlum ; I knowed it cooled ye off when ye was het, an' het ye when ye was cold : I knowed all that, o' course — any fool knows it. But will ye bleve it ? — I was mor'n twenty-one years old, a man growed, 'fore I foun' why 't was that way. "

From *Fishin' Jimmy*, by ANNIE TRUMBULL SLOSSON.

# CONNECTICUT, MASSACHUSETTS, AND RHODE ISLAND.

C. M. TURNER . . . . . . .
{ Black May.
Red Spinner.
Coachman.
Alder, etc.

J. H. FARNHAM . . . . . . .
{ Brown Hackle.
Red Hackle.
Yellow May.
Coachman, etc.

O. E. BORDEN . . . . . . .
{ Montreal.
Coachman.
Jenny Lind.
Polka.
Perch Fly.

A. J. COLLINS . . . . . . .
{ Silver King.
Raven.
Black Prince.
Scarlet Ibis, etc.

S. PROCTOR THAYER.

CHARLES E. H. HIGGINS . . . .
{ White Miller.
Scarlet Ibis.
Royal Coachman.
Yellow May, etc.

ANDREW S. MARCH . . . . .
{ Silver Doctor.
Parmacheene Belle.
White Miller.

ROBERT C. BOURN . . . . . .
{ Grizzly King.
Montreal.

|  |  |  |
|---|---|---|
| *Connecticut.* | Black May.<br>Red Spinner.<br>Coachman.<br>Alder.<br>Soldier, etc. | Trout. |

C. M. TURNER, Lakeville, Conn.

For Dutchess County, New York, and Litchfield County, Connecticut, I would use for May the following flies : —

| | |
|---|---|
| Black May. | Red Spinner. |
| Coachman. | Alder. |
| Soldier. | |

For the month of June : —

| | |
|---|---|
| Great Dun. | Dark Stone. |
| Black June. | Shoemaker. |
| Governor. | |

And later in June I find nothing better than the White Miller, particularly in the latter part of the day.

In small streams and clear water any small fly is a better choice than a large one. If the day is gloomy, I would want a mist-colored snell. If the day is bright and the water clear, the lighter color the snell is, the better. I always use single strands for this locality, and medium-sized loops.

The best hook is made from a sewing needle; the bend is like the genuine Limerick, except to turn the point to one side. Size of hook No. 10.

| *Massachusetts.* | { Brown Hackle.<br>Red Hackle.<br>Coachman.<br>Yellow May.<br>Abbey. | { Trout. |

J. H. Farnham,                    Spencer,                    Mass.

The result of my experience in fly-fishing is to make me a stronger advocate for it than ever, both for the increased amount of pleasure over bait-fishing, and the larger and better fish obtained by this method. I repeatedly proved this to myself as well as to my companion in my rambles, who is an adept in the art of bait-fishing. In numbers his creel may have exceeded mine, but in size mine averaged much higher.

My best sport was obtained by using Brown and Red Hackles with palmer bodies. One rainy afternoon in July I remember especially, when the fly proved *the* lure. My friend, fishing with bait, caught only a few small ones, while I had good success fishing with the Brown Palmer Hackle and the Coachman.

On another afternoon I was out alone on a small brook, so small I could easily jump across it most of the way, and one that was "fished to death;" there came up a violent thunder-shower, but in spite of this I caught my best trout of the season immediately after it ceased, a fourteen-inch trout, very broad and deep and beautifully colored, — this on a Brown Hackle. While it rained hard I caught some on a Canada, and after the sun came out clear had some sport with a Coch-y-Bonddu and a Red Hackle.

On another trip in late July, a cloudy, overcast afternoon, I did fairly well with a Yellow May and Royal Coachman. In August, on a bright, sunny afternoon, in some deep, sluggish water, I caught some half-pounders and one fish weighing a pound, with the Abbey and a little "buzz."

To sum up: I found, during the best season, the Brown and Red Hackle the best for my fishing, with the Coachman for a second, and took trout occasionally on the other. The poorest fly in my small collection, I think, was the Grizzly King. I do not remember that I had a rise to it on any occasion. I tried one of the floating flies, but it was a failure in my hands.

When I use bait, I prefer Carlisle hooks for trout fishing to all others; they should be snelled on single short strands of gut, and used with a clear leader. I use single gut for all my snells and leaders; the leader should have loops for attaching flies.

I prefer Sproat hooks for flies, No. 10 and No. 12, and only use two flies on a cast. I would rather change than have more on at a time.

---

| *Massachusetts.* | Montreal.<br>Coachman.<br>Jenny Lind.<br>Polka.<br>Perch Fly. | Trout and Black Bass. |
|---|---|---|

O. E. BORDEN,                    Fall River,                    Mass.

The most of my trout fishing has been done in the Rangeley and Seven Ponds region, and my fishing for bass in this vicinity. My favorite fly for all-round fishing, trout and black bass, at any and all seasons, is the Montreal, and if I were obliged to restrict my choice of flies to one I would rather have it by half than any other fly ever made; of course there are times when some other fly takes better.

I recall a Maine trip when the Coachman did more execution, and another when the Jenny Lind did far more work than the others, and the Coachman was of no use whatever. But through all the " vicissitudes of changeful time " the Montreal is always reliable; for black bass fishing in this region it is one of the best, ranking with the Polka, which for black bass, I think, is unexcelled.

I make my own flies, and have done so for years, so I have had abundant chances to experiment with new combinations of colors; but I must confess that the result was to make me stick to a few established patterns, finding I cannot, as a rule, improve on those that years of experience have proved good.

In this locality the white perch rise freely to the fly during the latter part of June and the first of July, and I have had better luck with a fly of my own make for them than with any other I have ever tried. Finding that white perch took the Red Ibis well, and the flies that had yellow in their make-up, I tried a combination of red, yellow, and white, generally a white body with gold tinsel, a wing of mixed yellow and red, or red, yellow, and white, with a bright yellow hackle, and it proved a most alluring creation for white perch. I have not given it a name, but simply call it a perch fly; and as the perch is hardly a game fish, perhaps the fly deserves no other.

I have never had much luck with large flies. I have stopped making them on hooks larger than No. 3 Sproat for bass, and have taken bass as readily on No. 4 or No. 5 hooks as on larger. I have tried many experiments with large flies, but in this locality they are of almost no use.

I generally use Sproat hooks, but do not know that they are any better than the O'Shaughnessy. I make my leaders of stained gut, but I cannot truthfully say that I think it makes much difference. I have used them both ways, and believe that if fish feel like biting they will do it with equal gusto whether the gut of the leader and snell is stained or clear.

|  |  |  |
|---|---|---|
| *Massachusetts.* | { Silver King. <br> Raven. <br> Black Prince. <br> Scarlet Ibis. <br> Gray Hackle. | { Black Bass <br> and Suckers. |

A. J. Collins, Fall River, Mass.

In August last, my brother and myself were fishing together in a small lake in Rhode Island. The day had been quite warm, and we had done no fishing during the afternoon. About six o'clock we took the boats and ran along close to the shore for perhaps a half mile; as my brother did not understand fly-fishing, he took his place at the oars, and I did the casting myself. I started out with a White Miller for tail fly, Silver King for second, and Gray Hackle for third, all hung to short leaders; the fish would rise almost in an instant, and we captured forty-eight bass, two small pickerel, and two sunfish before dark. None of the bass were very large, the largest not over one pound. It was the second time in my life that I had taken pickerel with a fly.

The next morning we went out again at sunrise, and I started out with Black Raven for leader, for second a Green Ibis, and Scarlet Ibis for third. I took five small bass with the scarlet fly, but not a rise could I get to anything else, though I tried repeated changes. Then I took my place at the oars, and Jim took his rod and put on to his line a small spoon hook, and I rowed back over nearly the same ground, and he captured thirty-two bass and four or five large white perch before ten o'clock; one of the bass weighed three pounds. Jim laughed at my fly-fishing so much that I took good care not to repeat it when he went fishing with me afterwards.

One of the most curious things that I ever saw about fly-fishing

happened to me the 6th of October, 1881.   On that day a party of
three of us were fishing for pickerel in a lake just below Worcester,
Mass.   The day was quite warm, with hardly any wind.   There
were plenty of small gray flies that seemed to come out of a swamp
near by and settle on the water.   We saw fish rise to these flies at
short intervals, and supposed them to be small perch, as there were
no bass in the pond at that time.   Just for fun I fastened two flies
to my line, a Brown Hackle and a Grey Miller; at the third cast
a fish rose to the fly, and when I struck him I found that I had
quite a fish to deal with.   I thought that I was fastened to a
pickerel, but when I reeled him in, instead of a pickerel I was
fastened to a large sucker, and he had the fly in his mouth, too.   I
caught two more after that, and each one had the fly inside of his
mouth.   Query, did the fish rise to the fly or not?

I have caught eels, horned pouts, and one small mud-turtle with a
spoon hook, but I never before caught suckers with a fly.

---

|              |   | Grizzly King. |   |        |   |
|--------------|---|---------------|---|--------|---|
|              | { | Stone Fly.    |   |        |   |
| *Massachusetts.* | { | Fin Fly.   | { | Trout. |   |
|              | { | Red Hackle.   |   |        |   |
|              |   | Red Ibis.     |   |        |   |
|              |   | White Miller. |   |        |   |

S. Proctor Thayer,                     North Adams,                     Mass.

I have fished for several seasons in the Adirondacks, in Maine,
New Brunswick, the Provinces, and elsewhere, both for trout and
salmon.   My favorite flies for this locality, Massachusetts, are Yellow Professor, Red Hackle, Grizzly King, Stone Fly, Fin Fly, and
the Gnats, using small flies and the smallest size of mist-colored gut.
It is of great importance to have well-made flies.   Poorly-made,

cheap flies are an abomination. Where trout are as wild as they are around here, nothing will do but the smallest and most delicate line, leader, and fly. Your flies, etc., meet all requirements. It is difficult to answer your questions briefly, as so much depends on the stream, etc. In general, I should say, use the very smallest size of hook and the lightest gut possible, single, mist-colored, in long strands. It is frequently of advantage to have two or three extra leaders in readiness, so that when one becomes water-soaked and heavy, a new one which is light and dry can be put on the line, and will float nicely on the water.[1] Then, again, perhaps the only way in which trout can be taken will be by sinking the fly under water and drawing the fly along with a sinuous motion. In a great many instances the only thing that attracts trout is the novelty of the fly. This is noticeable in localities that have been persistently fished. I have very frequently observed this. A friend of mine at the Rangeley Lakes, at a time when there were plenty of good fishermen about, who cast and cast without success, put on a bright yellow fly, something that no one there had, or had seen, and had very good success. As a general thing, however, better success in the long run will be had by sticking to the best of the standard flies, which are well known. The best all-round fly I have found to be the Red Ibis, although it does not *take* around here as far as I have been able to observe. Of course dark waters require light flies, like Gray Hackle and White Miller, etc., and light waters the reverse. The more transparent the water and the wilder the trout, the more invisible should be the line, leader, and fly. I once fished the Clear-

---

[1] A dry leader is liable to break, therefore we cannot refrain from a word of caution against this advice. To cause a leader to float well, oil it lightly with red deer fat, or mutton tallow. — M. E. O. M.

water, a tributary of the Miramichi, where fishermen very rarely go. The water was extremely clear, and I found that I could only take trout there by using some of the smallest flies which I happened to have with me. I expect to fish with the fly every year as long as I am able to throw one, and I am sure that I shall find something new every season that I may cast a line.

---

| Massachusetts. | { White Miller.<br>Scarlet Ibis.<br>Royal Coachman.<br>Yellow May.<br>Parmacheene Belle.<br>Silver Doctor.<br>Seth Green. | { Trout and<br>Bass. |

CHARLES E. H. HIGGINS, D. D. S.,      Worcester,         Mass.

The love of angling must be born in a man; anglers are not taught. If an angler takes up fishing late in life, it is only the blossoming of the late flower; the germ was there, although dormant, perhaps, through the pressing duties of business life.

A true angler is the happy product of the Creator's will, and he is happiest when, by the brook-side, rod in hand, he communes with nature and pursues his quiet way through woodland and meadow, dropping the fly at the foot of that rapid water, or in the little pool where the stream enters the meadow land; taking a trout now and then, or, if his creel be not made heavy, delighting in the surrounding scenery, the green sweet-smelling grass-lands, the blossoming flowers, the song of the birds, the chattering of the squirrels, and above all the tremulous delicate apple-blossoms that every wind sends floating about him like so many snowflakes.

My experience has led me to favor small flies for such brooks and streams as are sufficiently clear of brush to permit fly-casting. In Worcester County they are few indeed. I prefer the White Miller, Scarlet Ibis, Royal Coachman, and Yellow May, tied on No. 12 hooks or smaller, and for bass fishing about here I choose flies tied on hooks not larger than No. 8. For the latter the flies are White Miller, Scarlet Ibis, Parmacheene Belle, Silver Doctor, and Seth Green.

I have a decided preference for the flies tied with expanded wings. I well remember an instance when, after repeated casting with a White Miller tied in the ordinary way, I substituted a White Miller with expanded wings, one of my own tying, which was successful immediately in taking bass. Whether the principle is equally applicable to all patterns of flies I am not prepared to say, but I can say that such of my flies as are tied with the concave of the wing outward I find to be more taking than the others.

Among hooks, I consider Pennell eyed Limerick is worthy of the first place, and the straight-backed Sproat a strong second. Anglers should distinguish between the straight and hog-backed Sproat. I use stained gut, not dyed, and rather lighter than most that is used.

There is much satisfaction to be derived from using fine tackle, especially fine leaders. I have some leaders that I made from fine drawn gut, each strand of gut being fifteen inches long, which I consider the *par excellence* of leaders, as the length of each strand dispenses with about one half the usual number of knots to be found in common leaders.

I am decidedly in favor of flies tied with a short loop at the head, or, better still, tied on Pennell eyed hooks.

*Massachusetts.*  {  Silver Doctor.
Parmacheene Belle.    } Trout.
White Miller.

Salmon Flies.    { Land-locked
Salmon.

ANDREW S. MARCH,                    Boston,                         Mass.

I find great enjoyment in the woods and in casting a fly. I
do not know that it makes much difference what the fly is, if it is
only the right size. For trout, I am partial to the Silver Doctor,
Parmacheene Belle, and White Miller, according to the day; and if
for land-locked salmon, a brilliant Salmon fly.

---

*Rhode Island.*    { Grizzly King.
Montreal.

ROBERT C. BOURN,                 Providence,                        R. I.

For my favorite cast for small-mouth black bass upon inland lakes,
after trying many different casts many different years, my mind has
settled itself upon this as my standard one; change, of course, being necessary upon occasion : the Grizzly King with Ibis shoulders
dressed on No. 2/0 Sproat, or, better yet, the reliable O'Shaughnessy
hook. This used as a tail fly at the end of a good six-foot leader is
the whole thing. I know that it is a large fly, but I believe in it.

One fly of that size used with forty feet of line and whipped
with seven ounces of rent bamboo, is all the strain a good trout rod
can bear comfortably, and more than a poor one can. I believe that
allowing the fly to sink a foot or so after the cast, in bass fishing,
secures many fish that would not look at a fly cast upon the surface,
as in ordinary trout casting. A tremulous motion imparted to the
fly upon the surface, especially in the absence of a ripple, I deem of
great importance.

After many experiments, I have come to the conclusion that there is nothing better for leaders than the best of round, even, unstained gut. I tried an experiment last spring in local trout fishing in mounting my Carlisle hooks instead of binding the gut on with silk, as usual. I bought the eyed hooks, and fastened my leader, after soaking, with half a double water-knot directly to the hook. During a week's constant fishing, in which time I took about five hundred trout, I did not lose a fish by breakage at the knot. It was far easier to change in case of lost barb or broken hook by cutting the leader close to the eye and tying on another hook. I told a friend of mine my experience, and he tried it, and was delighted.

Care should be taken, when dressing flies tied with simply a loop of gut to the hook, not to have the loop too long, or it will twist badly. Sneck bend hooks may have good penetration, but I prefer to see my flies stand straight upon the water.

After a dozen different trips to the Moosehead Lake region, Maine, I have no one fly that I place beyond every other. I have had good success with many at different times. I am a Jonah upon the subject of the Montreal. I have caught fish on it, but it has never been a success with me, either for land-locked salmon, trout, or bass. Friends of mine laud it to the skies, but I cannot, though it seems such a favorite.

| *Rhode Island.* | Blue Jay.<br>Grasshopper.<br>Montreal.<br>Wm. H. Hammett. | Trout and<br>Bass. |

WILLIAM H. HAMMETT,　　　　　　　Newport,　　　　　　　R. I.

I have before me at this writing two large fly-books. In the pockets I find many a worn fly, and among them the greatest prize of all, a Blue Jay that captured my first large trout in the Rangeley Lakes in 1882. While at Kennebago Lake, Maine, I found the Blue Jay, Grasshopper, and Montreal flies the most taking, and also used with great success a fly that I invented some years ago while fishing in the south part of Rhode Island. Observing that the bass were rising to a large green fly, I used some green worsted for a body and tail, with a red and white wing, and have since found it successful as an all-round fly for trout or bass. The fly has since been given my name.

In regard to the rod, I handle some very good split bamboos ranging from 5½ to 10 ounces, and none pleases me more than my favorite 10½ foot rod, weighing 6½ ounces.

As regards hooks, my preference is the Sproat, reinforced when above No. 3. I pay more attention to the quality and smoothness of the gut than to color.

For trout fishing, three flies are ordinarily used, though I generally prefer two on a six-foot looped leader, using judgment as to size, according to the water fished. I usually select a cast from the Montreal, Professor, Coachman, Grasshopper, Canada, Cheney, Grizzly King, Blue Jay, and the Hackles.

For lines, I always use an enameled braided silk, and level, as I do not like the tapered; size to compare to weight of rod.

## PLATE I.

No. 60. Parmacheene Belle.      No. 63. Cunningham.

No. 61. Nicholson.      No. 64. Lord Baltimore.

No. 62. Nameless.      No. 65. Orange Miller.

No. 60.   The Parmacheene Belle was invented by Mr. Henry P. Wells, and named after Parmacheene Lake, in Maine.  Mr. Wells's first mention of this fly is in his interesting paper on " Fly-Fishing in the Rangeley Region " in the second edition of " Fishing with the Fly."  Later he writes of it again in his valuable book, " Fly Rods and Fly Tackle," saying : " My first favorite is the ' Parmacheene Belle.'  Perhaps I am too partial to this fly, since it is in a measure my own child.  John and I seldom fish between half past eleven and four o'clock.  That interval is passed prowling about the woods, or shooting at a mark with a rifle, or in some similar way.  Often the fly-tying box is produced, and the word is, ' Well, John, what shall we tease them with this afternoon ? '  Thus, on joint suggestion, very many different combinations have been tried, and so some seven years ago was the ' Parmacheene Belle ' born.  It was a success, and since then I have used it four fifths of the time when fishing the headwaters of the Androscoggin River.

" Unless I am deceived, these large trout take the fly not as an insect, but as some form of live bait.  If this is true, an imitation of some favorite form of food is in itself sufficient under all circumstances, provided it is so conspicuous as readily to be seen.  To test this theory the fly in question was made, imitating in color the belly-fin of the trout itself.

" Place the whole catalogue of known flies on the one hand, and this single fly on the other, and force me to choose and confine myself to that choice, and for fishing in those waters I would choose the ' Parmacheene Belle ' every time.  I have tried it in sunshine and rain, at noonday and in the gloaming, and at all times it has proved successful."

The Coachman for many years was probably as universally popular in this country as any fly one could mention, but the Parmacheene Belle has come to be its strong rival, and we have astonishing reports of its success in all waters.

Mr. Wells also recommends the Parmacheene Belle for sea trout.

A fly called the Parmacheene Beau has lately appeared.  It is practically the same as the Parmacheene Belle, with the addition of jungle-cock feathers as shoulders, and is an infringement upon the former pattern and name.  We feel sure Mr. Wells is not responsible for this latter device.

No. 61.  The Nicholson, sometimes called the Blue and Brown, has for many years been popular for salmon as well as for large trout.  Thaddeus Norris wrote : " The Blue and Brown, or Nicholson, is named after an old salmon fisher, ' a broth of a boy,' of St. John, New Brunswick.  The wings, of mallard, according to Mr. Nicholson's style of tying, stand well up.  The large hook is for high water, when the dubbing and hackles are of lighter shades ; as the water falls the hackles and dubbings should be darker.  On low water and bright weather dark brown and purplish blue are best ; the hook decreasing in size as the water falls.  In fact, trout hooks Nos. 3 and 4 O'Shaughnessy are, as a general rule, large enough for the rivers of Canada ; Nos. 1 and 2 are full size for high water."

No. 62.  The Nameless is supposed to be a reminder of Mr. W. H. H. Murray's enthusiastic account of his experience in fishing for trout in " the Nameless Creek," a part of his " Adventures in the Wilderness," — the book that did so much to attract invalids and sportsmen to the Adirondack region.  The fly was made and named by Mr. John Shields.

No. 63.  Mr. G. V. Cunningham, of Cohoes, N. Y., was the first to tie this combination, and requested us to give it a name ; we therefore called it after him, " the Cunningham."

No. 64.  Lord Baltimore.  In the extract from Dr. Henshall's book, wherein he relates the origin of the Oriole bass fly, is also told the story of the Lord Baltimore ; but Professor Mayer has said that this fly was invented for fishing in the lakes of Maine, where he has found it as successful as other fishermen have else where for black bass.

Professor Mayer, its inventor, will also be gratefully remembered for his further good work for sportsmen in the compilation of the beautiful book of sketches, published by the Scribners, entitled " Sport with the Rod and Gun."

No. 65.  The Orange Miller is so distinguished because of its color and form, and is held to be useful for either trout or bass.

With what words shall I be able to make you see what we saw? The air was pure and clear as a newly-cut diamond, white and colorless as mountain air always is, — a perfect lens, through which, with unimpeded eye, we saw the marvelous transfiguration from day to night go on. Five thousand feet beneath us Lake Placid slept, verifying its name. In the south, a hundred mountain peaks were ablaze with the peculiar red sunset light. For a hundred miles the wilderness stretched away, — a deep green sea, across whose surface the sun was casting great fields of crimson. Amid the darker portions eighty patches of gold flashed, representing as many lakes. Eastward, the valley of Champlain lay in deep shadow. To the north, bounding the vision like a thread of silver, gleamed the St. Lawrence. In the valley of the south lay the martyred dust of him who died on a Virginia gallows, that American manhood and American liberty might not perish. The closing moment had now come. The heavens to the west were swathed in the richest tints of scarlet and orange. A thousand colors lay on forest and lake. The mountain summits flamed. The sun, like a globe of liquid fire, quivering in the intensity of its heat, stood as if balancing on the western pines. Down into them it burnt its way. Pausing for a moment, and only for a moment, it poured its warm benediction upon the forest, bade a crimson farewell to each mountain top, kissed the clouds around its couch, quivered, dropped from sight! And there in the crisp air we thus stood, and gazed in silence westward, until the shadows deepened along the sky; the fog crept in and filled once more the valley at our feet; and the wilderness which had been to me and mine a nurse and home, and which we feared we should never see or enter together again, lay wrapped in silence and in gloom.

W. H. H. MURRAY.

# NEW YORK.

T. V. ALLIS . . . . . . . . { Trout Flies.

J. M. JOHNSON . . . . . . .
{ Beaverkill.
Queen of the Water.
Professor, etc.

JOHN H. OSBORNE . . . . . .
{ Griffith.
Black Gnat.
Cow Dung.
Queen of the Water.

A. P. VAN GIESEN . . . . . .
{ Brown Hen
Coachman.
Yellow Professor.

REV. ARTHUR LAWRENCE . . . { Blue Professor.

WALTER S. MACGREGOR . . .
{ Magpie.
Silver Doctor.
Reuben Wood.
Gov. Alvord, etc.

IRA S. DODD . . . . . . . .
{ Van Patton.
Grizzly King.
Ginger Hackle.

H. A. PRIDE . . . . . . . .
{ Brown Hackle.
Black Hackle.

GARDNER LADD PLUMLEY . . .
{ Beaverkill.
Queen of the Water.
Coachman, etc.

S. J. BRYANT . . . . . . . .
{ Brown Hackle.
Reuben Wood.
Babcock, etc.

T. P. PROCTOR . . . . . . . { Proctor Fly.

JOHN LYMAN COX . . . . . .
{ Brown Hackle.
Coachman.
Red Ibis, etc.

WILLIAM E. WOLCOTT . . . .
{ Green Drake.
Soldier Palmer.
Red Ibis, etc.

| | |
|---|---|
| A. M. GOVE | { Brown Hackle. / Ginger Hackle. / Blue Jay. |
| DR. J. R. ROMEYN | { Brown Hackle. / Scarlet Ibis. / Seth Green. / Romeyn, etc. |
| JOHN DAVIDSON | { Davidson Hackle. |
| WILLIAM J. CASSARD | { Bass Flies. |
| FRANK PIDGEON | { Royal Coachman. / Grizzly King. / Professor, etc. |
| E. T. STRONG | { Brown Hackle. / Quaker. / Green Drake, etc. |
| H. C. WILCOX | { Black Gnat. / Claret. / Queen of the Water, etc. |
| G. V. CUNNINGHAM | { Cow Dung. / Governor. / Professor, etc. |
| CHARLES VAN KIRK | { Montreal. / Coachman. / Green Drake, etc. |
| GEORGE H. PAYSON | { Governor. / Beaverkill. / Van Patton. / White Miller, etc. |
| JOHN D. QUACKENBOS | { Brown Hackle. / Green Drake. / Orange Miller. |
| C. E. FRITTS, M. D. | { Brown Palmer. / Coachman. / Professor. |
| A. R. FULLER | { Brown Hackle. / Red Ibis. / Coachman. / Alder. |

*New York.*          Trout Flies.

T. V. ALLIS,                    New York,                    N. Y.

There seems but little room for new patterns of trout flies. The greatest skill is required to choose among the varieties already tied, without getting too large an assortment. I prefer a few good standard flies, with two or three dozen of a kind in my fly-book, to a varied assortment with only two or three of a kind, as there is nothing more annoying than to run out of a taking fly, as one is apt to do if fishing an overgrown or rocky stream. I have made it a rule to confine myself to twelve varieties, with a dozen flies of each tied on No. 8, 10, and 12 hooks, making three dozen of each kind. As fast as I find one kind or size getting low I replenish it.

It is difficult to say what are "standard flies," as I find extraordinary luck is apt to establish the prestige of some particular fly. My experience, however, has been that the quiet, or gray and brown shades, are the best for general use in eastern New York, Massachusetts, and Connecticut, increasing in brightness as you go north towards Maine and Canada. For instance, I find bright colors suit the taste of Vermont trout better than Massachusetts trout, and even brighter colors can be used more successfully in Canada than in Vermont.

I use a taper line and tapering leader, the large end being as near the size of the small end of the line as possible. I also have the snells of the flies stained to match the leaders, making as little contrast as possible.

I believe a fly closely imitating a grasshopper will take well in all waters during the grasshopper season, but I have never yet found a satisfactory fly of this kind.

| | | |
|---|---|---|
| *New York.* | Beaverkill.<br>Queen of the **Water.**<br>Professor.<br>Coachman.<br>Cow Dung.<br>Quaker. | **Trout.** |

J. M. JOHNSON,               Binghamton,               N. Y.

### PART I.

It would seem an easy matter, for any one who has had much experience in fly-fishing, to name his favorite fly or flies, but this I have not found to be the case. On the contrary, one of the most perplexing things, for a small matter, that I have undertaken for many a day has been that of naming my three favorite flies. I thought at first it was a very simple thing to do, and that but little thought or consideration would be required to make a selection, but in that I was mistaken. I put the question to myself in this way: If I could have but three kinds of flies when I went trout fishing for a week or two, which three would they be? I must take with me none except the three I selected, and must depend wholly upon them for success. It was rather an arbitrary rule, but I could see no other way of so fairly answering the question. That view of the matter presented quite a serious question, and I must make no mistake in my choice.

My trout-fishing experience has been almost wholly confined to the counties of Delaware, Sullivan, and Ulster, in the State of New York. The streams where I have cast my lines have been the Beaverkill and Willowemoc and their tributaries, in Sullivan and Ulster counties; Front Creek, Baxter Brook, the Loomis, and the Sharuck, in Delaware.

That I might deal fairly with the question presented, and also fairly with the many beautiful flies which I have used with greater or less success at different times, I thought I would lay out before me all of the kinds I had (and they were many), and instead of selecting three from the collection as the favored ones, I would lay aside one after another, until only three remained. So I brought out my book, and took from it one fly of each kind I possessed. What pleasant memories arose as I laid them out carefully and affectionately! Here was one, worn and frayed, the tinsel gone and the feathers ragged, and I thought of the rare sport I had had with that little imitation, while standing at the head of a noble pool in the Beaverkill, and with it had brought to my basket many a beautiful trout; and this wreck of the little dainty thing I put on my leader I remembered to have cast time and again among some big rocks in the Willowemoc with much success, and I loved it for what it had done. But I must not be sentimental.

From the different flies spread out before me I commenced to lay aside. It was easy at first, for I presume I am like other fishermen, and have in my book many flies of but little value, except on some rare occasion, when for that particular day they may be taking. One fly after another I had compelled to "stand aside," until only six remained. Then the really difficult work commenced. The six were the Beaverkill, Professor, Coachman, Queen of the Water, Brown Hackle, and Cow Dung. Each had its merits, and none was I willing to give up. I must smoke over the matter, and, lighting my pipe, I went over my fishing trips. First I bade good-by to the Cow Dung, but not without remembering the days when the fickle fish seemed to want no fly but that. Then the Brown Hackle was laid aside with regrets. But how could I do without all the others? I recalled the bright days when the deepening shadows made it difficult to see clearly, and I had put on a Coach-man with its bright wings. I remembered the day when, just at night, I cast a Coachman into the pool above the rocks back of the Dutchman's house on the Beaverkill. There was a splash, and I struck, but failed to hook the fish ; a second cast a little farther over under the overhanging trees where all was dark, and he came again, and this time he was hooked. My delicate rod bent and quivered as he rushed down the stream. Not there, my friend, the rocks are too plentiful and the current is too swift. I turned him, and, with a rush that made the reel sing a merry tune, he started up the pool where I could manage him. It was a gallant fight, but the pliant rod never failed, and hook and line held fast, and the finest trout of the day topped out my creel.

But thinking again of the days (and there were many of them) when the other three had landed nearly all my catch, while other flies had failed me, I must lay aside my loved Coachman, and there remain but three, the Beaverkill, Queen of the Water, and Pro-fessor, which I cannot give up, and they are my three favorites.

In making the selections named, I have not forgotten that there have been many days when the three named flies had no attractions at all. The trout would have none of them. But at the same time, they would not rise well to any fly that I could offer ; so, all things considered, early in the season as well as late, one day taken with another, I have had better success in the water named with these than with any other.

The decision made, I quickly gather the for a moment discarded flies, and place them in my book again, telling them it was only in fun ; that none of them shall be left, but shall stay with me, and next May and June shall tempt the beauties of the Beaverkill and Willowemoc.

PART II.

The waters where I have cast my lines have been within a somewhat limited territory, as my fishing has been almost wholly within the counties of Delaware, Sullivan, and Ulster, in the State of New York, and the streams have been the Beaverkill and Willowemoc and their tributaries, Front Creek and Baxter Brook. It has not been my good fortune to have the pleasure of fishing the many streams and lakes of the Adirondacks, the Rangeley Lakes, or the famed Nipigon. Of those waters I only know from what I have read or "heard tell of," but I am cherishing a well-grounded hope that erelong I may know something of them from personal experience. Of the streams before mentioned, where I have passed so many delightful days during the past ten years, I flatter myself that I have a pretty thorough knowledge. I think I have learned "where the trout hide" there, and that equally important knowledge, where not to fish ; for I have never seen a trout stream which did not have stretches of water, beautiful to look at and tempting to an angler, but where it would be a waste of time and strength to whip with a fly.

My choice of flies must of necessity refer to the streams where my fishing has been done, and in naming my selection I do not forget that there have been many days, or portions of days, when the fickle fish would not have them, and then I would have to try others, with varying success. I remember one day last May, when, with a friend, I was fishing the Willowemoc. I had had fair success during the early part of the day, which was warm and bright, but about midday my good luck deserted me and I could take scarcely anything, which I attributed to the fact that it was the middle of the day. After lunch and a long rest, I tried it again, but with no success. I tried all my favorite flies and some which were not favorites, until I think I must have tried at least twenty. If I took a fish, it seemed as if it was by accident. About five o'clock I sat down at the head of a beautiful pool in which I knew there were plenty of trout, as they were jumping the whole length of the pool; I watched them to try and discover what they were taking. I noticed coming down the stream a fly, which, when it reached the pool, would quickly disappear as some fine fellow rose for it. Going above, I caught one of the flies and compared it with the flies in my book, but could find nothing to match it closely. The fly that came nearest it was a fuzzy-looking little Quaker, No. 12 hook. I put it on as a leader, with a Beaverkill and Queen as droppers, and wading out until I could cast where the trout were jumping, as a forlorn hope, I sent the little Quaker out. Gently it struck the water, where it rested but an instant, when it was taken with a greediness that delights the heart of a fisherman, and the fun commenced. From that moment until dark I brought the fish in until I had nearly filled my basket, and I blessed the maker of it for that little fly. The Quaker did the business for me that day. At another time, during the same month, on the Beaverkill, I found I could do more with the Red Fox than with any other, and I have at times put on a Reuben Wood with good results. But the success which I have had with these or other flies has been spasmodic and on some particular occasions, and unlike that had with my three favorites. The Coachman ranks well up with the three named, and to it I am indebted for many fine fish. I recall days which were dark and gloomy, if any days on a trout stream can be gloomy, and bright days when the deepening shadows at nightfall made it difficult to see clearly, and I had put on a Coachman with its white wings with which to close the day's sport.   Casting to the farther side of some pool under the overhanging bank where all was dark, I have frequently topped out my creel with the best fish of the day.

I have sometimes thought that the preference as to flies was to a certain extent due to the fact that one fisherman would be using those of one maker, while another would be using those made by some one else.   A comparison of standard flies of the same name, tied by different makers, will very often show a marked difference, and yet both answer to a general description.   The bodies of the flies are usually very nearly alike, but the color of the wing will differ so much that one might reasonably doubt the correctness of calling them the same; and often there is just difference enough to make one taking and the other not, under the same circumstances and in the same waters; the result being that one fisherman would declare the fly to be no good, while his friend, fishing with the same named fly, but made by another maker, would stoutly maintain it was just the fly he wanted.   I have had just that experience.

I like a small hook.   For a fly with a slim body, like the Beaver-kill, I use a No. 12.   If the fly has a bulky body, the Reuben Wood for instance, I use No. 10.   It may be only a notion of mine that a bulky body requires a little larger hook than a slim body, but so I think.   I prefer a mist-colored leader rather than pure white. This is perhaps another notion.

Upon consulting with my friends, some or all of whom have accompanied me wherever I have fished the streams mentioned, I find their favorites for those waters to be as follows: Colonel H. G. Rodgers, Beaverkill, Queen, and Coachman; Honorable S. C.

Millard, Reuben Wood, Brown Hackle, and Grizzly King ; A. R. Tweedy, Beaverkill, Queen, and Professor ; C. W Sears, Beaverkill, Queen, and Coachman.

To sum it all up, for early and late fishing, days light and days dark, for early morning, midday, and twilight, if I could only be permitted to take with me but three kinds of flies, they would be the three first named, the Beaverkill, Queen of the Water, and Professor. But still I like a well filled book. I would take a good selection to cater to the whims of the trout on those special occasions referred to.

---

| *New York.* | Griffith.<br>Black Gnat.<br>Cow Dung.<br>Qeeen of the Water. | Land-locked Salmon and Trout. |
| --- | --- | --- |

JOHN H. OSBORNE,　　　　　　　　Auburn,　　　　　　　　N. Y.

In 1886 I was on the Saguenay for " Winanish " (land-locked salmon), and my friend, Mr. Creighton, president of our club, whose article in the May number of " Scribner's Magazine " for 1889 you may find interesting, showed me a fly of his own invention, named by him the Griffith, which was a very killing fly. I inclose specimen and description of them furnished by Mr. Creighton : —

"THE GRIFFITH." (*Tie with yellow silk.*)

*Tag.* — Gold tinsel (would be better in twist).

*Butt.* — Yellow seal's fur.

*Body.* — Black mohair, with three to four turns over it of gold-colored floss silk.

*Hackle.* — Black, tied in at shoulder only.

*Wings.* — Black crow, jungle-cock two thirds up on each side. (Leave gray butts of jungle-cock on.)

*Topping.* — Golden-pheasant crest.

*Head.* — Of yellow tying silk.

I also inclose specimen of a fly that has proved very killing for the small native trout in Balsam Lake (on a small tributary of the Beaverkill, near its head).[1]  I do not know the name of the fly, or whether it has any.

I have found the Black Gnat, Queen of the Water, and Cow Dung also very effective on the same waters.

---

| *New York.* | { Brown Hen.<br>Coachman.<br>Yellow Professor. | { For Trout. |
|---|---|---|

A. P. VAN GIESEN,                    Poughkeepsie,                    N. Y.

More than elsewhere I have fished in the streams of Ulster and Sullivan counties, New York.  If I could have but one fly, that one would be the Brown Hen, as described by Thaddeus Norris.  If I could have but two, the second would be the Coachman.  If I could have but three, the third would be the Yellow Professor.  As a general rule, I have found that when a cast made of these three will not take, nothing will take.

---

| *New York and Canada.* | { Blue Professor. |
|---|---|

REV. ARTHUR LAWRENCE,                    Stockbridge,                    Mass.

Last year I found in the northern Adirondacks that the gray drake wings on a blue body (Blue Professor) were extraordinarily effective.  At the Laurentian Lakes, in Lower Canada, there was nothing so killing as a brown fly, of which I cannot give the name, but to which the Seth Green with a red body would be the nearest.

---

[1] The fly sent as the one found killing at Balsam Lake had white wings and tail, scarlet chenille body, pale ginger hackle, and was dressed on a No. 11 Sproat hook. — M. E. O. M.

## PLATE J.

No. 66. Oquossoc.

No. 67. Klamath.

No. 68. No Name.

No. 69. New Lake.

No. 70. Tomah Jo.

No. 71. Prince Edward.

**No. 66.** The Oquossoc is a combination made and named by Mr. John Shields, and intended for fishing in Maine.

**No. 67.** The following extract from a letter written to Mr. Orvis by Major Henry McEldery, U. S. A., will be an explanation of the Klamath: " I left dear old Fort Klamath in 1876, that paradise of fishermen sportsmen. Let us call the trout fly that I am going to describe to you by the name of 'the Klamath,' in honor of that post, for it was there I had my great success with it. I usually tied the fly on No. 3 or 4 Limerick hook straight. Body, of copper-colored peacock herl, made rather full; tail, of the barred wood-duck feather, with sometimes a little bright red ibis added; tip, gold tinsel; head, of black ostrich herl; wings, of the black loon feathers with white spot on either side. By varying the size of the white spots I found the fly did equally well for day or evening fishing, or for bright or dull days, or for clear or dull waters. I had more success with this fly with the salmon-trout on the Williamson River, ten miles below Fort Klamath, and in the streams about Fort Klamath, than any fly I ever fished with. Among the officers, it soon became noted for its killing properties. I could catch larger fish with it than any other fly I had."

**No. 68.** The No Name was first tied by C. F. Orvis, in about 1880, at the request of a fisherman, whose name we have forgotten, who wished to try a variation of the Professor. The fly proved successful, and as it had not been named we often wrote on the card underneath the fly No Name, until in time we found it was being called the No Name. It has been a favorite fly from the first.

**No. 69.** The New Lake was a fly designed and named by Mr. Lorenzo Prouty, of Boston. There is also a valuable fly for Maine fishing called the Prouty. Mr. Prouty was not only a skillful fisherman, but a man who left hosts of friends who remember him with loyalty, and grieve that he could not have lived out his days of usefulness and happiness. The following is a portion of a letter from the venerable Mr. John Shields, who will be glad, we are sure, to have us print this tribute to one whom he remembers so faithfully : —

" Few, if any, are more deserving of a notice in your book than Lorenzo Prouty. It is doubtful if to-day any person has as large a circle of fishing friends in New England as Mr. Prouty had. His long experience in the tackle trade had given him a wide reputation among anglers in general. His integrity and abiding attention to their wants secured for him the entire confidence of his patrons, who invariably left the selection of flies and other articles needed in their outfit to him. Mr. Prouty was a capital angler and an expert woodsman. The writer had the pleasure of spending many pleasant days with him on the Maine lakes. In the death of Lorenzo Prouty I lost a good and kind friend."

**No. 70.** The fly called Tomah Jo was first made by Miss Sara J. McBride, of Mumford, N. Y., and named by Mr. Charles W. Stevens, of Boston, who introduced it to the public in his pleasant little book entitled, " Fly-Fishing in the Maine Lakes." In his trips to Maine Mr. Stevens was often accompanied by an Indian guide, of whom he writes as follows : —

" Tomah Joseph, the son of his father, who still, at an advanced age, occasionally acts as guide, is now about forty years of age, is himself the father of several embryo guides, and as 'cute an Indian as ever paddled a canoe. To enumerate his several accomplishments in his particular line would require more space than we can afford to give here at this time. In casting a fly I have never seen him excelled, scarcely equaled. In mending rods he is an adept. I think, after seeing him run the rapids on the stream, Mr. Murray would preach a sermon from that text, and Tomah Jo would always say, " When you come to Maine bring plenty wood-duck-wing-fly, yellow body."

This fly is beautiful, but its special interest to us, beyond its success, lies in its name, for that awakens a remembrance of the wonderful Wabanaki traditions that the elder Tomah Joseph has related and so helped to preserve. A collector has said of them : " This Wabanaki mythology, which was that which gave a fairy, an elf, a naiad, or a hero to every rock and river and ancient hill in New England, is just the one, of all others, which is least known to the New Englanders. When the last

Indian shall be in his grave, those who come after us will ask in wonder why we had no curiosity as to the romance of our country, and so much as to that of every other land on earth."

The Algonquin was one of the six great divisions of Indians in North America: its people spoke forty different dialects, and extended from Labrador to the far south, and to Newfoundland on the east. The eastern division of these was known as the Wabanaki, the word suggesting that they lived near the white light, or rising sun. They were subdivided into the Micmacs of Nova Scotia, the St. Francis Indians of Canada, and some lesser clans, and the Penobscot and Passamaquoddy tribes of Maine. Tomah Joseph belonged to the latter, and was Indian governor at Peter Dana's Point. Mr. Charles G. Leland, who was greatly interested in collecting and preserving all the Indian traditions possible, to aid in their future study, has said of them: "The Indians were as fond of recitations as the white man is of reading, and their memories of stories were wonderful."

Arthur Wentworth Eaton in a pretty little poem tells us something of their habits and their God in the " Legend of Glooskap," which concludes as follows: —

> But the old Acadian woods and shores,
> Rich in beautiful legend stores,
> Were once the home of an older race,
> Who wove their epics with untaught grace.
>
> .    .    .    .    .    .    .
>
> The Micmac sailed in his birch canoe
> Over the Basin, calm and blue ;
> Speared the salmon, his heart's desire,
> Danced and slept by his wigwam fire ;
>
> Far in the depths of the forest gray
> Hunted the moose the livelong day,
> While the mother sang to her Micmac child
> Songs of the forest, weird and wild.
>
> Over the tribe, with jealous eye,
> Watched the Great Spirit from on high,
> While on the crest of Blomidon
> Glooskap, the God-man, dwelt alone.

No matter how far his feet might stray
From the favorite haunts of his tribe **away,**
Glooskap could hear the Indian's prayer,
And send some message of comfort there.

Glooskap it was who taught the use
Of the bow and the spear, and sent the **moose**
Into the Indian hunter's hands ;
Glooskap who strewed the shining sands

Of the tide-swept beach of the stormy **bay**
With amethysts purple and agates gray,
And brought to each newly-wedded pair
The Great Spirit's benediction fair.

But the white man came, and with ruthless **hand**
Cleared the forests and sowed the land,
And drove from their haunts by the sunny **shore**
Micmac and moose, for evermore.

And Glooskap, saddened and sore distressed,
Took his way to the unknown West,
And the Micmac kindled his wigwam fire
Far from the grave of his child and his sire ;

Where now, as he weaves his blanket gay,
And paddles his birch canoe away,
He dreams of the happy time for men
When Glooskap shall come to his tribe again.

All the old Indians, male or female, retain stories and songs of greatest interest, and as Mr. Leland says of our Eastern Indians: "The Wabanaki have in common the traditions of a grand mythology, the central figure of which is a demigod or hero, who, while he is always great, consistent, and benevolent, and never devoid of dignity, presents traits which are very much more like those of Odin and Thor, with not a little of Pantagruel, than anything in the Chippewa Manobozho or the Iroquois Hiawatha. The name of this divinity is Glooskap, meaning, strangely enough, the Liar, because it is said that when he left earth, like King Arthur of Fairyland, he promised to return, and has never done so. It is characteristic of the Norse gods that while they are grand they are manly, and combine with this a peculiarly domestic humanity. Glooskap is the Norse god intensified. He is, however, more of a giant; he grows to a more appalling greatness than Thor or Odin in his battles; when a Kiawaqu' or Jötun rises to the clouds to oppose him, Glooskap's head touches the stars, and, scorning to slay so mean a foe as an equal, he kills him contemptuously with a light tap of his bow." All through it, this American mythology of the north bears a wonderful resemblance, perhaps we are safe to say relation, to the Edda of the old Scandinavians; there is said to be hardly a song in the Norse collection which does not contain an incident found in the Indian poem-legends, while in several there are many such coincidences. To quote again from Mr. Leland: " Thus in the Edda we are told that the first birth on earth was that of a giant girl and boy, begotten by the feet of a giant, and born from his armpit. In the Wabanaki legends, the first birth was Glooskap, the Good principle, and Mālsum, the Wolf, or Evil principle. The Wolf was born from his mother's armpit. He is sometimes male, and sometimes female. His feet are male and female, and converse. We pass on only twelve lines in the Edda (Vafthend-nismal, 36) to be told that the wind is caused by a giant in eagle's plumage, who sits on a rock far in the north 'at end of heaven.' This is simply and literally the *Wochowsen*, or Windblower, of the Wabanaki, word for word, — not the 'Thunder Bird' of the Western Indians."

As Tomah Joseph has been one of the principal narrators of these traditions, the time may come when his name will be of special consequence, as the interest in Indian archæology grows deeper, and the enthusiasm over these myths, legends, and folk-lore greater, among ethnologists, as they seek to follow up these traces of affinity between the northeastern Indians and the Eskimo. The subject was, perhaps, too large even to mention in these pages, but we cannot resist giving in this connection one of the less wild, more homely beliefs, telling Tomah Joseph's own story as he handed down the tradition, from his forefathers, of the origin of the fishes in the sea; for surely this native legend of New England must be of interest to the fishermen who know its rivers. Mr. Charles G. Leland has divested it of its broken English, but is careful to give it in other respects as nearly as possible in the form in which it was rendered by the old Passamaquoddy Indian. It is called —

*How Glooskap conquered the Great Bull-Frog, and in what Manner all the Pollywogs, Crabs, Leeches, and other Water Creatures were created.*

(Passamaquoddy and Micmac tradition.)

*N'karnayoo*, of old times, there was an Indian village far away in the mountains, little known to other men.   And the dwellers therein were very comfortable : the men hunted every day, the women did the work at home, and all went well in all things save in this.   The town was by a brook, and except in it there was not a drop of water in all the country round, unless in a few rain-puddles.   No one there had ever found even a spring.

Now these Indians were very fond of good water.   The brook was of superior quality, and they became dainty over it.

But after a time they began to observe that the brook was beginning to run low, and that not in the summer time, but in autumn, even after the rains.   And day by day it diminished, until its bed was as dry as a dead bone in the ashes of a warm fire.

Now it was said that far away up in the land where none had ever been there was on this very stream another Indian village ; but what manner of men dwelt therein no one knew.   And thinking that these people of the upper country might be in some way concerned in the drought, they sent one of their number to go and see into the matter.

And after he had traveled three days he came to the place ; and then he found that a dam had been raised across the rivulet, so that no water could pass, for it was all kept in a pond.   Then asking them why they made this mischief, since the dam was of no use to them, they bade him go and see their chief, by whose order this had been built.

And when he came to him, lo, there lay lazily in the mud a creature who was more of a monster than a man, though he had a human form.   For he was immense to measure, like a giant, fat, bloated, and brutal to behold.   His great yellow eyes stuck from his head like pine-knots, his mouth went almost from ear to ear, and he had broad, skinny feet with long toes, exceeding marvelous.

The messenger complained to this monster, who at first said nothing, and then croaked, and finally replied in a loud bellow : —

" Do as you choose,
　　Do as you choose,
　　Do as you choose.

" What do I care ?
　　What do I care ?
　　What do I care ?

" If you want water,
　　If you want water,
　　If you want water,
　　Go somewhere else."

Then the messenger remonstrated, and described the suffering of the people, who were dying of thirst. And this seemed to please the monster, who grinned. At last he got up, and, making a single spring to the dam, took an arrow and bored a hole in it, so that a little water trickled out; and then he bellowed : —

" Up and begone !
　　Up and begone !
　　Up and begone ! "

So the man departed, little comforted. He came to his home, and for a few days there was a little water in the stream; but this soon stopped, and there was great suffering again.

Now these Indians, who were the honestest fellows in all the world, and never did any harm to any one save their enemies, were in a sorry pickle. For it is a bad thing to have nothing but water to drink, but to want that is to be mightily dry. And the great Glooskap, who knew all that was passing in the hearts of men and beasts, took note of this, and when he willed it he was among them; for he came as the wind blows, and no man wist how.

And just before he came all of these good fellows had resolved in council that they would send the boldest man among them to certain death, even to the village which built the dam that kept the water which filled the brook that quenched their thirst, whenever it was not empty. And when there he was either to obtain that they should cut the dam, or do something desperate, and to this intent he should go armed, and sing his death-song as he went. And they were all agog.

Then Glooskap, who was much pleased with all this, for he loved a brave man, came among them looking terribly ferocious; in all the land there was not one who seemed half so horrible. For he appeared ten feet high, with a hundred red and black feathers in his scalp-lock, his face painted like fresh blood, with green rings round his eyes, a large clam-shell hanging from each ear, a spread eagle, very awful to behold, flopping its wings from the back of his neck, so that as he strode into the village all hearts quaked. Being but simple Indians, they accounted that this must be, if not Lox the Great Wolverine, at least Mitche-haut, the devil himself in person turned Wabanaki; and they admired him greatly, and the squaws said they had never seen aught so lovely.

Then Glooskap, having heard the whole story, bade them be of good cheer, declaring that he would soon set all to rights. And he without delay departed to the bed of the brook; and, coming to the town, sat down and bade a boy bring him water to drink. To which the boy replied that no water could be had in that town unless it were given out by the chief. " Go, then, to your chief," said the master, " and bid him hurry, or, verily, I will know the reason why." And this being told, Glooskap received no reply for more than an hour, during which time he sat on a log and smoked his pipe. Then the boy returned with a small cup, and this not half full, of very dirty water.

So he arose, and said to the boy, " I will go and see your chief, and I think he will soon give me better water than this." And having come to the monster, he said, " Give me to drink, and that of the best, thou Thing of the Mud ! " But the chief reviled him, and said, " Get thee hence, to find water where thou canst." Then Glooskap thrust a spear into his belly, and, lo! there gushed forth a mighty river; even all the water which should have run on while in the rivulet, for he had made it unto himself. And Glooskap, rising high as a giant pine, caught the old chief in his hand and crumpled in his back with a mighty grip. And, lo! it was the Bull-Frog. So he hurled him with contempt into the stream, to follow the current.[1]

And ever since that time the Bull-Frog's back has crumpled wrinkles in the lower part, showing the prints of Glooskap's awful squeeze.

[1] It may be observed that the Indians commonly say that wherever the bull-frog is to be found in summer there is always water. It is not to be understood, in this tale, that the bull-frog is supposed to have merely drunk up the river. It is the river which has become incarnate in him. It is the ice of winter penetrated by the spear of the sun, that is, Glooskap. Thus, in another tale, a frozen river tries, as a man, to destroy the hero, but is melted by him. The Passamaquoddy name for the monster who swallowed the stream is said to be *Hahk-lee-be-mo.*

Then he returned to the village ; but there he found no people, — no, not one. For a marvelous thing had come to pass during his absence, which shall be heard in every Indian's speech through all the ages. For the men, being, as I said, simple, honest folk, did as boys do when they are hungry, and say unto one another, " What would you, *you* like to have, and what you ? " " Truly, I would be pleased with a slice of hot venison dipped in maple-sugar and bear's oil." " Nay, give me, for my share, succotash and honey." Even so these villagers had said, " Suppose *you* had all the nice, cold, fresh, sparkling, delicious water there is in the world, what would *you* do ? "

And one had said that he would live in the soft mud and always be wet and cool.

And another, that he would plunge from the rocks and take headers, diving into the deep, cool water, drinking as he dived.

And the third, that he would be washed up and down with the rippling waves, living on the land, yet ever in the water.

Then the fourth said, " Verily, you know not how to wish, and I will teach you. I would live in the water all the time, and swim about in it forever."

Now it chanced that these things were said in the hour which, when it passes over the world, all the wishes uttered by men are granted. And so it was with these Indians. For the first became a Leech, the second a Spotted Frog, the third a Crab, which is washed up and down with the tide, and the fourth a Fish. Ere this, there had been in all the world none of the creatures which dwell in the water, and now they were there, and of all kinds. And the river came rushing and roaring on, and they all went headlong down to the sea, to be washed into many lands over all the world.

We have had three motives in repeating this old Indian tradition. First, because it was given to posterity by Tomah Joseph ; second, because it is of New England, " my ain fair countree," and relates to the origin of fishes, and they are the motive of all there is in these pages ; and third, to repeat and enforce the work so enthusiastically and intelligently begun by Mr. Leland. In his book of Algonquin legends he said : " I sincerely trust that this work may have the effect of stimulating collection. Let every reader remember that everything thus taken down and deposited in a local historical society, or sent to the Ethnological Bureau at Washington, will forever transmit the name of its recorder to posterity. Archæology is yet in its very beginning; when the Indians shall have departed it will grow to giant-like proportions, and every scrap of information relative to them will be eagerly investigated. And the man does not live who knows what may be made of it all."

Who will have better opportunities for adding to this information than those who are annually fishing and hunting? Around the camp-fire or in the floating canoe will be heard scraps, now and then, that should be remembered and recorded, for each may be a blaze on the tree to point farther on, or show whence came the unknown.

No. 71. An account of the Prince Edward fly will be found in the letter from Mr. Francis C. Green.

| | | |
|---|---|---|
| *New York.* | Magpie.<br>Silver Doctor.<br>Reuben Wood.<br>Royal Coachman.<br>Black Gnat<br>Polka Dot.<br>Professor.<br>Seth Green.<br>Gov. Alvord.<br>Ferguson.<br>Orange Wren. | Trout and<br>Black Bass. |

WALTER S. MacGREGOR,                    Syracuse,                    N. Y.

I have always found it difficult, if not impossible, to determine in advance the proper cast of flies for either trout or bass, at any season of the day or year.

So much depends on the condition and temperature of the water, and of the air and sky, whether the water is cold or warm, clear or discolored, high or low, smooth or rippled, still or swiftly moving, and whether the sky is overcast with dense or fleecy clouds, or clear and dry, or warm and humid. Then, again, much depends on the capricious tastes of the fish themselves, and on the insects on which they may be feeding at the time.

I am one of those who believe that under any or all of these circumstances, if the fisherman is patient and skillful, and has a sufficient variety of flies, he can catch more and larger fish than with any other lure.

I suppose every practical fly-fisherman has a few favorite flies, the reliables on which he depends, as the basis of his cast, and these will differ according to individual taste and experience, or locality. But to be successful, one needs, I believe, a great variety of flies, of different colors and combinations of colors.

It has repeatedly been my experience, while bass fishing from a boat, with a companion, to find none of the standard flies attractive, while some solitary specimen in my fly-book proved a killing bait. My companion, without that fly, was helpless, no matter how skillfully he cast.

For trout fishing my favorite fly has always been the Brown Palmer Hackle, wound on red worsted body;[1] next in their order, the Reuben Wood, Royal Coachman, Black Gnat, and Polka Dot, Professor, and Seth Green. These have almost always proved taking flies in the North Woods.

In bass fishing, the best early fly is the Silver Doctor with green hackle. This has also proved a most excellent fly throughout the season. Next, the Reuben Wood, the John Mann, the Magpie, Gov. Alvord, Montreal, Ferguson, Orange Wren.

Next to the Silver Doctor, the Magpie has proved the best general fly throughout the season, in all kinds of weather. I have been surprised to find it an attractive fly until long after sundown, in fact as long as you can see to fish, — much more so than the light-colored flies. Of course, these are but a few of many excellent patterns.

With the single exception of the Silver Doctor, my experience in bass fishing in Central New York has proved that bright, gay-colored flies are not nearly as taking as those of subdued colors, with light or dark brown, gray or black wings, brown, black, or green hackle, and orange, yellow, red, purple, black, or white bodies, or combinations of these colors.

I have never had much success with Hackles or Palmers in bass fishing. But with me success has largely depended on a great variety of flies from which to select the cast for the particular day and season.

[1] Soldier Palmer.

Made by C.F. ORVIS, Manchester, Vt.

PLATE I: DESCRIPTION PAGE 157

Made by C.F. ORVIS, Manchester, Vt.

PLATE J: DESCRIPTION PAGE 171

Made by C.F. ORVIS, Manchester, Vt.

PLATE K: DESCRIPTION PAGE 189

Made by C.F. ORVIS, Manchester, Vt.

PLATE L: DESCRIPTION PAGE 199

|  | Van Patton. |  |
|---|---|---|
| *New York.* | Grizzly King. | For Trout. |
|  | Ginger Hackle. |  |
|  | Coachman. |  |

IRA S. DODD, Riverdale, New York City.

My experience last season was confined to the Beaverkill River, Sullivan County, N. Y.

I was there twice: first for a day or two in June, when I found the Van Patton a good fly; and then I spent a month in that region, beginning with the second week in July. I then found the Van Patton of little use; in fact, no fly with white in it seemed wanted in the middle of the day. The Black Gnat was good, and on one day, after a rise in the water, the Grizzly King seemed to be the thing. But the best fly was a small drab fly (tailless), with a nearly black body wound with a fillet of gilt, and leaden wings; the hook, I think, was about No. 13. I do not know the name of this fly. I bought it of Mr. Pritchard, who died last winter.

A fellow-angler had excellent success, one day, with a curious light blue fly which I never saw before. I took some large trout (large for that stream), over a pound in weight, toward evening, with a good-sized Ginger Hackle, orange body, No. 7 or 8 hook, and some after dark with a Coachman.

---

| *New York.* | Brown Hackle. | Trout. |
|---|---|---|
|  | Black Hackle. |  |

H. A. PRIDE, Holland Patent, N. Y.

Favorite flies are Black Hackles first, and Brown Hackles next, and no others. Hooks, Kendall sneck bend; snells, single and white.

New York. {
- Beaverkill.
- Queen of the Water.
- Coachman.
- Governor.
- Van Patton.
- Black Hackle.
} { Trout.

GARDNER LADD PLUMLEY,                    New York,                    N. Y.

My favorite flies on the streams of Ulster and Sullivan counties, where I feel most at home, are the Beaverkill, Queen of the Water, Coachman, Governor, Van Patton, and Black Hackle.

The Queen of the Water and the Beaverkill, in the early season on those streams, are also certainly very successful flies. The Coachman as an evening fly seems always the best possible. Late in the season, when the water is very low and clear, or in the middle of a warm day in June, sometimes, the Governor seems better adapted to "raising 'em," as I now sadly remember, from an incident of several seasons ago, which may possibly prove instructive to my readers, as it was to me.

In the latter part of June I was fishing the headwaters of the Neversink, in Ulster County, in company with a friend who is a master in the art. The middle of the day was very hot, with a cloudless sky. I was ahead, and had carefully fished over a fine pool without a rise; I say carefully, for I had tried most of the dark flies in my book. I gave it up for the time and went down the stream some little distance and found a cool spot. From time to time I looked up stream for my friend. Finally I could see his rod flashing in the bright sunlight over the pool I had just left. From where I sat I could not see the fisherman, so, after waiting a long time, I concluded he must somehow have had luck, so I went back to him. I found him standing nearly up to his waist in water, and seemingly greatly interested in the pool which I had found so barren. He was anxious to show me the results, so brought his creel to me, and in it I had the pleasure (?) of counting seven good trout, all taken from that stand. He then told me that, finding everything else to fail, he had tried a Governor with a bit of red on the body, and with this he was successful. Why, though, those fish would not take my Black Hackle I shall never know.

I believe in a Sproat hook, and a dark, almost black leader.

---

| *New York.* | Brown Hackle. Reuben Wood. Red Ibis. Babcock. Brown Stone. Montreal. | Trout. |

S. J. Bryant, Wallingford, Conn.

My experience has been confined to the Adirondack waters in the vicinity of Bisby Lodge, of which I am a member.

I feel fully equipped for that section if supplied with the Brown Hackle, Reuben Wood, Red Ibis, Babcock, Brown Stone, and Montreal. I have mentioned the foregoing in the order of my valuation.

They are all well known, unless it be the Babcock, named after a most expert and experienced fly-caster of Bisby Club. Mr. Babcock originated the fly which more nearly resembles the Montreal than any other; it has quite a circle of white in the body, and the other colors are brighter than the Montreal.

I most decidedly prefer the short loop, about two inches long, made of clear, heavy gut. Hooks should be of medium size.

| *New York.* | Proctor Fly. | Trout. |

T. P. PROCTOR,    Utica,    N. Y.

My fishing is all done at the lakes owned and controlled by the Bisby Club.

Having had good success with the Reuben Wood fly, and thinking it might be improved upon, I made some suggestions for the making of it which are embodied in the inclosed fly.

Many of my friends have had good luck with it, and they have named it the Proctor fly. I hope you will give it a trial, and let me know what success you have with it.

NOTE. — The Proctor fly is similar to the Reuben Wood, except that the body is made with chenille of a pale pink tinge tipped with three turns of olive-brown chenille.

---

| *New York.* | Brown Hackle.<br>Coachman.<br>Red Ibis.<br>Professor.<br>Montreal.<br>Grizzly King.<br>Orange Miller. | Trout. |

JOHN LYMAN COX,    Orange,    N. J.

The unfortunate destruction of my notes, which I was in the habit of keeping each day, and recording the catch made and flies that caught it, makes me dependent upon my memory for facts, but I may be able to mention one or two points of interest.

My experience has been confined wholly to the Adirondacks between June and September.

For general work, at nearly all hours, both morning and evening, three flies have done the best, — Brown Hackle, Coachman, and Red Ibis.

Four others are also killing, — Professor, Montreal, Grizzly King, and Orange Miller.

I incline to the belief that it is the red in the Montreal that does the work, for when that fly has taken well the Red Ibis has perhaps taken better. The Professor and Brown Hackle, similarly, have gone together.

I have not had as much success with other flies as with those enumerated.

It is a very general belief that a light-colored fly must be used to kill at night. My experience, certainly in one instance, was not confirmatory of this. I was fishing on Lake Colden, on the Adirondack Club preserve, about August 20th, a few years ago. There was quite a strong wind blowing, and the sky was somewhat overcast, about six o'clock. Until after sunset the trout would not rise, but then took the fly poorly. As the darkness increased the fish rose better, and I had fine sport when it was so dark that I could not see the flies, which were all dark, though I do not now recall which they were. Instinct seemed to tell me when to strike, and the sport was very exciting, though the fish were small. I had been advised to try dark flies by a New York gentleman who had been through the same experience.

For Adirondack trout, flies tied on No. 8 Sproat hooks have seemed to me quite as large as desirable, and my judgment on this has been confirmed by some of the best fishermen among the guides. I suppose every one is troubled by snells breaking close to the hooks; for this reason looped hooks would seem to offer advantages. One fly that I never succeeded with is the Black Hackle for late August fishing, though I have been told that it was absolutely the only fly taken on very hot days.

|            | { Green Drake.    |          |
|------------|-------------------|----------|
|            | Soldier Palmer.   |          |
| *New York.* | Red Ibis.        | Trout.   |
|            | Coachman.         |          |
|            | Professor.        |          |

WILLIAM E. WOLCOTT,                    Utica,                    N. Y.

From my experience in angling for speckled trout in the waters of the Adirondack region in the State of New York during the past eighteen or twenty years, I will briefly state the following conclusions. My favorite here for trout in the smaller streams, and on the rifts in the larger ones, is the Brown Hackle, although the Soldier Palmer is perhaps its equal. In lake fishing for speckled trout the Coachman and Professor are the more reliable flies, and on one particular lake at the headwaters of the south branch of the Moose River the Green Drake is unsurpassed for killing qualities. Time and again, in the early evening hours, have I filled my basket on this lake with beauties ranging from one half to a pound and a half in weight, and four out of the five would be taken on the Green Drake fly.

The Scarlet Ibis takes well as a tail fly in almost any of the Adirondack waters during the summer months.

Many anglers claim superior merits for a fly having brown wings, orange body, red game-cock hackle; and it certainly averages well. I use mist-colored leaders and quite large flies.

# PLATE K.

| | |
|---|---|
| No. 72. Silver Doctor, H. P. Wells's pattern. | No. 75. Spider. |
| No. 73. " " J. G. Shearer's " | No. 76. Seth Green. |
| No. 74. " " C. F. Orvis's " | No. 77. Silver Ibis. |

No. 72. The Silver Doctor has been subjected to many variations. John Hailey, who first taught us how to tie an artificial fly, said : " There is no better fly than the Silver Doctor; make it with a silver body, and put a little of everything you can find in the wing, and you will have a Silver Doctor." This rule was unorthodox and not to be indorsed, even though it apparently expressed the practices of many. The best pattern is that given as a salmon fly in Plate B ; the more closely one follows this dressing, the more correct will be the result. In Plate K will be seen three dressings that are much used. We believe Mr. Wells now adds the gallina hackle outside the blue hackle on the lake fly as well as on the salmon fly, but this was learned too late to be shown in this plate.

Mr. J. G. Shearer, in his letter, gives testimony regarding the second dressing. The third was one of our first attempts at fly-making, but it immediately became popular, and so was retained as a form of the Silver Doctor, though we do not uphold it as the correct pattern, and can only claim for it that it has been used with much success, and was therefore thought too good to be abandoned. We have often wished that it had been called by some other name, but it is now too widely known to recall and rename. Another variety is made with a bright green hackle ; it is then sometimes known as the Silver Ferguson, but the fly is more like the Silver Doctor than a Ferguson. All of these patterns have proved of especial value under varying circumstances, and therefore each has its friends.

No. 75. Spider. To our mind this is the poorest possible representation of a spider, and we can see no sufficient reason why that name should have been given to it ; but the fact remains that it is called " the Spider," and when made on the larger hooks is much liked for large trout, and sometimes for black bass.

It must be remembered that in these plates we are endeavoring to give the *favorite* flies, the general *favorites ;* not those we admire as most beautiful, taking, or durable, but those that are most widely known and approved. The only criticism we can make in regard to this successful fly is that it was named "the Spider," but then Charles Dudley Warner has said : " The trout fly is a ' conventionalized ' creation, as we say of ornamentation.  The theory is that, fly-fishing being a high art, the fly must not be a tame imitation of nature, but an artistic suggestion of it."

No. 76.  The Seth Green fly is made with either a gray wing or one of cinnamon brown ; the latter seems to be chosen for black bass, while the gray wing is preferred when fishing for trout.  A representation of the fly, with light brown wings, can be seen in the colored plates of bass flies in " Fishing with the Fly ; " that shown in this plate is the one so much used for Lake Superior regions and in the far West.  Some years ago, Mr. Seth Green, in a letter to the " New York Express," gave his favorite cast of flies, with directions for using the same.  It may be well to repeat them here, that they may not be lost.

" There are two kinds of fish, both kinds called black bass, in different localities. I designate them as black and Oswego bass.  They look very much alike to amateurs.  The Oswego bass has the larger mouth, and lies in still waters where there are weeds, flags, and pond-lilies.  He takes a spoon, a frog, or a minnow.  They are the poorer table fish of the two kinds, and lack the game qualities of the black bass, which live only in pure lake or river water with a rocky bottom, and are taken with fly, or dobsons, or crawfish, or grasshoppers, which are their favorite food, but will take minnows or a spoon sometimes.  Trolling with flies in large waters, I use a twelve-foot leader made of single gut, and four flies, and two B shot and two small brass swivels on the leader ; one swivel at the upper end and one in the centre, and two shot about equal distance from each end of the leader ; put the flies an equal distance apart.  I have used hundreds of different kinds of flies, and have kept sifting them out until they have got down to four kinds.  They are the killers.  My upper fly is red body, white wing, and white hackle, with gold tinsel stripe.  My second is a fly called Grizzly King.  It has a green body and mottled wing of a mallard or red-head.  It is called by fly-makers the 'Under-Wind.'  The hackle is grizzly, and it has a red ibis tail.  My third fly is called the Governor Alvord, in honor of our worthy statesman.  The wing is made of two colored feathers, cinnamon and drab ; the cinnamon is used for the under wing.  The body is made of peacock herl, and has a red ibis tail, and a red hackle from a red rooster.  The fourth fly I call the Seth Green.  The body is green, with a large yellow stripe ; the hackle, chicken red ; the wing, either gray or light cinnamon brown.  I do not cover the body of my flies with the hackle; the hackle of all my flies is put on at the head of the fly. The flies are tied on a 'two-aught' (00) hook; the body of the fly is one fourth of an inch in diameter in the largest place in the body. When trolling with flies for bass, your boat should be rowed one third slower than for any other kind of fish. The flies should be allowed to sink within three or four feet of the bottom, and when you have a strike take plenty of time to reel him in, as there are ten fish lost by reeling them too fast where one is lost by reeling him too slow, and you are likely to take some more on the lower flies. If the fish is on the lower fly you will not take any more, but if he is on one of the upper flies you will be sure to take more if there are any in sight.

"When casting for black bass in a river where there is a current, you should cast abreast the current and let the flies swing round with the current without drawing them in, only just enough to keep the line taut; and when it has swung round so far as to be directly below you, draw it gently toward you as far as you can, and recover your line for another cast. Great care should be taken to have your tackle as fine as you can and answer the purpose."

Mr. Seth Green will long be remembered by American fishermen for his labors and success as a fish culturist; his work is now faithfully continued by his brother, Mr. Monroe Green.

No. 77. The Silver Ibis, sometimes called the Tinseled Ibis, receives its name from its silver body and red ibis wing. This pattern was first made and introduced by Mr. C. F. Orvis, about 1884. It is a very durable fly. This fact, added to its brilliancy, has caused it to be liked for deep, rough waters, and large fish.

|            | Brown Hackle. | |
|            | Ginger Hackle. | |
|            | Blue Jay. | |
| *New York.* | Scarlet Ibis. | **For Trout.** |
|            | Alder. | |
|            | Grizzly King. | |
|            | Silver Doctor. | |

A. M. GOVE,                    Lebanon,                    N. H.

Brown, Ginger, and Red Hackles are my favorites, yet in some localities and at some times winged flies are very taking, — the Blue Jay, Scarlet Ibis, Alder, Grizzly King, and Silver Doctor and Coachman.

The White Miller that so many are partial to I never caught a trout on in my life, and now never carry this fly in my books.

As you must know, in four seasons some particular fly may be very taking. For instance, in the month of August, 1879, while fishing in the Adirondacks, the Scarlet Ibis was the most taking fly of the season. I had but two with me, and was offered for one of them five dollars! Money could not buy the fly, but I gave it to the person desiring it, for you know a fisherman deserves contempt who is not willing to divide.

Another season I was given a half dozen royal purple Hackles by an old friend of mine, Mr. Prouty, who you may know as an ardent lover of the " gentle art," and a friend to all of its disciples. I found in one pool I could take trout with these hackles, as the saying goes, " right out from under the noses" of far better anglers than myself, for no other fly would allure the fish.

The next season I stocked my book with some more of them, but they were poor; the dye was not permanent, and washed out immediately on coming in contact with the water.

In 1878, while fishing in the Adirondacks late one afternoon, I took fifteen trout, the combined weight of which was thirty-three pounds; twelve were taken on the Brown Hackle, and three on the Alder.

In 1881, from the same pool I took twelve trout that weighed twenty-one pounds; ten were taken on the Ginger Hackle, and two on the Silver Doctor. At this time Nessmuk was visiting my camp.

In 1884, I took from another pool twenty trout, none less than one pound in weight; all were taken on the Brown Hackle.

This last season, I went out one morning for trout for breakfast, and brought in three, the combined weight of which was seven and a half pounds, all taken on a Brown Hackle.

These are only a few of the cases that occur to me, but from these records you may judge what I think of hackles.

I prefer the O'Shaughnessy hooks, sizes from No. 6 to No. 9.

I always tie my own leaders, and prefer a clear to a colored one, and as light as a good snell will tie. Of course, in buying a lot of gut a large portion is of no use for leaders. I always weight them after they are tied, and the ones that will stand two pounds dead weight without parting I consider good for from six to eight pounds of fish.

I have tied only two flies myself, and both were successful at the time. One had a red flannel body, made of a piece cut from my shirt, wound with silver thread from an old guitar string, brown hackle legs, and wings from the speckled feathers of the ruffed grouse, white tail and black head.

The other fly was purple, wound with a bit of brass tinsel, and had tiny wings from the mottled feathers of the loon, and a scarlet head.

|            |                    |         |
|------------|--------------------|---------|
| *New York.* | Brown Hackle.<br>Scarlet Ibis.<br>Seth Green.<br>Cow Dung.<br>Coachman.<br>Fiery Brown.<br>Montreal.<br>English Blue Jay.<br>Governor.<br>Bee.<br>Romeyn. | Trout. |

DR. J. R. ROMEYN,                    Keeseville,                    N. Y.

The foregoing list indicates my favorite flies among those well known. In fly-fishing in the Saranac Lake region, early in the season, I use the Brown Hackle, Seth Green, and Scarlet Ibis, always using the Brown Hackle as the tail fly, and change, say in June, the two upper flies to suit the whim of the trout; and as trout are as fickle as some of our maids, I change often to please them. I take many trout with the Seth Green in June. I do not put much faith in theories advanced regarding the day and season.

The Romeyn fly was named after me, and devised by the late Dr. W. S. Ely. It has proved very successful towards evening, and in quiet waters.

In my thirty-seven years' trouting in the Adirondacks I have tried all kinds of hooks, but for all purposes give me the good old O'Shaughnessy. With it I can hook a trout more successfully, and save him too, than with any other. I think its peculiar shape and its larger wire commend it over the Sproat.

I use No. 7 for all my flies, and always have my snells 4½ inches long, as then they do not wind around the leader, as the longer ones are apt to do. I prefer them stained if they would last stained, but all that I have ever used, or seen used, will lose their stain after being used, and return to their original white color. I want heavy gut, white and round, and single strands.

The number of flies made is legion. I have a very large number, but with one dozen flies of one dozen in variety I can take all the trout I want to or ought to, and have flies left over at the end of the season.

---

| *New York.* | Davidson Hackle. | Trout. |
|---|---|---|
| John Davidson, | Elizabeth, | N. J. |

For twenty-eight years I have fished the Salmon River at Edrington Park, New York, for brook trout. I go there every year with my friends, Dr. Kempshall, Mr. Abram B. Knapp, and my brother, Mr. James Davidson. Our usual catch for a summer is about four thousand five hundred to five thousand fish.

Our favorite flies are Brown Hackle and the Davidson Hackle. The latter is an invention of my own. It is dressed on a No. 10 O'Shaughnessy hook, with a single gut stained a light brown; the body is thick, and dark orange in color; hackle, light brown near the hook, shading off to a yellow. This fly takes in all seasons from June to September 1st. Whichever flies we have on our lines, a Davidson is sure to be one of them.

---

| William J. Cassard, | New York, | N. Y. |
|---|---|---|

My personal experience in fishing for black bass in the St. Lawrence has proved that the flies most effectual are as follows: —

| | |
|---|---|
| Caddis, cork body, drab wings. | Parmacheene Belle. |
| White Miller, best of all. | Cheney. |
| Orange Miller. | Orange Brown Hackle. |
| Yellow Professor. | Tinseled Ibis. |

| | |
|---|---|
| Reuben Wood. | Ferguson. |
| Silver Doctor. | Oriole. |

Later experience added to this list the

| | |
|---|---|
| Golden Doctor, salmon pattern. | Golden Duke. |
| Golden Dustman. | Moisic-Grub. |
| Oconomowoc. | |

---

| | | |
|---|---|---|
| *New York.* | Royal Coachman.<br>Grizzly King.<br>Professor.<br>Brown Hackle.<br>Ginger Hackle.<br>Cahill.<br>Green Drake,<br>  and others. | Trout and Bass. |

FRANK PIDGEON,　　　　　Saugerties,　　　　　N. Y.

To name my favorite flies as they have been of service to me, I should place them in the following order, with but little difference allowed in the first half dozen: Royal Coachman, Grizzly King, Professor, Brown Hackle, Ginger Hackle, Black Hackle, Cahill, Abbey, the Midges, all the Fox flies, Hackles, Cow Dung, Montreal, dark Green Drake, Ronalds Stone, Dark Stone, Soldier, Kingdom, Captain, Brown Hen, Oak fly, Alder, Gen. Hooker, Golden Spinner, Shoemaker, Caughlans, Great Dun, Queen of the Water, May-fly, etc., according to season and time of the day; but I have had experience which proves to my satisfaction that one cannot formulate cast-iron rules for regulating a trout's appetite, or his want of it.

I have caught trout with a Royal Coachman at the regulation twilight hour, and on dark days, and I have also caught them in the finest of weather at high noon. Again I have tried my favorite Coachman in the gloaming, and would take only one or two with it, finding it was the Professor that had the call, until it was so dark that nothing could be seen unless held to the sky line. The Professor has always been a favorite fly of mine through the middle of certain kinds of days, and towards the evenings of others, but it was a revelation to me when I first found a Coachman discarded for a Professor in the dark.

I have caught trout when the snow still lay along the mountain streams, and when it was snowing and hailing, with a Grizzly King.

I favor small flies, as a general rule, for this section. They should be tied on Sproat hooks, and no other, No. 8 to No. 13. I think the Sproat hook the truest in draught, and best proportioned in size of wire to size of hook.

I favor a single-strand tapered leader as light as I can get them, and in as long lengths as possible, the whole about nine feet long, mist-colored. I detest a twisted leader for this kind of fishing. I think slipping the ends of snells into a leader wears them out quicker, although it is the method I use; but it is better to have a short length of gut to fasten the dropper fly to.

For black bass I prefer, also, single gut leaders, nine feet in length, but of heavier quality. Flies should not be too large, Nos. 3, 4, and 5. I think most of the black bass flies sold as such are trash. A year ago last July, one morning when the sun was shining brightly, I caught a black bass on a Coachman tied on a No. 10 Sproat hook, with light trout tackle, lightest kind of a leader, and a split bamboo that weighed $6\frac{3}{4}$ oz. ; as the tackle was made to use as well as to sell, the fish was landed from water running like a mill-race, instead of adding to the list of departed big fish that always get away. This one weighed 3 lbs. 2 oz., and was drowned and landed in water over three feet deep without the help of a net, which, of course, I had forgotten on that particular morning.

I prefer for black bass the following flies : Royal Coachman, Lottie, Silver Doctor, Reuben Wood, Brown, Black, Ginger, Red, and Gray Hackles, Governor, Brown Hen, Grizzly King, Professor, Abbey, Seth Green, Gov. Alvord, Ferguson, and many of the trout patterns, all to be used according to season, time of day, or weather. I do not think a hook fly should ever be tied " fluttering," *i. e.* at the bend of the hook, for the reason that the larger quantity of long wet feathers make a heavy mass that will turn inside out and cover the hook with a wad, changing all the original design of form and color. I can see, though, that there may be some advantage in this method of tying smaller trout flies.

A better and more sportsmanlike feeling is gradually growing here in regard to the protection of fish and game. I hope the day may yet come when fishing with the worm will be looked upon with as much horror in the community as the use of an old " Queen Anne " in potting a bevy of quail upon the ground.

---

|  |  |  |
|---|---|---|
| *New York.* | { Brown Hackle. Quaker. Green Drake. Coachman Red-tip. | { For Trout. |

E. T. Strong,                    Elizabethtown,                              N. Y.

The popular fly here is the Brown Hackle. I have had better success by sticking to it for one of the cast, but for the last two seasons I have done better with more variety. I should, with my slight knowledge, name the Quaker, Green Drake, and Coachman Red-tip as my favorites till the middle of July; after that time would prefer the Brown Hackle and Black Gnat.

Two years ago, a nice string of young California trout was caught in the Bouquet, in June, with a gray fly similar to the Quaker.

Made by C.F.ORVIS, Manchester,Vt.

PLATE M: DESCRIPTION PAGE 221

Made by C.F. ORVIS, Manchester, Vt.

PLATE N: DESCRIPTION PAGE 239

Made by C.F.ORVIS, Manchester,Vt.

PLATE O: DESCRIPTION PAGE 255

Made by C.F.ORVIS, Manchester,Vt.

PLATE P: DESCRIPTION PAGE 277

## PLATE L.

No. 78. Split Ibis.

No. 81. Sheenan.

No. 79. Saranac.

No. 82. Webster.

No. 80. The Tim.

No. 83. F. G. Simpson.

No. 78.  The Split Ibis is so designated from the construction of its wing, it being made of the fibres of white and red ibis ; a portion of these are put on under the hackle, and the balance over it.  Mr. H. P. Wells has recommended this split or shredded effect in making the Parmacheene Belle.  The method is very manifest in the Lake George fly shown in Plate BB of bass flies.

No. 79.  The name " Saranac " always arouses a memory of one of the most stirring descriptions that we ever read, — that of the boat-race between " John Norton the trapper, the guides of the woods, the professionals, and the Lad," written by W. H. H. Murray in " Adirondack Tales."  No fresher, more vigorous word-painting ever existed ; though enjoyed again and again, it always holds its strong, wholesome excitement ; and this little fly brings to mind Saranac as it was on that autumn day, — the crowds that had gathered at the summer hotels on the lake, the intensity of feeling in the race that followed, the sweet odor of the dry leaves, and the exhilaration of the atmosphere.  William Cullen Bryant, in his poem on " The Death of the Flowers," perhaps voiced the prevailing sentiment of mankind regarding the closing of the year, when he wrote : —

> " The melancholy days are come, the saddest of the year,
>     Of wailing winds, and naked woods, and meadows brown and sear.
>     Heaped in the hollows of the grove the withered leaves lie dead ;
>     They rustle to the eddying gust and to the rabbit's tread.
>     The robin and the wren are flown, and from the shrubs the jay,
>     And from the wood-top calls the crow through all the gloomy day."

But we who live in the Eastern States find in these days a keen joy and glory that are almost matchless, a joy for sight and for all the senses that Murray had a vision of when he wrote the following : " It was high noon at Saranac, and a brighter day was never seen.  The sky was so intensely blue that it fairly gleamed, as if, like woods of compact fibre, it was capable of taking polish. In it the sun stood, and shone with self-asserting brilliancy. It glistened, it scintillated, it sparkled, as if its rays were actually frosty. The sky above was wintry. The cold of the North was journeying southward, like her feathered couriers on lofty wings. The upper atmosphere was chilly, but on earth summer still tarried with its hazy warmth and slumberous airs. The heat came from the earth rather than from the sun, and it lingered like a happy child near the mother that gave it birth, and from whose bosom it would not fly. The lake had not stirred a ripple. It took its mood from the atmosphere, and matched it perfectly. Perhaps it said to the wind, ' Oh, let me rest to-day ! You have blown me about and kept me moving, until I am weary. Do give me a little peace. Come, dear, sweet wind, if you love me so, do let me have one day of rest !' And the wind, thus coaxed by the sleepy beauty, had humored her luxurious whim, and stood all day holding his very breath. The air was thickened as with golden-colored smoke. It was not common air ; it was incensed, aromatic, pungent. The nose found strange, spicy scents in it, and breathed it in slowly, as a delicate mouth receives cream, not to swallow, but to taste. No one could breathe such air for the purpose of ordinary life, — mere respiration, — but as one breathes perfume ; receiving its delicious sensation as a luxury, and drawing each breath, not for life's, but for joy's sake. In front of ' Martin's,' across the lake, the hillside fairly flamed. The leaves had a ripened glory, rich as that which the old painters, with their ardent colors, painted into the faces and around the heads of their saints. Along the shores, blown by previous winds, the bright-colored leaves lay thick ; some lying limp and flat, — patches of crimson on the dull water, — some half immersed, while others, curled and curved, floated jauntily on the surface, as if they could scarcely bear to touch the element on which they rested. Nature, on tree and water, and in the air, was lavish of her highest tints ; until the gray moss on the rocks, and the gray rocks themselves, looked, with the golden colors on them, almost gorgeous."

After the spirited descriptions of the race and shooting-match came the affecting scene when "the Lad" played on the violin for the dancers, and a farewell that awed them by its pathos and sweetness. We cannot resist quoting the account of the later farewell that took place between the three friends that night, as they sat by the camp-fire under the pines near the lake ; for though so differently expressed, it urges the same idea of "affiliation with Nature" and independent observation so earnestly spoken of by Packard, Lubbock, and nearly all successful scientists : —

" I 'm sorry, Henry, that ye must leave us to-morrer," said the Trapper, breaking the long silence that had preceded the remark ; " but you say ye must go, and I suppose we must give ye up.  There be many in the settlements, I dare say, that love ye and long to see ye ; and it 's but right for ye to go.  But ye won't quite forgit us, boy, when ye 're livin' in the great city, and the han'some and the rich be round ye ? "

" I shall never forget you, John Norton, nor the Lad either," responded the young man ; " I owe my life to both of you, and while I live I shall remember it. My life was saved here in the woods, and here would I live, were I not bound to civilization by ties I cannot in conscience break.  But I mean to have you both visit me this winter.  Do you know it is only two days' travel from this island to my city home ? "

" It is n't distance, Henry," said the Trapper, after a moment's pause, " that makes a visit likely or onlikely atween friends.  I footed it from the shore of the Horicon to the shore of Ontario once, jest to call on a comrade I heerd was campin' on the Big Water.  No, it sartinly is n't distance, Henry, but difference in ways of livin' that keeps friends apart.  Lord bless ye, boy, if miles was all that lay atween us, me and the Lad, and the pups there, could make ye a visit eenamost any time arter the snow has crusted ; for the trappin' is onsartin then, and the snow-shoes be famous things to travel on.  But ye live one way, and we another ; and, though ye be a nateral woodsman, and take to our way of livin' as easily as a young otter takes to the crick, yit I conceit it would be different with me in the settlements, and that yer way of livin' would n't suit an old man whose days have been passed in the woods, and whose ears hate the noise of the clearin's."

" I don't know about that, John Norton," replied the young man ; " you should live as you wished with me, and I would do everything I could to make your stay pleasant."

" Aye, aye, Henry," responded the Trapper ; " I understand the goodness of yer heart and the openness of yer hand ; and if anything could make me contented with the ways of the settlements, ye sartinly could do it.  But natur' and habits be stronger than wishes ; and my natur' and habits be agin it.  Why, Henry, I should smother in the city ; for I 've heerd that the cabins be made of brick and stun, and stand so nigh together that they act'ally tech ; and that the smoke of the fires be so thick that ye can't tell when the sun rises or sets ; and that the carries from p'int to p'int be covered with folks; and that the trails be thicker with people than the trunk of a bee-tree when the bees be swarmin'. Is it raally so, boy?"

"Yes, the houses do stand side by side," replied Henry Herbert, "and the streets are full of people from morning till late at night, and the noise and jar of cars and carts are continuous."

"That's it," interrupted the Trapper, "that's it. The noises would eenamost kill me; for beyond the crack of a rifle, or the sound of an axe cuttin' wood for the camp, my ears hate noises, onless it be such as Natur' makes. For when the ears be full of noise the eyes can't observe, nor the heart meditate on the things around. It is n't what folks tells us makes us knowin', but it's what we find out for ourselves. It's the blaze on the tree that the hunter sarches and finds with his own eyes that he never forgits; and I have never seed a city man yit that knowed anything, of his own self; for his edication was what he larnt by others or had read in books. And ye know, Henry, that the raal wisdom of Natur' has never been printed in books yit."

"I think you are right, there, John Norton," returned the young man; "the best wisdom has never been printed; for scholars, as a class, never study for the new, but for the old, and the present generation only recites the same lessons that the fathers had recited."

"Yis, Henry, that's it; and queer enough it seems to a man of the woods. Lord! I guided a man a year or two ago that knowed everything that books could tell a mortal. He was as full of figgers and facts as a hedgehog is of quills, and if ye poked him up a leetle with a question or two, he'd shed 'em faster than ye could pick 'em up. But when ye got him right down to it, he did n't know nothin', Henry. He could n't tell the p'ints of the compass on a cloudy day, nor keep the trail on a carry, nor tell a doe's track from a buck's. He did n't even know how to dress out his venison nor cook a pancake. And I do believe the creetur' would have starved to death when the Lord had made plenty around him. And it made me thankful for my gifts and larnin' as I observed his ignorance."

"And yet," replied Herbert, "he was, very likely, a wise man in his way."

"Sartinly, sartinly," admitted the Trapper. "But the way was n't a good un, Henry; for what's the use of bein' knowin' if ye can't make it sarve ye? The larnin' that don't help a man find his way when he is fetchin' his trail through the woods, and don't tell him where to find the spring holes, or the spawnin' beds, or the places on the mash where the bucks feed, or how to cook his venison arter he has got it to his camp, is n't wuth much to a mortal, for sartin. For larnin' is given to us, as I conceit, as the scent is given to the nose of the hound, for the parposes of life ; and larnin' that don't tell a man when he is in danger how to git out of it, or when he is hungry how to satisfy the cravin's of his natur', is of no raal use to a man, as I jedge."

" The Bible says," interrupted the Lad, " ' Take-no-thought-of-what-ye-shall-eat-or-what-ye-shall-drink,-or-what-ye-shall-put-on,- for - after-all - these - things-the-Gentiles-seek.' "

" Yis, yis," said the Trapper, " them Gentiles always seemed to me to have the right idees of it. And I never could understand how the Lord could think they was off the trail, if they was honestly sarchin' for victals and clothin' to kiver their nakedness. No, I never could see how they was wrong in doin' jest what every man has to do to keep body and soul together. What did He mean, Henry, when He told them not to think about their victals and their garments ? He did n't mean to have them go naked, did He, or trust to luck in the matter ? "

" No, by no means," responded Herbert. " The phrase ' take no heed ' means not to be *anxious ;* not to *worry* about it."

" Well, well," said the Trapper, " now I git the direction of the trail. Lord-a-massy ! how different the Scriptur' looks from one pint than it does from another ! It sartinly don't do any good to worry over a thing. Many be the nights, when I used to be out scoutin', that I 've gone to bed in the leaves hollow as a horn without a karnal in it, wonderin' where I 'd find breakfast in the mornin' ; but worryin' never brought a partridge to the snare yit, or a trout to the hook, and there 's but one way for a mortal to act when he 's in a pickle, and that is to do the best he knows how and trust to the Lord for the rest. But the doin' must be put under the trustin', as the powder is under the bullet, as I conceit."

The Saranac fly was made by Mr. John Shields, and named after the lake made famous by story, and noted as a health resort.

No. 80. The Tim. Legend hath it that when the " Pine-Tree State " was yet an unexplored wilderness, three trappers, Tim, Jim, and Sutton, came to it annually in search of game. Separating where Eustis now stands, Tim went to the west, and followed Tim Brook up to what is now called Tim Pond ; Jim went to the north, and Sutton to the south. At the end of the season they met and related their various experiences. Tim Pond lies two thousand feet above the level of the sea, and is to-day a favorite camping and fishing ground ; the forests guard its sparkling waters, and the man who gave it its name sleeps by its side. The following verses, written by M. J. Messner, are familiar to all who frequent the lake and know the story of

### TIM.

I love a man whose deeds are earnest,
Whose heart is faithful, whose words are true,
And little it matters where God has placed him,
Or what is the work that is his to do :
Whether he sits in halls of marble,
To make the laws for a mighty land,
Or hears in the forest the wild birds warble,
And grasps an axe in his brawny hand.

Just such a man was Tim the hunter,
A guide, with record without a stain ;
Who knew like a book each brook and river,
And loved every tree in the woods of Maine.
For forty years, through pathless forests,
He followed the moose and the caribou ;
But never again shall we hear his rifle,
Or, piercing the darkness, his loud halloo.

For Tim is at rest ; his life-chase ended,
He sleeps 'mid the scenes that he loved so well,
By the side of the tranquil mountain lakelet,
Whose beauty the tourists with rapture tell.
And his memory lives in that sheet of water,
Though his spirit rests in the great beyond,
And will live as long as the wavelets ripple,
For 't is known to the world by the name Tim Pond.

**No. 81.** The Sheenan, sometimes called the Sheehan, is probably not of American origin, but is a copy of some one of the many "Shannon flies." There is a very beautiful fly pictured in "Ephemera's" "Book of the Salmon" that is king of them all, called "the Shannon fly," but there are many other patterns known vaguely as "Shannon flies," one of which the Sheenan may resemble, and the name have been misunderstood or misspelled, until the fly came to be generally known as the Sheenan, instead of Shannon fly.

No. 82.   The Webster is spoken of in the letter relating to fishing in Maine, by Mr. John W. Webster, of Waterbury, Conn., after whom the fly was named.   Mr. Webster is an angler of long experience and much success, whose judgment of a fly has great weight with his many friends.

No. 83.   This fly has been found especially effective for fishing in Winnipeg. Mr. F. G. Simpson was the first to introduce it to us, and recommend it to other anglers ; we therefore identify it by his name.

New York.
{
Black Gnat.
Claret.
Queen of the Water.
Coachman.
White Miller, etc.
}
{ Trout.

H. C. Wilcox,                    Friendship,                    N. Y.

ON THE GENESEE.

This certainly is an auspicious day for trouting. The hazy atmosphere and clouded sky are forerunners of spring showers. The leaves on the birches are about the size of a Coachman's wings. Our old landlord advises me that the water is at the proper stage. I have a supply of garden worms and grubs from decaying timber, which are not to be ignored when flies prove unattractive, or in places where casting cannot be properly adhered to. " And mark me now," that man who scorns the use of other lures on all occasions will often be compelled to satisfy his appetite with codfish; or he will make his appearance with flies or leader attached to his rod after using worms to fill his creel, and blandly inform you that he only uses flies, when perhaps the color of the fish exhibited will locate them up some mountain stream where flies could not be used.

While fly-fishing is preëminently the proper method and infinitely more enjoyable, there are times and places where it fails absolutely. On such occasions, trout caught with worms, if properly served, will be found palatable, at least to a hungry fisherman; so we will not be sentimental to the extent of returning with empty creels because forsooth the fish prefer a diet of worms. Here is room in my box for your leaders, and the damp felt will keep them in condition for immediate use upon our arrival, after which coil them inside your hat, thereby avoiding the corkscrewing resulting from close coils. My old friend M—— will not forget his first experience in this practice. He is a most persistent and skillful angler, observing and quick to adopt seeming improvements. My plan came under his notice, and the first change found his leader resting securely inside his hat. While busy fishing in a difficult place he felt a fly seeking to obtain a foothold on his eyebrow. This familiarity was resented, and a vigorous slap impaled the fisherman on a " Queen " which had innocently worked out of the hat. A surgical operation, performed on the spot, extracted the hook from his finger, and ever since he forswears Queens.

Yes, this is the West Branch. We will drive up and fish down ; there is a millpond five miles above, which has twenty feet of water, and some fine trout lurk in its depths. Before it was completed I located a large spring near the bottom, and that knowledge has been valuable since. Last year I fished that particular place for hours without a nibble, but the absence of the smaller fry strengthened my conviction, that some old residents were in possession of the premises. Experiments were in order, and in addition to a white grub on a No. 3 Sproat hook I placed a lively worm on the point. This soon attracted a minnow, who proceeded to scurry the whole combination through the water in all directions. Suddenly the tip was drawn down steadily under water, the hook set with a sharp jerk, and work was commenced on strictly business principles ; that fish had to be brought above the sunken logs and brush without delay. It was a trying time for both angler and rod, and possibly for the fish, for he was compelled to come up, although evidently against his wishes. He was a beauty of $1\frac{1}{2}$ lbs., and was quickly followed by another of $1\frac{3}{4}$ lbs. How nicely they topped off the basket, and how small the others looked which heretofore were fair sized.

Below the old mill is a famous pool : make your cast for it, Queen, stretcher, Coachman and Red Hackle, droppers; mine, Professor, Cow Dung, and Ginger Hackle. There was a rise above you near the fall. Try and drop your stretcher exactly where he rose. Missed it? Well, "pick your flint" and try again. Now bring him away from the bank into clear water. "A good fighter?" Lead him this way. He weighs about twelve ounces. We have done fairly well, and the sun is shining here. We will move down to the woods. Change your cast to darker and smaller flies, the Egg, Claret, and Black Gnat, with Brown Hackle, Hawthorne, and Leadwing Coachman for another cast. Note which are the killers.

Approach carefully; try the shady places under the banks, close to old logs, in the eddies where the current naturally gathers the food; there will be found the much sought prizes. Do not allow your shadow or that of your rod to fall on the pool. Don't touch that old log; it projects into the stream, and the jar would alarm every fish in that vicinity. Cast across the current, allowing your flies to drift to the eddies in a natural manner. There you have him! He took the Claret; try the same eddy again. Missed it? Cast lower down; trout often drop down to recover lost flies. There, be careful; he is larger than the first one. "Lost?" Well, he will not patronize you again soon. You gave him slack line. "Going below?" Very well, I will try that place where the foam covers the dark water. Observe how near the stretcher will cut the edge. Did you see that! He took it later, about fourteen ounces!

In that pool below you, where the old tree lies along the edge, I once caught a trout after my stretcher fly had caught in the log, leaving the droppers dangling in a very tempting manner over the water. One was seized by a fish, which made it necessary to detach the stretcher at once or lose the fish ; this was successfully accomplished. It is still a mystery how that No. 10 Sproat hook held its victim through the struggles, but he came to creel, and weighed a pound.

Frequently the excitement of hooking and landing a large fish brings on well-defined cases of " buck fever." Once, while fishing a spring hole on the Genesee, when making the first cast, the leader was stiff, and when the second dropper was drawn under it caused the stretcher to describe a circle and the fly to be taken by another trout immediately upon its alighting. Here was a little of the excitement approaching " buck fever." This appeared to be the first time these fish had been " hitched up " together, and they made it warm for the teamster, but we ran them into the fence finally, and scored fourteen and sixteen respectively.

Some time back in the seventies, about the middle of July, Judge F—— and myself were casting over this stretch of water, and were caught in a sudden shower. It was brief, and although the water was not swollen, it was highly colored. We had decided that to fish with bait was our only chance, but for the fun of it I said, " Now see me take a trout from the mud-hole with a fly." Proceeding to cast, much to our surprise a trout generously impaled himself upon a Professor, quickly followed by another. This was a revelation in fly-fishing, and with flies of rather gay colors, and in the scorching sunshine, we filled our creels with fair-sized fish. Occasionally one would leap entirely clear from the water.

I have never since experienced such fly-fishing, but no doubt under precisely the same conditions the results would be similar.

Here by this spring is a favorite place to lunch ; under the shade of this birch-tree we have met with fair success. The sun is bright and the water so clear that we cannot add much to our catch until three or four P. M. This pool below the spring is a favorite place for large trout. They will assemble near the outlet of the spring after dark. It does not signify that we cannot get a rise now; the water is deep near the opposite bank where the driftwood is lodged; the bottom is covered with sunken logs, large boulders, and brush. Select a favorable place from which to make casts over the entire pool, and experiment to ascertain if any brush needs trimming to give flies free swing behind. Select your place to land your trout and remove any obstructions which might interfere with landing. Now place a flat stone at the exact spot where you wish to stand, that you may find it after night. Here will be no striking at a rise; you must feel a strike, and frequently it will be almost imperceptible, while the sound of a rise will often direct your cast. Yet trout will usually hook themselves securely after dark. Give no line where possible to land them; otherwise " it 's a fight in the dark," and impossible to know what dangerous places the fish is aiming for. Reel in and land quickly; you will lose fish by any other process. A piece of wax candle or small pocket lantern will often be useful for changing flies or disentangling snarls in the line or leaders.

Take plenty of luncheon; the fish will take their own time, and hungry fishermen are handicapped by a well-fed trout. I often remain out all night. As a rule, trout will not rise in deep water; but once in a while, experimenting to see how far I could cast from a position about ten feet above the surface of the water, I have noticed some trout near the bottom, in about twelve feet of water, that were apparently getting interested in my operations, and were slowly working up toward the surface; and soon one made a dash, and, upon being landed, proved to be an eight-ounce trout, which had appeared of not more than four ounces in the deep water. Eventually several were taken. The sun was shining into the pool from the southwest, it being about three P. M. This was at a "splash-dam" on Pine Creek, in Potter County, Pennsylvania.

On another occasion, while fishing a pool surrounded by weeds, the leader and flies were allowed to lie quiet until I could light my brier pipe. Upon attempting to withdraw for another cast, the White Miller was fast to a large trout; the flies must have settled two or three feet below the surface.

For clear water and a cloudless sky, a leader of single horsehair, with midges tied on No. 16 hooks, will often take trout when ordinary tackle will fail. Such tackle must be enforced by a flexible rod and careful angler, or a large fish will not endanger his liberty seriously, even if hooked. Keep out of sight as much as possible, and if trout are rising in any particular portion of the pool make casts elsewhere until you have the distance measured and the flies can fall like snowflakes. Then cast directly to the spot and be prepared for a rise at once. When a fish is fast, get him away from that particular spot quickly, so as not to unduly alarm others. When a trout rises and turns back without touching your flies, change your cast and try again. I once hooked a fine fish at the foot of a rapid, which immediately made a dash for the deep water below, and in his effort to free himself hooked one of the flies into the back of a huge sucker. What a mismated pair, sucker and trout at one cast!

With all their natural caution, trout act strangely at times. Not many years ago, I lost a portion of my leader, stretcher, and dropper

with a trout. He was caught next day with a worm, and had my
property in his possession. It is my belief that large trout, after
the spring runs, can be found in nearly the same place day after
day, except that they may go on the rapids to catch flies, and then
return to the old haunts, usually the most inaccessible portion of
the waters. Well do I remember one old fellow that selected an
abiding-place close under an old tree-top which hung conveniently
near the water, and where it was impossible to cast a fly; whence
he could rise easily and take whatever pleased his fancy. Hooking
the stretcher through a leaf, I floated it below him, and when it
stopped the droppers danced in a bewitching manner directly over
him; soon the thumping made by that fish in my basket was sweet-
est music.

If your hook becomes fast under that old log, don't break it;
reel up and allow the tip-ring to follow down just as you would use
a disgorger; when the ring finds the hook push it loose; you have
saved time, hook, and temper. When it is time to return to our
night-pool put on larger hooks, — a Miller, Coachman, and Queen.
Did you tie your line securely to the reel this morning? Well, do
it now, before some fish swims away with the whole cast. Now tie
your leader by that knot, which will not slip, but can be taken off
easily. No, I am not tying to the wrong end of my leader; the
loops are designed to stand toward the line, so that the droppers
will not cling to leader, but stand clear and consequently are more
easily taken. Throw your leader out into the water to soften, while
we lunch and smoke. There was a rise from a large one! You
notice he did not break the water, but the swirl was similar to one
from an oar. We need not hasten; eat heartily. Now try the
foot of the rapids first. That was a fine one! Keep cool; don't

let him cross to the driftwood; lead him carefully to the place selected for landing. Good for a pound at least! Enticed by a Coachman. Trout will take the fly when it is so dark that only by feeling can you know anything about how or where you cast; however, with a familiar rod and line it is easy to tell when you are doing good work.

Do not move about unnecessarily; the grinding gravel under your feet will not benefit us. My fish took the Professor. Will change the Queen for a Miller. Let them sink a trifle when first alighting. That was only a water-rat; trout rise more quietly, making very little splash! If you feel anything touch your flies, strike instantly and firmly; if trout break water after being hooked, keep them up and reel in rapidly, — it is your best chance. Lost that one? Reel up and see if your flies are all right. Coachman gone? Come over to my lantern and repair damages.

We have plenty now; let us finish our luncheon, take a whiff, rest ourselves and the fish. I once took twelve pounds of trout after twelve M., no fish having risen before midnight.

As in conditions of wind and weather favorable to fly-fishing, there are as many exceptions as rules. I have often been successful when all conditions seemed unfavorable, — cold winds and not an insect in the air. Again, when the air was sultry, and filled with bugs and millers, very few would notice my flies. I reason that when there are no flies to choose from except those on your leader there are no comparisons to make, and if they accept yours you fill your creel more rapidly than when different conditions prevail. Usually trout will not rise in moonlight, but I have found excellent fishing moonlight nights when a shady place could be selected to cast over.

Well, it is late, and we will return. Did you mark the way? Follow me. I noted the direction carefully, and can follow the course. You have proved an apt scholar, and the size of your fish shows a marked improvement over your last. We left plenty of fish in that pool, never fear. Did it ever occur to you how many fish each good pool furnishes each fishing season? You can usually get a few each day from each favorable place, and your catch will be duplicated many times during the year.

Once while fishing a long rapid with both flies and worms, without taking a fish, I had concluded that place, at least, was fished out. While debating the question mentally there came a swarm of deer flies, and they commenced to settle upon the water, when "presto!" the water commenced to boil, and there were fish in the air, "fish everywhere," so long as the flight lasted. This circumstance convinced me that where a few are taken plenty are left for a good fry, even though they refuse to be fried.

Trout do not seem to hear, but they manage to get sounds by some sense. The usual theories of wading down a stream I do not advocate except when the trout are uneducated. Then you can often walk up in plain sight and they will accept the offer, although not tendered in the latest approved style; while among the initiated they will disappear at the first sight of the angler, or the sudden appearance of roily water from above; to them in a majority of cases it means an enemy.

Notice where this tree projects into the deepest portion of the pool; approach slowly to where you can look into the deep water. Did you notice any disturbance among the fishes? "What did I do?" Scratched on the log with a pin. You will now see why caution is necessary in approaching the haunts of trout. Well, the sun is about where we saw it yesterday morning on our arrival, and for one day we have had quite an experience.

Perfection in fly-fishing will be acquired when you can make the trout leave the natural fly and accept the artificial, which has not yet been claimed by reliable anglers.

Trout feed at the upper or lower portions of pools alternately, without apparent reasons for making the changes. You will find it difficult to take them from the lower portions except by fishing up stream and keeping below the fish. I had supposed that the Red Hackle was an imitation of the small red caterpillar, but the veteran Nessmuk affirms that it resembles nothing below or above. It is his favorite bug, and that settles the question. Occasionally a fly which begins to get frayed and ragged will be taken with renewed vigor. This teaches us that in its bedraggled condition it more closely resembles the natural fly, and often leads to changes in tying additions of tails and other extras.

My first tying of flies furnished plenty of the extraordinary patterns, and some proved killers, for reasons before stated; others faded; and a new combination of colors appeared, often improving their taking qualities. I never troubled myself about their resemblance to other flies, provided they filled the creel. Flies may look differently after wetting, or upon being viewed from below.

A moving bait will often attract, and when drawn quickly up a rapid will be seized at the first pause by a pursuing fish. Twenty-five years ago, while casting on Pine Creek, I saw trout come within six feet of me and take the fly, even when I was wading the stream. But I have no expectation of that now. The least suspicion of a shadow or disturbance of the water will send them to cover, and terminate your chances for those particular fish.

|  |  |
|---|---|
| *New York.* | Cow Dung.<br>Governor.<br>Professor.<br>Grizzly King.<br>Henshall.<br>Reuben Wood.<br>Orange Miller.<br>Ferguson.<br>Seth Green.<br>Cunningham. |

G. V. CUNNINGHAM, Cohoes, N. Y.

The flies that I use are the Cow Dung, Governor, Professor, Grizzly King, Henshall, Reuben Wood, Orange Miller, Ferguson, Seth Green, and Montreal. These flies are used between the hours of three and eight P. M. in the Mohawk River.

I have tied a new fly that I have great luck with for bass : body, seal-brown wool, ribbed with silver tinsel; tail, a wisp of green parrot, scarlet ibis, and mallard; hackle, dark ginger; wings, wood-duck or partridge. Is there any name for this fly? If so, I wish you would be kind enough to tell me.[1]

I use No. 7 or No. 8 Sproat hooks. I prefer natural color to the stained gut, and single gut leaders with loops.

---

|  |  |  |
|---|---|---|
| *New York and Pennsylvania.* | Montreal, with deer-hair hackle.<br>Coachman.<br>Green Drake.<br>Dark Stone, etc. | Bass and Trout. |

CHARLES VAN KIRK, Ithaca, N. Y.

I am sorry to say that in Cayuga and Oneida lakes, where I fish a great deal, and in the Susquehanna River, the largest bass are caught with bait, and all sizes rise indifferently to the fly.

---

[1] We have named this fly the Cunningham, after its maker. See Plate I. — M. E. O. M.

I use 7 and 8 oz. rod, F and G silk lines, make my own leaders of best selected gut, clear and single snells; also a clear, long strand on dropper, and short loop on tail fly. For the waters above mentioned, for bass, I place the Montreal fly first, followed by the Professor, Grizzly King, Seth Green, Scarlet Ibis, Coachman, White Miller, Caddis, Ferguson, Gray Drake, and "fluttering black fly" for tail on stretcher. In Cayuga Lake the Montreal has never failed me from June 15th to September 1st, but the hackle should be tied of deer hair *au naturel*, as the body and tail give plenty of color without staining the hackle. A strip of skin and feather cut from the neck of a Dominick rooster will make an attractive lure when there is a good ripple on the water, but should be carefully trimmed and tied to a medium-sized hook. For hooks, I prefer the Sproat, medium and small sized, and in addition to the foregoing have always used the common hackles more or less.

For trout, I use the Coachman in all its variations, and White Miller at dusk or on dark days, Cow Dung, Fern, Red Ant, Professor, Black Ant, Abbey, Seth Green, Dark Stone, Grizzly King, Evening Dun, Scarlet Ibis, Brownstone, Yellow and Green Drakes, Palmers, Alder, Yellow May, Black June, Red Fox, Soldier, Oak, Beaverkill, Quaker, the gnats and hackles, all on small Sproats for this section; but larger for "John Brown's tract," where the larger and more gaudy flies can be used to good advantage. Last season the trout here seemed to take well to small hackles and gnats, colors of red, black, dun, and yellow predominating. I purchased from a German, resident of Scranton, two scale-wing flies, something akin to a blue-black water-bug, different in make from anything I have ever seen, very glassy in appearance, with which I had splendid success for larger trout, by allowing them to sink well to the bottom in deep pools.  Unfortunately, I have lost the address of the maker, and do not know where I can send to replace them

---

| *New York and Pennsylvania.* | { Governor.<br>Beaverkill.<br>Van Patton.<br>White Miller.<br>Black Hackle. | { Trout. |

GEORGE H. PAYSON,　　　　　　Englewood,　　　　　　N. J.

As you know, the " fish fever " is a more difficult disease to get out of an angler's system than malaria, and can only be cured, and that temporarily, by eight ounces of fly rod and several days' soaking in running water.  I regret that I have not had a wider experience from which to draw replies to your questions concerning flies.

Doubtless every angler has his favorites, which he regards with a sort of holy veneration ; and when persistent casting with these charmed lures fails to produce even a rise, there must be something wrong with the universe.  My fishing has mostly been done in the much-fished streams of Pennsylvania and New York, where fish are small, and high scores difficult to obtain.  I find that the Governor, the Beaverkill or Van Patton, which are very much alike, and a Black Hackle have been the most effective for the time of year when I do my fishing.  When the waters are low, and, with the exception of some of the tan-colored streams of Pennsylvania, of crystal clearness, I prefer small flies, a No. 12 Sproat hook seeming to be the most satisfactory.  But to upset this theory, I remember that once, having wearied myself casting with a delicate trio of flies, on a bright day, I put on a White Miller, tied on a bass hook, in sheer desperation. It struck the water such a spat as I was convinced would scare any trout in that neighborhood, but, to my unutterable surprise, was taken at once by a trout which weighed nearly a pound. So much for pet theories. For two or three years I have used coffee-colored gossamer leaders, and do not believe them a particle better than a fine mist-colored one, while their extreme lightness makes them most difficult to handle. Of course I do not advocate a bass leader for fine trout fishing, but I do think that the rage for hair-like tackle is mostly nonsense. If a trout does not see you and is on the feed, he will rise to the fly without much regard to leader or snell; but if he is scared or not hungry, coffee-colored leaders, green leaders, mud-colored leaders, or any other artful combination of man will have no effect on him. I have seen an old he-trout caught out of a hole by a man standing in full view, armed with a big hook and a lively worm, when two of us had wasted all our science and flies in vain; and, as I again say, so much for pet theories. Every year, when I come back from my fishing trip, I am convinced that I know less about the true inwardness of the elusive trout than ever: and the old couplet regarding a woman's whims seems to apply equally as well to those of a trout : —

> "For if she will, she will, you may depend on't;
> And if she won't, she won't; so there's an end on't."

*New York.* ⎰ Brown Hackle.
⎨ Green Drake.          ⎰ Trout.
⎱ Orange Miller.

JOHN D. QUACKENBOS,              New York,                    N. Y.

My favorite flies are the Brown Hackle, Green Drake, and Orange Miller. If I can have three, give me these; if I can have but one fly, I will take the Brown Hackle every time. I prefer a small hook, full hackle, and gut either white or mist-color, I really do not think it makes any difference which. For all-round flies, as regards locality, time of day, and season of year, I do not think a better selection could be made than that I have named.

---

*New York.* ⎰ Brown Palmer.
⎨ Coachman.
⎱ Professor.

C. E. FRITTS, M. D.,              Hudson,                    N. Y.

Favorite flies are Brown Palmer, Coachman, and Professor on No. 6 and 8 Sproat hooks, and light stained single snells. These flies seem best at all times and seasons.

---

*New York.* ⎰ Brown Hackle.
⎨ Red Ibis.
⎨ Coachman.          ⎰ Trout.
⎱ Alder.

A. R. FULLER,              Meacham Lake,                    N. Y.

The best flies are Brown Hackle, Red Ibis, Coachman, Alder. If trout will not take one or more of them, they are N. G., and I have no use for them. Regarding color of snells, I doubt if it makes any difference.

# PLATE M.

No. 84. Alder.

No. 85. Abbey.

No. 86. Alice.

No. 87. August Dun.

No. 88. Allerton.

No. 89. Adirondack.

No. 90. Bowman.

No. 91. Brown Gnat.

No. 92. Black May.

No. 93. Beauty.

No. 94. Ben Bent.

No. 95. Brown Adder.

No. 96. Black June.

No. 97. Blue Jay.

No. 98. Bee.

**No. 84.** The Alder. The original of this fly is hatched from the egg laid by the mature insect upon the leaves of trees or bushes bordering the water, preferably alder-bushes. The natural fly was first imitated in Great Britain, where it was much used, early in the season, as an evening fly. In this country it seems effectual throughout the summer, and wherever the " trout lepyth."

**No. 85.** The Abbey. In America, the Abbey is credited to, and named after Mr. Charles Abbey, of Abbey & Imbrie, a New York firm of fishing-tackle dealers. The fly has been popular in this country many years. It is claimed that it is an English pattern of old standing, which received its name from a building, not from an individual; also that long before it was called the Abbey fly it was in general use, known as the Jew fly.

**No. 86.** The Alice was copied from a fly sent to us by Mr. T. V. Allis, of New York city. The fly was one that experience had proved valuable, but it had never been named. We called it the Alice, as being approximate in sound to the name of its donor, Mr. Allis.

**No. 87.** The August Dun belongs to the order Ephemeroptera, the natural insect existing only two or three days in a mature state. It was first copied and named by English fly-makers, being called the August Dun from the month of its appearance. In this country we have adhered to the English name and dressing. The fly is not as well known here as other patterns, though it possesses many merits.

No. 88.   The Allerton was named after Mr. Robert G. Allerton, of New York city, treasurer of the Oquossoc Angling Association, a club having a fine preserve and club buildings in Maine.   The fly, perhaps, should be dressed on a larger hook than that shown in the plate, and classed among the lake flies, but it is frequently made small, and thought to be better adapted to brook trout.

No. 89.   The Adirondack is a fly that has been used for many years in the waters of northern New York, or the Adirondack region ; hence its name.   In some of the lakes and streams of the wilder portions of the State, better success seems to be attained by using flies of larger size and brighter color than one would select for the more thickly inhabited sections.   This fly is valued for such conditions.

No. 90.   The Bowman is a quill gnat, *i. e.* a fly having the body made of a strip of quill.   It was named after Mr. William H. Bowman, of Rochester, N. Y., associated as Fish Commissioner for the State of New York with General R. U. Sherman, R. B. Roosevelt, Eugene Blackford, and Seth Green, men well known to the angling fraternity for the efforts they have so constantly and generously made to further all fishing interests.   Mr. Bowman is a skillful fisherman as well as an able fish commissioner.   A fly indorsed by his name is without doubt good.

No. 91.   The Brown Gnat is one of the immense order Diptera, similar in shape to the Black Gnat, but brown in hue.

No. 92.   The Black May is an imitation of one of the two-winged flies, or Diptera.   In some species, the bodies are covered with shaggy gray hair.   These flies are loath to leave the water, and will walk or float on its surface with great agility, a tantalizing vision to the trout.

No. 93.   The Beauty is a fancy fly having a modest dress that would suggest use as well as attractiveness.   We know but little of it further than that it is a pet fly with several successful anglers.

No. 94.   The Ben Bent was first made in 1884 by C. F. Orvis, and named by Mr. A. N. Cheney after Colonel Frank S. Pinckney, whose *nom de plume* was " Ben Bent."   A pleasant circumstance in connection with the naming of this fly was, that the first time Colonel Pinckney tried the new fly named for him he caught on it the largest trout he ever captured, one weighing nearly five pounds.

**No. 95.** The Brown Adder is a fly that has been long in use, but we have not been able to learn who first made or named it. We can only testify that it is one of the "tried and true." It resembles closely several forms of the Phryganidæ, or flies coming from caddis cases, and in this resemblance probably lies its charm for the fish.

**No. 96.** The Black June is an imitation of one of the caddis flies appearing upon the water in the month of June. Its color is so much darker than the other flies of this order that it is called "black," and "June" from the time of its appearance. It seems especially good in the mountain streams of the New England States.

**No. 97.** The Blue Jay flies are not imitations of any insect, but derive their names from the feather of their wings, obtained from the plumage of either the common American blue jay (*Cyanocitta cristata*) or that of the English blue jay (*Garrulus glandarius*). The color and markings on the feathers of the two birds are equally beautiful, but quite different, though apparently equally effective.

The under portions of most of the feathers are without the blue and black bars, but they give some fine dun shades, of most delicate transparency, for small gnats and "floating flies." The fly No. 14, in the accompanying plate, is made from the English blue jay feathers; that in the plates in "Fishing with the Fly" from those of the American jay.

**No. 98.** Imitations of bees have been made since early times with no special restrictions as to material, so each maker has chosen his own. The one illustrated in the plate of trout flies, also in the plate of lake flies in "Fishing with the Fly," was first made by C. F. Orvis, in 1878, for use in the streams west of the Mississippi River. The peculiar burnished effect of the upper feather of the wild turkey used for the wings, and the alternate rings of chenille which permitted a bulky, bee-like body without too much weight, has been so satisfactory that it now seems to be the generally accepted method.

Up i' the early morning,
Sleepy pleasures scorning,
Rod in hand and creel on back, I 'm away, away !

Not a care to vex me,
Nor a fear to perplex me,
Blithe as any bird that pipes in the merry May.

Out come reel and tackle,
Out come midge and hackle,
Length of gut, like gossamer, on the south wind streaming.

Brace of palmers fine,
As ever decked a line,
Dubbed with herl and ribbed with gold, in the sunlight gleaming.

WESTWOOD.

# PENNSYLVANIA, NEW JERSEY, AND DELAWARE.

JAMES B. CHANDLER . . . . .
{ Queen of the Water.
Hamlin.
Bright Fox, etc.

M. E. DOYLE . . . . . . .
{ Trout Flies.

C. A. BABCOCK . . . . . . .
{ Silver Doctor.
Polka.
Seth Green, etc.

DR. J. C. BIDDLE . . . . . .
{ Red Fox.
Stone Fly.
Cow Dung, etc.

J. M. ANDERSON . . . . . .
{ Black Gnat.
Coachman.
Cow Dung, etc.

H. H. LANE . . . . . . . .
{ Polka.
Silver Doctor.
Yellow Sally, etc.

ROBERT H. BUCKMAN . . . . .
{ Gray Hackle.
Jenny Lind.
Queen of the Water, etc.

GEORGE W. PECK . . . . . .
{ Professor.
Brown Palmer.

C. M. HOSTETTER . . . . . .
{ Montreal.
Professor.
King of the Water.
Lord Baltimore, etc.

EDWARD K. LANDIS . . . . .
{ Flies for Black Bass
and Chub.

T. S. MORRELL (" Old Izaak ") . .
{ Grizzly King.
Queen of the Water.
Coachman.
Bishop, etc.

G. L. BRYANT . . . . . . .
{ Coachman.
Cow Dung.
Frogs.

HOWARD GARRETT . . . . .
{ Live Bait.

|                              | Queen of the Water.  |         |
|:----------------------------:|:---------------------|:-------:|
|                              | Hamlin.              |         |
| *Pennsylvania*               | Great Dun.           |         |
| *and*                        | Bright Fox.          | Trout.  |
| *New York.*                  | Dark Fox.            |         |
|                              | Grizzly King.        |         |
|                              | Red Spinner.         |         |

JAMES B. CHANDLER,                    Philadelphia,                    Pa.

My experience has been principally in the trout streams of Pennsylvania and the Adirondacks, but extends back to a period when trout were very abundant, thirty years ago.

1st. My favorite flies now are Queen of the Water, Hamlin, Great Dun, Bright and Dark Fox, Grizzly King, Red Spinner. My leader has a representation always from that list. Although I have a large assortment of flies, comprising almost every variety, I am not without the experience of most fly-fishermen, viz., that one season a fly may prove a great catch, whilst the same fly, in the same locality and under similar circumstances, another season will utterly fail. I instance the Shoemaker, a beautiful fly, with which, on the Lycoming, one season, I took nearly all my fish, large and small, bringing in full creels. I ordered largely for the next season, with the result that I have never taken a fish on a Shoemaker since, a period of ten years. Perhaps this is personal as to that particular fly, but it will apply equally to like experiences with other varieties. I believe that faith, as well as skill, is necessary in trout fishing. A man is doubly armed who believes fully in his cast. The care, precision, and necessary delicacy of handling come spontaneously to the conviction, — " The fish lies there, and I have the fly he wants."

2d. The Great Dun, Hamlin, and Queen will always take good fish, but the Dun and Hamlin are especially adapted to early in the season. The Bright Fox is the best imitation of the natural fly in all the list of flies, and is suitable for evening during the entire season.  I use it as an upper dropper.

3d.  The Hamlin was invented by the late Dr. Up de Graff, author of " Bodines," and a surgeon of great celebrity, but, better than all, an excellent fly-fisherman.  He named it after his friend and co-laborer in outdoor sports, Mr. S. S. Hamlin, of Elmira.  The fly has a great record.  I would be at a loss without it.

I have abiding faith in the " fly on the water," and attribute much of my success to watching the changes in the Ephemera, and selecting from my large stock the same, or a near imitation.

I fish with long leaders, carefully made, and I color them by immersing them for an hour or two in weak alum water ; then drop them into a boiling preparation of logwood and water with a little powdered alum, allowing them to remain twenty-five seconds ; then drop them immediately into cold water, and wipe them dry ; then moisten the thumb and finger with sweet oil and run the leader through ; then stretch for a few hours, either between tacks or with light weight attached.  I like my snells the same color as my leaders.  The only difficulty I have ever had with hooks has been in the tempering, which is bad in too many.  As to size, that varies with locality and season and stage of water ; low clear water and bright weather call for small flies.

---

*Pennsylvania.*          Trout Flies.

M. E. DOYLE,          Shenandoah,          Pa.

My favorite flies are those of subdued colors, in browns, blacks, and grays.  I find at all seasons that these colors, when neatly tied, will kill well. Of course there are times when trout are considered "queer," and when they may be induced to rise to something bright. As a rule, however, I have found the colors mentioned to be very efficacious.

As to new flies, I would take no stock in them. Possibly their greatest advocates are anglers who visit unfrequented trouting regions, where the trout are plentiful, and where they can be induced to take anything. They would hardly be efficacious or prove tempting, in my modest judgment, where fish are scarce and shy, where they are constantly on the alert both for food and their enemies, and where, on the slightest cause, they scurry to their hiding-places.

The size of hooks upon which flies are tied, I should say, cannot be too small, while consistent with the size of the insect represented. The largest trout I have ever taken or seen taken were upon the smallest hooks known to fly-makers. The size and color of leaders and snells I regard as a matter of taste, my own inclining to the lightest in texture and color.

A large variety of flies may be necessary to the average fisherman, as far as filling his book is concerned, but for actual service I think they could be greatly reduced. The angler — and I do not consider him a success if otherwise — who is an observer of things about him while in the haunts of the trout, must, of necessity, see that no gaudy flies, no representatives of the tropics, are ever within view; that in color they represent the tints already suggested, and that in size they never reach above the proportions of those tied upon a No. 10 hook. These he must copy in his mind's eye, duplicating them (artificially) on his leader, and casting here and there with greater or less success, until his creel is filled. These ideas,

modestly advanced, may be scouted at by many anglers of broader
experience, but they are the result of many years' experience in the
mountain streams of this section of Pennsylvania, and are given
with a view toward the honest exchange of opinion upon a topic in
which I am much interested, rather than to air a very limited knowledge upon a very broad subject.

---

|  |  |  |
|---|---|---|
| *Pennsylvania and New York.* | Silver Doctor.<br>Polka.<br>Seth Green.<br>McLeod.<br>Triumph.<br>White Miller.<br>Reuben Wood.<br>Californian.<br>Yellow Sally.<br>La Belle.<br>White and Jungle Cock.<br>No Name.<br>Montreal.<br>Ferguson. | Black Bass and Trout. |

C. A. BABCOCK,                    Oil City,                    Pa.

The fly-fishing here is mostly bass fishing, the trout streams being
generally small and thickly overhung with bushes, and the trout
themselves scarce and small.    The bass fishing is, however, excellent, two good bass streams being within easy reach by rail ; a half
hour's ride will place one at good points on either the Allegheny
River or French Creek.

During June and early July, the fly that kills the most bass is
the Silver Doctor ; following, and in about the order named, are the
Polka, the Seth Green, McLeod, and Triumph ; and for dark days,
and just before dusk, White Miller, Reuben Wood, Californian,
Yellow Sally, White and Yellow Hackle, La Belle, and White and

Jungle Cock. Later in the season, in the latter part of July and in August, the Grizzly King is by far the best fly. I speak of the one with wings tied with concave side out. Last August, in about two hours, I took twenty-seven fine bass at the head of one eddy in French Creek, nineteen of them upon a Grizzly King, and then stopped, not because the fish had ceased to bite, but because my creel and pockets would hold no more, and I had already returned six to the water. My other experiences in July and August are similar as regards the merits of this fly.

I have not found the White Miller a good evening fly here, except during June and the first part of July. In these months there is, in this locality, a light-colored fly greatly resembling the White Miller, or perhaps a shade darker, swarming upon the water at sundown and a little after, upon which the bass feed freely. A White Miller or Reuben Wood, dropped upon a spot where the twirl of a bass was lately seen, is almost sure to be taken. Last July, just after sunset, standing in an eddy and following the indications of the feeding bass, I took nine, averaging over two pounds each, about as fast as I could reel them in, all upon a White Miller. Later in the season, the yellow flies have proved the best for evening. The Brown and Ginger Hackles and the Coch-y-Bonddu are good at all seasons.

In regard to hooks, I think the Sproat or Pennell decidedly the best, and between the two I cannot choose. Perhaps the Pennell is the more certain to "engage," or hook, but I think, on account of its greater bend or narrower space between point and shank, the fish is not hooked so deeply in the jaw, and is therefore more likely to get away after being once hooked. Such, at least, is my experience: on a given number of strikes, I hook more bass with a Pen-

nell than with a Sproat, but more get away after being hooked. If
the Pennell hook were as far in the jaw as a Sproat, I think it
would hold better; but does not its bend make this impossible?

By all means, I would have the snell a very short twisted loop.
One word about leaders. In these waters floating grass is quite
common. At first I used mist-colored or uncolored leaders. I next
tried grass-colored leaders, with better results. Next, I made my
leaders, the first two feet grass-colored, dyed with aniline; the next
two feet mist-colored, dyed with logwood and copperas; the next
two grass-colored, with the best results of all. There was a decided
improvement in the catch following the introduction of the party-
colored leaders. I argued that a continuous green line of six or
eight feet in length was unusual, but one of two feet was not, and
I believe the bass thought so, too. This, of course, applies only
to times when the light is good. At sunset or after, the color of
the leader is of no account.

Last summer, during a trip to the Adirondacks, I found that
the best flies for the trout of that region were the Silver Doctor,
Montreal, Ferguson, No Name, and a Brown Hackle with a red tail.
I caught upon the last-named fly, in one afternoon, seventeen trout
whose aggregate weight was twenty-seven pounds  My guide, who
has been a guide for the last twenty-five years, confirmed my judgment in regard to the flies.

|  |  |  |
|---|---|---|
| *Pennsylvania.* | { Red Fox.<br>Stone Fly.<br>Cow Dung.<br>Black Gnat.<br>Queen of the Water, etc. | } Trout. |

DR. J. C. BIDDLE,                    Fountain Springs,                    Pa.

On several occasions I was able to kill a number of trout on the Red Fox trout fly. In rapid-running waters, I prefer, early in the season, the Stone Fly and the Cow Dung; late in the evening, the Black Gnat; in the latter part of the season, the Queen of the Water and the Royal Coachman; where the water is deep, one of large size. In making a cast, give the line plenty of time on the water, very seldom making a " dry cast; " in fact, I often allow the fly to sink some distance, and then by a " quiver " of the rod give the fly motion. When the trout are feeding on the larvæ, they will not rise for surface fishing. When the trout are feeding on land flies, I make a " dry cast," if possible.

Allow me to suggest that if you have opportunity you urge all true fishermen to stock the streams.

---

|  |  |  |
|---|---|---|
| *Pennsylvania.* | { Black Gnat.<br>Coachman.<br>Cow Dung.<br>Grizzly King.<br>Queen of the Water.<br>Great Dun.<br>Stone Fly.<br>White Miller.<br>Hackles. | } Trout. |

J. M. ANDERSON,                    Pittston,                    Pa.

For fourteen years I have followed that most enchanting pursuit, fly-fishing; and it seems to me that I grow more and more enthusiastic over it every year.  If from any cause I should become incapacitated, so that I could no longer wade the brook and cast my flies, the one genuine pleasure that I have every summer would be taken from me.

The greater part of my experience in trout fishing has been confined to the mountain streams of northeastern Pennsylvania which are tributary to the Susquehanna and Delaware rivers.  I have cast my lines in some of the streams of Colorado, yet the time spent there was too limited to form a factor in the following remarks.

The streams in this locality are such as are found in all mountainous regions, the water clear and cold, flowing over stony beds, full of holes and plenty of long, deep pools.  The water in a few of the streams is of a dark, discolored nature, owing to their taking their rise in some tamarack swamp.  But of whatever color it is, great care must be exercised if the angler wishes his creel to show a moderately successful catch.

In the use of flies, I have found that the time spent in using gaudy, highly colored flies has been about thrown away.  The natural flies which abound on our streams are all of a sombre hue, and the artificial lure that, with me, has proved most taking and most successful is the one that conforms the nearest to the natural fly on which the trout are accustomed to feed.

With us trout are scarce and wary, and fishermen plentiful and persistent, so that during the season scarcely a day passes that does not see one or more anglers industriously striving the one to outdo the other, in enticing from the rippling waters that most beautiful of all game fish, the mountain trout.  Indeed, on one famous stream in this locality, Bowman's Creek, I have counted thirty fishermen in one day, each intent upon his favorite sport.  And as they all wade the streams, you will readily perceive that the fish become exceedingly shy and wary from being so much disturbed.

My experience has been that the dull or moderately colored flies are the most successful for these waters; consequently, when I replenish my stock each spring, I confine myself to these and to a very few varieties. The Black Gnat, Coachman, Cow Dung, Brown and Gray Hackles, Grizzly King, Queen of the Water, Great Dun, Stone Fly, Coch-y-Bonddu, and White Miller comprise my list.

When I first commenced fishing, my fly-book was replete with a large variety, ranging from the modest Black Gnat to the gaudy sham which was like nothing that I had ever seen before or since, and which seemed to me to scare the trout and fill them with distrust rather than to entice them. Then I spent much time changing my flies from dark to light, from sombre to gay, and the various combinations of the same. But years of experience have taught me that this time was uselessly spent. Now I confine myself to the few flies enumerated above; and if the trout refuse to be taken in by these, then I am satisfied that nothing made by the deft fingers of man will entice them that day.

The conditions stated above, as making trout scarce and wary, render it necessary that tackle should be fine and delicate, yet strong, for once in a while you will strike one of those big fellows that will test the strength of the tackle and the skill of the angler to the utmost.

I prefer the small hook that drops lightly upon the water, making hardly a ripple. If the water be still, clear, and glassy, this is an absolute necessity, though in the ripples not so much so; but as one meets all conditions of water in fishing a mountain stream, he must be prepared for the most difficult emergencies.

My leader is made of clear gut, the best I can get, and is about nine feet long. I tie it myself, and have loops for but two flies, the tail fly and dropper. I did use three flies, but was continually bothered with the middle fly clinging to the leader. Now I use but two flies, and tie the loop for the dropper pointing up the line and about three feet from the tail fly. Since adopting that plan I have never been bothered with flies clinging to the leader, and having the trout strike and not being able to hook them. I also prefer my leader to be of medium weight single gut; heavier, if possible, next the line, and lighter at the end. I cannot conceive of any conditions in this locality that would call for twisted gut in trout fishing.

I like the evening fishing, and, late in the season, the early morning fishing. At the commencement of the season it is usually too cold in the early morning; the fish are sluggish, and not till the sun comes out bright and warm do they bite with any vim. At any period of the season the evening fishing has been to me the most enjoyable and the most successful.

On one occasion last summer, I remember going up a small tributary of the main stream which I had been fishing. Just below a bridge which crossed the stream was a long, shallow pool, which I fished, but did not obtain a rise. I passed on up the stream for a short distance, and from almost the first hole I landed a fine fat trout. As the evening shadows were beginning to gather, I retraced my steps and returned to the pool below the bridge. At the first cast I had a strong strike and hooked my fish. Then commenced a contest between the fisherman on the one hand and the trout on the other, wherein the skill of the fisherman and the strength of his tackle were matched against a lusty trout fighting for his life. As is my custom, as soon as I found I had him securely hooked, I began to look around for a place to land him, so that I might gradually work him towards that spot; but I quickly discovered that the edges of the pool were so thickly overgrown with small trees and brush that not a single opening in the dense foliage presented itself, and as I was without a landing-net I was in a quandary. The gallant trout rushed hither and thither, while the leader cut the water like a knife, and as the pressure of the pliant rod became too great he would leap from the water and shake himself as only a frantic trout can. There is a limit to the endurance of all nature, and the rushes of my prize came less frequent as his strength failed him, and after repeated attempts I was enabled to gently reel him in and slip my open basket beneath him. Five times was this operation repeated without moving from my tracks, but so much time was consumed in playing and killing each trout that I could no longer see where to cast, so gave it up for the day.

It is the memory of such scenes as this which to me makes the evening fishing preferable. On very bright, sunny days I use mostly sombre-hued flies, but if the day be cloudy, then I try my lighter-colored flies with success. There are days, though, when the fish will look at nothing, as I have often found out; when, after carefully casting over a pool without receiving a rise, I have seen a half dozen or more trout dart under the rocks as I passed down the stream. But even under the most adverse circumstances, patience, care, and sticking at it will oftentimes work wonders and turn defeat into victory. Many fishermen give up too quickly, and if the trout don't show the same eagerness to be caught that they do to catch them, they say the stream is played out and there are no more trout there. That sort of spirit will succeed no more in trout fishing than it does in anything else. I always fish a stream carefully, and am not in too great a hurry. Often have I seen promising chances spoiled by a too careless approach to a pool. Trout are so wary and so easily frightened that the utmost care must be used to insure even moderate success.

---

|                    |   |
|--------------------|---|
| *Pennsylvania.*    | ⎧ Polka. <br> ⎪ Silver Doctor. <br> ⎪ Brown Hackle. <br> ⎨ White Miller. <br> ⎪ Grizzly Hackle. <br> ⎪ Royal Coachman. <br> ⎩ Yellow Sally. |

H. H. LANE,                     Oil City,                     Pa.

The fly I consider the best at all times, and especially on a bright afternoon, is the Polka, my next choice is the Silver Doctor, next a Brown Hackle (seal brown, with a black body wound with silver tinsel). This hackle I originated myself, and almost always use it as a dropper in clear waters and a bright day.

For early morning a White Miller, Polka, and floating Grizzly Hackle are my favorite trio ; later, remove the White Miller and substitute the Royal Coachman. At sunset, the Silver Doctor, Brown Hackle, and Yellow Sally.

These flies are the ones I favor, but, like all fishermen, when " down on my luck " I go all through my fly-book.

PLATE N.

No. 99. Black Ant.

No. 100. Brown Ant.

No. 101. Black Gnat.

No. 102. Black Gnat.

No. 103. Blue Dun.

No. 104. Bright Fox.

No. 105. Beaverkill.

No. 106. Bluebottle.

No. 107. Brown Caughlan.

No. 108. Chantrey

No. 109. Bissett.

No. 110. Bicknell.

No. 111. Caperer.

No. 112. Cheney.

No. 113. Cinnamon.

**No. 99.** The Black Ant is too well known to require description. It is sometimes made with gray, and sometimes with black wings; the latter is pictured in the plate, because in this country it seems to be the style generally preferred, even though the gray wings are more true to the natural insect.

**No. 100.** The Brown Ant belongs to the same order of insects as the Black Ant, and is usually made with gray wings, though not always. See Wilson's Ant in another plate, and the letter in the California division from Mr. Ramon E. Wilson, regarding his preference for a different dressing.

**No. 101.** The Black Gnat, or midge, may often be seen in swarms over the brooks in May or June, when it is frequently termed the " fisherman's curse," for the annoyance it is to anglers at a time when the fishing is usually at its best. English fly-makers always, and correctly, make it with dark, lead-colored wings, but in America it is customary to make the entire fly black, which seems even more successful than when made in the old way. It is properly very small, yet exaggerated copies are used in some parts of the West and North, and with much effect.

**No. 102.** The Black Gnat, No. 102 of the plate, is a representation of the insect made with black wings, as is sometimes preferred by American fishermen.

**No. 103.** Blue Dun. Perhaps no other fly is known under a greater variety of names, or dressed in a greater variety of methods. First and foremost, it is one of the cocktails or drakes, and should always be made with three black hairs, representing the stylets; these should stand well up, and somewhat reversely. In Ireland it is a Caughlan, while in other parts it is known variously as the Blue Bloa, Blue Drake, Hare's Ear, Hare's Fleck, the Blue Upright, Early Dark Dun, and other names.

The natural fly varies somewhat in different temperatures and seasons. David Forest regards the Olive Dun as the same fly, and writes of it: " The Olive Dun makes its first appearance in February, when it is known as the Blue Dun, or February Flopper. It then presents a dead lead color; the inclement weather, then seasonable, causing the fly to assume so sombre a hue. A few weeks later, if the weather be more genial, it is a shade lighter upon the body, when it is styled the Cock-winged Dun. By the beginning of April it is of a general olive color, with a yellow-ribbed body, upon which rests a bloom like the ripe Muscat grape; but upon dull days this is replaced by a rust-like fungus, which gives a ruddy appearance to the whole body at first sight. It is then known as the Yellow Dun of April, light and dark.. In April, in the cold water near the springs or source of streams, more especially in limestone districts, the fly appears of a light blue tint. This is designated the Pale Blue Dun. A few weeks later, again, and the Blue Dun of February appears as the Yellow Dun of May, and in ungenial weather as the Hare's Ear Dun. This, like most of the numberless appellations, takes its name from a part of the material used in the construction of the artificial." Cotton, when writing of this fly, advises you to " take a small tooth comb, and with it comb the neck of a bluish greyhound, and the down that sticks in the teeth will be the finest blue that ever you saw. The wings of the fly can hardly be too white."

Later methods permit other materials to be used for the body, but always of the bluish mouse shade with the soft light dun wings that are combined and create its name.

No. 104. The Bright Fox is one of a suite of flies originally tied with bodies of fox hair, whence the name. Makers have sometimes substituted other hairs and wools for the bodies, but they retain the old colors. All of the Fox flies were intended to imitate insects of the order Neuroptera, in their first appearance from the pupa, when they are of the palest shades, with delicate translucent bodies, and transparent, iridescent wings. After existing for a time in this, the sub-imago or pseudo-imago stage, they again cast their skins, and appear in deepened, more brilliant colors. Logically, these flies should be used early in the season, as they are the first or early development; but the class has many forms, and some of them appear in successive broods, so that the sub-imago of one may be contemporary with the perfect insect of another species. The fisherman must therefore adapt his selection by observations at different times, places, and seasons.

No. 105. The Beaverkill is a fly having hearty advocates. It is generally used in the small sizes ; indeed, owing to its wing feathers, it cannot be properly made on larger than No. 6 or No. 7 hooks. Feathers from larger birds are sometimes substituted for the delicate curlew feathers, but with doubtful effect. We can best give the history of this fly by an extract from a letter written to us by Judge Fitz James Fitch, author of " Sea Trout " in " Fishing with the Fly," and other sketches, written under the *nom de plume* of " Fitz," that have given much pleasure and information to many readers. In this letter, dated March 22, 1886, Judge Fitch writes : —

" The opinion of an angler as to the merits of a fly does not amount to much unless founded upon his experience in its use. Sometimes I have bought flies new to me because they looked ' taking,' and have found them so ; but more frequently I have found them ' no good.' The three flies with which I have caught the largest number of trout are : first, the Gray Hackle, with scarlet body wound with silver tinsel ; second, Coachman for evening fishing ; and third, the Beaverkill. The latter fly I introduced and named. About forty years ago my first fly-book was filled with English flies of great variety, there being generally but three of a kind. Among them was a fly unknown to me, which I chanced to put on with two others to fish a large and beautiful pool under a high fall on Mill Brook, Delaware County, N. Y. ; within an hour I took upon this fly alone, from this pool, thirty-two trout, ranging from four ounces to sixteen ounces each. My two companions, both older, better, and more experienced anglers, did nothing in comparison until I gave each of them one of the two remaining flies, when their sport became good. When the bout was over, the best preserved of the three flies was given to Harry Pritchard, with an order to make three dozen Beaverkills like it. It has proved an excellent fly ; not always the best, but more frequently so than any I have used, except the Gray Hackle. I have used it on all the streams hereabout, in Massachusetts and in John Brown's Trout, New York, and other places, and generally with success.

" A few years ago I was in Pritchard's, selecting flies.  As I was taking from the case and counting out a dozen or two of Beaverkills, a gentleman, whom Harry introduced to me as Colonel S——, remarked to me : ' I think that the best fly in the world.  My cousin brought me from London some English flies.  This was among them.  I gave one to Harry, and he has made and sold thousands of them.'

" I looked smilingly at Harry, when he, in his slow way, said : ' Colonel S——, that gentleman [pointing to me] was the one that introduced that fly, more than thirty years ago.  He showed me the first one I ever saw, and named it.  That fly that you brought me as a sample was made by me ; I recognized it in a moment.  Whether your cousin bought it in London or not, I made the fly.'

" The colonel looked rather crestfallen and left.  Harry then said : ' He has been telling that story for years.  I did n't undeceive him, because I did n't care anything about it, and he is a good customer ; but when he told this to you, who knew better, I thought I had better tell him the history of the fly.' "

No. 106.   The Bluebottle, or " flesh fly," scientifically known as *Musca vomitoria*, deposits its eggs upon decaying animal matter ; from them are hatched the maggots that fishermen call " gentles."   There are several nearly allied species of the " blow fly," all laying their eggs, or " blows," in immense numbers upon flesh, a single female sometimes as many as twenty thousand ; these hatch in a short time, often in two or three hours, and grow with extraordinary rapidity, having been proved to attain in twenty-four hours to two hundred times their first weight.   The larvæ, or " gentles," when fully grown, leave the substance upon which they feed, and seek to bury themselves before passing into the pupal state, from whence they emerge the " flesh " or " blow " fly.   One species of the flies may be distinguished by its golden green or bronze color ; this is the *Musca cæsa*, common in both America and Europe.   Another species, troublesome to housekeepers, is the *Musca lardaria*.  The latter is more frequently seen toward the end of autumn ; its thorax is white, banded by black stripes, abdomen of bluish gray.  The Bluebottle is also called the Shade fly.

No. 107.   The Brown Caughlan is one of the favorite drakes or cocktails, called in Ireland the " Caughlans."   It was copied there, and as the original was also found in the Ephemeridæ of this country, the same copy was adopted here.  The Gray Caughlan is one of the same order, only a different species, deriving its name in the same way. An illustration of the latter fly may be found in one of the plates of trout flies in " Fishing with the Fly."

No. 108. The Chantrey was well known in England many years ago, and was a favorite with the sculptor, Sir Francis Chantrey, who was a skillful angler. Owing to his frequent use of this fly it was named after him. The Brown Hen bears so close a resemblance to the Chantrey that they are now considered practically the same. The Brown Hen receives its name from its wings, formerly made from the dark feathers of the mottled brown hen. The wild turkey of America furnishes such perfectly marked brown feathers that they are now often used in place of the more variable hen's feathers and with the best possible effect. It is shown under the name Brown Hen in " Fishing with the Fly."

No. 109 was made and named after Mr. Thomas M. Bissett, a member of the firm known from 1875 to 1881 as Conroy, Bissett & Mallison, dealers in fishing-tackle, New York city.

No. 110. The Bicknell received its name from a fisherman living in California. It is recommended for general use in the streams of that State.
See letter from Mr. Ramon E. Wilson, in the California division.

No. 111. The name Caperer is applied to an insect that may be seen toward dusk, flitting or capering from the bank to the water; its apparently aimless motions justify the name. A smaller and similar fly is called the " skip-jack." The imitation of this erratic insect, whether dressed large or small, is an enticing lure in midsummer.

No. 112. The Cheney. For a history of this fly see the notes accompanying the bass flies. The wing of the Cheney trout fly differs from that of the bass fly, the former being made of the peculiar stiff feathers from the jungle-cock's wing. This feather is durable, holds its position well, and does not absorb the water, all of which are desirable qualities for the wings of artificial flies designed to do work that shall entitle them to a place among the souvenirs that brighten the memory, creating " day-dreams and evening musings of warm air, blue sky, bursting buds, open streams, green grass, June days, and time to go a-fishing."

No. 113. The Cinnamon receives its name from its prevailing color, a rich, soft cinnamon shade of brown. The name embraces several species, some larger than others. The larger species may often be found running about on the beams of bridges, or on old posts at the water's edge. They are duns or caddis flies, and properly to imitate this form the wings should be folded about the body in rather a drooping manner; but it seems to be the preference with fishermen to have the wings of nearly all flies tied well on top of the hook and standing up smartly, better to represent the fly when poised for flight, or struggling, as often seen upon the water. Made in this way, the feather fly seems to float better and have a more lifelike appearance than when all the feathers are gathered too closely about the hook, where they would cling a sodden mass, resembling nothing, and serving only to weight the hook. Therefore, though it is perfectly easy to copy the folded, drooping position of the wings of the duns, it is oftener avoided than attempted, the color and size being thought to be more important features.

| | | |
|---|---|---|
| *Pennsylvania and New Jersey.* | Gray Hackle.<br>Jenny Lind.<br>Queen of the Water.<br>Coachman. | Trout. |

ROBERT H. BUCKMAN,                     Phillipsburg,                     N. J.

My fishing is confined to the streams of Monroe and Pike counties, Pennsylvania, and Warren County, New Jersey, and as my territory is limited, so is the list of my flies. I mention nearly all when I say that I rarely stray away from the use of the Gray and Brown Hackles. Early in the season, my first choice is a Gray Hackle, lemon body wound with a crimson thread; in fact, I may say this is my choice at all times. I constantly use it as my stretcher fly. Next follows a fly with a dun wing and yellow body, in imitation of a May fly; this approximates in color, at least, to the Gray Hackle above described, and does not make a marked difference. Then come the Queen of the Water and the Coachman. These, with the Brown Hackle, comprise my list.

One of our party had great success, last year, with a monstrosity in the shape of a blue, yellow, and red fly, called the Jenny Lind. He was fishing the still water of the Tunkhannock, in Monroe County, at a place called the "Duck puddle." It was a warm day early in July. He had fished this place every year for a generation, and knew there were trout there, but after hours of ceaseless work and constant changing of flies until his book was exhausted, he had met with indifferent success. In desperation he put on the Jenny Lind, when lo! the whole scene changed; the place was alive with trout.

In describing the scene, he said he was never in the habit of talking to himself, but on this occasion, on making a cast he would say, "Here comes another." He had taken some ten or twelve, ranging from fifteen inches down, when the hook pulled off and was lost.

Quiet reigned again, except in his breast, and although he went the weary round of his book the fish would have none of it. This fly had been given him that morning by a passing fisherman; there was none other in the neighborhood, and as our season closed on the 15th, he was obliged to leave off with that single experience. Talking with him to-day, he told me he was "itching to get up there with a Jenny Lind."

In conclusion, regarding the fly question, it is my belief there is more in the way you fish than in what you fish with. The man who goes down the stream with the sole disturbing thought on his mind of what is the kind of fly demanded by the trout this morning, and attributing his ill success to unfortunate selection, is outdone by the man who puts on a fly he knows to be good ordinarily, and then gives himself up entirely to watching the stream and his manner of casting.

---

| *Pennsylvania and Adirondacks.* | { Professor. Brown Palmer. | { Trout. |
|---|---|---|
| GEORGE W. PECK, | Roselle, | N. J. |

In May, in Pennsylvania, the Professor, and in early September, in the Adirondacks, the Brown Palmer with a red tail, are the flies I rely upon wholly. These as "tail flies" have never failed me. Other flies I have tried with only indifferent success. Hooks about No. 8 in size.

| *Pennsylvania.* | Montreal.<br>Professor.<br>King of the Water.<br>Coachman (brown wing).<br>Lord Baltimore.<br>Brown Hackle (yellow body). | Black Bass. |
|---|---|---|

C. M. HOSTETTER,        Pittsburgh,        Pa.

Taking my cue from Mr. Marston's inquiry of Scotch salmon anglers, I asked the following old bass anglers, Dr. James McCann, Dr. Joe U. Dickson, Mr. H. I. A. Stewart, and Charles A. Dick, Esq., "What six flies do you consider the best for black bass?" The following six were the favorites: —

| | |
|---|---|
| Montreal. | Coachman (brown wing). |
| Professor. | Lord Baltimore. |
| King of the Water. | Brown Hackle (yellow body). |

This refers to the waters of western Pennsylvania, southern Ohio, and West Virginia. Medium-sized flies and Sproat hooks are preferred.

---

| *Pennsylvania and West Virginia.* | Flies for Bass and Chub. |
|---|---|

EDWARD K. LANDIS,        Brewster,        N. Y.

I have fished for bass this season altogether with the fly, and in the Juniata River, between this place and Williamsburg. My favorite fly is what I suppose you would call the "Polka Dot:" it is a fly with a very dark polka dot wing, and black hackles and body with a green tail. I was fishing, one evening in the latter part of August, and had tried a number of flies of different shades, but with little success, when just at sunset I attached this fly to my leader as the tail fly, and the first cast I made I hooked and landed a twelve-inch bass. The fish rose to it greedily, and in less than an hour I landed nine very nice fish, ranging in size from nine to fourteen inches. (We judge our fish by inches up this way, and not by weight.) The next morning I started out early, using the same fly, and in a small stretch of water, just below a riffle, I landed three nice fellows, but in testing the fly after landing the last one I broke the snell off close to the head; it was worn out. As I had but that one, I attached a Black Gnat in its place, but had not as much success with it, although it is a very killing fly in these waters. We have a fly here called the Potato Bug (made by a local fly-tier), which is also very killing at times; it has a dark brown wing (wild turkey), dark maroon body, and dark brown hackle, the body being wrapped with gold tinsel.

Some of our anglers have great success with the Red Ibis, but I never took to it. I have met with more success with the dark browns and the blacks than with any others; I landed two twelve-inch and one ten-inch bass in less than twenty minutes, one afternoon last summer, and caught them all on a small Black Gnat.

I inclose a fly made by me three years ago, while fishing on the Potomac, at Shepherdstown, W. Va. It was taken with the greatest avidity by bass, sunfish, and chub. It seemed to please the fish more than any others I showed to them. We had had muddy water for some time, and I thought that a bright fly would probably do better than the regular standard flies, so I made this fly, and was delighted with the results. Have not had a chance to try it in Pennsylvania and New York waters but expect to do so this summer, and will let you know the results.[1] Our Pennsylvania bass

[1] The fly inclosed closely resembled the Alexandra, except that it had a heavy scarlet hackle. It would, no doubt, be effective in many waters for bass, as the Alexandra is used with much success. It is thought that the fish take the latter to be a small minnow, owing to its glittering silvery body. — M. E. O. M.

prefer a quiet-colored fly, being perhaps imbued with a touch of Quakerism. At least that is the result of my observation.

I desire to call your attention to what seems to be a curious similarity in regard to the coloring of birds, fishes, insects, etc. I allude to the " mimicry of nature." Professor Drummond, in his book on Central Africa, noticed that the insects most prized as food by the birds always closely imitated some natural object, which imitation afforded them a means of concealment from their enemies. He also noticed quite a number of very brilliantly colored insects flying about, which the birds never, or very rarely, touched. If a bird did catch one, it was speedily rejected. Drummond concludes, from his observations, that these insects had acrid juices offensive to the bird's taste, so there was no necessity for their concealing themselves, like the edible insects.

During the holidays I noticed an article in one of the illustrated magazines (I do not now remember which one) on " Fishes of the Indian Ocean," in which the writer states that all the brightly colored fish are very poisonous, while the sober-colored ones are all edible. He draws the same conclusion that Drummond does.

I have found the same rule to hold good for flies, with a few exceptions. In general, the more sober-colored the fly, the better. This is especially true of clear water, and perhaps the reason that fish take a brighter fly in cloudy water is because they have more difficulty in finding their prey, and readily seize on anything that comes to hand ; and as under such circumstances they can see a bright fly further than a sober-colored one, the former fly has a better chance of success. Size of flies has a bearing on the subject, too. I always tie mine on a No. 6 hollow point Limerick or No. 4 Pennell for the largest, and four sizes smaller for clear water and educated fish. I am speaking now of bass, for the trout streams here are small and too thickly wooded to allow of fly-fishing. Most dealers sell flies that are large enough to frighten any bass.

I much prefer the Pennell eyed hooks to all others, and use rather light unstained gut, as, when frayed, it can readily be changed, whereas with the old style of fly a helper is necessary, and I have often lost flies by the gut breaking off just at the head of the fly, although apparently all right. In my opinion stained gut is no better than unstained gut.

With regard to size and color, I don't think that color has as much to do with success in catching fish as size. I prefer a small-sized fly, and frequently use trout flies for bass. Do not think the Sproat hook equal to the hollow point Limerick or Pennell for a fly-hook, as I have pricked and lost more fish with a Sproat than with either of the others.

Here is a little experience I had one day last summer. I was fishing in the Juniata, just below Cone Forge, in as fine a stretch of water for fly-fishing as one could wish. I had whipped the stream for upwards of a mile without a rise, and was thinking of giving it up, when I spied a little toad on the shore. I picked it up and hooked it on a large Brown Hackle and put two No. 2 shot on the leader for a sinker, and threw it in. The toad had not sunk two feet when I got a tremendous run. I gave my fish a little line, then "struck," and landed a fifteen-inch beauty which weighed 1¾ pounds. I found some more toads, and in a very short time I caught three more fifteen-inch bass and one eleven-inch one, and lost two others in playing them. Ever since that day, when I cannot catch fish with the fly, I hunt toads.

|  | ⎰ Grizzly King.<br>⎱ Queen of the Water.<br>Cow Dung.<br>Red Spinner.<br>Coachman.<br>Oak Fly. | ⎱ Trout. |
|---|---|---|
| *New Jersey*<br>*and*<br>*Adirondacks.* | | |
|  | Bishop. | ⎰ Bass and<br>⎱ Lake Trout. |

T. S. MORRELL ("Old Izaak"),              Newark,              N. J.

On account of age and disability I have done very little " wading the stream " for a number of years. I cannot say that I have any special favorite flies, as all depends upon the condition of the water, the weather, temperature, etc. Still, to test myself, I have rigged three casts, regardless of all conditions. For the first the stretcher is a Grizzly King, the first dropper a Brown Hackle, and the hand fly an exceedingly small Coachman. The second cast is : Queen of the Water for a stretcher; first dropper, the Oak or Cow Dung.; hand fly, Red Spinner. The other cast is: stretcher, a Cinnamon; first dropper, a Grizzly King ; and hand fly, a Queen of the Water. From this it would seem that I have a preference for a Grizzly King and Queen of the Water, yet I assure you I am not conscious of it in practice. One thing I am particular about, — the flies must graduate in size, the stretcher the larger, and the snells of the flies must vary in length ; the hand fly should be the longest, and the gut should be stained to match the leaders.

In lake fishing, trolling in the Adirondacks in May for lake trout, brook trout, or black bass, often found in the same waters, I have found the Bishop to be the most taking fly : body, white chenille ; wings, white and red ibis ; red tail and brown hackle.

| *New Jersey.* | { Coachman. <br> Cow Dung. <br> Frogs. | } Black **Bass.** |

G. L. Bryant,                      High Bridge,                      N. J.

We have inland lakes, but they are so deep that it is hard to get a large black bass to come up to the fly, very early, some seasons. They rise to flies finely in Lake Hopatcong, but they are so capricious that I have not been able to ascertain the most alluring fly for all times. The large mouth take a Coachman well, while at times the Guinea does well for the small mouth. I believe, on the whole, that colors about like the Professor, and some darker browns, do well for the latter fish. I have seen bass of $3\frac{1}{2}$ lbs. taken on a trout Cow Dung fly, but as a rule the fish are so strong in this lake that nothing short of a very heavy Sproat will hold them. I have seen even these bent out, or broken, and in summer fishing, when frogs are used for bait, a single leader will not hold, if they get into rocks. The most experienced guide on the lake uses twisted gut, with Edgar barbless hooks, while using frogs for bait, as these hooks will admit of taking the frog off to rest without maiming him.

My experience is, that the best colored leader for this water is stained almost a black by some sort of writing fluid. Lines should be the same; as the water is very clear, the fish are very wary and hard to lure, although they roam about in schools of hundreds, and are taken over six pounds in weight, *i. e.* the small mouth.

*Delaware.*    Live Bait.    Bass.

HOWARD GARRETT,    Wilmington,    Del.

There is little to be said upon fly-fishing upon the Brandywine, the only available bass stream hereabouts. While many prefer to use the fly only, the fact is that all are universal bait fishermen. Occasionally an angler from a distance will use the fly in the early morning and late in the day, but as a rule the fish caught are much smaller than when taken with bait.

Bass fishing is tolerable from Rockland Dam, three miles above the city, to the forks of the Brandywine, which are within a few miles of West Chester, Pa., some sixteen miles above.

For bait, shrimp, hellgamites, crawfish, toads, and minnows are the best for September and October.

Hooks and snells are immaterial to a great extent.

# PLATE O.

No. 114.   The Coachman is, perhaps, the most general favorite of any fly used in America, although it did not originate in this country, but was brought to us from England.   Mr. David Foster gives a description of the inventor in his book, the " Scientific Angler," which we will quote, as it is undoubtedly correct, and the best history that can be given of the origin of the fly.   In his directions for fly-casting, he remarks : —

" A thorough command of the rod and line is as essential and important as the wielding of the whip in the case of the tandem or four-in-hand drive.   We are reminded of this analogy that the most skillful cast we ever knew wielded the whip.   We refer to the famous royal coachman, Tom Bosworth.   Old Tom had, in the early part of his life, driven three successive British sovereigns, namely, the Fourth George, the Fourth William, and finally, for a lengthened period, Her Majesty Queen Victoria.   As a successful fisherman, old Tom, when known to the writer, was unsurpassed.   He would often fish in the wake of several rodsters, whose energy would exceed their skill, and would extract, not infrequently, three times over the weight of fish, by skillful and careful casting over the awkward and most unlikely-looking spots, which the majority of anglers would never dream of trying.   A favorite freak of his with the whip was to take the pipe from the teeth of a passing pedestrian by a carefully calculated whirl of the whip, and his aptitude was as remarkably exemplified for a limited distance in his use of the rod. Bosworth originated the Coachman fly so much appreciated for night fishing. This artificial has recently been much used as a fancy fly, for day fishing, and with considerable success.   The Red-tip Coachman and Leadwing Coachman are merely imitations of the original White-winged Coachman made with a touch of red in it, or with the dark wing, because it is thought under some circumstances they might be more successful.

**No. 115.**   The Gilt Coachman, with its bright gold body in place of the proper one of peacock herl, was a response to a request from a fisherman living in Wagon Wheel Gap, Colorado, who wrote saying: "The Coachman appears about the best fly used about here, but it ought to have more gilt on it.   Make some with all the gilt possible on them."   They were accordingly made with bodies almost wholly of gilt tinsel.   These were tried, reported to be an improvement, and the Gilt Coachman came to be a standard fly for some of the Colorado waters.   It is occasionally tied with silver tinsel in place of the gilt, and is then called Silver Coachman.   I have also seen it with a middle of orange silk, and called Orange Coachman.

**No. 118.**   Henry Guy Carleton is an American author of more than the average directness and humor, who never fails to be strikingly lucid and interesting. When we first saw the fly to which he has given his name, we admired it greatly, but said to the man who gave it to us: " Do you know, it reminds me of the fly called the Volunteer, that appeared with the Thistle, just after the notable race between the two yachts of those names; the flies were ephemeral, — no one ever saw them after that one appearance, but I think I will mention them in connection with Mr. Carleton's fly."   " No, you better not," he said.   " Henry Guy Carleton stammers a little sometimes when he gets excited, but you know *he can write!* "

There is no question but that this fly is honored in bearing the name it does, and in consequence will greatly interest fishermen, and we hope that Mr. Carleton will not write us either up or down because we were " only reminded," for we are heartily glad of the opportunity in this connection to quote some of Mr. Carleton's own words regarding fly-fishing, printed in a book issued by William Mills & Son. It is hard to choose among his very explicit directions, but perhaps portions of his little essay entitled " The Artificial Fly," and his graphic description of " Striking the Tarpon," either of which are types of his originality of purpose and expression, will manifest his knowledge and experience as a fly-fisherman.

## THE ARTIFICIAL FLY.

The artificial fly is a fish-hook to which variously colored feathers have been tied, and is supposed to be easily mistaken by a fish for a real fly. If this be true, it is a strong proof that a fish has n't sense enough to come in when it rains, and does n't deserve to live.

Real flies may be obtained at most watering-places much cheaper than artificial flies, but for some purposes they are not so useful.

Artificial flies are all named. There are the " Professor," the " Hackle," the " Ibis," the " Yellow Sally," and several other breeds. Whenever a bilious angler has no luck, and nothing to do, he sits down and concocts a new swindle in feathers, and christens it with a nine-jointed Indian name, and at once every angler in the country rushes in and pays two dollars a dozen for samples.

To cast the artificial fly well requires practice, and some persons are more skillful than others. The first thing I ever caught on an artificial fly was a large and muscular friend, who was sitting in the stern of the boat, and who was narrow-minded enough to make coarse remarks while we were rowing back to camp for surgical assistance.

Oysters do not rise readily to the artificial fly, particularly during the spawning season.

Tackle-boxes are now thrown upon the market in great numbers, and are of several sizes. The smallest is made to contain chewing-tobacco and fish-hooks well mixed together, but the larger kinds have more compartments than a tenement house, and will hold lines, hooks, reels, sinkers, gangs, poker-chips, and other necessaries with ease.

## CONCERNING THE BLACK FLY.

The black fly is not as large as a bull-dog, but he can bite with both ends. There is not a single black fly in the Adirondacks. All the black flies there are born married and have large families.

The black fly earns his living by raising lumps like the egg of a speckled hen on the forehead and behind the ears of a man, who will simultaneously wish that he could die and be out of his misery. One hundred and seventy black flies can feed comfortably on each square inch of a man's ears, but the simple-hearted natives of Maine, the Adirondacks, and Canada do not mind them until they settle down nine deep.

The lumps raised by a black fly will grow seven days, and then burst into a rich dark red bloom, which is much admired by the angler when he sees himself in a looking-glass trying to shave.

There are mosquitoes and deer flies also in these localities, but they are mere toys to the man who is wrestling with several million free-and-easy black flies.

Camping - out is a noble and improving sport, but should be indulged in with caution. Should he discover during the night that he had accidentally spread his blankets upon a nest of large and polygamous ants, he should at once arise and move camp. No angler should be cruel to dumb animals.

I had a friend who went camping in the North Woods for two weeks, and he says he enjoyed every minute of his stay; but rather than go again he will go to state's prison for nine years.

### STRIKING THE TARPON.

The best bait for tarpon is half a mullet, tied on to the hook with a string. The fisherman may sometimes prefer other bait, which is just as effective on days when the tarpon are not biting.

The tarpon bites by taking the bait into his mouth. This theory is not disputed by advanced naturalists. He then swallows it, closes his eyes for a few moments in meditation, and proceeds to move off. At this juncture the careful angler will wake up.

To strike the tarpon properly, wait until he has proceeded about fifty feet, when, raising the rod and tightening the line, a strong, triple yank will set the hook firmly, and the tarpon will show his sudden interest by a jump of seven feet for fresh air. At this moment a kick and a few well-chosen words will arouse the nigger, who will weigh anchor. The anchor must be weighed at once, or the tarpon will never be.

A tarpon's first desire, on finding that his hunk of mullet contains a gift with a string tied to it, is to bite a hole in the sky, and then to visit Brazil or Iceland and arrive that day. This excursion must be promptly discouraged by pressure on the line and an industrious combination of nigger and oars, or the angler will lose fish and salvation simultaneously.

Failing to reach Queenstown or Rio Janeiro, the tarpon again takes a hurried view of the scenery and starts for Aspinwall, changes his mind, throws four hand springs, heads for New Orleans, exhibits himself once more in mid-air, makes a break for Havana, and then, getting warmed up, proceeds to show what he can really do. A bewildering series of complicated evolutions follows for two hours, at the end of which time he is alongside, and the nigger skillfully knocks him off the hook with the gaff, and the proud and happy angler returns to the hotel to cuss.

Sometimes a tarpon turns out to be a fourteen-foot shark, who makes a bee-line for Patagonia and gets there on time, with four dollars' worth of line and twenty-one dollars' worth of language trailing after him. Sometimes he is a jew-fish, sometimes a stingaree, or a devil-fish, or a case of delirium tremens with fins. An angler may start out in the morning with perfectly honorable intentions to fasten to nothing but tarpon, and acquire during the day only a large assortment of large-sized what-is-its, and then lose his rod, reel, line, and soul on some unknown variety of submarine insanity, of which his only recollection is a bite, a whiz, and a sense of goneness forever.

A year ago, I took one hundred and twenty-seven dollars' worth of tackle, including a thumbstall worth thirty cents, to Jupiter Inlet, for a few days' tarpon fishing. In four hours I caught nineteen pieces of active bric-a-brac, some with stings, some with warts, some with horns and legs, and all with types of beauty which proved that they should have been sand-bagged when they were born; and then a twelve-foot something with a violent desire to go round the world in sixty days laid hold and borrowed all of my tackle but the thumbstall.

I shall not go to Florida this year. If the few little precepts I have given can be of use to the young anglers who will read them, I shall be glad. They have been of no use to me.

No. 119.  The Carmen was introduced by Mr. T. V. Allis, of New York city. That the trout found it so captivating perhaps suggested its name, — a name that weaves a spell, and brings us visions of the reckless, fascinating witchery of Carmen the Gypsy. An echo of the Havaniase, with its quaint waltz-like melody, sings itself in our ears, passion and tenderness flit again before us, and again we sigh as we think of poor Gorges Bizet cut down just as he had learned the joy of success.

No. 120.  The Dark Claret and Bright Claret are two species of the same form, but their distinctions are frequently ignored, and, to reduce the number of patterns, their chief characteristics are blended in a fly called the Claret. These flies belong to the order Diptera, and are of a class frequenting the headwaters of small brooks and springs where the temperature of the water is most uniform. The larvæ are slender and worm-like, sometimes of a deep red color, and live in the sand and water, burying themselves deeper when about to change to the pupæ. Their pupa skins harden, and they are for a time apparently dormant, but the body is slowly contracting and changing ; it finally floats to the surface of the water, splits open above the thorax, and the two-winged fly emerges.

Their usual time for appearing is the forenoon. Most species breed twice a year.

No. 121. The Cahill. Mr. John Shields writes to us that " the Cahill was named after a Dublin fly-maker of that name, who would occasionally, after making a fly, put it to the writer's ear and inquire if I heard it *buzz*."

This fly is claimed as an American pattern, but we are confident that Mr. Shields is correct in his statement of its birthplace.

No. 122. The Cow Dung fly. Tradition declares that this fly should be used on windy days, as the natural fly is found upon the water only when blown there by strong winds ; but it has been proved that the fly is often successful at other times, and actual observation shows the wind theory unreliable.

The larvæ of these flies feed upon the excrement of cattle, and the females may be seen hovering in its vicinity, as they lay their eggs near or upon it. The females are short-lived and do not wander, but it is stated that the male flies prey upon smaller insects, especially the tiny water-flies, which they hold with their anterior feet while they suck the blood of the bodies. In their greed they often venture too far, and fall into the water, where they furnish a fat morsel for the waiting trout.

Their color is a brown similar to the tints of many of the caddis flies, — that favorite food of the trout and grayling, — so that they are likely to be successful in any streams where the Phryganidæ are familiar food to the fish.

No. 123. The Equinox Gnat was first made by C. F. Orvis in the summer of 1889, and named after a pretty little sheet of water that lies close at the base of Mount Equinox, where it mirrors to the " everlasting hills " their grandeur and beauty, in winter reflecting to them their blue, deeper than that of the skies, broken here and there by the masses of white that seem almost to be clouds come to earth and materialized.

These we may watch for a time, until by the power of the sun-god they slowly

EQUINOX: THE EDGE OF THE SHADOWS

vanish from sight, again to assume intangible forms overhead as they are lifted up and away, leaving only the trees and the rocks.

When the clouds have gone back to the winds, the arbutus and the violets begin to stir and strive to peep up through the cover of last year's fallen leaves, that they may speak again to the waving branches above, which look to us, who are down in the valley, like a veil spread over the whole form of the mountain. This veil gradually changes, beginning with a faint yellowish-green fringe of color way down at its edge, that goes creeping up and up, day after day, all the time growing darker farther down as the gray meshes of the interlacing twigs yield to the buds and leaves.

We rejoice to see the mountain cast aside this wonderful veil of nature and reveal the fullness of a beauty to which we can never weary of turning, be it in the unfolding or when all charms are mature. Then in calm gladness she breathes out the spirit of rest and welcome that beckons all to her, the clouds softly hover near, the winds hasten to carry her messages and healing, and the sun reaches down to glorify and exult in a possession that is supreme.

By and by the frost-king comes to contest this gentle rule, with a wild power awakening a glow and warmth and joy that hold our gaze in wondering sympathy.

All this the little lake mirrors day after day, finally showing how again the shadowy veil seems drifting down, this time from the upper heights. When it quite meets the stretching fields we realize that the blushes and glow are gone and the mountain is sleeping. Soon the clouds draw nearer, laying over all a warm coverlet, and then we know we must wait for the awakening.

We love the little lake that has so tenderly reproduced all this wonderful change, and like often to linger near it.

The tiny fly, named because of its success in the lake which bears the name of the mountain at whose feet it lies, recalls memories of both, and brings to us recollections of many an hour of twilight fishing, and we whisper the prayer that Redlaw learned to utter, " Lord, keep my memory green."

No. 124. The Emerald Gnat is a small fly receiving its name from the emerald green of its body.

No. 125. The Camlet Dun. This fly was originally known as the Camlet fly because made of a soft wool called in olden times camlet (*i. e.* camel's hair).

Cotton suggests the fly for the latter part of May and all through June, saying, " It is shaped like a moth, with fine diapered water-wings. The artificial is made of a dark brown, shining brown camlet ribbed over with a very small light green silk, the wings of the double gray feather of the mallard, and 't is a killing fly for small fish." He also recommends for September the Camlet Brown, " the dubbing pulled out of the lime of a wall, whipped with red silk, and darkish gray mallard feather for the wings."

But in later years the modest Camlet Dun, somewhat different in appearance, has taken the place of the old Camlet fly and Camlet Brown. As the name implies, it is now more of a soft dun hue, though yet made with the wool body. This later type is one of the best and most satisfactory of our flies, and is especially taking in the mountain streams of Vermont.

**No. 126.** The Deer fly. It is probable that calling the fly pictured in the plate the Deer fly began with a mistake by some one, but it has been persevered in so long, and the little green and white fly (that is very like one of the little millers or moths we often see in summer-time) has come to be so widely known and so much used as the Deer fly, that we can only follow the fashion, as we do so frequently with no better reason than to do as others do.

Flies made with deer's hair are also called Deer flies, and we have heard a fly called a Deer fly because of its delicate fawn color ; but the green and white fly is the one most widely distributed as the Deer fly. It is sometimes stated that the name arose from its imitating the little flies troublesome to the deer in warm weather, called deer flies, as we speak of horse flies, buffalo gnats, etc., but this is doubtful. However it received its name, it is an addition to a collection of flies, and seems especially taking in some portions of the far West.

**No. 127.** The Dark Stone. Reference has been made to this fly in the mention of Theakston's First Class or " Browns." The name stone fly is applied to a class of natural insects, and arose from the habit of those flies to hide underneath flat stones, or in their crevices. These flies have always been great favorites with fishermen, whether natural or imitated. They are valuable food for trout and grayling, and are eagerly sought by them. The Light Stone is named from its color.

No. 128. The Dorset was made in 1883 by C. F. Orvis, after a description given by Mr. Emmet Tuttle, of Manchester, Vt., who had observed an insect greedily taken by the trout on a small pond in the town of Dorset, Vt. As the name of the real fly was not known to him, the imitation was named after the town wherein the fish seem to enjoy the original, and approve the artificial representation when it is offered to them. The fly has been found equally successful in other waters, chiefly during the month of June.

And oh ! the gleam of the birches' stems,
  And the new green of the pines,
And the hemlock fringes sweeping low,
  Till they touched the creeping vines !

And every bank was studded thick
  With wild flowers sweet and rare ;
While the ferns seemed made of spirit-stuff,
  They were so slight and fair.

  .    .    .    .    .    .

Could it be, I thought, in the world with this
  There was dust and heat and glare ?
Could it be there was sorrow and hate and sin,
  And terror and wild despair ?

Alas ! it could ; but for this one day
  I would live as if it could not ;
I would dream that the world from end to end
  Was only this one dear spot.

CHADWICK.

## VIRGINIA AND WEST VIRGINIA.

M. C. TREIBER . . . . . . . . { Trout Fishing.

RUSSELL ROBINSON . . . . . . { Jock Scott.<br>Lord Baltimore.<br>Green and Gold, etc.

COLONEL W. L. BUMGARDNER . . { Black Gnat.<br>White Miller.<br>Queen of the Water.

T. S. DOYLE . . . . . . . . . { Hackles.<br>Queen of the Water.<br>Red Ibis.<br>Blue Dun, etc.

JOHN M. KINNEY . . . . . . { Coachman.<br>Queen of the Water.<br>Professor.<br>Hackles.

S. H. HENKLE . . . . . . . . { Trout Flies.

CHARLES H. HASWELL . . . . . { Yellow Fly.

JAMES BUMGARDNER, JR. . . . . { Queen of the Water.<br>Coachman.<br>Hackles, etc.

F. R. WEBB . . . . . . . . . { Coachman.<br>Hackles.<br>White Miller.<br>Queen of the Water, etc.

NEIL ROBINSON . . . . . . . . { Cow Dung.<br>Montreal.<br>Scarlet Ibis, etc.

E. D. BOWLY . . . . . . . . . { Queen of the Water.<br>The Owner.

A. P. TALLMAN . . . . . . . . { Hackles.<br>Coachman.<br>Royal Coachman.

*Virginia.* Trout Fishing.

M. C. Treiber, Staunton, Va.

Our mountain waters abound in brook trout, and they commence to take the fly in early June. The best fly-fishing begins about the latter part of July, and the largest trout, often averaging twenty inches in length, are taken mostly, in my experience, by fishing up stream. I assign the following reasons: —

Trout usually lay with their heads up stream, and are more easily approached from behind. By gently casting ahead and allowing your flies to float back to you with the swift current of the waters, you will find the fish seldom escape. Your hook will not miss his mouth, as so often happens when fishing down stream, the jerk of the line being directly against his mouth and all the resistance he has, while it is the reverse in fishing down stream.

One of my favorite modes of fishing, in which I have been very successful, is simply to take an average-sized trout hook, with a light, clear snell and leader and only one hook (using two or three hooks at a time only tends to confuse the trout); procure a spool of fine red silk, the best make, so that you can depend upon the silk retaining its bright red color; then wrap your hook very closely with the red silk, knitting it on just as you would in fastening a hook to a snell, and leave the two ends of the silk to dangle over the point about an inch. Some of the largest trout are taken in this way. It is always advisable to have a quantity of these hooks properly prepared before going out for your day's sport. I would further advise, on a cloudy day to use the brightest red silk. On a clear day, a dark maroon color answers better.

This information may be old to most sportsmen, but to those

who have never tried it I would urge its use as being very effectual
and convenient.

---

| | | |
|---|---|---|
| *Virginia.* | ⎧ Jock Scott.<br>⎪ Lord Baltimore.<br>⎨ Green and Gold.<br>⎪ Grasshopper.<br>⎩ Yellow Sally. | ⎰ Black **Bass.**<br>⎱ |

RUSSELL ROBINSON,　　　　　　　Wingina,　　　　　　　　Va.

I am at the foot-hills of the Alleghanies. Trout, and plenty of
them, in a reach of fifteen or twenty miles, but a pound specimen is
a week's talk. They are not educated (?) trout. The streams are
open, no obstruction to casting, and the grasshopper the bait. I
notice little difference in the day's result as to flies, if the grasshopper colors are used. Green and Gold, Grizzly King, Yellow
Sally, Green Mantle, all are equally taking. Later on, the Montreal,
and particularly the Blue Jay, seem to take their fancy. The
region is unknown to outsiders, — a rough, unkempt, brave, but
hospitable people, given to a little "moonshining" (illicit distilling),
and suspicious of strangers, unless well placed by letters; it is not
a highroad for the fancy trout fisher, and though at the "Crab
Tree Falls" there is a six hundred feet cataract (or fall, I should
say), — next to the "Yellow Stone" the highest we have, — it is
comparatively an unknown region. Deer, bears, turkeys, ruffed
grouse, wildcats, and rattlesnakes are plenty; you can take your
choice in the hunting line. The natives are prone to the use of the
old "bamboo" stocked rifle of about seven feet and exceedingly
small calibre, wonderfully expert in its use, and "ugly" in every
sense, from want of education and long provincialism, unless you
are placed. An hundred trout a day is not unusual with them, with

their native cedar rods and grasshoppers, or the long round worm found under the bark of the pine. Few of the fish reach a half pound. The banks are clear on the upper waters of the Tys and Rockfish rivers, and the stream are filled with boulders, evidently from a glacial drift of long ago. My best luck has been with the Grizzly King and Green Mantle, and late in the day with a Coachman. For years I have been there with friends, and found the fish only too plenty. An eight-ounce split bamboo, a very few flies, and that cheerful and contented spirit that should be a part of every angler, make the yearly trips pleasanter and pleasanter as time goes on.

As to bass (small-mouthed), they were put into the James River some twenty years ago, or less. The big-mouthed (*G. salmonaides*) are native. The James is a rapid, "unsartin" river, full of ledges, rocks, falls, and islands, but given to jump up at any time six to ten feet, without provocation, from a sickly-looking cloud somewhere west, and bring down a mass of red, muddy stuff that hangs on for weeks before it clears again. The bass are increasing rapidly; the fishing, when the water is favorable, is good, very good. The minnow is the usual bait, preferably the long, red-eyed gray "chub" of the creeks; next the crayfish. I have tried legions of flies, and yet have not made up my mind. The Montreal (red body), Polka, and Grizzly King, all take. I have had good success at times with the Bee fly of lake trout size. Reading Mr. Henry P. Wells's book on " Fly Rods and Fly Tackle," wherein he speaks so strongly of his tests under water of the " top-knot " of the golden pheasant, I last season sent for a half dozen small-sized (No. 3 Sproat hook) Jock Scott salmon flies. My success was bewildering for some days; all I took were on the Jock Scott; then the fish became tired I imagine, because they would take nothing but the Oriole.

The most successful bait is the minnow, and as casting the minnow on the "Henshall" rod is beautiful, but the minnow troublesome to get, and keep, etc., I "evolved" an idea. I took a very thin piece of rubber packing, cut in shape of fish, and sewed to it feathers; that is, commenced at the tail and put on a scale of feathers, overlapping the next row, and so on to the head. I used white (pigeon) except at the middle and near the head of the fish; there I put in a lap of ibis feathers. This. made an exceedingly light minnow, easily cast with fly-rod, and was and is wonderfully successful. Anything can be used for the body that is waterproof and tough. I simply used rubber because I had it, as I use it on my engines at home. This may be patentable (if the fluttering fly of Imbrie is, anything is); if so, I present it to you. You cast it just as you would a fly, letting it sink a few inches and recovering. I have had more success and caught larger fish with it than with anything else I have tried. I think it advisable to tie the snell so the hook is about two thirds from head of minnow; not at tail, unless the minnow is made very small (and I have tied them small enough to take " yaller bellies," sun perch).

Another point: the new lines (size H) for minnow casting are elegant. You get a piece of paraffine (if your shops don't have it, get a few paraffine candles); cut it up, put it in a bottle, all you can get in, and fill this up with coal naphtha, the benzine of the shops, at a temperature of say 100° (put the bottle in hot water); it will nearly all dissolve. Put the line in, poke it around for some time, so as to saturate it thoroughly, take it out, hang it in the sun for twenty-four hours, then go over it with a rag and chamois skin, and you will have a semi-waterproof line that casts a minnow twice as far, lasts longer, and in every way is more pleasant to use than any other. By washing it in benzine, if dirty water or dust bothers, and re-paraffining, you can always keep a clean line if necessary. Try this. I think, after soaking the line, the paraffine solution is better to be left until it cools or thickens before the line is taken out, as there is more paraffine precipitated in the fibres of the line. The difference in amount of paraffine wax the benzine will dissolve, between say 50° and 150°, is simply wonderful.

"Sproat" I cling to as a fly-hook, though for bait fishing I have for the last year or more used the Pennell Limerick, cutting off the eye and tying on loops with great success.[1] I think the long projection of point in use of minnow an advantage. It's a splendid hook for bait. Sproat is good enough for me for flies. I think the fancy of "mist-color," etc., is more fancy than anything else. Any neutral color will do. I use "Arnold's ink dye" (see H. P. Wells's book), and had used it before Mr. Wells wrote of it.

One trouble I have had, the tips, — one or three ringed. Agate jewels are all right until cracked. I got a "Dutch" jeweler, friend of mine, to make me a few jewels of steel. They work beautifully. Of course you must wipe them off at night, preferably with an oily rag. They weigh not more than the jewel, and are, as far as my experience goes, perfect.

Now, sir, thanking you for many pleasant hours passed in reading your "Fishing with the Fly," I hope, if you should ever come down to this benighted country, you will send me your card, so I can reach you, and show you a little of the "Old Virginia" not yet entirely dead.

---

[1] The writer does not appear to understand that Pennell Limerick hooks are made with plain shanks, or "tapers," as well as eyed. — M. E. O. M.

| | | |
|---|---|---|
| *Virginia.* | { Black Gnat. <br> White Miller. <br> Queen of the Water. | { Trout. |

COLONEL W. L. BUMGARDNER,                    Staunton,                        Va.

The letters I inclose are from some of our best sportsmen, and if you wish to make use of their contents you are at liberty to do so.

My experience corresponds with Captain Doyle's report. I use all the flies that he speaks of, same-sized hooks and snoods, and a leader nine feet long. I have had good success with the Black Gnat; and in the West Fork of the Greenbrier, as late as seven o'clock in the evening, when I could scarcely see my cast, I have caught with White Millers, and a small fly with a dark body and white wings, as many as three trout at one cast.

The largest trout I ever took was twenty-one inches long, but I had nothing to get his weight. This was taken on a Queen of the Water, in the middle of June, in the West Fork of the Greenbrier.

The North Fork of the Shenandoah is the stream I have been re-stocking for the last four years, and will put more fry in this fall and early spring. You will see from Mr. Henkle's letter what the re-stocking has done; some of the boys had fine sport last spring; larger catches than his have been made. It is about twenty-two miles northwest of Staunton. Fine livery can be had here, and the people are hospitable; they charge from one to one and a half dollars a day. They also have hounds, and can give fine deer hunting in season; there are plenty of pheasants and partridges. The Greenbrier is about seventy-five miles due west; a good hotel, the Traveller's Repose, is situated right in the forks of the river. (A battle was fought there during the late war, called the Greenbrier fight. Not long ago a musket was found in the mountains, the bayonet sticking in the ground, and all well preserved.) The West Branch comes from the Great Cheat Mountains, and the East from the Alleghany Mountains. The fishing is good from April to August.

We have numbers of smaller streams from fifteen to twenty miles, both east in the Blue Ridge, and west in the North Mountain and the Alleghanies.

---

| *Virginia.* | Hackles.<br>Queen of the Water.<br>Red Ibis.<br>Montreal.<br>White Miller.<br>Blue Dun.<br>Cow Dung. | Trout. |

T. S. DOYLE,         Staunton,         Va.

The trout is, as you know, a very capricious fish. At one season he likes one fly, at another season he likes another fly. One day he takes your flies, next day he will not look at them.

Before June, I have always fished with red worms. Grasshoppers and black crickets are deadly later in the season.

A fly-book for Virginia waters should contain an assortment of dark flies.

1. The Hackles, Brown, Gray, Red, and Black.
2. Queen of the Water or the Montreal fly.
3. Red Ibis.
4. White Miller.
5. Blue Dun.
6. Cow Dung.

All should be of medium size, Sproat hooks. I like about a No. 9 or 10 and a four-inch snood. Hook *always* dark. I prefer the brown leaders, six to nine feet; however, they come in three-feet lengths, and you can splice them to any length.

*Virginia.*
$\left\{\begin{array}{l} \text{Coachman.} \\ \text{Queen of the Water.} \\ \text{Professor.} \\ \text{Hackles.} \end{array}\right.$
$\left\{\text{Trout.}\right.$

JOHN M. KINNEY,                    Staunton,                              Va.

The most killing flies used by me in the waters of the North Fork of the Shenandoah River, Augusta County, Virginia, and in the East Fork of the Greenbrier River, in West Virginia (the only streams I fish in), I find to be the Coachman, Queen of the Water, and Professor, the best for May and June fishing; also the Brown and Gray Hackles. These are good for any time of day at those seasons.

It is, in my opinion, very little use to fish with any kind of fly in these waters before the first of May, as the fish feed from the bottom until the insects get well abroad.

The flies I have named are good for all of the summer months as well as May and June. I once saw a fly, made by an amateur, with the feathers from the neck of a female mallard duck, interspersed with white. It was a very deadly fly in the waters I have named, especially late in the season. It was made like a hackle; the ordinary Brown Hackle is something like it, only the fly mentioned had more white in it; the body was peacock green.

I have had some success with the Black Hackle and Black Gnat, but combinations of brown, peacock green, or blue and white, also the colors used in the Queen of the Water, all with the addition of some gold or silver tinsel, seem to be the favorite colors with these fish at all times.

I have had the best success with flies tied on medium-sized hooks. I like the snells and leaders to be tea-colored.

*Virginia.* Trout Flies.

S. H. HENKLE, Staunton, **Va.**

Last year I took over two hundred and fifty trout, and used therefor very dark to light brown and gray until late in the evening, when I used very light colors. I am sorry I cannot give you a more definite account as to exact number taken with each fly; another time I will keep a tabulated record. The size of the hook I prefer is about No. 8, 9, or 10 Sproat.

Many bass are also taken here with the fly.

---

*Virginia.* Yellow Fly. Striped Bass.

CHARLES H. HASWELL, New York, **N. Y.**

I have fished much at the lower falls of the Potomac, and successfully for striped bass, with a yellow fly which is like a fly common in Virginia waters in the spring of the year, except that it is larger and the wings somewhat lighter in color. I send you specimen of the same.

NOTE. — The fly sent was on a No. 4/0 hook, and had a full, yellow body and gray wings.

## PLATE P.

No. 129. Ethel May.

No. 130. Esmeralda.

No. 131. Egg.

No. 132. Fin Fly.

No. 133. Francis Fly.

No. 134. Fern.

No. 135. Green Drake.

No. 136. Furnace.

No. 137. Gosling.

No. 138. Golden-eyed Gauze Wing.

No. 139. Golden Spinner.

No. 140. Greenwell's Glory

No. 141. Great Dun.

No. 142. Grayling Fly.

No. 143. Grizzly King.

No. 129. The Ethel May was first tied as an experiment by C. F. Orvis, in 1884. One was sent with others to Mr. John Henry Applegate, of San Francisco, Cal., who wrote in response: " I see that one of the flies you sent me has no name. My little daughter is always greatly interested in all my flies, and we would like to call this one the Ethel May, after herself." So the fly was named that has since proved successful in Adirondack waters.

No. 130. Esmeralda. We do not know the story of this fly, but its name always reminds us of the pretty little song with its dancing refrain. The fly must have been named " under the spreading greenwood tree," while to the accompaniment of rippling waters somebody sang : —

"A home among the free, Esmeralda, —
Esmeralda, — Zingara ! "

No. 131. The Egg, sometimes known as the " Little Egg," is a fly at one time recommended by Miss Sara J. McBride, a careful student and fly-maker, who for some years continued in her own name the business established by her father, John McBride. She advised the use of the " Little Egg " as a trout fly for the month of July.

No. 132. Fin fly. Those who fish the least are often the most positive regarding ways and methods, and it would almost seem at times as though their intuitions availed to bring them rewards not granted to the more faithful. Mr. Albert

Walker, of Bennington, Vt., is a brisk, cheerful old gentleman, delighting in "all outdoors," and who "goes a-fishing" once or twice a year, when the season first opens, with all the enthusiasm of a boy running away from school with a bent pin and piece of twine.   One day, in the year 1882, when the apple-trees were growing pink, forgetting their years and gnarled joints, he came hurrying into the fly-room, in his hand his "pole," as he had called it for over seventy years, and " now did n't propose to change its name," saying : " I want you to make me a fly to catch fish.   I don't want any of your fancy notions ; when I go a-fishing, I go to bring home something besides stories, and if you will make a fly just as I tell you I 'll show you some fish worth seeing.   I have always used a Coachman, and fastened to it a bit of the fin of the fish, and I want a fly to take the place of that. Make it just like the Coachman ; only make the body of a soft red shade, as near the color of a fish's fin as you can get it."

The " fish-fin bait " was an old idea, but a fly made to represent it and the Coachman together was a new one.   The flies were made on No. 6 and 7 hooks, and the old gentleman went off exulting to the river-side to prove his theories.   His prophecy of a good catch came true, and he yet relies upon the Fin fly, which he declares ought to do away with all other patterns.

Mr. McGregor (" Rob Roy ") wrote in the " Forest and Stream," some years ago, regarding his success with a fly, the description of which was almost identical with that invented by Mr. Walker, though Mr. McGregor did not say what he called it, or that there was any connection in his mind between it and a fish's fin.

No. 133.   The Francis fly originated with and is named after Mr. Francis Francis, an English writer, whose contributions to angling literature are among those most highly valued.   He is the author of many books and papers, chief among which is his " Book on Angling," which every fisherman should own.   Regarding the fly of his name, we quote from this book what he has written of it : —

" The Francis Fly.   It may seem egotism in me to place this fly first on the list ; but, since its invention, from the accounts I have had of its qualifications, from all quarters of the globe where *Salmonidæ* are found, it certainly appears to have gained, as I hope, a well-earned reputation.   I first found it would kill well on the Welsh rivers, where I tested it severely against the far-famed Coch-y-Bonddu ; and in whatever position it was placed, whether as stretcher or dropper, it killed about three fish for one by the Coch-y-Bonddu.   I therefore brought it into public notice, and it was greatly favored. But, neglecting it for a season, I did not use it much; by accident, however, I tried it subsequently in other quarters with greatest success; and since that time, wherever I have gone, I have found it an unfailing resource when any other favorites failed.

" It should be dressed, of course, to suit the water; small for light waters, and large for heavy water or for evening fishing. I have killed well with it dressed on a No. 11 or 12 hook. It is an excellent evening and night fly dressed on a No. 7 or 8 hook, owing to the lively and attractive play of the hackle-point wings. Dressed large, it kills sea trout well, and it has even slaughtered many a lordly salmon; while I have seen large numbers of it, dressed like huge moths, sent out to India to kill mahseer amongst the Himalayas.

" An acquaintance once told me of a prodigious take of very big fish which he made on the Kennet with it dressed large."

No. 134. The Fern. English fishermen know a natural insect resembling a beetle which they call the fern fly. There are two varieties of these: one with blue wing-covers, and the other with more of a red and orange hue; the latter is the one usually imitated. These insects are commonly known as " sailors and soldiers," owing to their colors. They may be found on the water-plants, from which they often drop off into the streams and are seized by the fish.

As they are imitated in varying ways, confusion has arisen in regard to the Fern fly, which has been increased owing to the fact that the fly generally known in this country as the Fern fly is quite unlike the English fly of that name. Ours is an imitation of a tiny moth often found during the daytime, with tightly closed wings, clinging to the under sides of fern leaves, or other brook-side weeds. This Fern fly, or moth, seems best as an evening fly, at which time the natural moths are most restless. It would seem better to have called this the Fern moth, and so avoided confusion by not using a name already appropriated. Charles Cotton described the original imitation of the beetle, saying the body should be " of the fur of a hare's neck; that is, of the color of fern or bracken." He advised it for August.

No. 135. The Green Drake is called " the superior fly of the drake tribes," and every writer on angling seems roused to eloquence when discoursing of the first appearance of this little insect.

An outline sketch of the drakes has been given in Part I. The green drake, like all of its class, is bred in the water, first as an egg, and then as the larva. It usually rises to the surface some time during the month of May, when the pupa skin splits open and the fly emerges. Their length varies slightly, averaging about three fourths of an inch. The body consists of slender joints, tapering to the end, where it terminates in three stylets. It has a pair of oblong wings of delicate green, slightly veined and mottled; when it rests, these stand upright, like the wings on a butterfly; at the base of the larger wings are two tiny rudimentary wings. One wonders to see these flies apparently springing from all parts of the water, but on looking closely we may discover the empty pupa skins floating away with the current. They continue to hatch for three or four weeks, until all are matured. At first they fly but slowly, and seek to rest upon the nearest blade of grass or overhanging bush.

The green drake is the pseudo-imago or sub-imago, as later the fly undergoes yet another change, casting away the garb of delicate green, and appearing in one of soft gray, the wings becoming more transparent and sparkling, and the fly more active in this its final existence. It is then known as the gray drake.

Trout that feed in streams where the green drakes are plentiful are thought to be finer than all others, being firm in flesh and brilliant in color; but " when the green drakes are up," that is, upon the water, it is almost impossible to get the attention of the fish. It is claimed that the natural fly is the only attraction, and many are the successes related of fishing with the same when imitations had failed; nevertheless, imitations are made and used. Those who practice fly-fishing frequently find occasions when the Green Drake seems the only fly of service.

Experiments have been made endeavoring to transplant the natural flies from one stream to another, and it has been found that it can be accomplished. This may become quite a feature in the fish culture of the future. These flies are some-times spoken of as May flies.

Since writing of the green drake there has been published in the columns of " Shooting and Fishing " a very interesting paper on the May fly, its value as fish food, and the possibility of transplanting it to waters hitherto unfrequented by it. Mr. A. N. Cheney, the editor of the fishing department of this journal, is the writer of the article, and we have obtained from him permission to reprint his most able contribution to the history of the green drake, or, as it is called by some anglers. the May fly, hoping that further experiments may be made in the propagation of this desirable insect, for thereby is undoubtedly a means greatly to increase pleasure and profit in fly-fishing.

## STOCKING TROUT WATERS WITH THE MAY FLY.

We read much about stocking or re-stocking waters with different species of fish, but little, in comparison, about stocking waters with fish food.  At one of the meetings of the American Fisheries Society, a fish culturist said : " There is a popular idea that fish can live on water, an idea that it is unnecessary to tell this association is erroneous.  That fish will live long without food is shown by that persecuted fish, the gold-fish, which is kept for months in glass globes without food, the owners declaring that they live ' on what they get from the water.'  That newly hatched fish and small species get some microscopic food in ponds and small streams is well known, but a fish of a quarter of a pound weight requires something more substantial ; besides, fish do not breathe in their food, at least our game fishes do not, but see it first, and then seize it.  It is doubtful if a trout or bass of a quarter of a pound weight can see the minute daphnia and the other small animal life on which it first fed."

Something like ten years ago, I engaged a man to bring me some bait, either gold shiners (bream) or suckers, for the spring lake trout trolling in the month of May, and when he delivered it I found that it consisted of suckers only, and the number he brought and the price he demanded were both large.  To insure a future supply I paid for all that he offered, with the understanding that he should keep in a spring for me all that I did not wish to use at that time.  I did not think of the bait again until October, when I desired some bait larger than common for late black bass fishing on the rocks in deep water, and drove out to get my suckers, and a sorry lot I found.  I then for the first time saw the spring, which was very like a well containing four or five feet of water.  The poor suckers had big heads, a backbone covered with skin, and nothing more.  The man was astonished, as he " thought they would suck in enough to keep them fat ; " and so they would had there been anything to " suck in."

According to Beaumont and Fletcher, —

> " What 's one man's poison, signor,
> Is another's meat or drink."

This is rather too strong an illustration when applied to the matter of food for fishes, but fish of different species, and fish of different ages of the same species, require a diversity of food to arrive at their best conditions.

Upon the character of the food that it eats depends the quality of the flesh of the trout, and of other fishes as well.  This is exemplified by the trout of Wilmurt Lake, in the southern part of Hamilton County, New York. This lake contains no fish life except speckled trout, and the food is entirely insect and crustacean. The lake is on the top of a mountain nine hundred feet above West Canada Creek, and nearly three thousand feet above tide-water, and is made up of springs, which enter from the bottom and sides. The trout are well fed, red-meated, with creamy curds between the flesh flakes, like a fresh run sea salmon, and connoisseurs — men who have eaten all kinds of trout at home and abroad — pronounce them the most delicate and rich in flavor of all the trout kind. General Richard U. Sherman, after a visit to the lake, said : " There is something in the character of the food that, with its abundance, gives the trout not only a rapid growth, but a peculiar richness and delicacy of flavor. I have never known an ill-conditioned fish taken from the lake, and any one who has known much of the Wilmurt trout can recognize them at sight from their plump and symmetrical form and their brilliancy of coloring." This, be it remembered, is caused by a diet of insects in larval and winged stages, and shellfish.

Bourn Pond, situated on the top of one of the spurs of the Green Mountains in Vermont, was once favored as Wilmurt is. The trout of this pond were confined to a diet of insects and crustaceans. The trout were all red-meated, plump, and well fed ; most pleasing to eye and palate, and as delicious as the Wilmurt trout. Perhaps twenty years ago some fishermen went to Bourn Pond in winter to fish through the ice, using for bait live minnows, which they carried with them. When their fishing was over they turned into the water all the minnows that were unused and alive. These minnows have increased, and the flavor of the trout has deteriorated upon a diet of insects, crustaceans, and minnows.

I visited this pond about ten years ago, and there was then but a blazed line through the woods from the wagon road to the pond, and it was so faint and imperfectly blazed that twice it was utterly lost. Some of the trout I found to have red flesh and creamy curds, but others had white flesh and flesh varying in shades of color between white and red, showing the influence of the introduced fish food. Minnows were everywhere abundant in the water, but I noticed all about the pond, where I could see the bottom, that it was fairly paved with the creeper cases of the dun flies. Never before had I seen in any water such a display of creeper cases, nor such evidence of the abundance of insect life.

The creeper cases are hollow cylinders, smooth inside, composed of bark, bits of wood, straws, gravel, etc., all held together by an adhesive substance which the creeper or larva uses in the construction of its tough covering. Each of these cases had once contained a creeper, the larva of a fly, excellent food for trout, and in all probability there was crustacean food as well, for the color of the flesh of the trout plainly indicated it. The sight that I then beheld has ever remained pictured in my memory. The cases, from their size, appeared to be those of the red dun, the largest of the tribe, which flies chiefly at night; but the May fly, the drakes, may have been there as well, but they have no cylindrical cases, like the duns, and they had left no sign.

I have planted fresh-water shrimps for brook trout food, crawfish for black bass food, and urged the planting of smelts and frost fish for the food of land-locked salmon and lake trout, and desired to transplant insect food, although I have not until now seen the way clear to do so.

Last summer I spent nearly two months at Lake George, where the May fly is found in greatest abundance. How abundant I can better tell by relating a fact. The Fort William Henry hotel stands square across the south end of the lake, facing north. It is a five-story structure, with a lake frontage of about three hundred and fifty feet. One year when the May fly was rising, there was a north wind which drove the flies against the hotel. Windows, doors, and all openings on the lake front were closed in consequence of this sudden visitation of choice fish food, but the flies increased until they actually covered the windows and plastered the house until the whole front was stuccoed with green drakes. Last year when I reached the lake the main flight of the May fly was over, and favorable winds would bring the creeper cases to our shore until they formed windrows on the beach ; but one morning I noticed quite a number of flies just liberated, and it occurred to me to see how long they would live for the purpose of transporting them. First, I got an empty biscuit box of tin, put cross-pieces of wood inside for perches, made a number of holes for ventilation, and caught and put into it as many flies as it would comfortably hold. The inner part of a bait bucket made entirely of woven wire caught my eye as it was drying in the sun, and putting down some dried branches from a brush pile into it, I filled that with flies. Some were green, some gray, and a very few were of a purple tinge.

The May fly, or green drake, as the largest of the tribe is called, is familiar to all anglers. The gray drake is the metamorphosis of the female green drake, and the purple or blackish drake is the metamorphosis of the male green drake. I caught the drakes in the morning, soon after breakfast, and twenty-four hours later I looked at them. Some few were dead in the bottom of the box and bucket, but the larger part of them were alive. I was called away that day, and did not see them again, but I was satisfied that they could be transported on a journey of at least twenty-four hours, if taken when they first emerged from the water, which is long enough for all ordinary purposes, and that the experiment of transplanting them would be well worth trying.

The last issue of the "Fishing Gazette," just at hand, contains an article upon stocking trout waters with May fly, written by Major W. G. Turle, and as it contains the only information upon the subject that has ever been printed, so far as I know, I quote from it sufficiently to show the method adopted, and that Major Turle was successful in his experiment.

" It is a well-known fact, of which most fishermen are aware, that the May fly is very eccentric in its choice of habitation. Whilst in one place they will be thick on the water, a hundred yards higher up not a trace of them is to be seen. . . . After thinking the subject well over, I determined to try the experiment — as far as I was aware, a novel one — of transferring the May fly from one part of the river to the other. . . . It was absolutely necessary that the flies should be transferred alive and uninjured. Catching them was easy enough, for they simply swarmed on the bushes like bees in a hive, but to keep them free from damage and unimpaired was 'another pair of shoes.' They are so exceedingly delicate, especially about the wings, and the least injury to the latter would have entirely upset my calculations. It was evident that I required some kind of a cage, well ventilated, and so constructed that no two flies should press against each other ; in fact, what I wanted was a series of perches, on which the flies could rest, like chickens in a fowl house. . . . I procured about six bandboxes and several small baskets, as I calculated sufficient to contain about five thousand flies. With a long thread of worsted I made numerous horizontal lines across the boxes, repeating the rows of worsted at intervals of about two inches until they reached within a short distance of the lids. For ventilation I perforated the boxes in numerous places, and cut a little door, some two inches square, in the lid to drop the flies through. Finally I provided small plugs of cotton wool to prevent their escaping, and then my preparations were all complete."

When the May fly season began, Major Turle employed some boys, and started for grounds frequented by the flies, where he found them early one morning hanging in myriads, on bushes and shrubs, being the " hatch of the previous day." It was a simple matter to pick up the flies, put them in the boxes, " when they generally fell to the bottom, and then climbed up on one or other of the numerous lines. We continued our work until each box was filled with rows and rows of insects, perched like swallows on a telegraph wire." The boxes being filled, they were taken to the place where it was desired that the flies should establish themselves, and where the water was fringed with sedge and alder bushes. " On these I shook out the flies, and watched them for a short time, till I was quite certain they had taken to their new abode. Next evening I went down to see how they were getting on, and rejoiced to find them dancing about in the air, as is their wont, before they drop their eggs in the water ; therefore, in a couple of years (the time generally supposed requisite for the maturing of the eggs) I might reasonably hope to see a rise of fly on that part of the river. In due course my hopes were realized. I congratulated myself that my care and trouble had not been wasted, for the May fly was firmly established."

Later, quite by chance, Major Turle discovered that by transporting the larvæ of the May fly the same result might be obtained as in the case of the transported flies : " From my own observations, I now feel sure that not only a river can be supplied with May fly, but also, if the larvæ is put down in the spring, there will be rise of fly the same year. . . . The May fly is a valuable addition to any stream, for it not only gets the trout into first-rate condition, but also affords those who are not specially skillful with the small fly a good fortnight or three weeks by means of the larger and more easily manipulated one."

Major Turle's experiments demonstrated that the May fly season can be lengthened. In some waters they rise earlier than in others, and if the earlier-rising flies are trans-planted to waters containing the same fly which rises two weeks later, the transplanted fly will continue to rise on the same date as in the original water, thus lengthening the season in the new water by two weeks. The ordinary season of the May fly is three to four weeks, although there will be some rises earlier and later, but the great flight proba-bly is not more than during two or three weeks.

Major Turle has made it plain that there is a margin of at least forty-eight hours in which the fly can be safely transported, and its establishment in new waters secured, and the operation is such a very simple one that it is well worth trying wherever there are brook trout waters lacking the May fly. This is a matter that must be undertaken by anglers, and the result to be obtained by successfully adding this fly to the food supply of the trout will certainly warrant the time and trouble necessary to bring it about. The question of food for our game fishes is one that will demand more attention from the anglers in the future than has been accorded it in the past.

No. 136. The Furnace fly is one of the oldest patterns. It is sometimes made without wings, the peacock body wound with a furnace hackle, but the winged fly seems oftener preferred nowadays. The "furnace hackle" wound to make a palmer body is the chief feature of the fly, and the source of its name.

No. 137. The Gosling receives its name from its soft yellow tinge, akin to that of the young goslings before their feathers have fully appeared. It is usually made quite small, and esteemed for midsummer fishing for trout.

No. 138. The Golden-eyed Gauze Wing, or the Chrysopa, is spoken of in Part I., and drawings of the eggs, larva, and mature form may be seen in the plate giv-ing the sixth class, or beetles. According to Comstock, " the female, before laying an egg, emits from the end of her body a small drop of a tenacious substance ; this is drawn into a thread by lifting the abdomen, then an egg is placed on the tip end of the thread. These threads or stalks (see engraving, Part I.) are often attached to the leaves of plants infested with aphis. The larvæ hatch from these eggs, and feed upon tiny plant lice. Gardeners appreciate them highly because of this fact."

After feeding for a time the larva spins about itself a tiny round silken cocoon having a little lid over a small opening; through this opening the fly emerges. There are several species; those most desired are of a pale apple-green tint, or a lighter and yellower shade. They vary somewhat, also, in size, and possess an unpleasant odor. They are numerous during the summer months from early in June. These flies can be well imitated by means of the fish-scale wings.

No. 139. The Golden Spinner should properly be made very small and light, but, like so many other well-known patterns, a combination of colors has been found effective, heavier waters and strong fish calling for more substantial tackle, and so copies are exaggerated until they lose much of their resemblance to the natural insects. Personally, we think most of the Spinners should be dressed as hackles, or with the most slender, delicate wings; but the popular dressing of this fly has proved so serviceable that a strict observance of nature must yield to practical demonstrations, though only a similarity of color seems to be preserved to recall the original insect from which it was named.

No. 140. Greenwell's Glory, introduced to the fishermen of Durham by the Rev. Canon Greenwell, is a fly well known to British anglers, and is in considerable favor in this country also. Mr. Francis, in his "Book on Angling," advises its being dressed on the "smallest possible hook," and affirms that "it will kill well in the hottest weather."

No. 141. We are indebted to Charles Cotton for the Great Dun, which he describes in his addition to the "Compleat Angler" as follows: "We make use, in this month (February), also of a Great Dun, made with dun bear's hair, and the wings of the gray feather of a mallard near unto his tail, which is absolutely the best fly that can be thrown upon a river this month, and with which an angler shall have admirable sport."

No. 142. The Grayling fly is the one sent to us by Mr. G. Henry Shearer, of Bay City, Mich., who wrote of it, "The Grayling fly I inclose was copied from a fly found on the Au Sable River some years ago by my friend, F. L. Westover, and our success with it was so good that we have used it ever since."

We have in this country three species of grayling. The first was discovered in 1819 by the Sir John Franklin expedition to the North Pole, and was named by Sir John Richardson. The origin of the name he gives as follows: " Its highly appropriate Esquimaux name (' Hewlook Powak '), denoting ' wing-like,' alludes to its magnificent dorsal, and it was in reference to the same feature that I bestowed upon it the specific appellation of *signifer*, or the ' standard-bearer,' intending, also, to advert to the rank of my companion, Captain Back, then a midshipman, who took the first specimen with an artificial fly. It is found only in clear waters, and seems to delight in the most rapid parts of the mountain streams." It was some years after this, in 1860, grayling were discovered in Montana by Surgeon J. F. Head, of the United States army, and were described by Professor Milner, in 1874, as *Thymallus montanus*. Professor Manly Miles, in 1864, sent to Professor Cope specimens of grayling from streams in Michigan. These fish had heretofore been known as " Michigan trout," but Professor Cope classified them as *Thymallus tricolor*. It was not until several years after that general interest was awakened in this beautiful fish, of which Mr. Fred Mather has written : " The very name of my beloved fish calls up a picture that, above all others, is the most cheerful adorning memory's wall. . . . The trout fisher needs no special directions or tackle to fish for grayling ; he may cast in the usual manner, only remembering that the fish has a very tender mouth, and must be treated with this fact ever in mind. . . . I have killed, I believe, every game fish in America east of the Rocky Mountains, except the salmon, for which I have a rod in readiness that I hope to use soon ; and I can say that while I do not think the grayling the superior of them all for gameness, yet there is something of romance in the remembrance of the grayling, a kind of sentimental retrospect, that endears the fish to me above all others. Whether it was owing to the pine woods and the genial companionship I do not care to consider, but each year there comes a longing to repeat the pleasant experiences of the Au Sable and its delicate grayling."

The grayling found in the colder streams of Europe is practically the same as the American grayling ; only experienced eyes can detect the differences. It was in earlier times called the "umber." This *Thymallus vulgaris*, or European grayling, grows to a larger size than the grayling found in America, and is in consequence, perhaps, somewhat less spirited. This may account for Andrew Lang's assertions in his charming "Confessions of a Duffer," wherein he relates : "I once did manage to make a cast correctly ; the fly went over the fish's nose ; he rose ; I hooked him, and he was a great silly brute of a grayling. The grayling is the deadest-hearted and the foolishest-headed fish that swims. I would as lief catch a perch or an eel as a grayling. This is the worst of it, — this ambition of the duffer's, this desire for perfection, as if the golfing imbecile should match himself against Mr. Horace Hutchinson, or as the sow of the Greek proverb challenged Athene to sing. I know it all, I deplore it, I regret the evils of ambition ; but *c'est plus fort que moi.* If there is a trout rising well under the pendent boughs that trail in the water, if there is a brake of briers behind me, a strong wind down stream, for that trout, in that impregnable situation, I am impelled to fish. If I raise him, I strike, miss him, catch up in his tree, swish the cast off into the briers, break my top, break my heart, but — that is the humor of it. The passion or instinct, being in all senses blind, must, no doubt, be hereditary. It is full of sorrow and bitterness and hope deferred, and entails the mockery of friends, especially the fair. But I would as soon lay down a love of books as a love of fishing.

"Success with pen or rod may be beyond one, but there is the pleasure of the pursuit, the rapture of endeavor, the delight of an impossible chase, the joys of nature, — sky, trees, brooks, and birds. Happiness in these things is a legacy to us of the barbarian. Man in the future will enjoy bricks, asphalt, fog, machinery, 'society,' even picture galleries, as many men and most women do already. We are fortunate who inherit the older, not 'the new spirit,' — we who, skilled or unskilled, follow in the steps of our father Izaak, by streams less clear, indeed, and in meadows less fragrant than his. Still, they are meadows and streams, not wholly dispeopled yet of birds and trout ; nor can any defect of art nor certainty of laborious disappointment keep us from the water-side when April comes.

"Next to being an expert, it is well to be a contented duffer : a man who would fish if he could, and who will pleasure himself by flicking off his flies, and dreaming of impossible trout, and smoking among the sedges Hope's enchanted cigarettes. Next time we shall be more skilled, more fortunate. Next time! 'To-morrow, and to-morrow, and to-morrow.' Gray hairs come, and stiff limbs, and shortened sight ; but the spring is green and hope is fresh for all the changes in the world and in ourselves. We can tell a hawk from a handsaw, a March Brown from a Blue Dun, and if our success be as poor as ever, our fancy can dream as well as ever of better things and more fortunate chances. For fishing is like life ; and in the art of living, too, there are duffers, though they seldom give us their confessions. Yet even they are kept alive, like the incompetent angler, by this undying hope : they will be more careful, more skillful, more lucky, next time. The gleaming untraveled future, the bright untried waters, allure us from day to day, from pool to pool, till, like the veteran on Coquet side, we 'try a farewell throw,' or, like Stoddart, look our last on Tweed."

No. 143. The Grizzly King is similar to the Professor, except that it has grizzly feet, or hackle, and a green body. It is supposed to have been a favorite fly with Professor James Wilson, a brother of John Wilson (Christopher North), and to have been named by him. It appears to have become even more generally used in this country than in England and Scotland, being of service here for black bass as well as trout, the size being varied to suit the fish and the locality. This is the fly mentioned by Mr. Seth Green as one of his favorite cast, and sometimes called by him the " Under Wind."

Mr. Wakeman Holberton has sent to us a fly similar to the Grizzly King, but with " cheeks " or side feathers of red ibis placed over the mallard. It is known to some fishermen, when dressed in this way, as the " Bass Grizzly," and is similar to the fly shown in the plate as Holberton II. The two flies are undoubtedly the same, confusion having arisen from the alterations made by some fly-maker. It is probably needless to add that the Grizzly King, when tied for black bass fishing, is made on much larger hooks than the fly shown in this list.

*Virginia.*
$$\left\{\begin{array}{l}\text{Queen of the Water.}\\\text{Coachman.}\\\text{Hackles.}\\\text{Black Gnat.}\\\text{White Miller.}\end{array}\right.$$
$\left\{\begin{array}{l}\text{Trout.}\end{array}\right.$

JAMES BUMGARDNER, JR.,                    Staunton,                    **Va.**

My experience is confined to the streams of the mountains of Virginia and West Virginia, of which the headwaters of the Greenbrier River are the best. My fishing has generally been in the months of June and July.

Ordinarily, I use but three flies, viz., the Queen of the Water, the Gray or Brown Hackle, and the Coachman. In the middle of the day and in the bright sunshine, I substitute the Black Gnat for the Coachman ; and in very dark days and late in the evening I use the Miller in place of the Coachman. The mountaineers of this region, who are unscientific, but very successful, use the Queen of the Water alone, and will buy or accept no other.

I have tried in this vicinity all the well-known flies, and all are useless except the varieties above named. I have been most successful with flies of small size.

All of my experiments with new flies, *i. e.* new patterns, have resulted in failure. I have gone, during each of the last five or six years, with a party of six, to the upper Greenbrier River. After trying all of the ordinary flies in use, we have come to the conclusion that the Queen of the Water, Coachman, Gray and Brown Hackles, with the Black Gnat in bright sunshine, and the Miller in dark days and late in the evening, are not only the most efficient, but are all that are necessary.

On our last trip our catch was 1,248, in about five days of fishing, of which over half were taken with the Queen of the Water.

I prefer clear snells to the stained, and as small in size as will give strength to hold the fish. They should be single, with short loops.

---

|            |                                                                                        |         |
| ---------- | -------------------------------------------------------------------------------------- | ------- |
| *Virginia.* | Coachman.<br>Brown Hackle.<br>Queen of the Water.<br>White Miller.<br>Black Gnat.      | Trout.  |

F. R. WEBB,        Staunton,        Va.

For trout fishing in the North Fork of the Shenandoah River, Va., and the Greenbrier River during June and July, I find the list of flies given the most effective. Large-winged white flies in particular are more useful in the evening. I get more strikes at the tail fly (fly at end of the line) than any other, regardless of kind of fly.

---

|                  |                                                            |             |
| ---------------- | ---------------------------------------------------------- | ----------- |
| *West Virginia.* | Brown Hackle.<br>Cow Dung.<br>Montreal.<br>Scarlet Ibis.   | Black Bass. |

NEIL ROBINSON,        Coalburgh,        W. Va.

The Gauley, Elk, and Coal rivers are tributaries of the Great Kanawha. Over these streams and the James I have fished for a number of years for black bass. After trying all kinds, characters, and descriptions of available flies, I have settled down to the following as better than all others combined: first and foremost, a medium-sized Brown Hackle; then in order, Cow Dung, Montreal, Black Hackle, Gray Hackle, and Scarlet Ibis. I have tested the value of these flies by using one at a time in connection with something different, changing position on the leader and counting strikes on each fly. While still using a variety, it has almost become a rule with me to use one Hackle, a Montreal, or a Cow Dung all the time.

Heavy single gut leaders and single snells, smoke-colored, with a light hook, seem to answer better than anything else, as a general rule. In case of a strong wind, one small shot, used while the wind lasts, will overcome any objection to the use of the single gut and light hook.

I have never had any success with hooks larger than No. 3 or No. 2, unless in trolling, and even then No. 2 is about the best size. This is our experience with bass ranging from three fourths of a pound to three pounds.

---

| *West Virginia.* | { Queen of the Water.<br>{ The Owner. | { Black Bass. |

E. D. Bowly,          Shepherdstown,          W. Va.

The Queen of the Water I have invariably found the most killing for large-mouth bass in the Potomac River, whereas the Grizzly King did better in the Shenandoah, although the bass of the latter stream are so eager to take anything in the shape of a fly that it is very hard to make a choice. I have also had good luck with a fly which is known in this locality as the Owner, being the invention of a very dear friend of mine by that name.

He makes this fly fully as large as the drawing,[1] and it is astonishing how small-mouth bass will take it when the water is slightly "milky," especially on the Potomac. With this fly as a stretcher and a Queen of the Water as a dropper, I raised and killed sixteen good bass in eight casts, not consecutively, and within a half hour,

[1] The drawing inclosed in letter appears to be of a No. 4/0 Sproat hook.

Made by C.F.ORVIS, Manchester,Vt.

PLATE Q: DESCRIPTION PAGE 297

Made by C.F.ORVIS, Manchester,Vt.

PLATE R: DESCRIPTION PAGE 315

Made by C.F.ORVIS, Manchester,Vt.

PLATE S: DESCRIPTION PAGE 327

Made by **C.F.ORVIS**, Manchester,Vt.

M. Bradley Co.Lith.

PLATE T: DESCRIPTION PAGE 349

taking also within the same time six others singly, all of which took the Queen. I may state here that I tie my Queens of the Water with much lighter yellow bodies than those usually sold. My reason for so doing is the fact that our river (the Potomac) is very seldom perfectly clear when the fish are rising at their best, and I think the light color more easily seen by them. I have tested this myself, by lying flat on my back in three or four feet of water of all shades of murkiness, and I found the light yellow showed yellow, while the orange might have been any other color; hence I am a strong advocate of all the lighter colors, especially for the bodies. The wings show true to their color, minus a slight clouding; the hackles also show better than the bodies. As regards size, I have invariably found a medium fly, as well as hook, to be the best for all waters that I have fished. A hook the size shown here (about No. 1) is my favorite and I think the Sproat the only hook suitable for flies.

I am partial to flies with very narrow and short wings, and made stiff enough to stand up well when wet; there are hundreds of flies on sale that are beautiful when dry, but wet them and this is what you have: a thing that might pass for a " bag-worm," but the fish could never mistake it for a fly.

I would advise all anglers to tie their flies to stand out well in the water, without regard to their appearance when dry.

Another killing fly for our waters is a modification of the colors entering into the Queen of the Water, yellows, browns, reds, grays, (mottled) and gold and silver, made into palmers and hackles, tied so as to make the hackle stand out well.

I use the usual four-inch snell reinforced at the hook; by being reinforced at the end of the hook, the gut does not bend and wear where it joins the shank of the hook, as the long limber space above the reinforcing piece is the only part that bends much, and that is long enough to prevent short "kinks," which are so fatal to gut-snells when often repeated.

I also find that the farther from the leader the dropper fly is, the better.

I stain the gut by saturating a piece of sponge with ink, and drawing the snells over it before knotting them, and then drying.

I think a ribbing of "arrasene" (wool chenille) on the bodies of flies adds to their deceptive qualities.

---

| *West Virginia and Colorado.* | { Coachman. Royal Coachman. Brown Hackle. Black Hackle. | { Trout. |
|---|---|---|

A. P. TALLMAN,         Bellaire,         Ohio.

My favorite flies among the well-known ones are the White Coachman, the Royal Coachman, and the Brown Hackle. I rarely use any others. I find them the most successful where I have tried the fly in late years, namely, in West Virginia streams and in Colorado. In the latter named waters, especially the upper Rio Grande, the Coachman, and the Black Hackle wrapped with silver tinsel, are the flies used by almost every one, but I have never been successful with a black fly in the West Virginia waters.

If I were to formulate a theory in regard to flies, leaders, loops, seasons and propitious times of day would be evolved from my experience season after season in West Virginia waters; but to tell the truth, I have no theories. I have thought at times I had, and that I could afford to give some sage advice as to the points noted above, but a subsequent experience " knocked them all out."

Many years of June outing told me that June is the time of all others ; then the very next season in July upset everything, and showed July to be just as good a month as June, in some years. As to time of day, I find there is no use to settle down upon some favorite hour. I have taken just as many trout at noon as at any hour of the morning or evening.

# PLATE Q.

No. 144. Governor.

No. 145. Golden Monkey.

No. 146. Royal Governor.

No. 147. Gray Drake.

No. 148. Grannom.

No. 149. General Hooker.

No. 150. Hare's Ear.

No. 151. Southside.

No. 152. Hofland's Fancy.

No. 153. Hamlin.

No. 154. Great Red Spinner.

No. 155. Hawthorn.

No. 156. Hoskins.

No. 157. Hod.

No. 158. Iron-blue Dun.

No. 144. The original of the Governor is supposed to have been, not a fly, but a small beetle. The imitation was first popular in the south of England, but has since been heartily adopted in America, with a slight change in its composition; in England the Governor being usually made with a yellow or bright orange floss tip, while in America it is made with a tip of brilliant red silk. There they have also a variation called the *Mackerel* Governor, but this distinction is not observed in this country.

No. 145. Golden Monkey. The history of this fly is obscure, and attempts to account for it are rather guesswork than the assertion of positive facts. It is a favorite because often successful, and probably successful because similar to many other reliable patterns. We wish, however, that it had been given a more reasonable name, and one less baffling to inquiries, as our best efforts have elicited only the facts that it is, has been, and probably will continue to be a favorite fly.

No. 146. The Royal Governor is only a variety of the old Governor just mentioned. The fashion of making it with a band of red silk in the middle of the body, à la Royal Coachman, originated in the Western States. The silk strengthens and brightens the fly, and by many is thought to be an improvement. The designation "Royal" was derived from the application of the same term to the Coachman when made in a similar manner. This dressing is better known west of the Mississippi than in the East, being especially popular in Colorado and Montana.

No. 147.  The natural Gray Drake is the perfection or last transition of the female Green Drake.  Its existence is short, but in compensation it seems endowed with superior animation and delicacy.  The wings are transparent and iridescent, with fine black veinings, and the segments of the body are distinctly defined. Swarms of these flies may be found in the vicinity of the streams in early evening, each fly in continuous motion, and often approaching the water that will receive the eggs and convey them into some resting-place until the tiny creeper is ready to venture forth, and in turn become a perpetuator of the species.

The parent fly, or Gray Drake, survives but a short time after laying its eggs, and as it becomes weaker and less vigorous in its flights often falls into the water, and becomes an easy prey to the watchful, waiting fish.

The imitation of the Gray Drake has long been used as an evening fly, and in this respect is valuable, the trout frequently seeming to distinguish and prefer it to that of the Green Drake, but the latter is generally considered more successful. The theory is that the trout are more familiar with the aquatic larva or creeper, and the Green Drake, when first emerging from the pupa, is somewhat sluggish in its movements and an easier victim to its enemy the trout, who then pursue it to the exclusion of all others ; indeed, by some fishermen it is thought useless to attempt to lure the fish when the Green Drake is "on" or rising, but a successful imitation will often score an astonishing catch.  After the fly is well "up" and the metamorphosis complete, and the Green Drake becomes the Gray Drake, the fish find uncertainty in their pursuit, and are less determined in it ; this is perhaps a reason why an imitation of the Gray Drake is less apt to raise them, though it seems astonishing that the fish appear so often able to distinguish the slight difference between the two ; however, at times the Gray Drake will awaken an eagerness accorded to but few other flies.  Properly it should be made small, but in America, like most of the well-known trout-fly patterns, it is often tied on a large hook, and the exaggerated copy successfully used in heavy, deep waters.

No. 148.  The Grannom, also known as the Green-tail and Shell fly, is an imitation of one of the duns, order Trichoptera.  It is peculiar in appearing in some seasons in multitudes, while in other years but few will be seen ; the cause of this is yet to be ascertained.  When first hatched, the insects are much paler in color than after they have been some time exposed to the air ; consequently they are frequently imitated in different shades, and each maker seems to vary the representatives to suit his own fancy. That in the plate is thought to be the one best liked in this country. The tiny tuft of silk suggests the cluster of eggs that are always apparent in the female of this species of caddis flies.

No. 149. The General Hooker, whether named after the famous general in the war of the rebellion or as a play upon words, is undoubtedly of American origin. Miss Sara J. McBride is the only writer who refers to it, though the fly has been well known for some time. She mentions it as an effective imitation of one of the Phryganidæ, or stone flies, or browns, as Theakston calls them. We have understood that this fly was one of Miss McBride's own designs, but of this we have no positive information, although the first fly of the name that we ever saw came from Miss McBride when she was located at Mumford, N. Y.

No. 150. To give the complete history of the Hare's Ear, sometimes called the Hare Lug, would be to write of the season's changes and review the angling literature of centuries. It will be easier to state that the name arises from the material composing the body of the artificial insect, namely, the fur or down from the inner part of the hare's ear, and that it is an imitation of one of the many forms or shades of the drakes or cocktails, called by Theakston the Blue Drake, but to the confusion of many also known as the Blue Dun. Each author gives his favorite method for copying these drakes or "blue duns," until the multitude of copies almost rivals in numbers their prototypes. Mr. Francis writes : " This is, perhaps, one of the best known and most generally used flies in the kingdom. It is known equally as the Early Dark Dun, the Hare's Ear, and the Cocktail. In Lancashire, Cumberland, and that district, it is the Blue Bloa ; in Yorkshire, the Blue Drake ; in Devonshire, the Hare's Pluck, the Hare's Fleck, and the Blue Upright ; in fact, its names are as endless as those of the salmon fry, and it is a common favorite upon every river from Caithness to Cornwall. It varies slightly in color, according to temperature and season. If the day be cold and bleak, it has a darker tinge than in warmer and more genial weather. Grizzled fibres pulled from the hare's ear are favorite materials for the body, and these are warped in sometimes with yellow silk and sometimes with olive silk, so that the color may be seen which gives the variety required."

There are but few writers mentioning artificial flies who do not describe and recommend several varieties of the blue duns, sometimes giving a list of imitations to cover the entire season, each varying slightly to accommodate the weather or month. Reference has been made to the variations in these imitations in the note upon the Blue Dun. All these designs are useful; the one shown in the plate is only one of the popular types. The Gold-ribbed Hare's Ear is another that is much liked.

It is in their attention to detail that the fly-fishermen of Great Britain differ from the majority of those in America; the former observing more closely the originals, and copying more carefully their variations and gradations, while the anglers of this country have so far been content to depend upon a few standard types to represent a class.

In conclusion, it may be interesting to those who have not happened to see Mr. David Foster's "Scientific Angler" to read his very original assertion in connection with the Drakes and Browns, showing, as it does, the opposing conclusions arrived at by different observers. We cannot, however, wholly indorse Mr. Foster's opinion and reduction of the species, but he may be wise in an inclination to limit them more than is done by other naturalists, and respect should certainly be felt for his years of observation. His statement is as follows : " In taking, first, the most important order of naturals (the Ephemeridæ family), we deal with what has hitherto been made a most intricate and formidable list of insects, modern naturalists dividing and subdividing into sections and sub-sections, until the poet Pope's "thousands of winged insects" threaten to descend from the ideal into stern reality. Personal observations, extending over a period of fifty years, lead us to affirm the greater part of this extensive classification to be perfectly needless. There are, in fact, but four different species of up-winged insects, these forming the Ephemeridæ family. The prevailing temperature of the atmosphere and the water at the time the larva and pupa are arriving at the state of maturity is largely instrumental in influencing the color, the body of the insect being susceptible to change from these effects." He then states at length the order of change in some forms to illustrate his assertions, that of the Blue Dun, or Cock-winged Dun, according to his theories, being a notable instance.

No. 151. The Southside Club has its preserve and club houses on Long Island. Its members, as a rule, are men of wealth, and everything possible is done to make the appointments perfect in all that conduces to the pleasure and comfort of the members and their guests. The ponds of the association are splendidly stocked with large trout, and fortunate is the angler who is privileged to fish in them. The flies and other tackle used are generally fine, and the Southside fly, named after the club, is a fair representative, in size and color, of those most successful on these fishing-grounds.

**No. 152.** In the " Fly-Fishers' Manual," by T. C. Hofland, published in London in 1839, the author writes as follows regarding the Hofland Fancy: " This fly, from its having been my great favorite for many years, has, by my friends, been named as above, and I am convinced of its excellence as a general fly. I am content to adopt it. Mr. Willingham, formerly of the Strand, sold great numbers of them under this name. I have had sport with it in most parts of England. . . . I rarely use any other fly as a stretcher. I have killed trout with this fly at Farmingham when the May fly has been strong on the water, and the fish had refused any other I could offer. It may be used after sunset, in any part of the kingdom, and in any season."

**No. 153.** Dr. Thaddeus Up de Graff first introduced the Hamlin to the public in the pages of his book entitled " Camping Out, or Bodines." He relates graphically his pleasures and triumphs, some of which were due to the Hamlin, so named after a friend who shared with him many of his experiences. As Mr. Up de Graff in his book describes distinctly the construction of this fly, it would seem that there could be no question regarding the correctness of it, yet there is a large showy fly, somewhat resembling the Gold Doctor, that has been used of late at Middle Dam, Maine. It is utterly unlike the Hamlin, yet for some reason which we cannot ascertain is known by that name, causing confusion and error regarding the true Hamlin as described by Dr. Up de Graff.

**No. 154.** The Great Red Spinner has, from earliest times, been much noticed, imitated, and used by fishermen, but confusion exists regarding its name.

The natural insect is the imago of the March Brown, belonging to the order Ephemeroptera, and from its shape is one of the drakes. Herein is where Theakston's nomenclature proves itself consistent and intelligible, for he very properly calls the fly the Red Drake, in accord with its color and shape.

Observe here the contradiction and carelessness of the common parlance. The ever popular March Brown, if we accept its shape and color as a guide for naming it, is a Brown Drake, and in the course of its development undergoes a change in color, when it becomes the Red Drake. This is in natural sequence and easy to comprehend and remember, but, according to the old method, the fly, when it issues from the pupa, is called a March Brown ; after existing a short time in the sub-imago, it passes into the next state, becomes more active and brilliant, and of a reddish hue, but for some unknown cause, suddenly and mysteriously, its entire name is changed, and it is no longer known as the March Brown, or any name by which we may trace a relationship to its early existence, but is called the Great Red Spinner.

No one could imagine any possible connection between its two forms under these two names. It may be said that it is not needful that the angler should be fully informed, but we assume always that greater pleasure is felt in using all imitations intelligently, and curiosity often aroused regarding the originals of the imitations, and sometimes fuller information sought. It is much easier to acquire the latter when not confused by misleading terms.

Some writers are more reasonable, and call the sub-imago of the Great Red Spinner the Dark Mackerel, and the imago the Light Mackerel ; why Mackerel we cannot say, unless from some association with a " mackerel sky," as the March Brown (Dark Mackerel) and the Great Red Spinner (Light Mackerel) are both more apt to be upon the water during a shower or windy weather ; being lively, strong-flying insects, they sustain themselves well in the air until driven down to the water by wind or rainfall, when the trout will seize them ravenously.

Like the sub-imago and imago of the Green and Gray Drakes, the Brown Drake or March Brown, *i. e.* the first form of the fly, is thought more alluring than the second, the Red Drake or Great Red Spinner, but both, whether in the natural or artificial forms, are favorites of the trout.

We cannot resist once more calling attention to the confusion existing by the old haphazard way of naming, and the puzzle created for the beginner when he seeks to learn something of the angler's entomology, — one moment a fly is a Brown, the next a Mackerel or a Spinner. We cannot expect to undo what has been established, but can we not seek to avoid further confusion, and hereafter let some portion of a designation be the same for all forms of the same insect, whether speaking of it as larva, pupa, sub-imago, or imago, and then distinguish each form by a name indicating its chief characteristic at each period of its existence, — this characteristic may be of color, action, or abode, — and so, in the angler's entomology, let all forms have an appropriate family name and a prefixed name, corresponding to the surname and Christian name of mortals? The Latin language provides perfectly for these distinctions, but the English can be made to convey simply and clearly all that is needful. Furthermore, why not let the naming be always as complete a description as possible of the insect, reserving other and fanciful appellations for flies that are not imitations of natural insects?

The copy shown in the plate is somewhat incorrect in resemblance to the natural fly, which is more amber or orange red in tone; but this is the dressing that has proved very successful, and is widely known and fished with as the Great Red Spinner.

No. 155. Hawthorn. Dame Juliana Berners wrote of "a bayte that bredyth on a hawthorn;" and later, Izaak Walton mentions as useful " the smal black fly, or hawthorn fly, which is all black and not very big, but very smal, the smaller the better, to be had on any hawthorn-bush after the leaves be come forth."

The hawthorn bush is not as common in America as in England, but the insect is often to be seen, and its imitation has been used with success, especially in the mountain streams of Pennsylvania. An American writer says of the habits of the hawthorn fly on our own streams: "Its life is beneath the surface of the earth eleven months of every year, but it finally comes crawling, creeping out of the ground on warm June mornings, appareled in new livery. After resting awhile on low herbage, all, as if by one impulse, fly to the nearest stream. We have kept these insects for weeks in confinement, and they would neither eat nor drink. But every morning, for hours, they congregate over streams; keeping time with the ripple of the water, they hold a dance; darting hither and thither, occasionally touching the waters to go down with the current, or else down the throat of a fish. When these bright creatures are holding high carnival above, the trout positively refuse other enticement."

No. 156. The Hoskins, named after a gentleman living in western New York, well known as a successful angler, is a fly greatly depended upon by those accustomed to using it. The wings should be hyaline and very slightly mottled; the tail, or stylets, of genuine golden-pheasant crest, not a dyed feather; and the hackle a true dun: these, with the delicate yellow body, make a most desirable combination, resembling some of the drakes or Ephemeroptera.

**No. 157.** During our first acquaintance with trout flies, the Hod was given to us by Mr. Henry Morse, of Rochester, N. Y., who stated that it was an excellent fly for the Caledonia Creek and Ulster and Sullivan County streams of his State; also that he believed it to be the invention of Miss Sara J. McBride. She mentions it in an essay as " one of the most familiar imitations of the Phryganidæ," or caddis flies. Mr. Morse was a wonderfully graceful fly-caster, and perhaps as skillful a fisherman as we ever met. A favorable opinion from him of the merits of any fly was most convincing.

**No. 158.** Mr. Francis Francis, in his " Angler's Book," has written such an explicit and entertaining account of the Iron Blue that, after his enthusiastic description, any other attempt must seem utterly commonplace; we therefore beg any one interested in the fly, if they have not already done so, to read what Mr. Francis has written of it. Other authors have written of this attractive little member of the Ephemeroptera, till there seems no end to the names applied and the endeavors to imitate it correctly.

In Yorkshire, the Iron Blue is called the Little Dark Watchet, and Mr. T. E. Pritt, in his book on Yorkshire trout flies, gives four different methods for its imitation, and says of it: " The Dark Watchet is one of the daintiest morsels with which you can tempt a trout, and one of the most difficult to imitate satisfactorily."

Mr. Frederic M. Halford, in his illustrated book on " Floating Flies," also gives four careful dressings for this much-discussed fly.

Ronalds, Aldam, Jackson, Wade, Foster, almost every writer on artificial flies, give special attention to the fly and its various imitations. It is spoken of by them as the Iron-blue Drake, Little Dark Blue, Little Dark Dun, Dark Watchet, etc.

After their existence as aquatic insects, the natural flies arise from the pupæ in multitudes as iron blues, arousing the appetites of the trout. At the end of their short lives as iron blues they cast their sub-imago skins, and attain their last and perfect forms, when they are known to anglers as jenny spinners. While iron blues they vary in hue, and, to accommodate different localities and seasons, it is recommended that every fly-book contain imitations of several different shades. The correct imitations should always be small.

The fly shown in the plate is a very dark specimen, but one that has been generally popular, though many other dressings are used here as well as in Great Britain.

I call to mind the summer day,
   The early harvest mowing,
The sky with sun and clouds at play,
   And flowers with breezes blowing.

I hear the blackbird in the corn,
   The locust in the haying,
And, like the fabled hunter's horn,
   Old tunes my heart is playing.

                   WHITTIER.

# OHIO.

Dr. James A. Henshall . . . { Golden Dustman. Henshall. Oconomowoc. Polka, etc.

Hugh Hardy . . . . . . . { Gov. Alvord. Chippy. Lake George, etc.

Jeptha G. Dunlap . . . . . { Gov. Alvord. Lake George. Grizzly King, etc.

J. B. McKimm . . . . . . . { Holberton I. Alexandra. Oriole.

George W. Upton . . . . . . { Brown Palmer. Bee. Seth Green. Coachman, etc.

John L. Miner . . . . . . . { Silver Doctor. Professor. Royal Coachman, etc.

S. M. Harper . . . . . . . { New Flies for Black Bass.

H. A. Shirwin . . . . . . . { Gray Hackle. Brown Hackle. Montreal.

S——— . . . . . . . { Professor. Governor. Golden Pheasant. Coachman, etc.

Ohio.
⎧ Golden Dustman.
⎪ Montreal.
⎪ Polka.
⎪ King of the Water.
⎨ Abbey.          ⎰ For Florida Fishing
⎪ Henshall.       ⎱ and Black Bass.
⎪ Oconomowoc.
⎪ Oriole.
⎪ Lord Baltimore.
⎩ Red Ibis.

DR. JAMES A. HENSHALL,                 Cincinnati,                 Ohio.

Replying to your questions anent flies, will say that I restrict my assortment to about a dozen, which I find answer usually all the requirements of fly-fishing.

For black bass I find the best " general flies " that can be used with a great prospect of success, almost anywhere and at any time of day, are Montreal, Polka, King of the Water, and Abbey. These are all red-bodied. Next to these I reckon Professor, Oconomowoc, Grizzly King, and Oriole, which are nearly as good, especially on shady streams.

On very dark days or for late afternoon, Coachman, Henshall, Oriole, White Miller are not to be excelled, I think.

Golden Dustman, Lord Baltimore, and Red Ibis are good, especially on open waters, or lakes, ponds, and wide streams, on light days.

The Henshall and Oconomowoc, when about the size of trout flies, cannot be excelled for " crappies " or " fresh-water striped bass."

For Florida fishing I have found the Golden Dustman, Professor, Polka, and Montreal very good on bright days; but for evening or dark days, the Coachman, Oriole, White Miller, and Henshall seemed somewhat better.

The following are original with me, and the date of their designing: Polka and Oriole, 1870; Henshall and Oconomowoc, 1872;
Golden Dustman, 1883.

I am partial to Sproat hooks, — size, No. 2 to No. 4 for black
bass, except in Florida, No. 1 to No. 2.   I like unstained single
leaders, and loops for flies instead of snells.

In regard to shape and size of flies, you know already.

You can, of course, use anything in my books on the subjects, as
I have not changed my opinion on anything written there.

---

|  |  |  |
|---|---|---|
| *Ohio.* | Gov. Alvord.<br>Chippy.<br>Lake George.<br>Seth Green.<br>Royal Coachman. | Black Bass. |

HUGH HARDY,                    Columbus,                    Ohio.

We have seven natural black bass streams in our immediate vicinity, all of which are streams composed of irregular pools, ripples,
and stretches of water full of boulders, and are consequently the
very cream of fly-fishing.   Wading is the proper thing in all.

In the middle of April, when our fly-fishing begins, I am partial
to dark flies, preferring the Black June or Gnat, accompanied by
one other fly of lighter color.

In proof of this, — at that time, our water is a little off color,
and the dark flies show better than light ones.   Our first insects
appearing are black or very dark brown.   One of these is a large
black flying ant that hovers over the water.   The Cow Dung,
Brown Hen, Jungle Cock, Montreal, Grizzly King, are also very
good flies.

Made by C.F.ORVIS, Manchester,Vt.

PLATE U: DESCRIPTION PAGE 363

Made by C.F.ORVIS, Manchester,Vt.

PLATE V: DESCRIPTION PAGE 379

234    235    236    237    238    239

M. Bradley Co. Lith.

Made by C.F. ORVIS, Manchester, Vt.

PLATE W: DESCRIPTION PAGE 389

Made by C.F. ORVIS, Manchester, Vt.

PLATE X: DESCRIPTION PAGE 401

Then from May 1st to June 15th fishing is forbidden. After that our streams are low and clear, so that more care and skill must be used in order to be successful. We must cast a little farther, let the flies drop more carefully, and be ever ready, as then the bass strikes quickly, and very often the instant your flies alight on the water. From this time until the last of September I never rig a cast without a Gov. Alvord as one of them. I have had phenomenal luck with this fly during the last three years. I remember, just this last September, when I took in an hour's fishing six nice black bass, and every one of them with the Gov. Alvord.

The last one I saw jumping in the edge of some weeds. I went over carefully, made a cast, and plainly saw this bass, a $2\frac{3}{4}$ pounder, pass right by the tail fly (a Royal Coachman) and take the Gov. Alvord.

In company with this fly, I rig my cast with one that is brighter, a Royal Coachman, Chippy, Lake George, Seth Green, or such flies. All these flies are tied on No. 4 Sproat hooks, single fine gut snood without helper. In October, when the bass start into the deeper water, I use large gaudy flies tied on No. 1/0 or 2/0 hooks, and of patterns Gov. Alvord, Silver Doctor, St. Lawrence, Golden Drake. I have found that I can catch good strings of bass with these large flies when the smaller ones will not be noticed.

You generally get the big fellows at this time of the year, but you must allow your flies to sink a little below the surface of the water.

You will know all the flies I have mentioned except the Chippy, probably. This fly was gotten up by Colonel Park, of this city, and several fishermen helped him name it Chippy, because it looks so giddy. It has an orange-yellow body, with a narrow band of gold tinsel; black hackle at head, and white wings, covered partly by red wings. Its combination of color has proven a killing fly, especially for large trout in Northern waters.

Leaders should be six foot, fine single mist-colored gut.

I do not like flies tied with helpers, because they make a fly fall flat and heavy; and as for strength, I think if you buy a good quality of flies, a single strand of gut, well tied, is capable of standing more strain than a light fly-rod can put upon it. I like the snood instead of a loop, because the loop tends to make the fly heavy and unnatural just at the point where you want the fish to think there is nothing attached to the fly. All gut, snoods, and leaders should be colored instead of white.

I have used the same flies and tackle in lakes and streams of northern Wisconsin, Michigan, and Canada. and found they do as well there as here.

---

| *Ohio.* | { Gov. Alvord.<br>Lake George.<br>Grizzly King.<br>Scarlet Ibis. | { Black Bass<br>and Rock Bass. |
|---|---|---|

JEPTHA G. DUNLAP, Cedarville, Ohio.

I am heartily in sympathy with the plan and publication of the work which you propose, and regret that I have but a limited supply of information from which to draw for your benefit, owing to the fact that my experience in fly-fishing is confined to two seasons, in which I had to acquire the art in all its details without the slightest aid except such as I obtained from books.

The streams in which I have used the fly lie between cliffs of solid limestone, and are consequently of a very rocky character. They are occupied by the small-mouthed black bass and the rock bass (red-eye, goggle-eye, etc.), and these, but more especially the first, have been the object of my wiles.

My list of flies up to the present time has been comparatively limited, but selected from those advised by the various writers on black bass angling. Of those that I have tried, not more than six or seven have been of the slightest use, and only three or four a marked success. In the season of 1887, my best fly, while it lasted, was one which I sent you to imitate, and which you informed me was at one time a favorite in Lake George waters, but not known by any special name: body, dark orange or brown, ribbed with gold twist, if I am not mistaken ; hackle, scarlet ; wings, very finely mottled duck, resembling mottled mallard, but I think finer or clearer mottled than that, and therefore better ; tail, scarlet and white, tied with black thread ; hook, about No. 14 Kinsey. If this fly really has no name, I prefer to give it one. Next in merit was the Scarlet Ibis. Why the fish take that fly, so unlike anything in nature, is a problem. Certainly it is not for food, for I took with it large rock bass so full of crawfish that in more than one instance there was no room for another, even the mouth being partially filled.

These two flies were by far my best for that year. I took a number of fish with a brown fly which I have not seen described, and a few with the Grizzly King, but with the Yellow Palmer, Yellow Professor, White Miller, and a number of others of good repute I failed entirely. One day's experience taught me that fish are very exacting at times in their demands, and the importance of using a fly which happens just then to suit the fancy of the fish. In company with a friend who used a Henshall minnow rod and a fine silk undressed minnow casting-line instead of suitable fly tackle, and who could not by any means project his flies more than twenty feet, I spent the greater portion of a day on one of our streams fly-fishing for bass. I tried on this occasion the Gov. Alvord, Grizzly King, Ferguson, Yellow Professor, Yellow Palmer, Red Ibis, New Page, White Miller, and I did not catch a fish. My companion used a fly with dark crimson chenille body, tipped, and I think ribbed, with gold tinsel; hackle, scarlet; wings, very finely mottled duck, like those of the Lake George fly referred to above; tail, scarlet; hook, about the size of a No. 1 or No. 2 Sproat: and with this he took eight bass. Once in a while a bass would follow my flies, but by no motion that I could give them could be induced to take them. On one of these occasions my friend happened to be not far away, and I called him to try his fly on the fish. He walked in plain view to within twenty feet of where the fish was lying, threw his fly, not to say cast, and it was immediately taken. This was a day so fraught with instruction that, notwithstanding my bad luck, I enjoyed it greatly.

Last season, my best fly every day, from the first to the last, was the Gov. Alvord, with which I had no success whatever the year before. Next in merit was the Ferguson. The Grizzly King, not, I think, a good type, had but two or three fish to its credit. The Lake George fly, so great a favorite the previous season, took but two or three fish, and they were taken late in the evening. Whether this failure was owing to the slight variations made in imitating the original fly I cannot say, though I think it was, the difference being in the size and shape of the body, which in the original was plump and smooth, while in the imitation it was thinner and shaggy. The wings of the former were of a very finely mottled feather, giving a grayish effect, while those of the latter were of mottled mallard, a feather more clearly defined in its markings, and in this particular case making, I am inclined to think, a marked difference in the result. The Scarlet Ibis, so good a fly the year before, took not a single fish. The yellow flies have, so far, been an entire failure, proportioned to the amount of yellow in combination with other colors.

One evening, with a dark fly, Gov. Alvord, for stretcher, and the imitation of the Lake George fly, one of light color, for dropper, when so dark that I could scarcely see where the flies touched the water, I took a two-and-a-half pound bass on the lighter fly. Five minutes later, when so dark that I could not see, I took at the same place another on the Gov. Alvord. What is one to conclude from this? That the fish see a dark fly at night quite as well as a light one? Hardly, perhaps, but it shows that one of these fish did see the dark fly, and preferred it to the light one.

As all my theorizing has been in favor of clear gut for clear water, and as its superiority over the various shades of silk thread leaders, which I used to make and experiment with in bait-fishing, has been established in my mind, I have used no stained gut, and therefore can say nothing practically in its favor. I have, however, from some observations made in bait-fishing in roiled water, been led to believe that something else than clear gut would be better. I have thought that even an ordinary drab-colored linen or silk line, if fine, was better in such cases.

The deductions which at present I am inclined to make from my above limited experience in fly-fishing are: that flies which are best one season may, on the same stream, the next season be worthless, and those which were worthless the first season may be supreme the next; — that, so far as I have tested it in these waters, the favorite feathers are very finely mottled white and gray; duck, brown mottled turkey, scarlet ibis, and those of dust color; for bodies, dark orange or a shade of reddish brown, scarlet, crimson, and especially peacock herl; for hackles, scarlet and brown; for tails, scarlet and white mixed, or all scarlet; — that yellow has not so far, in these waters, proved a desirable color, and that I cannot yet say much in favor of green except in the form of peacock herl; — that the indiscriminate use of mottled mallard, pintail, wood-duck, etc., for making a particular fly is a mistake, and that a very slight difference in the form or color of a fly may sometimes make a very great difference in the effect. Of course, these ideas are more or less subject to modification by further experience, but I offer them as the best that I can give you at present.

## PLATE R.

No. 159. The Imbrie was named after and introduced by Mr. Charles F. Imbrie, of the firm of Abbey & Imbrie, fishing-tackle dealers, of New York city. The fly won and has held popularity ever since its first appearance.

No. 160. The wings of the Jungle Cock fly suggest its name, as they are taken from the frill or neck hackles of the wild fowl of the jungles of India, from which our domestic fowls are descended. These wild cocks have peculiar feathers, some of them terminating in a stiff, shell-like growth, especially those about the neck and upon the head, and at the joint of the wings near the body. They are much used by fly-makers, particularly on salmon flies. These feathers are also convenient in imitating "lady-bugs" and small beetles, resembling wonderfully the structure of the hard glassy wing covers of these insects. The narrow feathers on the back of the head of the jungle-cock are marked with a small eye or white spot, which appears specially taking to the fish. Therefore, two of these feathers are laid together, or "matched," for the wings of a trout fly, and the body is made according to fancy or to suit the locality. Red, with a touch of black and white, seems to be the combination most widely used for trout, consequently, it is the one depicted in this plate. Purple is probably liked next, and gilt and green have each many advocates.

No. 161. The Josephine. Mr. O. D. M. Baker, of Poughkeepsie, N. Y., was the first to give this fly a distinctive name, as he relates in his letter. His daughter was the first to make it for him, and he named it after her. He found it of much service in the streams of the Catskills.

Previous to Mr. Baker's having named the fly, it had been used by other fishermen, unknown to him, and called the "Red-winged Coachman." Mr. W. J. Cummings, of Bishop-Auckland, England, mentions it in his catalogue with the Coachman, saying: "But I have varied the original fly by substituting a delicate red wing in place of the white one; thus dressed, it kills twice as well, and I am certain will be found useful on any stream." Thus, it will be seen that two fishermen, widely separated and unknown to one another, arrived at similar conclusions; but we do not expect ever to see this fly a greater favorite than the ubiquitous Coachman.

No. 162. Jenny Lind, lavender wing. We understand that when first tied the Jenny Lind was made of blue feathers only, but it is now as frequently seen with lavender wings as with blue, so that in speaking of the fly one is obliged to state which color is intended. Either appears effective for both trout and bass, and for no good reason that has ever been defined.

No. 163. The Jenny Spinner is the imago of the Iron Blue, and in this, its final state, is one of the most delicate flies in form and color on the angler's list. The imitations of it vary somewhat, and each maker confesses his failure to reproduce the insect to his entire satisfaction. Although familiarly called the Jenny Spinner, it is one of the drakes of the order Ephemeroptera. Theakston very properly calls it the Pearl Drake, the wings, portions of the body, legs, and stylets all being of a pearly tinge and nearly transparent. The head and end joints of the body are brown; therefore Ronalds and Theakston make the fly with a middle band of white, terminated at either end by brown. There is so much difficulty in representing the extreme delicacy of the wings, that fly-makers have generally abandoned the attempt, and give it a gauze-like effect by making it "buzz," using for the purpose some tiny light gray feather, that of the sea swallow being an excellent tint. For the bodies some makers use horsehair in place of silk, but the commonly accepted dressing is that shown in the plate, which has been found generally useful.

It may be well to remind our readers once more that many of the flies shown in these plates are depicted in exaggerated sizes, in order better to display the colors and outlines.

No. 164. The Jenny Lind was first made and named by Mrs. O'Connell, of Halifax, Nova Scotia. It is now used for both trout and black bass. We have previously mentioned the variation in the color of the wings.

No. 165. The King of the Water dates back of " the three brothers that came over in the Mayflower," and is an old, well-known fly that has outlived its records. When it was first used, and by whom it was named, we cannot say ; but it ranks well with the Professor, Grizzly King, Great Dun, Red Hackle, and other flies known to all anglers.

No. 166. The Katydid is of the order Orthoptera ; the imitation shown in the plate is one first made by C. F. Orvis some eight or nine years ago, receiving the name chiefly on account of the color, and as a reminder of " grasshopper time." Every one who listens to the summer chant of this companion of the fairies has a pleasant thought for the tiny green katydid. Oliver Wendell Holmes has expressed this feeling, that is almost universal, in his own gentle, kindly way, in the following verses, which we venture to quote from his book of poems, because they were in our mind when we borrowed the pale green feathers from the parrot and bound them to a hook.

> " I love to hear thine earnest voice,
>     Wherever thou art hid,
>   Thou testy little dogmatist,
>     Thou pretty Katydid !
>   Thou mindest me of gentlefolks, —
>     Old gentlefolks are they, —
>   Thou say'st an undisputed thing
>     In such a solemn way.

> .    .    .    .    .    .

> " O tell me where did Katy live,
>     And what did Katy do ?
>   And was she very fair and young,
>     And yet so wicked, too ?

> .    .    .    .    .    .

>   Pray tell me, sweetest Katydid,
>     What did poor Katy do ?

"Ah no ! the living oak shall crash,
    That stood for ages still,
The rock shall rend its mossy base
    And thunder down the hill,
Before the little Katydid
    Shall add one word, to tell
The mystic story of the maid
    Whose name she knows so well.


"Peace to the ever-murmuring race !
    And when the latest one
Shall fold in death her feeble wings
    Beneath the autumn sun,
Then shall she raise her fainting voice,
    And lift her drooping lid,
And then the child of future years
    Shall hear what Katy did."


**No. 167.**   The Kingdom is a well-known English fly, also sometimes called the Kindon.   T. C. Hofland makes special mention of it in his book, published in 1839, saying: "It is much in use in the Hampshire streams, and is a good general fly also, as are most woodcocked-winged flies."   This has been proved true by the way in which the fly has continued in favor through the succeeding years.


**No. 168.**   Mr. John Shields writes to us that the Jewell is one of his patterns, "named after a Boston gentleman, a good angler."

Mr. E. A. Cooley, of Bay City, Mich., writes to us as follows : —

"The Jewell fly was first tied by Thad Norris, on the banks of the Au Sable River, Michigan, and named by him after a favorite guide and boatman, Leonard Jewell, late of Bay City.   It is a most successful fly at all times of day and in all seasons."

We can only say, — "Who shall decide when doctors disagree ? "


**No. 169.**   The Lowry.   We have received contradictory information regarding the name of this fly, the first affirmation being that it was given the name of an expert fisherman ; but an old fly-maker, in whose knowledge and memory we have great confidence, tells us that it was first made from the feathers of an Oriental species of parrots, — a most curious and interesting group of these attractive birds called the Lories. There are several species known under this name, some of the smaller being termed Lorikeets. The change in the spelling of the name of the trout fly is, undoubtedly, a corruption of the name of the parrot feathers originally used for the fly ; but as there is a chance that this theory is not correct, we do not venture to interfere with the name of the fly, and give it as it came to us, though inclining to the belief that the old fly-maker's statement is to be relied upon, and the name should be the Lorie. However this may be, it is an excellent fly for brook trout, and is specially popular on the Long Island and Pennsylvania streams.

No. 170. The Lake Green is a modification of the Professor and Grizzly King flies. It is not as highly esteemed as either of those patterns, though sometimes found to be a valuable substitute. It is an old, well-tried pattern of good standing.

No. 171. The Laramie. Eight or nine years ago a fisherman living in Laramie City, Wyo., sent to us a fly like the one in the plate, saying that it had no name, but had been found successful in that vicinity. We copied the fly, and in order to distinguish it and locate its usefulness called it the Laramie because it first came to us with its record from that place. Since then it has been much used in the far West, and seems adapted to the streams of that section of the country.

Nos. 172 and 173. The Lady Martha and Lady Sue are patterns given to us by Mr. Benjamin Allan, of Nashville, Tenn. The flies originated with him, and he could, doubtless, tell us something interesting of the names conferred upon them. He only told us, however, that they were captivating flies.

| *Ohio and West Virginia.* | { Holberton I. Alexandra. Oriole. | { Bass Fly. |
|---|---|---|

J. B. McKim,                    Wellsville,                    Ohio.

I have found the Holberton [1] a most taking fly for black bass on the South Branch of the Potomac in West Virginia, and I attribute it to the very heavy hackle on this fly. This is a point for you.

I think a heavier hackle on all casting bass flies would increase their killing qualities. Bear in mind, the Holberton was not the only fly used, as I took fish with the Alexandra and Oriole, and with the Conroy. To these flies, and others in the cast, the fish would rise indifferently; but with the Holberton in the cast, no matter with what other flies, that was the killing one. Increase the hackle!

---

| *Ohio.* | { Brown Palmer. Bee. Seth Green. Coachman. Professor. | { Black Bass, Rock Bass, and Yellow Perch. |
|---|---|---|

George W. Upton,                    Warren,                    Ohio.

In the Mahoning River (Ohio) small bass rise eagerly to Brown Palmer Hackles. I catch eight out of ten on a Brown Hackle. I always have one of the three flies on my leader. I catch a few with Red Ibis, or a bass insect made to look like a bumble-bee (yellow). In the water it is undoubtedly taken for a young crawfish. I catch an occasional fish on any other fly that happens to be on the cast,

[1] The Holberton mentioned in this letter is the one with a gray mallard wing and heavy gray hackle. Mr. Wakeman Holberton now indorses another fly as the true Holberton, and calls this a modification of the Grizzly King. (See Plate Z.) But as the gray-hackled fly has been known to so many for so long a time, we shall venture to refer to it as Holberton I. ; the other as Holberton II. — M. E. O. M.

— Seth Green, Coachman, Professor, etc., but the Brown Hackle is *the* fly for such muddy streams. Rock bass rise to the Hackle and the bass insect eagerly. At Punderson's Lake, Geauga County, Ohio, black bass (large mouth) rise to the Hackle when wind is right; and at twilight speckled bass (calico or strawberry bass, Syn.) rise furiously, near shore, to the Brown Hackle, and nearly as well to the Ibis.

I caught a few small black bass (small mouth) and some rock bass and yellow perch with the Hackle and Ibis in the Detroit River this summer (August), fishing over a sunken wreck. My experience can be summed up in a few words. In the Ohio lakes and rivers *always* use one Brown Palmer Hackle to fish with; change the other two on your leader for amusement and experiment, and to please the eye, as occasion suggests.

---

|  | | |
|---|---|---|
| *Ohio.* | Silver Doctor.<br>Professor.<br>Royal Coachman.<br>King of the Water.<br>Soldier.<br>Soldier Palmer.<br>Luminous Fly. | Black Bass. |

JOHN L. MINER, Windham, Ohio.

The only fly-fishing in this vicinity is for the small-mouth black bass in the headwaters of the Mahoning River. The water is yellow and dull generally. My experience has been limited to these streams, except in Canada. My favorite flies are in order named: Silver Doctor, Professor, Royal Coachman, King of the Water, Polka, Soldier, and Soldier Palmer. There must be considerable red in the fly, either in the body or hackle, not in the wings. I don't think I have taken a bass on a Scarlet Ibis or a Scarlet Hackle. May and June are the best months, and early in the morning, or from an hour before sunset until dark, the time. The by all odds most killing fly I had last season was a Silver Doctor with the "luminous body."

They are very roughly tied, but are certainly very killing in these waters. The ones I had were tied on No. 2 Sproat hook, and I caught bass freely on them, and with other flies No. 4 Sproat is the best size. I have never had any success with ordinary flies tied on larger than No. 3 or 4.

Now I think ordinary flies, or some of them, could be improved by making the bodies larger; not longer, but thicker. I consider the Sproat hook the best, O'Shaughnessy next. I prefer short loops to snells, by all odds, but not short enough to prevent their being looped on without waiting to soak them out; heavy single gut is always preferable to light double. I am looking forward to better sport this spring, as bass were very plenty laté last fall; but bass will not take the fly in the fall, as the waters are always dull here at that season.

---

| | | |
|---|---|---|
| *Ohio.* | { New Flies for | { Black Bass,<br>Pike, Sunfish,<br>and Roach. |

S. M. HARPER,                    Mechanicsburg,                    Ohio.

My fly-casting has all been in Ohio and West Virginia, with rods and flies of my own make. Seeing much to interest me in the "American Field" and other sportsmen's papers relating to angling with the artificial fly, I decided to try my hand, and therefore procured some lancewood and Bethabara wood, and made a three-jointed fishing-rod, with which I cast my first fly. I used it for several seasons, then presented it to a friend.

I tied my own flies on hooks of various sizes, some as small as No. 8 Sproat, and for black bass on hooks as large as No. 2/0 and 3/0. My first attempts at fly-tying produced something that looked as much like a toad as a fly; but by practice I succeeded in making a fly which was and is a success as a killer, though rude in its appearance. I have tried it along with many others, and never have found any that were its equal.

By continual experimenting I hit upon a combination of colors and material that have proved very attractive and lasting; with one single fly I took more than six hundred fish. Sunfish, roach, pike, rock bass, and big-mouth black bass were in the number. With three flies I captured twenty-five pounds of the before-named fish and a common *bat*, all in fifty-five minutes, from sundown to dark. This was on a small inland lake of about four acres, and thirty feet deep, surrounded by spatterdock.

The fly is tied on a No. 8 Sproat or Limerick hook; body, lemon; wings, of the coverts of the turtle-dove and meadow lark tied on crossways, and flat; legs, of black tying-thread. I use woolen yarn, raveled from a Brussels carpet, which I wind on so as to shade in the proper colors. The tail of this fly extends farther down and over the bend of the hook than that of any other fly I have ever seen, and my experience proves that it hooks fifty per cent. more fish than do the other flies used.

The large fly for bass has a tag composed of the red feathers of the blackbird's wing and the yellow feathers of the meadow lark's breast in equal parts; legs and under wings are made of the hackle feathers from the Plymouth Rock rooster; the upper wings are made of the white feathers from the tame pigeon's wing and tail feathers of the whippoorwill. The last-named feathers are the most killing for black bass that I ever used, but they are not strong or durable; therefore, as a substitute, I use the wing feathers of the meadow lark.

The evening hours are the best, unless there is a good ripple upon the surface during the day; southwest wind, with cumulus or cotton-ball clouds.

Best months, September and October; next best, May and June.

---

| *Ohio.* | { Gray Hackle.<br>Brown Hackle.<br>Montreal. | { Trout. |

H. A. SHIRWIN, Cleveland, Ohio.

My favorite flies among those well known are, first, Brown Hackle; second, gray flies, including hackles and flies of various other names which a novice might call gray, preference being given to white and silver bodies; third, Montreal.

Regarding locality, I have found my favorite flies working similarly in different parts of the country where trout are found. The most peculiar fact connected with it is, that, at certain times, not seasons of the year, but certain years or certain days at the same time of the year, I have found that trout would rise only to the Brown Hackle and at other times only to the gray flies. For instance, one whole season of several weeks' fishing on the north shore of Lake Superior, I could find success only by using Brown Hackles, and on the succeeding year, in same months and location, Montreals, or flies similar (sometimes with a little more red, even if crudely reinforced by a shred of red flannel), were the killing flies. I have also found for a whole season's fishing at Moosehead Lake the most successful fly, by odds, was the Gray Hackle.

I have not found these peculiarities so strikingly brought out in stream fishing, but the same flies have been the successful ones where I most frequently fish, that is, in Cold Creek, Castalia, Ohio, the only trout stream of any consequence in this State. While I have fished for trout in most of the Western and New England States, including the Adirondack wilderness, in the streams and small lakes, I have not observed any peculiarities on this subject worth further mention here.

I wish I might have one fly left to send you as a sample of what we have found very killing at the Castalia Club, which is called the Castalia Hackle, and I believe was originated by our president, Mr. Fayette Brown, several years ago. It is possible you have made them, but my impression now is that I have always had mine made by one or more of the New York tackle houses. It is very similar to the ordinary Gray Hackle, but has some colors introduced in the body which seem to make it just to the taste of our very critical trout.

As to my theories regarding hooks and snells, I have not been especially particular about the make of hook, using the regular Sproat mostly. Have had no experience with eyed hooks, but intend to try them as soon as convenient. For snells and leaders, I decidedly prefer the darkest stain I can get.

|  |  |  |
|---|---|---|
| *Ohio.* | { Professor.<br>Governor.<br>Coachman.<br>Golden Pheasant.<br>Cow Dung.<br>Grizzly King.<br>Black Gnat.<br>White Miller. | { Trout. |

S———,　　　　　　　　Cleveland,　　　　　　　　Ohio.

To be safe, I will give only individual experience. Away back in the forties, the first trout I caught in Lake Superior waters was on the Professor, and he did not wear the gaudy red caudal appendage that to the trade now seems indispensable.

For the last decade, my first cast on the waters where I now fish is, regularly (beginning with the stretcher), Professor, Governor, and Coachman, and varied only with occasional changes to the Hackles, Golden Pheasant, Cow Dung, Grizzly King, and Black Gnat, with the White Miller for evening.

I have just prepared one book with less than a dozen varieties in it for use; two or three other books have an endless variety to give away from.

As to theories on the many things connected with fishing implements, I am almost destitute, as my fishing has been in waters where we could always keep the larder supplied without being compelled to revert to extraordinarily fine work. In the matter of colored snells and casting-lines, I have little faith in their superiority over clear gut.

And as for hooks, I do not believe any are superior to the old Limerick, but we take the "goods the gods provide, and are thankful" that they do the business.

PLATE S.

No. 174. March Brown.

No. 175. Lady of the Lake.

No. 176. Maurice.

No. 177. Morrison.

No. 178. Marston's Fancy.

No. 179. Montreal, old pattern.

No. 180. Neversink.

No. 181. Oak Fly.

No. 182. Olive Gnat.

No. 183. Orange Dun.

No. 184. Orange Black.

No. 185. Pale Evening Dun.

No. 186. Prime Gnat.

No. 187. Portland.

No. 188. Peacock Fly.

No. 174. March Brown may be said to be next to the Green Drake in importance to fishermen. Although for years it has been called the March Brown, this name is misleading, for it is not one of Theakston's first class, but is one of the drakes of the order Ephemeroptera. It is intermediate between the pupa and the imago of the Great Red Spinner. Here again will be seen the confusion in past naming. The March Brown is in reality a drake or cocktail; it exists for a time, then becomes more active, perfectly developed, and changes color as it matures ; in this perfect form it is given an entirely different name, and instead of being known as the March Brown is called the Great Red Spinner. All this is deeply confusing to one who investigates carelessly.

Theakston avoids these contradictions by calling the sub-imago, or March Brown, the Brown Drake, and the imago, known as the Great Red Spinner, the Amber Drake ; the term "drake" indicating the shape or species, brown and amber their color. By these names they may be much more easily identified than by the old and contradictory terms, and the student can readily study their habits and order of appearance.

There are many ways of imitating this fly. Mr. Pritt, in his book on Yorkshire flies, gives five different dressings for the March Brown, any of which are good ; other fly-makers have each their own methods of reproducing it, the general aim being to achieve for the copy of the male fly, a dark mottled brown of a chocolate tinge, and for the female a lighter tint and more of an olive hue. In America, a mingling of the two shades, producing an amorphous form having the darkly marked chocolate-brown wings of the male and the olive-green body of the female fly, is a combination supposed to possess the merits of the two types in one, and do away with the necessity of carrying two patterns; that is, copies of both the male and female.

The fly is known also as the Cob fly, Great Brown, and Dun Drake.

**No. 175.** The Lady of the Lake is a comparatively new fly, originating in America. It is usually dressed large and for deep waters.

The name originally belonged to the Alexandra fly, but when it was abandoned for that fly in favor of the name of the much-admired princess, it was appropriated for this new and dainty creation of the American fly-makers.

**No. 176.** The Maurice. Mr. Fitz-Maurice has been for many years manager of the fishing department of the old house of John P. Moore's & Sons, New York city, now known as Shoverling, Daly & Gales. By his cordial, energetic kindliness Mr. Fitz-Maurice has won for himself and his firm many friends. It is pleasant and fitting that the fly bearing a portion of his name should be looked upon also as being reliable.

**No. 177.** The Morrison was first made by C. F. Orvis in 1886, and was named after Colonel L. Morrison, of Lock Haven, Pa. The history of its origin and naming has been given in Part I. of this book.

Mr. Morrison has related great success with it, and declares it to be "the black fly of the future." Properly, it should always be dressed on a No. 10 or No. 12 hook, but larger sizes are frequently found desirable.

**No. 178.** The Marston's Fancy is a pet fancy of Mr. Robert B. Marston, the genial and able editor of the "London Fishing Gazette."

Anglers on this side of the Atlantic are indebted to Mr. Marston for many favors, and in introducing to them this little namesake he has added to their indebtedness, for the fly has proved an important factor in many a triumph by the river-side, winning praise wherever it is known.

**No. 179.** The Montreal is a much-questioned fly, and but few flies are more popular. The letters in this book speak often of its merits for all parts of the country. We are inclined to think that the Montreal with a claret body is the one usually intended by the writers. That fly will be found pictured in the plates in

" Fishing with the Fly," but there are many fishermen who continue to use what they call the " Old Montreal," and the " Gray Montreal." By the " Gray Montreal " is generally meant the fly now called the Portland. The following letters give the history of the original Montreal. It will be seen that they describe a fly with a gray wing, yet we find that anglers, when they speak of the " Old Montreal," oftener mean one like that shown in the plate than one with gray wings. Sometimes it is difficult to know just what they do intend. We have placed the Claret Montreal among the lake flies.

Mr. N. P. Leach, of Montreal, Canada, writes to us as follows : —

" My old favorite fly for trout, *S. fontinalis*, is, and has been for many years, the old original ' Montreal fly.' I have used this fly in many waters, from Prince Edward's Island to Vancouver's Island. In the northern waters I use it for the tail fly in making up my cast.

" *Re* the origin of this fly, we give the credit to the late Peter Cowan, Esq., of Cowansville, P. Q., who we think used it as early as 1850. He often had as fishing companions some of the English officers who were stationed here, and they sent samples of the fly home to England, and the tackle-makers there made and sent the fly into the market here as the Montreal or Canada fly. The latter name has recently been given to another style of fly.

" The Montreal fly as first made, and as I now have it made, has a *red body* with or without tinsel, *ginger hackle*, and *mallard wings, black head*. Sheriff Cowan also tied a most killing fly, a small slim black fly with long black streamers. I have killed hundreds of trout on the first black fly that he gave me."

The second letter is from Fish Commissioner E. B. Hodge, of New Hampshire : —

" PLYMOUTH, *May* 21.

" I have not time to answer all your questions, but will give you something in regard to the Montreal fly which may be new to you.

" This fly was first tied by Peter Cowan, of Cowansville, P. Q., who was for many years high sheriff of the district of Bedford. Uncle Peter first made this fly about the year 1850. He found it a killing lure, and presented some of them to the officers of the regular army then stationed in Montreal. Mr. Cowan could not devote his time to making this fly, and, the demand becoming great for them, he gave samples to a fly-maker in Montreal, who made them under the name of Montreal.

" The original Montreal was gray duck wings, red body, gold tinsel, reddish-brown hackle."

From these letters there can be no question regarding the original fly and its history; consequently the pattern with gray wings should perhaps have been depicted in this plate, but it seemed better to print the history and show the fly commonly, though erroneously, called the " Old Montreal," for there are many fishermen who have earnestly assured us that this was the original, the " Old Montreal."

No. 180.  The Neversink was made for and named after one of the famous trio of rivers in southern New York, the Beaverkill, the Willowemoc, and the Neversink.  We cannot learn with any certainty who first invented this fly, now known for many years to the fishermen frequenting this celebrated trout stream.

No. 181.  The Oak fly.  Walton, in his lessons of the " Fourth Day," after giving directions for making the May fly, adds: " Or you may make the Oak fly with an orange, tawny, and black ground; and the brown of a mallard's feather for the wing.  And you are to know, that these two are most excellent flies, that is, the May fly, and the Oak fly."

The natural flies belong to the Diptera, and may be found upon the trunks of the oak, ash, and other trees, and always with their heads turned down; from these circumstances they have received many different names, as the Oak fly, Cannon fly, Downlooker, Downhill fly, and the Woodcock fly, from the feathers used for the wings.

Modern fly-makers are inclined to make the body of a lighter shade than the " orange, tawny, and black " of Walton's day, but the brown speckled wings and dark brown feet are still combined with a deep yellow or pale orange, to create the fly thought good for May and June trout fishing; but perhaps its greatest fame in this country has been won by its success for grayling, in Michigan.

No. 182.  The Olive Gnat is one of the tiny gnats or midges, that are properly made on the smallest possible hooks.  They commonly receive their names from their colors.  The Olive Gnat is hardly as great a favorite as the Black, Brown, or Gray gnats, but by many it is thought useful.

No. 183. W. J. Cummings says of the Orange Dun: "I do not know of a better fly than this, if used when the waters are just clearing from a flood. I have seen it almost torn to pieces in such a condition of water; it is one of the best flies in use."

Ronalds describes and pictures this fly in the "Fly-Fisher's Entomology," and it has long been known as one of the standard patterns.

No. 184. The Orange Black is also an old pattern; indeed, Dame Juliana Berners describes a fly which may have been the original of this, but we name it from its colors, the orange body and black wing.

No. 185. Pale Evening Dun. Mr. Ronalds dresses the Pale Evening Dun with a dun hackle, but American fly-makers all seem to make the fly as shown in the plate. It is well known in this country and widely used, although it is an old English pattern.

No. 186. The Prime Gnat is a device of Mr. William C. Prime, author of "I Go A-Fishing," "Later Years," "Tent Life in the Holy Land," a beautiful book on Porcelain, and many other valuable and delightful works. Mr. Prime has also been for many years editor of the "Journal of Commerce," and vice-president of the Metropolitan Museum of Art; in short, he is acknowledged one of the most accomplished men of this generation and country; there seems no realm of interest which he has not invaded to gather treasures for his fellow-men. His insight and power as a *raconteur* are marvelous, but underneath the knowledge and cleverness are a strength and depth of tenderness of feeling that pervade all his writings. The fisherman, or any one else, who has not read "I Go A-Fishing" is to be envied the pleasure in store for him; yet perhaps the pleasure in the books is as great to the one who turns to them as to old and dear friends again and again, always to find in their pages companionship and suggestive thoughts to linger over, and never to leave but with an echo of the old Arabic greeting, —

> "Salaam Aleikoum Ya Effendi,
> Es salamak Ya Braheem," —

and a feeling of the peace that abides.

No. 187.   Miss Sara J. McBride, a noted fly-maker, for a number of years made and sold this fly as the Portland, sometimes tying it with stylets of blue macaw.   The fly bears a close resemblance to the original Montreal, invented by Mr. Cowan, of Montreal, and by many is yet called the Gray Montreal; but that form of the Montreal has been so contested by the later Montreal that it has seemed well to adhere to Miss McBride's nomenclature.   We do not know why she called the fly the Portland, but it seems well to distinguish this pattern by the name given to it by her, so long as we are unable to retain for it the original appellation.

No. 188.   Charles Cotton, in his list of flies for June, tells us: " We have then the Peacock fly; the body and wing both made of the feather of that bird."   The fly bears a resemblance to many of the small flies of the order Diptera, consequently has been in favor ever since the olden times, and wherever the fly-fisherman seeketh the

" Trout-dimpled pool, bright beck, and sighing sedge."

It is not every man who should go a-fishing, but there are many who would find this their true rest and recreation of body and mind. And having, either in boyhood or in later life, learned by experience how pleasant it is to go a-fishing, you will find, as Peter found, that you are drawn to it whenever you are weary, impatient, or sad.

From *I Go A-Fishing*, by W. C. PRIME.

There is always that distinction to be kept in mind between going to get fish and going a-fishing. There is no possibility of convincing the general run of people that the old angler has his enjoyment in the going for fish, and that the getting of fish is but a minor part of the day's pleasure. This distinction grows more and more marked as we grow older. The young angler, — I speak of young in experience, not young in years, — the angler who has not had many years of enjoyment in the gentle art, counts much on the fullness of his basket, on the rivalry with companions, on the glitter of his catch when spread out in the evening. So do we all. But as we grow older we learn more and more to appreciate the innumerable joys which dwell on the banks and in the waters of the rivers and lakes, and which are surely to be taken whenever one goes a-fishing. And therefore the old angler has always a successful day, catching that which he went out to catch with great certainty, and coming home with a load of beauty in his heart, and beauty to talk and tell about, though there be not a fish in his creel.

W. C. PRIME.

From letter to *Journal of Commerce*, June 23, 1890.

I have two or three hobbies : I have given a long life to the collection and study of early illustration in books. I have devoted a good deal of time to the study of ancient art. I have filled my house with a collection of pottery and porcelain. I live, when in town, among these associations, but all my life, my heart, is shut up in my rod case, until I get away from town, and then it escapes and enjoys its beating.

W. C. PRIME.

From letter to Mr. Robert B. Marston.

## MISSOURI, IOWA, INDIANA, AND ILLINOIS.

ROBERT E. M. BAIN . . . . . . {
Red Ibis.
Holberton.
Silver Doctor, etc.

A. E. FLICK . . . . . . . . . {
Black June.
Blue Bottle.
Coachman, etc.

J. J. ORVIS.

F. B. FLANDERS . . . . . . . {
Blue Bottle.
Yellow Hackle.
Professor.

A. W. HATCH . . . . . . . . {
Lord Baltimore.
Hackles.
Ferguson.
Black Prince, etc.

G. P. McDOUGALL . . . . . . . {
Lord Baltimore.
White Miller.
Yellow May, etc.

M. D. BUTLER . . . . . . . . {
Bucktail.
Lord Baltimore.
Jock Scott.
Silver Doctor, etc.

CHARLES H. PARKER . . . . . . {
Silver Fairy.
White Miller.
Scarlet Ibis, etc.

C. W. McCONANGHY . . . . . . {
Black Gnat.
Black Prince.
Lord Baltimore.
Brown Hackle.

G. R. WILSON . . . . . . . . {
Montreal.
Coachman.
Red Ibis.
New Flies.

J. W. RANSTEAD.

WILLIAM J. BROWN . . . . . . {
Polka.
Red Ibis.
Grizzly King.
Professor, etc.

CHARLES G. ELLIOTT . . . . . . ⎧ White Miller.<br>⎨ Coachman.<br>⎩ Montreal.<br>Californian, etc.

W. P. KENNETT . . . . . . . ⎧ New Flies.<br>⎨ Seth Green.<br>⎩ No Name, etc.

---

*Missouri.* ⎧ Red Ibis.<br>⎨ Holberton.<br>⎩ Silver Doctor.<br>Brown Hackle. ⎫ Black Bass.

ROBERT E. M. BAIN, St. Louis, Mo.

So far as the fishing in this immediate vicinity is concerned, the available waters are not such as would joy the heart of any follower of Cotton, but nevertheless I have caught some fine strings of fish solely with the fly.

The favorite fly here is the Red Ibis, it being the best " all-round " fly used; but it has a close pull with the Holberton and Silver Doctor, each having its admirers.

The fly-fishing grounds in this vicinity are mostly extremely shallow, and the bass are very shy. At Kid and Breeze lakes the only fishing done to amount to anything is with the fly, and on a good warm day in June, an Ibis, followed by a Brown Hackle, makes a killing cast. The best fishing is done from four to seven P. M., and I have caught with the two flies mentioned croppie, goggle-eyes, sunfish, striped bass, and all sizes of black bass.

I consider the Sproat hook king for all purposes. Snells with short loops, and double for the leader, and long single strands for the dropper flies, are the best.

|       |                                                    |                            |
|-------|----------------------------------------------------|----------------------------|
| *Iowa.* | ⎧ Black June. <br> ⎨ Blue Bottle. <br> ⎩ Coachman. <br> Miller. | ⎰ Trout and <br> ⎱ Black Bass. |

A. E. FLICK,                     Dubuque,                     Iowa.

Bass fishing is fine in this section, although it is a trout community, one club having recently planted a car of young trout.

Our favorite flies are Black June, Blue Bottle, March Brown, Coachman, and Miller. The first three are good any time up to three or four o'clock in the afternoon; we then use the White Miller and Royal Coachman.

The " Reed fly " is used largely around La Crosse, Wis.

The Sproat hooks No. 1/0 and No. 2/0 are used altogether for trout and bass flies.

---

*Iowa.*          Black Bass.

J. J. ORVIS,                     Fayette,                     Iowa.

The only " game fish " in this section are black bass, and for two years these have been very plentiful, though none I have seen taken weighed more than three pounds. As yet but few flies of any make are used. Live bait and spoon hooks have been used quite extensively, with odds in favor of live bait. I have used flies on several occasions, but with poor success. Whether it was my inability to make a good " cast," or whether the fault was with the fly, I cannot say.

On one occasion I remember having almost taken a " two-pounder " with a bright red fly. I had skated the lure into an eddy, until all my limited knowledge of " casts " was exhausted. The spot had a wonderfully fishy look, and I determined to try again. As carefully as possible, I floated the fly around the outer edge of the eddy, where I made a few jerky motions which caused it to skip out of the water gently. During one of these skips it was taken. In my excitement and surprise I allowed the bass to have a few feet of slack line. This occasioned the loss of a fly and my temper. The day was warm and looked showery. In fact, it had rained the night before, and the June morning was sultry and foggy. Having used the fly as an experiment, and having only the one with me, I had to resort to a collection of spoon hooks for further pleasure.

I found that a spoon with red and white feathers was the best that morning. Large bass cannot be taken with a spoon in clear weather in this stream, the Volga. There are quite a number of piscatorial sportsmen here, but they use live bait. Minnows, two inches or more in length, are preferable. During a day's fishing in this stream, with minnows for bait, I have taken over twenty bass, from half a pound to two and a quarter pounds. Next season I will make some experiments with artificial bass flies of standard makes, when I will be glad to inform you of the result.

In fishing with the spoon, I have observed that a small red one is better in shallow water, and in deep dark places a large, mostly white, feathered spoon is often used with success. A variegated water-beetle, with three hooks attached to a light snell, running from the head of the beetle a little past the tail (small spoon), is the best all-round spoon hook for use here. I have taken many a two-pound fish with it.

My experience with hooks of various kinds is such that I prefer in all cases a strong, small-sized hook with snell attached. Light, clear, double snells, long strands, are also preferable.

*Iowa.*  { Blue Bottle.  
Yellow Hackle.  
Professor. } { **Trout.**

F. B. FLANDERS,                    Dubuque,                    **Iowa.**

When the trout are feeding, my first endeavor is to ascertain what they are feeding upon, and then use a fly as near an imitation as possible.

The Professor has probably the best reputation on the creeks where I fish, and I have used it with some success; but flies of darker colors, even with a crow-black predominating, are my favorites.

The Yellow Hackle with a black head, at the proper season and in that part of the creek bordered by willows, is one of the best killers I ever used. The Blue Bottle, in season, is also one of the best flies I ever saw. The Blue Bottle is my favorite, having caught with that fly alone not fewer than one thousand trout during the past four seasons; the largest two pounds, and none smaller than six inches. I prefer my flies on No. 8 hooks, stained snells.

———

*Indiana.*  { Lord Baltimore.  
Hackles.  
Ferguson.  
White Miller.  
Black Prince.  
Silver Doctor.  
Scarlet Ibis. } { **Black Bass.**

A. W. HATCH,                    Indianapolis,                    **Ind.**

I will state that in heading the list with the Lord Baltimore (jungle-cock wings), I name the fly that nine out of every ten bass are taken with in this locality. I know of no one who does not prefer this to any, and I do not know but I may say all, other flies, as I think you will find it the stretcher on nine tenths of all casts.

This fly seems to be equally taking on clear and dark water, and at all times of the day and evening. On one occasion I took a bass on the Lord Baltimore when it was so dark I could not see the fly, and I have known fish to be taken in the moonlight with it on several occasions. Other quasi game fish also take it in preference to any other fly I know of. Other flies I would mention in order following : —

1. Ginger Hackles, Brown Hackle, and Deer Hackle (locally called " Bucktail ").

2. Ferguson, White Miller or Hackle, Black Prince.

3. Scarlet Ibis, Silver Doctor, Yellow Miller or Hackle, Royal Coachman (for very dark day or water).

4. I have found a fly with claret or purple wings quite taking in the middle of the day, when the sun was very bright and warm.

---

| *Indiana.* | { Lord Baltimore.<br>Brown Palmer.<br>White Miller.<br>Yellow May. | { Black Bass. |

G. P. McDougall, Indianapolis, Ind.

In response to your circular letter, I would say that I have tried all of the leading flies, and for Indiana waters I have discarded all but the Lord Baltimore, Brown Palmer, White Miller, and Yellow May. The Lord Baltimore I consider the most killing fly, and use it more often than any other ; and seldom go fishing without bringing in a good string of small-mouth black bass.

When the water is in good condition, I usually take one or two days' fishing each week from the first of July to October.

I prefer flies tied on No. 4 hook, and do not like those usually sold as black bass flies. They are almost always tied too large, and are intended to catch the eye of anglers who do not know what they want, but depend upon the recommendation of clerks who know nothing about fishing, and are only interested in selling their goods. I am glad you are getting out a book that will be a practical guide to amateur fly-fishermen, as such a book is much needed, and I believe will be appreciated.

---

| *Indiana.* | Bucktail.<br>Lord Baltimore.<br>Yellow May.<br>White Miller.<br>Brown Palmer.<br>Holberton.<br>Jock Scott.<br>Silver Doctor. | Black Bass. |

M. D. BUTLER,                    Indianapolis,                    Ind.

My favorite flies for bass fishing, the only fish I have taken with the fly, are the Bucktail, Yellow May Butterfly, or White Miller, Brown and Grizzly Palmers, Holberton, Jock Scott, Silver Doctor, and a Black Hackle tied over a yellow body. I do not know its name, but have had several strong strikes at the only one I ever had.

I have probably as much confidence in the Bucktail and Lord Baltimore, as a good cast for bass, as anything I could name. I have made and used the Bucktail for three or four years, and have been very successful with it. I am sorry I am not able to send you a sample that is tied in a more workmanlike manner, but the truth is my fingers have never become dexterous in the work of fly-tying, and you will see the fly is put together more for strength than for beauty.

We have probably a hundred fly-fishermen in Indianapolis, and among them some very successful ones. I hope they will give their experiences.

I do not take much stock in the " time of day," or like theories, believing that if you put an attractive fly near a bass, and keep out of his sight yourself, you will always get a rise.

To prove the efficacy of my fly, as the fishermen here call the Bucktail,[1] I will merely state that I have usually been at the head of the list in all the parties I have fished with since I began using it, and have, in four cases out of five, taken the largest bass and largest average and greatest number of fish, and nearly all the large fish took the Bucktail.

I took a number of bass this summer weighing from two to three pounds, and one of three and a quarter pounds, as handsome a bass as I ever saw. He fought about fifteen minutes.

I think the snells and leaders should be made as nearly invisible as possible, and in that regard the fisherman must be his own judge, and be governed by the color of the water he fishes in.

I want to say that some of the anglers with whom I am acquainted have taken trout both in the East, Maine, and the West, Rocky Mountains, and they all unite in saying the river bass are a long way ahead of the trout as fighters.

They say the trout is quicker, and fights lively for a short time, but has not the endurance and bull-dog tenacity of the black bass,

---

[1] The Bucktail fly is a deer-hair hackle with an orange body, the hair being tied on to extend far beyond the bend of the hook. Mr. W. C. Prime strongly recommends a hackle made in this manner, but has it made on very small hooks and with a short body. This latter fly, with the extremely long fibres, bears a resemblance to the insect commonly called "daddy-long-legs." Mr. Prime calls it a spider, and recounts great success with it in the waters of Vermont and New Hampshire. — M. E. O. M.

and that he seldom shows himself in the air when hooked, which a
bass almost invariably does, and usually several times.

*Indiana.*  { Silver Fairy.
White Miller.
Scarlet Ibis.
Hackles.
Yellow May. }   { Black Bass and
Striped Bass. }

CHARLES H. PARKER,                    Terre Haute,                    Ind.

For bass in Indiana I am in favor of light and bright colored
flies, and prefer Silver Fairy, White Miller, Scarlet Ibis, Gray
Hackle with green body, and Brown Hackle with yellow body.

In the early part of May, 1888, I fished in Tippecanoe River,
which, by the way, is fairly clear water, with a very dark bed. I
used a Scarlet Ibis and a Gray Hackle in the forenoon with very
good success, taking eight or ten nice striped bass and two black
bass, ranging in weight from three quarters of a pound to three
pounds. In the afternoon I met with rather indifferent success
until about five o'clock, when I changed my flies, using Silver
Fairy with White Miller at the end of leader, and from five o'clock
until dark I took nine fine bass, none less than a pound and a half,
all black bass but three. The black bass were taken almost invariably on the Miller, and striped ones on the Fairy; in the forenoon
most were taken on the Gray Hackle. A few days afterward I
used a Fairy and Brown Hackle in Lake Maxinkuckee. The water
is clear as possible. I took but two or three bass, and tried at least
eight different flies. The water was too smooth; a light wind
might have made it different. As for fly-fishing on the lakes, I
like a little ripple, not too much; too much is worse than none.
The next day I used live brook minnows very successfully.

I am very much in favor of small flies tied on hooks never larger than No. 4 Sproat, and generally smaller, using them as small as No. 8.

For snells and leaders I favor light double clear gut; I have no use for stained ones.

---

| *Indiana.* | Black Gnat.<br>Black Prince.<br>Lord Baltimore.<br>Brown Hackle. | Black Bass. |

C. W. McCONANGHY, La Fayette, Ind.

The past season has been quite a good one for fly-fishing here for those of us who enjoy it. My friend Mr. Segner and myself had a great deal of sport all season. We have the small-mouthed black bass in abundance, in the Wabash River and the larger streams that flow into it.

We have found the Black Gnat the best fly to use, especially late in the day when the water is clear. We have had good success with Black Prince, Lord Baltimore, and the Brown Hackle also. The bass, when in the humor, will rise well for any of the above, but we prefer a good stock of Black Gnats to any. We use the Sproat or the O'Shaughnessy hook Nos. 6 and 8, and have little trouble landing our fish.

August, September, and October have always been our best months; in fact, until the frosts seem to drive the fish down into deep water. We think here the condition of the water has a good deal to do with the color of the fly. After rains, until the water gets clear, a bright fly does better than the black ones. But as the water is nearly always clear, we find we have our best sport with the black flies.

Fly-fishing in this section is yet in its infancy, but will no doubt increase rapidly when it becomes well known what good grounds we have, and what a good supply of fine game fish is so near. I must certainly agree with Dr. Henshall that the black bass is the gamiest fish that swims.

---

|  |  |  |
|---|---|---|
| *Illinois.* | Montreal.<br>Coachman.<br>Red Ibis.<br>New Flies. | Black Bass. |

G. R. WILSON, Elgin, Ill.

The chief water in the immediate region is the Fox River, rising in southern Wisconsin, fed by the springs of the Waukesha and numberless others all along its course, and by an extensive system of lakes, including Geneva and Fox lakes. In its primitive state the Fox River must have been very near an ideal water for black bass and pike. At present there are some eight or ten dams within a space of forty miles; some have fishways, and others will be forced to put them in this season.

I do not think much fly-fishing had been done on the Fox until within the past five years; but illegal seining and set lines have been for a long time, and still are, employed to deplete the river, while the bait-fishing is very persistent from early spring until the latest open water in the autumn, especially on Sunday; on some Sundays last season there were more than forty persons fishing within a distance of half a mile. Under these conditions, it has seemed to indicate the prolific nature of the river that so many good bass are caught. I saw some few five-pound small-mouth black bass captured last summer, and have no reason to doubt that pike were taken last September weighing ten pounds.

My acquaintance with Fox River began less than three years ago, at first as a convalescent, in the boat of a friend; later, paddling myself, and floating; still later, wading and casting on the ripples, which can be done almost anywhere at medium stage of the water, outside the influence of the dams. I have never angled for bass earlier than the first of July.

Early in June, the fly locally called the "cisco fly" appears in untold numbers at Geneva Lake, at which time the cisco in said lake make their annual appearance. Again in August an exact duplicate of said cisco fly, only it is fully twice as large, appears all along the river.

During the last two seasons (in August, September, and October), it has been the custom of a friend and myself to drive some three miles to a series of ripples (our angling having been done mostly at one ripple), so as to cast an hour before dark; and we have almost always caught all the bass we needed, from three to eight or ten each, weighing from a pound up to three pounds; the pound and a half up to two pounds and a half being the larger proportion.

The cisco fly mentioned, together with a very small almost white fly, would be at sunset, on a quiet evening, in dense clouds, especially over our particular ripple. We understood why the bass were rising there, but we have not found why these flies were ten times more numerous over the rapid water than elsewhere.

The Montreal, Coachman, and sometimes the Ibis, proved good flies; also one with a red body, red and white tail, white wings and hackle, gold tinsel; with this (name not known) and the Montreal I have taken a good many pairs of bass, usually in September and October. One fly of yellow and orange mohair, gold tinsel, red tail, yellow hackle, and wild-goose wings (name unknown), and another with a light tan color body, blue and yellow tail, light brown hackle and wings (name unknown), also proved as good as any.

I have fished very little in midday, but have caught bass in the bright sunshine with all of the flies spoken of, but have not found the Brown Hackle or White Miller equal to any of the others mentioned.

I rarely use more than two flies, thirty to thirty-six inches apart. I dyed some gut with a decoction of the "shucks" of white walnut (butternut), producing a light shade of tan; also some gut with Arnold's Writing Fluid diluted. I am very well satisfied with these colors when not too dark, and prefer them to the white or clear. I prefer single leaders, fine rather than heavy, if the quality is good, and I generally use loops on them.

Have for a great many years used O'Shaughnessy or Dublin-Limerick shaped hooks, but the Alcock & Harrison made hooks of these shapes, in small sizes, have the shanks too short to suit me, and the Pennell Limerick eyed hooks seem to me a better shape; but I have not been able to see that those with turned-down eyes were any better than those with eyes that turned up. For the smaller flies I generally use snells; my large flies have short loops.

Incidentally, I have caught pike, pickerel, rock bass, and strawberry bass from the Fox River with flies. I should hardly claim that the flies, or any other personal preference stated, are better for me, or for this region, than others that might be named; still, I believe the preferences have at least a fairly good foundation, and two or three fly-fishing friends here, in their practice, confirm most of my assertions.

I will add only a little of my fishing experience to this elongated screed. Half a mile below the city are two iron railroad bridges, not more than eighty feet. Two years ago, late in October, and near sundown, I anchored my boat a hundred and fifty feet below these bridges. I then had rather large flies (probably tied by John Shields, twelve years ago, for a contemplated Lake Superior trip, but never used); they were on stout gut, apparently as good as ever. Not having any showy flies, I put one on, and soon hooked a large bass which made two or three grand leaps; and then, after a minute or so of wild tugging, my leader came back, showing the hook was broken from the snell. I put on another fly, seemingly in perfect condition, when the same routine was repeated. My rod weighs eight ounces, and the fish were played on the rod and reel. My patience was not exhausted, so I put on a third fly, — same result; then a fourth, — again the same result; the fish leaping every time, showing a good size. Now, of course, I wanted that particular fish, with his large stock of hooks. While affixing the fifth fly, this fish came out of the water, first on my right, then on my left, a hundred feet away, evidently trying to dispose of something he had no use for, but no further notice was taken of me. I have been inclined to think I hooked and played the same fish four times, but I cannot prove it.

Two evenings later, and half a mile from the other location, with tackle of my amateurish make, in two casts I landed two pairs of bass weighing six and a half pounds, and did not try for more. I cannot say which incident, as the years roll on, will become brightest in memory, but in one incident I have always felt that I was something less than a victor.

*Illinois.*          Bass Flies.

J. W. RANSTEAD,                          Elgin,                          Ill.

Black bass, in the Fox River of this State, have preferred dark flies.   I have seldom taken them with bright or yellow flies.

# PLATE T.

**No. 189.** The wings of the Pheasant fly are made of feathers from the English pheasant: hence the name of the fly which is a pattern that has long been in use.

**No. 190. The Puffer.** Mr. A. Nelson Cheney, of Glens Falls, was the first to announce this fly as successful. We can do no better than to quote his own words relative to it in one of his reminiscences of happy fishing-days, in which he has written: "A little brown-eyed maiden, once, looking into my fly-book, asked why I had the old, frayed flies tied up in separate papers, and marked, while the nice new flies did not show this care. Had she been of maturer years, I might have quoted Alonzo of Aragon's commendation of old friends; but, instead, I merely said: 'The nice new flies I can easily buy, but no one sells such old flies; therefore I take the greater care of them because of their rarity.'"

On another page we find him looking over these same old flies, and he says: "Take, for instance, this one, with the legend written on its wrapper: 'Puffer Pond, June, 1867. — Thirty-five pounds of trout in two hours. The last of the gentlemen that did the deed.' This, to me, tells the story of a very pleasant week spent in the Adirondacks. I remember, as I hold the ragged, faded fly in my hand, and see that it still retains something of the dark blue of its mohair body and the sheen of its cock-feather wings, that it was one of six flies I had in my fly-book that June day that stands out from other June days, in my memory, like a Titan amongst pigmies. That fly had no name, but the trout liked it for all

that, and rose to it with as much avidity as though they had been properly introduced to some real bug, of which this was an excellent counterfeit.   That glorious
two hours' time, with its excitement of catching and landing without a net some
of the most beautiful and gamy fish that ever moved fin, comes back to me as
vividly as though at this moment the four walls of my room were the forest-circled
shores of that far-away pond, and I stand in that leaky boat, almost ankle-deep in
the water that Frank, the guide, has no time to bail, occupied as he is in watching
my casts, and admiring my whip-like rod during the play of a fish or fishes, and
in turning the boat's gunwale to the water's edge to let my trout in when they
are exhausted.   It is sharp, quick work, and the blue-bodied fly is always first of
all the flies composing the cast to get a rise, until I take off all but the one kind,
and then, one after another, I see them torn, mutilated, and destroyed.   Later,
they will be put away as warriors gone to rest, and the epitaph written on their
wrappings, ' Thy work was well done; thy rest well earned.' "

The fly without a name, that awakens memories of that " June day that stands
out from other June days," is now called the Puffer.

No. 191.   The Parker.   In the Minnesota division of letters, Mr. W. P.
Andrus gives a most entertaining account of the origin of the Parker, which was
first used on Wild Goose Lake, in the Adirondacks, in 1877.

No. 192.   The Professor was named after the much-loved Professor John
Wilson (Christopher North), and the story of the fly is, that one time, when this
famous angler was fishing, he ran short of flies, and, to create something of a fly-
like appearance, he fastened the petals of buttercups on his hook, adding bits of
leaves or grass to imitate the wings of a fly.   This arrangement was so successful
that it led to the making of the fly with a yellow silk body, since then so widely
known as the Professor.

No. 193.   The Blue Professor is simply the old Professor made with a blue
body instead of yellow.   In some parts of the Adirondacks it appears more taking
than the true Professor.

No. 194.   The Poor Man's fly is, like many another offspring of poverty, one
to do faithful work when richer and more showy existences fail; it is modest in ap-

pearance, hailing from no one knows where, relied upon, yet not often extolled, but likely to survive with " the fittest." We speak often of " the blessings of poverty," the " necessity that is the mother of invention," yet seeing, day after day, its train of misery and desperation, there echoes time and again in our mind Murray's bitter protest against the fearful weariness of it all : " Oh, cursed poverty ! I know thee to be of Satan, for I myself have eaten at thy scant table, and slept in thy cold bed. And never yet have I seen thee bring one smile to human lips, or dry one tear as it fell from a human eye. But I have seen thee sharpen the tongue for biting speech, and harden the tender heart. Ay, I 've seen thee make even the presence of love a burden, and cause the mother to wish that the babe nursing her scant breast had never been born.'

No. 195. The Queen of the Water is credited to both Professor John Wilson (" Christopher North ") and his brother, the naturalist, Professor James Wilson. It is claimed by old fishermen that the Professor fly was made originally without the bit of scarlet ibis feather representing the stylets of an insect, and many experienced fishermen of to-day cut these fibres of ibis feather off, while others consider the fly useless without them. If, as is asserted, the Professor was first made without them, there was then very little difference between the Professor and the present Queen of the Water, except that the body of the latter is of a darker shade of yellow, almost an orange, and the hackle is wound the entire length of the body ; therefore it is reasonable to presume that the two are only variations of the original fly, that in time came to be known as distinct patterns.

The body of the Queen of the Water, being a palmer or caterpillar body, is not as durable as the plain bodies, but in its praise the following, written by Miss Sara J. McBride, who was a most careful investigator, will apply : " The larvæ of the moths is a favorite fish food, and consequently a successful bait. Hibernating larvæ are drawn from their retreats in warm spring days, and continue the pilgrimage they commenced the previous fall. In their wild journeyings on and on before spinning the pupa-shroud, they fall victims in attempting to cross streams. Hairy caterpillars feeding on the trees are blown off by the winds, or their silken thread is broken, and they hang under the leaves in shelter from the rain. Imitations of these, known to the American by the familiar term hackles, and to the accurate inhabitant of the British Isles by the correct name of palmers, are to be used after winds or during rain-storms, also that compromise between larvæ and imago known as the 'hackle fly.' Bristling with feet its entire length, and graced with a pair of wings, it offers a double attraction to the fish. No bait has ever been used that has given the general satisfaction of this anomaly. To look at it with the eye of a naturalist, one doubts the wit or wisdom of the fish that takes it, and concludes there are comparative degrees of saneness beneath the ripple of the wave."

History has proved, however, that the queens who attracted and gathered armies of followers are most wondered at for their bewildering combinations and contradictions; this little atom, then, with its inconsistency and its power to charm and draw the inhabitant of the " cool deep," is fittingly named the Queen of the Water.

**No. 196.** The Quaker, so named because of its modest drab-colored dress, is fast becoming a favorite for nearly all trout waters, though formerly it was used chiefly on the Caledonia Creek, that favored stream wherein has been proved so perfectly the possibility and wonderful success of pisciculture.

**No. 197.** The Quack Doctor. We regret that we cannot give a clear account of this fly. We have some notes regarding it, but do not feel that they are sufficiently reliable to be declared history. It is too late now to make any changes, but we greatly wish that we had given the place occupied by it in this plate to some other fly of which we could relate more, for there are so many others whose records we would like to preserve with those of the favorites already given: the Chauteaugay, which was a favorite with the late Dr. George Bethune, the Hopatcong, the Romany Rye and Romany Ree, the Water Sprite, the Mephisto, the Deacon, the Murray, the Dennison, the Tuxedo, and that new fly called the Chicago, which is attracting attention in the West. This last we especially regret not having in our plates, as it is a really handsome fly, and we receive excellent reports of it. The Chicago is a bass fly, and was first described by Mr. C. F. Johnson in the " American Field " as follows: " Body, thick scarlet worsted ribbed with gold and silver tinsel, showing section of gold and silver alternately the entire length of the body; wings and hackle, dark red; tail, white." It is usually made on quite large hooks.

As time passes, we fancy we shall learn many facts that we shall wish to add to these records, but that is inevitable, and should we wait to perfect our knowledge nothing would ever be printed; we must therefore let them go as they are.

No. 198. The Red Fox is one of the series of Fox flies, so named from the material composing the bodies. All are much-valued trout flies, well known to anglers on both sides of the Atlantic.

No. 199. The Romeyn was made by Dr. Ely, and named after Dr. J. R. Romeyn, of Keeseville, N. Y. Originally the fly had no red tip, but this improvement is a suggestion of Dr. Romeyn's that adds much to the beauty of the fly. Dr. Romeyn has fished in the Adirondacks for over thirty years, and is noted as a lover of the woods and a generous friend to all who, as Walton described them, " hate contentions, and love *quietnesse* and *virtue* and *Angling !* "

No. 200. The Red Ant. Charles Cotton recommended the Red Ant as a good fly for June. Fly-makers since his time have made but little alteration in the copy of this insect, though nowadays dark red silk is generally used on the body in place of the " brown and red camlet mixed," as first advised by Cotton.

No. 201. The Red Head is one of C. F. Orvis's patterns, designed in 1886 or 1887. It was named from the feathers composing the wing, they being the breast feathers of the red-head duck. The fly was first tried and proved successful in Wyoming, and has been more used in the Western States than in those of the East.

No. 202. A mistake was made in including the Red Ash in this list of flies, for, although it is an old fly and of good repute, named from its colors, the King of the Water and this fly are too nearly alike to both have been given a place ; either will probably do the work of the other, and the two patterns so similar are needless and uninteresting. The better fly to have shown in place of the Red Ash would have been the Red fly, or " Old Joan," known since Walton's time. The imitation of this is described by Alfred P. Ronalds as follows : " Body : the dubbing is composed of the dark red part of squirrel's fur, mixed with an equal quantity of claret-colored mohair, showing the most claret color at the tail of the fly ; this is spun on brown silk thread, to form the body. Wings : from the softest quill-feather of the pea-hen's wing which approaches the tint. Legs : of a claret-colored *stained* hackle. No feather of its *natural* color that I know of is of the proper shade. Clip some of the upper fibres off, that the wings may lie flat. The tint of the wings is that of a cake of glue held between the eye and the sun."

The Montreal and the Cow Dung flies have somewhat superseded this excellent fly, but it deserves a place in the list of favorites for its past services.

**No. 203.** The history of the fly to which was given the name of Reuben Wood has been related in Part I. The fly is widely used, and fishermen are glad to be reminded by it of the much-loved angler whose name it bears; but away up in the solitudes of the northern forests, at the inlet of a little lake, may be found another memento in the form of a natural monument of three blocks of granite, twelve feet high, standing silent and strong beside the ever-flowing waters. On it is this inscription : —

"In memory of Reuben Wood, a genial Gentleman and great Fisherman, who was fond of these solitudes."

In General D. H. Bruce's entrancing sketches of the Adirondacks, published in 1892 in the "Forest and Stream," we find this account of the monument : —

"A notably destructive event was the windfall of 1845, which began near Cranberry Lake, St. Lawrence County, and swept eastward some thirty miles, prostrating every tree in its path, from half a mile to a mile wide. Some parts of the land thus cleared are now under cultivation, but most of it is covered with underbrush which does not seem to have any ambition to replace the once stalwart forest. It was in this 'windfall' that A. Ames Howlett, so well known as a genial gentleman and accomplished sportsman, killed several bears. And in the inlet of Cranberry Lake, near by, he took his famous trout, weighing when some time from the water 5 lbs. 14 oz. It was upon this lake and surroundings that 'Uncle' Reuben Wood spent some of his pleasant days. Upon some stones of singular formation, piled one upon another in monumental form, and at a point well up the inlet, Justice I. G. Vann caused a suitable inscription to be cut, in memory of the man whom every angler loved. He was the soul of honor and truthfulness; he could not tell even a fisherman's lie.

"Many are the recollections of acquaintances I have made in my wanderings in the woods, as I think of my old friend. In a hundred places have there been such chance meetings, as many a camp-fire has burned the brighter for them. A long list of names recur to my mind, and so of many friends whose names I cannot recall, but of whom the pleasantest recollections remain. Many have passed over the river, a few remain. We are all mortal. Thousands of high-minded, devoted sportsmen have gone before; thousands are to follow. Life's great brook must be whipped for the last time, and the great whirlpool gathers us in. But we were the better for our communion with nature, and nature's gift of wood, stream, lake, and mountain.

" What a pleasure has fallen to our lot ! Yes, there was joy in the anticipation of the trip, in overhauling the equipment and supplying deficiencies. What zest in planning the trip and making engagement of guide and quarters. Long sketches of precious enjoyment could be read from the leaves of the fly-book, and certain flies seemed almost alive and anxious to drop into old haunts.

" And who among us is there who would not now prefer to spend an hour in the dear old wood, or follow the banks of the old brooks, to a day in any other place ? "

*Illinois.*  
{ Polka.  
Red Ibis.  
Grizzly King.  
Yellow Professor.  
Green Drake.  
Gray Drake.  
Coachman. }            { Black Bass. }

WILLIAM J. BROWN,            Batavia,            Ill.

What fly-fishing we have here is on the Fox River, mainly a prairie stream, broad and shallow, but still varying a good deal in character, so that while much of it can be fished by wading, much also can only be worked from bank or boat.

The main varieties of fish which take the fly in it are the small-mouthed black bass, rock bass, pike, croppie, and sunfish. Of course, those who do much fly-fishing are concerned mainly with the black bass. There are also large-mouthed bass in the river, but I think they are taken mainly with minnow, frog, or " grampus."

The best time of the season for fly-fishing seems to be July and August, though I think bass have been taken on the fly as late as November.

One fisherman, well acquainted with the river, says he has found flies in which prevailed one of the colors yellow, red, and black to be the most taking for bass, or a white fly at dusk.

Another says that the Brown Hackle has been more successful as an all-round fly for all seasons and circumstances than any other in his experience.

Another has found the Polka fly extremely successful.

A large Red Ibis fly has at times been very taking, and the largest bass I have ever taken in this river on a fly was on a medium-sized Red Ibis.

As for myself, I think I have taken more bass on a small-sized

Grizzly King than on any other fly, and it has seemed to take about as well at one time in the season as another. Another fly that I have taken a good many on is one with red body and white hackle and wings. The Yellow Professor has been another one quite successful, and the Green and Gray Drakes also.

By some, the Turkey Wing and White-winged Coachman are considered very good. As to size, the experience of others and of myself has been in favor of medium or small sized bass flies, down to the larger sizes of trout flies.

---

|  |  |  |
|---|---|---|
| *Illinois.* | White Miller.<br>Coachman.<br>Montreal.<br>Professor.<br>Californian.<br>Governor. | Black Bass and<br>Wall-eyed Pike. |

CHARLES G. ELLIOTT, Elgin, Ill.

The Fox River, which runs through this place, is a very pretty stream, also rapid. In many places it has long reaches of ripples, with plenty of deep pools. It is an ideal stream to wade, and I believe wading is the most satisfactory way to fish with the fly. I find that I catch the most bass out of water from one and a half to three feet in depth, running over a sandy and gravelly bottom, with weeds on either side. The bass seem to lie at the edge of the weeds.

I find that from five P. M. until it is dark is the time to take bass with the fly. I have been fishing eight or ten times this summer, never commencing until five o'clock, and with one or two exceptions have brought home from two to five bass, weighing from one to two pounds. I can tell you, a two-pound bass, caught in pure,

swift-running water, is somewhat of a fighter.   Generally I catch
a number of small bass, from six to eight inches; also quantities of
rock bass, which are always returned to the water if not badly hurt.
Black bass are usually hooked in the lip, where they ought to be,
but rock bass are apt to take a fly down as far as they can get it,
and are the cause of ruining many flies.

Nearly two weeks ago, after the moon was up, at about 8.30, I
took with a Coachman fly two bass, one weighing just two pounds,
the other one and a half pounds; since then, one evening after
nine o'clock, when it was so dark I could not see where my flies fell
upon the water, I took with the same fly two bass and one pike.
A few days after, two of my friends fished the same stream, and up
to sundown had not hooked a fish; from that time on until eleven
P. M. they caught seventeen bass and three pike, several of the bass
weighing over two pounds, and two of them three pounds.   Most
of these fish were taken on a fly with a Coachman body, brown
hackle, and brown turkey wings.[1]   These experiences lead me to
believe that bass are great night feeders, and are also very wary,
so that the large ones can be taken with a fly only at night, or by
being very careful.

That large bass will take the fly I am perfectly satisfied in my
own mind.   Wall-eyed pike rise to the fly quite freely at times, but
compared with bass are slow in their movements, and do not afford
a great deal of sport unless a large one is hooked.

I believe the best colors for bass are red, yellow, brown, and
white; I have never been successful with green.

The flies I have succeeded best with this season are the following:

[1] The fly the writer describes corresponds in description to the Governor, an old and
popular trout fly; or he may mean a Gov. Alvord, which is similar. — M. E. O. M.

Montreal, Coachman, Professor, Californian, Coachman, and White Miller. The two last named are certainly very good for evening bass fishing. The flies I have used this season have been tied on Nos. 2, 3, and 4 O'Shaughnessy hooks, with short twisted gut loops instead of snells. I think the flies tied on 1/0 and 3/0 hooks, which are generally sold as bass flies, are entirely too large, and are less liable to hook fish than the smaller flies. It may be necessary in some waters to have an elaborate assortment of artificial flies, but my experience has been that it is not.

I use a seven ounce, ten feet in length, all lancewood rod, which I find, if well made, has sufficient casting and holding power for bass fly-fishing. My reel is narrow between centre-post and edge of spool, so it takes up the line rapidly. I use a small leader, six feet long, of good, strong gut, with only two flies. I think it a mistake to use more than two flies in bass fishing, for this reason: the fish are taken mostly in shallow water, and if one has three flies on his cast the upper dropper will be attached at least five feet above the stretcher; a bass takes the upper dropper, and in his antics catches the tail fly on the bottom, the chances are that you will lose the cast, fish and all.

I hope that what I have written may confirm the bass fly-fishing experiences of others.

|  | New Flies. | |
| --- | --- | --- |
| | White Miller. | |
| | Coachman. | |
| | Grizzly King. | |
| | Raven. | |
| *Illinois.* | Red Ibis. | Bass. |
| | Professor. | |
| | Silver Doctor. | |
| | Seth Green. | |
| | No Name. | |
| | Yellow Drake. | |

W. P. KENNETT,					St. Louis,					MO.

My fly-fishing this year has been chiefly at a lake in the bottom-lands of the Mississippi River, in Illinois, about fifty miles south of St. Louis, Mo. Said lake is rented by a club of which I am a member. It is about half a mile from the river, and from one and a half miles wide to one and a quarter long; skirted by a dense growth of water-ivy, lilies, and spatterdock, extending from one hundred yards to half a mile from the shores. The bed of the lake is an immense bed of moss that grows to within a foot of the surface, only relieved here and there by beds of lilies and dock.

Our fishing is in holes or in clear places, apparently made by the fish, and around these lily and dock beds where the water is from two to five feet deep. The lake had an extreme depth of eight feet two years ago, but has been drained three feet by rapacious land-owners. Large-mouthed bass, croppie, sunfish, perch, buffalo-gar, and dogfish are the principal inhabitants.

July and August are the months we enjoy our best sport. June and September are the uncertain periods.

As a rule, we only fish for bass, and boat none under one pound. The sunfish are annoying at times, and occasionally, when the bass are not striking, we rig a light leader with four small flies, and gather in the sunfish galore. The croppie are seldom kept, as they average about half a pound, though we sometimes catch a pounder. The bass run up to six pounds, though from $2\frac{1}{2}$ to $3\frac{1}{2}$ is the usual size caught.

Eight to twelve bass, averaging three pounds, is a day's record which several of our members have made on various occasions.

Our ideas of tackle may seem at variance with yours, but they are adapted to our surroundings.

We use light rods, medium lines, heavy leaders, and large flies. Rods about seven and three quarters to eight ounces in weight, ten to ten feet six inches long, of split bamboo, greenheart, hornbeam (ironwood), and lancewood, with the last a strong favorite, sometimes with bamboo tips. Double leaders the rule, and twisted ones the exception, with single gut a *dernier ressort*.

Our flies range from 1/0 to 5/0, with 3/0 an average size used.

I inclose a few used this season. The White Miller, Coachman, and Grizzly King are our favorite morning and evening flies, with the Raven, Red Ibis, Montreal, Professor, Silver Doctor, Seth Green, No Name, Yellow Drake, and Cheney, or flies akin to them, our standards. We largely use home-made flies, that would doubtless appear nondescripts to you, and yet they are effective: a black or herl body with red wings, or black interspersed with white, we find successful, and vary the body with red, green, and yellow; again, a black-red or herl body, with dark wings interspersed with white, is taking; also dark wings alone. We use no hackles.

The Sproat and Limerick are our special hooks, with the former the favorite.

Rubber and German silver click reels generally preferred, though I myself and one other are partial to our automatic reels.

Tapered enameled waterproof lines E and F are those most liked.

Having used leaders of all the ordinary shades (mist, coffee, and ink-stained), we think the unstained gut as good for all practical results as any other.

I prefer a six-foot leader looped, and with an additional loop about two feet and a half above the tail loop.

We use two flies, as a rule. Our flies we have made with the feathers covering the barb of the hook, to prevent being caught in the moss and the dock leaves when casting.

All hooks are double snooded.

The hour after daylight and preceding dusk is our most successful time, though of course some days are exceptions. I should like to discuss the peculiar habit we have of handling our lines by using our left hand in controlling it and the fish, and show how it enables us to strike promptly and accurately, to feel easy motion of the fish with an added thrill that cannot be felt from the rod or reel alone, and to govern our fish more thoroughly and boat them quicker, at least on such fishing quarters as we have.

Having been unduly prolix, however, I refrain, and ask indulgence for the rather disconnected matter already penned.

## PLATE U.

**No. 204.** The Stebbins originated with and was named by Mr. B. M. Stebbins, of Owego, N. Y. Several years ago Mr. Stebbins wrote us an interesting letter, giving an account of his first use of this fly; but we have been unfortunate enough to lose the letter, therefore cannot repeat it here. In this letter he stated that the fly was a copy of a natural insect that he had observed the fish feeding upon. The imitations were first made by Miss McBride, and were very much liked by the anglers familiar with them.

**No. 205.** The feathers of the Scarlet Ibis (a description of which is given with the history of the Scarlet Ibis bass fly, Plate DD) furnish material for this fly; hence its name. Tied on a medium-sized hook, it has been very successful in the Adirondacks for trout.

**No. 206.** In the letter from Mr. Ramon E. Wilson, among those of the California division, will be found mention of the Shain fly and its use in the trout streams of the Pacific slope.

**No. 207.** The Silver Horns, sometimes called the Black Silver Twist, is one of the caddis flies, and in warm weather may be found in the vicinity of the streams, sometimes on the beams underneath old bridges, or on the willows. Its antennæ are extremely long, and of spotted silvery gray; from these the insect receives its name. Imitations of the Silver Horns have been used by fishermen for many years. Jackson and Ronalds each describe the natural insect, and give special methods for making the imitation.   Theakston also speaks of it in his notes, calling it the Dark Pied Dun.

No. 208.   The Sunset was given to us by Mr. W. P. Andrus, of Minneapolis, Minn.   We quote a portion of his letter accompanying it: "This fly has 'done me proud' on several occasions when I have been fishing in Wisconsin, about sunset; hence the name.   I sometimes use a yellow hackle in place of a white, as in this instance; also tip the body with peacock herl instead of green chenille."

No. 209.   Shad fly.   Some years ago, a gentleman, whose name we cannot recall, wrote to us from Holyoke, Mass., inclosing in his letter an artificial fly, saying of it: "I have taken many shad with flies like this one.   The shad rise freely at times and give the best of sport, but this is the only fly I know that is at all taking with them."   After receiving this letter we fell into the habit of referring to the fly spoken of in it as "the Shad fly;" later it was made on large-sized hooks and used for black bass and other large fish.   One of these large flies may be seen among the bass flies in the colored plates in "Fishing with the Fly."   There is much misunderstanding about this fly owing to its name; many imagine it to be an imitation of a natural insect that may be seen in swarms at the time the "shad begin to run," but this fly bears little resemblance to that other known under the same name. We regret ever having called it the Shad fly, and did so only in consequence of its use, and the controversy which had preceded its invention regarding shad, and whether they would "take the fly."

No. 210.   Wilson's Ant is named after Mr. Ramon E. Wilson, of San Francisco, Cal., who expresses his preference for this pattern in his letter just referred to in connection with the Shain fly.

No. 211.   Dame Juliana Berners recommended for July "The Waspe flye, the body of blacke wull lappid abowte with yelow threde, the wings of the boswarde." Ever since that far-away time anglers have continued to use imitations of wasps, and although it is maintained by some fishermen that trout will not notice the natural insect, the imitation appears effective.   That shown in the plate, we understand, is the most widely used copy of this familiar type.

No. 212.  The Widow.  Cotton, in his list of flies for April, suggests the Violet fly, "made of dark violet stuff, with the wings of the gray feather of the mallard." This is probably the same fly that later was called the Widow, from its subdued dress.  Thad Norris, in his book on angling, writes with delightful enthusiasm of the alluring qualities of this favorite fly.

No. 213.  The Yellow Drake is one of the order Ephemeroptera, receiving its name from its prevailing color.  It is not, perhaps, as great a favorite as the Green and Gray Drakes, but it is in general use, and at times more effective than its so-called superiors.

No. 214.  The White Miller, copied after the familiar moth, has been in use nearly ever since the time when anglers first learned to cast the delusive fly.

No. 215.  The Whimbrel is named from its wings, taken from the feathers of the bird of that name, one of the Curlew family.  The fly did not originate in America, but is much used here.

No. 216.  The Soldier Gnat is a tiny gnat.  It is called a Soldier Gnat because of its bright red body.  It appears to be useful on nearly all streams fished for brook trout.

No. 217.  Yellow May.  Flies innumerable have been created since the precepts of Walton and Cotton were first given to anglers, but it is strange that in so many ways their rules are yet followed, and the flies they recommended are yet favorites.  Many fishermen use them without realizing whence they came.

In some of the small New England towns of America that were settled by the English Puritans, we often find preserved English habits and terms that are now almost obsolete in Old England even, and are common in no other part of America. Here, isolated in a remote place in the new country, the people and their descendants have held fast to their early habits and speech.  So it is, we have sometimes thought, with artificial flies; patterns that have been transplanted have taken a fresh and stronger root in the new soil, and, though almost unused to-day in the land of their birth, having been superseded by later inventions, here in the new country they flourish as favorites, and so thoroughly American are they that, like ourselves, we forget often there is a history of their beginning back of their existence in this country. The Yellow May was described by Charles Cotton as one of his four favorite flies for the month of May. It has always been exceedingly popular in America, and is dressed on both large and small hooks.

**No. 218.** The Welshman's Button is an imitation of a small beetle.

When did we go to the Michigan woods?
        I only know
That the air was sweet with the low white clover,
And the honey-bee, the wild free rover,
        Had never far to go.

How long did we stay in the Michigan woods?
        I only know
That the fire-weed flamed crimson higher and higher
Till only one blossom crowned the spire,
While below the seeds lay side by side,
Ready to fly out far and wide
        As the winds might chance to blow.

How long did we stay in the Michigan woods?
        I only know
That the Elder-blossoms grew white, then brown,
Then the scarlet berries hung heavily down,
        Over the green below.

How long did we stay in the Michigan woods?
        I only know
That the thistle flung open his armor green
Till his silken vest was seen,
Then changed to a fairy in gossamer grace
That brushed with her silvery robes my face,
        As she floated high and low.

When did we leave the Michigan woods?
        I only know
That clusters of asters purple and white,
And the golden-rod like a flash of light,
        Had set all the roads aglow.

When did we leave the Michigan woods?
        I can only say
That the yellow poplars trembled over
Where the weary bee hunted in vain for clover
        The morning we came away.

                              ANNA C. BRACKETT.

# MICHIGAN.

W. DAVID TOMLIN . . . . . . { Trout Flies.

H. N. BOTSFORD . . . . . . . { Coachman. / Hackles. / Bee.

F. H. THURSTON . . . . . . . { Trout and / Grayling.

JOHN A. SEA . . . . . . . . { Professor. / Coachman. / Royal Coachman. / Hackles.

G. HENRY SHEARER . . . . . . { Coachman. / Grizzly King. / Professor, etc.

GEORGE M. KILMER, JR. . . . . { Professor. / Scarlet Ibis. / Coachman, etc.

HERSCHEL WHITAKER . . . . . { Professor. / Grizzly King. / Silver Doctor, etc.

FRANK N. BEEBE . . . . . . . { Silver Doctor.

*Michigan.*                    Trout Flies for summer fishing.

W. David Tomlin ("Norman"),          Duluth,                    Minn.

As favorite flies for trout for use in Michigan streams, I have learned to select the following : —

Black Gnat. — For early morning, clear weather.

Cheney. — For brush-grown streams, under shadows.

Cow Dung. — For swift-running waters, rapids, etc.

Coachman Red-tip.
Coachman Royal.
Coachman Gilt.
Coachman Leadwing.

Standards, using them at all times for changes, especially in cloudy weather or in the evening.

Fiery Brown. — Under rainy-weather conditions capricious trout will rise to March Brown and Fiery Brown when bright flies won't draw them.

Fire Fly. — Will raise trout in dark-colored streams, and ranks with Coachman as a killing fly.

Governor. — Always carry it, but find it useful only when trout rise to a dark brown : then it is a killing fly.

Grasshoppers. — A prime favorite under all conditions. Small trout are almost crazy to jump for them ; big trout never fool with them, but go for them with a snap.

Jungle Cock. — A good fly under certain conditions.

March Brown. — A good general fly.

Sand Fly. — A prime favorite ; have caught scores of trout with it, especially in Michigan streams.

Scarlet Ibis. — For trout in rapid waters, or at the eddies under falls or cascades, this is a killing fly ; for yellow perch or croppies in deep cold-water lakes they are a very drawing fly.

Seth Green. — At the mouth of rivers where a swift current races, there is not a finer killing fly than the Seth Green. Always carry them ; especially use them for large trout.

Widow. — This is a favorite, but the conditions for using it are peculiar. Sometimes you cannot get a trout to touch it ; another time you can get a dozen trout from the same pool with it.

Professor. — A prime favorite ; use it on almost all casts when I use more than one fly. When using a black tail fly, I use a brown fly and a Professor for droppers ; find it a good fly under general conditions, when using a Miller for tail fly ; then use Professor for droppers.

Yellow May. — As soon think of going without my reel as without this. Under circumstances where I could not kill trout with any other fly, I have caught them by dropping a Yellow May up stream and letting it drift down ; it kills sure. Trout, with all their cunning, cannot resist the seducing charms of a beautiful Yellow May.

For Lake Superior waters, ugh ! the beasties (?) like worms, bugs, and grubs. Peel the bark from a fallen half - decayed hemlock, and you find a white grub as big as the top of your little finger. Drop it into a pool, and every trout in that pool is yelling, Hello Central ! to the battery at the butt end of the communications. Hence hackles are my prime favorites : White Hackles, Black Hackles, Gray Hackles, Brown Hackles, and Deer-hair Hackles. I have cast every kind of fly in my books over them, and they would rise and hook themselves when they felt like it, but what good is that to an angler ? He wants sport as well as fish, and with small flies the pestiferous little wretches, the "fingerlings," are too previous ; they " get there" too soon. The uneducated little heathen have n't been to school, so perforce I took to using Hackles, big fuzzy Hackles, the uglier the better, and I now believe I can get larger trout and more of them with these Hackles than at any time in my experience. I presume I shall drift back again to a more classic style of angling, but I was so tired of trying to save little four-inch trout from suicide, — that 's what it really was, for they swallowed the small midges I offered them, and I had to kill them to cut my minute fly from their throats. In disgust, perhaps I have gone to the other extreme, for results are that I get fewer trout, but larger ones. I have been gradually drawn to the sneck bend hooks with clear unstained snells; have tried Sproat and O'Shaughnessy hooks, but like the sneck bend; think I lose fewer fish than with any other hook.

Fishing a stream that runs like a mill-race, I dropped a big Red Brown Hackle into the rapids. A flash of white rose and struck, and, without saying good-by, snapped my snell, — and I guess he 's going yet. He ran out thirty yards of line before showing any sign of his size; as I checked him he came to the surface, salaamed, and started on a new gait. My line and leader came in, but *S. fontinalis*, a big one, had gone, drawing a clumsy home-made Hackle across a pool that contained hundreds of trout. They jumped across and over one another in their anxiety to get possession of that embodiment of ugliness, something unlike anything in the air above, in the earth beneath, or in the waters under the earth. It was neither fish, fly, fowl, nor beast; its dress red silk, the hackle stripped from the wings of a fighting gamecock's feathers, made up on about a No. 6/0 bass hook. Was it any wonder they jumped at this when they had tried to swallow a big bass hook to which was tied a tag of red flannel? The unsophisticated little beauties! Go there in May, and probably you won't find one; the race has fallen victims to misplaced confidence; the "madding crowd" found that pool and cleaned it out.

| *Michigan.* | { Coachman. <br> Hackles. <br> Bee. | { Trout and <br> Grayling. |

H. N. Botsford,                    Port Huron,                    Mich.

My fly-book this season held Coachman, Professor, Bee, Blue Bottle, and Brown, Black, and Gray Hackles.   My fishing-grounds for 1889 were the Quigley and Big Two Hearted rivers, seventy miles west of the Sault, on the south shore of Lake Superior.   The Coachman was the old reliable, the Hackles next, then the Bee.   In 1888 I was on the Au Sable after grayling, and used the above flies with the addition of Grizzly King and White Miller.   I have been five years on the Au Sable, and found the above flies all that were necessary.   In 1887 I was on the north shore of Lake Superior, and found the above a good variety.   This was during the months of July, August, and September.   I like flies on Aberdeen hooks, No. 4 for trout and No. 6 for grayling, and use a leader three feet long with two loops.

---

*Michigan.*                 Trout and Grayling.

F. H. Thurston,                    Central Lake,                    Mich.

For sufficient reasons I have, for the most part, used bait of various sorts in my fishing in the Grand Traverse region, and though I often look longingly over my fly-books I seldom try their contents.

Our trout streams, or those which I have fished, are so overgrown with trees and filled with logs and brushwood that it is wearisome to attempt the use of the fly in such waters.   When I have done so, I have usually failed of success.   Only yesterday I tried green and yellow grasshopper flies on one of these brooks, only to see the trout scan them disapprovingly and sink out of sight. It was late in the day, and I wanted trout for breakfast, so I took off my leader, used bait, and caught a "mess." The water was clear and low. Had there been time, I should have tried the Brown Hackle, or a brown body with white wings. In my limited experience here, these are best. Red flies don't take well here, or on the Northern Peninsula. Grey Millers are good.

As to bass, they are not over-plentiful where I have fished, and I can ordinarily take several rock bass (which I don't want) to one *Micropterus*. I prefer the Sproat hook, and in some brooks I should use as large as No. 1, though that is large enough for bass. In other waters, very much smaller would suit me better.

I don't think it important to have stained gut, though I use it for leaders generally. I have done with gossamer gut, though there are waters where it might be the best.

There is a wonderful difference in the education of trout in different waters, as you know.

I have found that the dark green dragon-fly is attractive to the grayling in September.

---

| Michigan, Wisconsin, and the Northwest States. | Professor. Coachman. Royal Coachman. Hackles. | Trout, Grayling, and Bass. |
|---|---|---|

JOHN A. SEA, Independence, Mo.

My experience has been of few years' duration, but I have tried many and various waters since I have been inoculated with the virus of angling.

I first became a "practical angler," with all tackle built for serious service and warranted to hold anything from a sun perch to a forty-pound catfish, and I had caught many bass, before I read up on fishing. Since then I have made the acquaintance of Prime, Hallock, Scott, Orvis, Cheney, Norris, Walton, Harris, Pennell, Forester, *et al.*, and have read them with pleasure and profit; so much so that, preparing myself for an outing after trout, I rigged out in full from information they gave me; and with an eight-ounce fly rod, on the first evening I ever waded a trout stream, I took eighteen trout with the fly; largest, twelve inches, twelve about eight inches, and five under eight inches, and, having read it was the proper thing to do, returned the fingerlings to the water. While books do not make an angler, yet they send a man out prepared to see and understand many things that would otherwise escape his notice.

I went out with ideas of fancy flies, exact imitation and colorist theories, up stream and down stream, floating flies and sunken flies, and while I enjoyed myself and caught fish, I was on the watch constantly for *facts* that would enable me to build my theory and practice of fly-fishing. I have had my fly-books well filled, and although I have been many times a " disgruntled angler," I have never created any " nine-jointed, Indian-named bugs."

My wanderings, and those of my friends with whom I have fished, have covered many streams and waters in Michigan, Wisconsin, Minnesota, Missouri, and the mountains of the West, and our experience has tended to fix us in the use of but few kinds of flies, those the old standards : Professors, Coachman, Royal Coachman, and the various colored Hackles. I have found on rivers and waters named, that when new and fancy flies would be taken I could put on some of the above, especially a Brown Hackle, varying the size according to the fish rising and the time of day, and still take fish. I think, as a rule, our Western anglers use flies and hooks too large. I have fished with some of my friends in Wisconsin and used very small flies, especially on long, still reaches of the river and bright days, and taken fish when they, using larger flies but of the same pattern, could not get a rise. I have for trout used flies on hooks running from No. 12 to No. 5, the larger on the Western waters.

I have found for all places I have tried in the West and North-west that the old standards answered every purpose, and those smallest flies and midges that approached them more nearly in color, using light and dark according to the day, were best; sometimes an Ibis would be good, but I have found these better for bass than for trout.

I have caught more bass, both large mouth and small mouth, than I have trout. The Professors, the Coachman, the Ibis, and Brown and Yellow Hackles on 2/0 were all good. Those flies in which were black, yellow, red, and white, singly or in combination, were all good bass flies. Those tied on No. 2/0 hook were most satisfactory to me.

As to hooks I have a very decided opinion, and have been a care-ful observer of my own hooks and those of my friends. While any hook that is properly tempered will catch fish, and a skillful angler can hook, play, and land goodly fish with any such hook, yet I think the work can be done more easily and satisfactorily with certain kinds. My favorite for everything is the Sproat.

Our club, composed of gentlemen from Minnesota and Missouri, the Minnesouri Angling Club, have tried every bend and shape obtainable, Sproat, O'Shaughnessy, Limerick, sneck bend, Kendall sneck, Carlisle-Kirby, each having in the beginning its advocate; we are now, over twenty of us, unanimous in advocating the Sproat for all light fishing. Some of us like the O'Shaughnessy for heavy fish and large bait; otherwise the wire cuts out and tears up all live bait too much. Its action is about the same as the Sproat.

The sneck bend rakes out, as do the Kendall sneck and Carlisle-Kirby also, at the side of the mouth, or hooks in the thin cartilage, when a large hole is easily made, out of which the hook drops on the slightest strike being given. Limerick comes up suddenly at the point, does not set so easily as the Sproat; all the square bend hooks break more easily at the bend than Sproat. The Pennell hook is good so far as striking and setting are concerned, but those I have used were too highly tempered for the angler's comfort and went to pieces on the slightest provocation. We favor the Sproat for the following reasons: it is a central draught and " goes home " when you strike; the wire is small, and when bait is used does not cut up a frog or minnow, and we have found, after careful trial by all of our club, and after many discussions have fixed our attention on the way in which our fish, as they come to net, are hooked, that more than two thirds of all we take are hooked solidly through the upper or lower jaw, and we have grown so confident that they will be securely hooked when we use a Sproat that we are willing to count our fish as soon as we find him pulling after a strike. As to size, we find No. 12 to No. 5 for trout, and 1/0 to 3/0 for bass. I prefer for bass a 2/0, as I have found them large enough for any bass I have ever hooked, and I have fished where our catch of forty or fifty bass would average $2\frac{1}{2}$ pounds. I will say, however, that I like a Kirby or side bend hook for very small bunchy trout flies. like Black Gnat, Soldier Gnat, etc.

For snells, I like a mist-color, or the color produced by staining with Arnold's ink; but I have never been able to see that it made any appreciable difference in a day's catch whether leader or snell was stained or clear. In all cases of small flies and hooks I like a single snell, as light as can possibly be used; for large flies I like a single snell reinforced at the top of the shank, or a loop of heavy gut.

I use leaders of moderate length, three to six feet long, with loops for flies. In all cases I use for trout or bass a single leader and a single snell. I use single snells for wall-eyed pike and pickerel, and my experience has been that so few of them cut the snell that it is not worth the changing. A twisted gut snell is as good as gimp or wire. I have never seen one of them cut by pike or pickerel.

My theory for all fishing in the West and Northwest, and that which I practice for myself, is to use as light tackle as you can possibly without cruelty to the game, and I have tried to blend the "hold hard and kill quick" with the "fine and far off," and I think it makes a good working basis for the sportsman angler.

# PLATE V.

Criticisms have been made in the past, upon some papers that we contributed to the "Forest and Stream" and other publications, that in these papers we "wrote of English flies that were of no use in this country." This is a sweeping assertion that bears upon its face unfairness, for no one at all versed in the history of trout flies can deny our indebtedness to British anglers for many of our most valued patterns of trout flies. In future years I hope that we may be able to return these favors. At one period nearly all the tackle-dealers in America were of Scotch, English, or Irish birth, and had brought with them to this land their knowledge of the implements used in the "old country;" the flies they sold were all imported, and so the fishermen of this country came to know and use the flies most favorably known abroad. In time we invented methods of our own, copied the insects of our streams and lakes, and experienced fly-dressers grew up in this country; but it is nonsense and ungrateful to be unwilling to acknowledge our indebtedness to the older country. Its leisure class is greater than our own, and has thought out many things and experimented in many ways that we reap the benefit of. Some waters of America are quite unlike those of Great Britain, and so require different flies; but other streams and conditions are similar, and we are coming more and more, in the long-settled portions of the States, to adopt the delicate flies and gossamer leaders found effective in England.

We have especially endeavored, in these records of flies, to claim as ours no patterns originating in Great Britain, even though by long adoption they have come to seem to be our own.

As streams have become depleted, and the fish more shy, they need to be fished with greatest caution and skill ; there is, therefore, a demand for smaller flies, delicately tied in colors less gaudy than those needed for the flies used on wild, unfrequented rivers and lakes. Experienced anglers in England have generally advocated using extremely small flies, and have urged the observance of variations in colorings to accord with time of day, place, and season of the natural insects upon which the trout may be feeding.

Mr. Frederic M. Halford, in his valuable book entitled " Floating Flies, and How to Dress Them," has given explicit directions for making Quill Gnats and Floating Flies, and a list of the most " taking patterns." We have decided not to attempt to give anything of the histories of the flies that we have selected from his plates, fearing to make errors in quoting from authorities unknown to us ; we have merely chosen a few of his desirable patterns as types of the class. Mr. Halford, in writing of these, declares that " Before many years are past the old-fashioned fly, dressed on a hook attached to a length of gut, will be practically obsolete, the advantages of the eyed-hook being so manifest that even the most conservative adherents of the old school must, in time, be imbued with this most salutary reform. . . . Flies dressed on eyed hooks float better and with less drying than those constructed on the old system. . . . Some discussion has been raised lately in the press on the comparative advantages of turned-up and turned-down eyes, and much stress laid by some of our highest angling authorities on the direction of the pull of the hook. In down-stream fishing, with sunk fly, this point may certainly be of importance, but to the dry-fly fisherman, for whose perusal this work is intended, seeing that the smallest drag is at once fatal, it cannot be material. For attaching the flies, I am distinctly of opinion that Mr. Hall's form of the eye, inclining upwards, is more convenient, and therefore preferable."

Although Mr. Halford, in these words, so decidedly indorses the Hall eyed hook, many fishermen prefer the Pennell eyed hook. Some who like the Pennell hook in large sizes object to the small sizes, because there is so little space between the shank and the barb, that there is difficulty in hooking a fish with them. Hall's hooks have less of this objectionable feature, but they are Kirby bent, which, to many anglers, is a greater fault. We will not attempt in these pages to discuss the advantages and disadvantages of the various hooks. Difficulty is sometimes found in inserting the snell in the eye of any of the very small hooks, but this is only an inconvenience. We have great confidence in the strength and reliability of the old O'Shaughnessy hook, and frequently are moved to exclaim with Thad Norris, " O'Shaughnessy, you are the greatest hook ever invented ! " but we acknowledge the merits of many other shapes.

We would like to show some of the curiosities in novel-shaped hooks that have come to us : some with the barb on the outside of the hook ; some with no barb at all ; some with square angles in place of the more supple curve ; hooks made by blacksmiths, and hooks made by watchmakers : all showing thought and a *raison d'être.* The subject is an interesting one to all fishermen, and tempting to us, but there is a limit to the space we may occupy for our own theories. Mr. Wells gives, in his books, drawings of many different shapes, and reasons logically regarding them, as do numerous other writers. At the Columbian Exposition, in 1892, opportunity will be given to see and compare them all, from the hook crudely constructed of bone, by prehistoric man, to those of spring steel and hair-like delicacy.

Mr. Halford, in his " Hints on Dry-fly Fishing," writes : " For obvious reasons, it is well not to enter on any controversy as to the comparative merits of the two schools of fly-fishing, — the wet, or North Country style, and the dry, or South Country style. Each is, beyond doubt, effective in its own particular streams and under circumstances favoring its use, and a considerable degree of science is attained by the earnest followers of both. . . .

" To define dry-fly fishing, I should describe it as presenting to the rising fish the best possible imitation of the insect on which he is feeding, in its natural position. To analyze this further, it is necessary, firstly, to find a fish feeding on the winged insect ; secondly, to present to him a good imitation of this insect, both as to size and color ; thirdly, to present it to him in its natural position, or floating on the surface of the water with its wings up, or what we technically term ' cocked ; ' fourthly, to put the fly lightly on the water, so that it floats accurately over him without drag ; and fifthly, to take care that all these conditions have been fulfilled before the fish has seen the angler or the reflection of his rod."

Mr. Halford then gives advice for accomplishing all these points, toward the end of which we find, among others, these useful hints : —

" When new, the fly, of course, floats naturally, and the first throw with a new fly should accordingly be made with greatest care, as the most likely one to tempt the fish, and also because at each subsequent cast the probability of his suspicions being aroused by some slight mistake is ever increasing. After the fly has once been wetted, it must not be returned at once to the water, but thoroughly dried by making a series of false casts backwards and forwards in the air, so as to free the hackle, wings, and body from all moisture. In the art of 'drying the fly,' as this process of wafting it to and fro is called, as well as in the act of throwing, I need scarcely caution the experienced fly-fisher to give ample time to the line to travel out to its full extent before returning it, neglect of this precaution causing the fly to be 'cracked off,' and necessitating the loss of fly as well as time, and occasionally temper, in knotting on a fresh one. . . .

"A line, before being used, should be kept in a dry place for at least six months, and should be well rubbed over with red-deer fat from end to end, to render it perfectly waterproof. The deer fat makes the line float on the surface of the water, and the angler is enabled by its use to return, and consequently throw at least four yards more line than without it."

The last three flies shown in the plate are made with scale wings and bodies wound with silkworm gut.

Some time ago, in the English "Fishing Gazette," a correspondent signing himself "Bittern" wrote as follows : —

"What is really required for the wings of artificial flies is a substance which combines the lightness and buoyancy of the feather in the air as well as in the water with the toughness and power to retain the shape of the quill, together with the pliability, transparency, and texture of the gold-beater's skin, and the property of being easily stained or dyed, and this material, so far as I know, has yet to be discovered."

Later, it was found that the inner membrane of the scales of the shad, red-snapper, and other fish was a beautiful substance nearly answering this description. Flies made with wings of this membrane are extremely durable and lifelike in appearance ; the wings are too tough to be torn, but in the water become pliable and offer to the fish no resistance ; yet, attractive as they appear, they have not proved very popular with fishermen, owing chiefly, we think, to a slight rustling noise they make when cast through the air. It is doubtful if this sound is really any serious objection to these flies, but it seems to have been a fault that has prevented their extended use.

| | | |
|---|---|---|
| *Michigan.* | { Coachman.<br>Grizzly King.<br>Professor.<br>Hackles.<br>Bee. | { Trout and<br>Grayling. |

G. HENRY SHEARER,         Bay City,         Mich.

My experience in fly-fishing has been confined entirely to fishing for the grayling in Michigan, in the Au Sable and Manistee rivers.

I have fished these rivers for the past sixteen seasons. The grayling are now quite scarce, and unless something is done to protect them they will soon be a fish of the past, at least as far as the above rivers are concerned.

I use a split bamboo rod, ten feet long, an Orvis No. 1 reel, and thirty yards of silk line, F or E.

My fishing has been done during the months of June, July, August, and September, from about nine o'clock A. M. until four P. M.

My favorite flies, among those well known, are the Coachman, Grizzly King, Professor, Silver Widow, Black, Brown, and Yellow Hackles, and a fly that I call the Grayling fly, that was tied to order some three or four years ago for a friend of mine. It is a good all-day fly, and seems to take well at all seasons. I have also had splendid success some seasons with the insects, crickets and bees. The above comprise all I should take with me on a trip for grayling, in Michigan.

I use a two-yard leader, and one tail fly and two droppers. I inclose a grayling fly.

One season I had great luck with the Bee, the next year it was no good. The crickets (insects) have been of service.

I prefer the O'Shaughnessy hook to all others, as a grayling's mouth is very tender and tears easily, so that many fish escape by the hook pulling out; therefore it is better to have a hook with a thick wire, about a No. 6 hook, ordinary snells. I prefer the leader to have loops for attaching the flies to, being better to take off and put on, whether wet or dry. I make my own leaders.

Hoping that my rambling answers may be of some value to a brother fisherman in Michigan rivers, I will close by saying that a letter sent to Archie or Rube Babbitt, Grayling, Michigan, will bring any further information a party may need for a trip.

---

| *Michigan.* | { | Professor.<br>Scarlet Ibis.<br>Coachman.<br>White Miller.<br>Yellow Mary. | } | Trout. |
|---|---|---|---|---|

GEORGE M. KILMER, JR.,　　　　　　Lansing,　　　　　Mich.

I have fished ever since I could hold a pole and bait a hook, though I do not claim to be an expert.

There is some of the best bass fishing a man could wish about seventeen miles south of here, but they use live bait, minnows and frogs. The best fishing on the river commences in the fall or about the middle of August, and is open until the last of October.

Last year, two of us started September 2d for a two months' fishing and hunting trip, going up near the straits and lakes. They are full of fish of all kinds. The best fishing was in the Boardman Creek, in Kalkaska County. We caught three speckled brook trout that weighed five pounds each, and were told by people who lived there that fish had been caught weighing between seven and eight pounds. The law allows them to be caught at six inches in length, but it ought to be eight inches. We used live bait, grasshoppers, large flies, and White Millers. It is hard work in some places to reach the creek, but quite worth your while when you can get such fish. There is more fight in a half-pound trout than in a three-pound bass.

I am well supplied with tackle, any number of rods, and a trunk full of lines and hooks and flies and other tackle. I have my own horse and a light buckboard. I carry two tents: one is $10 \times 10 \times 40$ inches, 9 feet high; the other, $11 \times 14 \times 30$ in. wall, $7\frac{1}{2}$ feet high, with folding ridgepoles. That is my way of going fishing. You can stop where you wish, and as long as you please. It is said I have the largest and best outfit in the city (except in guns, as I cannot endure it to tramp all day in the woods).

I have fished all over lower Michigan and in the central part of Wisconsin, and have always had pretty good luck.

The flies we used most were the Scarlet Ibis, Coachman, White Miller, Professor, Yellow May, and a fly I made: body, bright green, white wings and hackle, brown tail, and a yellow thread-like collar, on a No. 1 Sproat hook.

The best time for fishing is from about three in the afternoon till sunset, although there is often good fishing in the morning. We used both double and single leaders.

| | Professor. | |
|---|---|---|
| *Michigan* | Grizzly King. | |
| *and* | Cow Dung. | { Trout and |
| *Lake Superior.* | Black Gnat. | { Grayling. |
| | Coachman. | |
| | Montreal. | |
| | Silver Doctor. | |

HERSCHEL WHITAKER,      Detroit,      Mich.

My fishing is done altogether with the fly,— the time covered by my outings being the month of August, and occasionally a few days in July,—and is confined to grayling and trout waters. One of the most killing flies for both trout and grayling in our waters is the Professor. The Grizzly King is another taking fly, as are also the Cow Dung and the Black Gnat. In dull weather I have had great success with the Coachman, and as an evening fly it is very successful. I have taken trout late into the evening, when casting was guesswork business, as late as nine P. M., with the Coachman, with trout rising at every cast. It is unnecessary to mention in the category of killing flies the Red and Brown Hackles. As well might you offer the affront to your grocer of asking him if he keeps sugar in stock as to ask the fly-fisher if he uses the Hackles, Brown and Red, in his outings. They are as staple as sugar, and fully as necessary.

For the past two or three seasons I have used with pleasure and with increasing admiration flies tied on " needle points," and with a line of proper weight, a cast rigged with good needle-point flies, when deftly thrown, is an eternal source of delight to me.

For " rock " and " reef " fishing on Lake Superior the Montreal and Silver Doctor are both very taking flies. Different conditions of weather suggest to the skillful caster necessary changes of his cast, but, with slight modifications, the flies above referred to have afforded me the bulk of my season's sport for a number of years.

My personal preference as to leaders is one stained a pale slate, single gut, of course, with loops for attaching the flies to the leader. A perfect single leader, with a proper handling of the fish, will take anything you are likely to hook when fishing for brook trout or grayling.

I have fished over the better portion of Michigan waters, and in Canadian waters upon the north shore of Lake Superior, with the flies above mentioned, and have no hesitation in recommending them for good results.

Michigan waters are teeming with *Salmo fontinalis*, which have been placed in the streams by the fish commissioners of the State, and sporting is constantly improving, so far as the rod and line are concerned. My summer outing of 1889 was the most successful I have ever enjoyed, both in point of numbers and size of fish.

---

| *Michigan and the Northwest.* | { Silver Doctor. | { Trout and Grayling. |
|---|---|---|
| FRANK N. BEEBE, | Columbus, | Ohio. |

The Silver Doctor is my favorite fly, used at all hours, clear or cloudy, at Castalia, Ohio, and in the numerous streams in northern Michigan, quite a number of streams in the Rocky Mountains, the Yellowstone particularly, and in Idaho, Washington, the Spokane, Snake, Clearwater, Cœur d'Alene, St. Joseph, and other waters.

As a special favorite, one is apt to look upon a fly, perhaps, as an owner regards his gun; that is, "the best there is, and 't will knock a 'squirl' out of the top of the highest tree in the woods." So with any little pet collections of feathers, hook, and tinsel.   I can recall but one singular coincidence in regard to my favorite.   During the summer of 1888 I spent the greater portion of the time fishing the streams of northern Michigan.   I went to one of my favorite grayling streams, the Sturgeon, where I had fished quite a number of times several years, before and always with good success. I started in with three flies on my leader, on Nos. 10 and 12 hooks, and fished a couple of hours with rather poor success, having only taken a couple of small grayling.   I changed the color of the cast with no better success, and finally, after casting several times over a very promising pool without a rise, concluded that I would try my favorite trout fly for grayling.   So examining my fly-book I found I had only Silver Doctors on about a No. 4 hook, but concluded to try one as a stretcher.   Making the change, I made a cast and had a strike ; another cast, a strike, and the fish hooked.   I could see that it was my Silver Doctor, but when I brought the fish to hand the wind was knocked completely out of my sails, — it was a trout. I had in this very stream, and along in this very locality, caught many grayling, but never before a trout.   I learned afterwards that a few years before a lot of trout were planted in the stream, and quite a number had been taken out of it since, of fairly good size.

I prefer a light weight, and detest a poor grade of hooks.

While believing that a white leader, or more properly, perhaps, a clear leader, is best, being nearer invisible in the water when looked at from the *under side*, still I use dark-stained leaders, and prefer stained snells, as they look to me so much better from the *upper side ;* and I have always had success sufficient to satisfy an angler who fishes for sport first, and fish second, perhaps better than if I were after fish first, and sport second.

## PLATE W.

No. 234. Academy.                    No. 237. Blue Bottle.
No. 235. Beaufort Moth.              No. 238. Cracker.
No. 236. Californian.                No. 239. Bishop.

**No. 234.** Of the Academy frequent mention will be found in the letters relating to bass fishing in Southern waters. It was first introduced to our notice in 1878 by Professor Thomas A. Williamson, of the Leesburg Academy, Virginia. He wrote that it was a combination of his own which he had found particularly successful for black bass in the Potomac River, and that he called it the Academy, after the institution with which he was connected. Professor Williamson considered the fly superior to all others for that vicinity, and thought it sufficiently large when dressed on a No. 3 Sproat hook, as the bass run smaller in that section, and seem to require smaller flies and more sober colors. He kindly sent to us a pattern fly and the materials for constructing a copy, that we might understand perfectly its arrangement.

A few years ago the professor contributed to the " St. Nicholas " magazine an interesting and concise article, giving easily comprehended directions for fly-tying.

**No. 235.** The Beaufort Moth was sent to us by Dr. Dawson, of Cincinnati, Ohio, who said the fly was named after his friend, the Earl of Beaufort, and that it had been found excellent for salmon as well as for trout and bass. The fly strongly resembles the Coachman, and seems to be an added proof of the universality of that fly.

**No. 236.** The Californian was first made by C. F. Orvis in 1878, and intended for black bass. For a time it had no name, but one evening, while criticising flies and chatting about them with Mr. Horace D. Dunn, of San Francisco, Cal., he said the fly ought to have a name, and proposed calling it the Californian, from its golden hue. It has been so called ever since, and has been a reminder of that other Californian, a " Forty-niner," and most interesting companion. Aside from his early experiences in California, he had lived a long time in Japan after its first opening to foreigners. His habits of careful, intelligent observation and correct conclusion, aided by a good memory, enabled him to acquire a fund of knowledge possessed by but few. Mr. Dunn gave us some beautiful little flies of Japanese make; also a line, float, and rod. The flies were all on tiny barbless hooks, exactly like those now indorsed by Mr. Monroe Green and his friends. The gut used on the flies and leader was peculiarly soft and flexible, and composed of numerous fine strands of a yellowish tint. The rod was a dainty affair, perfectly finished and proportioned, and far superior to the "blow-out" bamboos sometimes sold as Japanese rods.

No. 237. We intended to have no two flies of the same name in these plates, but the Blue Bottle was accidentally included in the trout flies as well as the bass flies. Its history is given with the trout fly representation, having been longer used in that form. This larger edition is now in particular favor for black bass in Wisconsin and Michigan, as will be seen in the letters from those States. This size is, of course, an unnatural Blue Bottle fly, but for some unknown reason it seems to be wonderfully effective.

No. 238. The Cracker is a fly with a record, and evolved by most careful study and experiment. It is intended for the coast and river fishes of Florida, and is named after the natives of that State, the "pore whites." Dr. George Trowbridge, of New York city, its designer, gives, in his letter, a full and most interesting account of the origin of this fly. Knowing, as we do, the skill and investigating spirit of Dr. Trowbridge, we feel that the fly with which he has made such surprising records is a valuable addition to an angler's assortment.

No. 239. The Bishop was first made by Mr. John Shields, and named for Bishop Bissell, of Vermont, whose acquaintance Mr. Shields made when salmon fishing in Canada. Once the opinion prevailed that red and white were the only reliable colors for successful black bass flies. However, the proof is now clear that others are of equal worth, though red and white are yet valued. The name of this fly carries a weight of dignity that should hold it above questioning, and command for it only confidence and respect.

Oh, the brave fisher's life,
It is the best of any,
'T is full of pleasure, void of strife,
And 't is beloved of many :
      Other joyes
      Are but toyes,
      Only this
      Lawful is,
      For our skil
      Breeds no ill,
But content and pleasure.
WALTON.

## MINNESOTA AND WISCONSIN.

W. P. ANDRUS . . . . . . . . $\left\{\begin{array}{l}\text{Gnats.} \\ \text{Millers.} \\ \text{New Combinations.}\end{array}\right.$

JOHN L. STOCKTON . . . . . . $\left\{\begin{array}{l}\text{Parmacheene Belle.} \\ \text{Montreal.} \\ \text{Coachman.} \\ \text{Deer Fly, etc.}\end{array}\right.$

A. GALPIN . . . . . . . . . $\left\{\text{Brown Hackle.}\right.$

F. C. SHATTUCK . . . . . . . $\left\{\begin{array}{l}\text{Leadwing Coachman.} \\ \text{Abbey.} \\ \text{Seth Green.} \\ \text{Academy, etc.}\end{array}\right.$

C. L. VALENTINE . . . . . . . $\left\{\text{Frank Gray Fly.}\right.$

| Minnesota, Wisconsin, Michigan, Adirondacks. | { Gnats, Miller, and New Combinations found effective. | { Trout and Black Bass. |

W. P. ANDRUS, Minneapolis, Minn.

The waters of this section of the country, as you doubtless well know, are so varied, that one cannot be sure of success with even his favorite fly, in different localities, as I have found by actual experience. In Wisconsin the Professor and Coachman are about a good average, but they are stock flies and good anywhere. On the Namekagon River I have taken some very fine trout with a sort of mongrel Professor (scarlet silk lower half of body, peacock herl upper half, small gray mallard wings, and gray hackle), but the most "all-round killer" on this river I found to be a fly invented by my friend, W. W. Leonard, which he has dubbed Ninekogen: body, brown or chocolate-colored worsted for lower half, yellow worsted for upper half; wings, brown turkey or pigeon; hackle, brown turkey; tinsel tip, no tail; body made fat; tied on a No. 6 to No. 8 Sproat. I have had lots of sport with this fly, and never start on a trip without a number in my book. Sometimes I tie a white top to the body, but usually a bright yellow. The flies I used on the Namekagon, in June and August, are better adapted for use from about three to six P. M., after which time a lighter color (Miller) is best.

On the upper peninsula of Michigan I have found the Gnats, Gray and Brown, very effective, tied on a No. 10 Sproat. At the Soo (Sault Ste. Marie), in the St. Mary's River, I found the Silver Doctor on a No. 4 and No. 6 Sproat very good; also the Grizzly King.

Last June (1888), in company with a friend (W. W. Leonard), I was on the Namekagon. We had whipped the stream all day with poor success, and were ready to stop (about 6.30 P. M.); but before leaving the stream I made a cast across to an old stump, a sort of "good-night cast," as it were, when, with rush and swirl, I saw my tail fly disappear, and a large fellow jumped clear out of the water and hooked himself. I knew he was fast, and so prepared for some sport. The water was deep, and there were no obstructions to prevent giving him a free rein. After playing him for about twenty-five minutes, I netted him. I cast again, and hooked another; in fact, I took four beauties out of that pool. When we reached our camp and put them on the scales, they were found to weigh just 1¼ pounds each. In this case I had on the mongrel Professor above alluded to.

When fishing in Lake Twitchell, in the Adirondacks, I found a fly that was made "on the spot" to be a great success. Body, red or scarlet mohair, not too fat, flat silver tinsel wound around the body; wings and tail, guinea hen; hackles, brown; tied on a No. 6 Sproat.

The history of the discovery of the above fly is as follows: In August, 1877, I was in the Adirondacks, at a small lake called Wild Goose Lake. Two of us had about exhausted ourselves by whipping the lake all around, and over some particularly attractive-looking pools had used nearly every sort of fly we had in stock, but with very poor success, as for our two or more hours' work we could show only about a dozen trout that would average five or six to the pound. We finally went ashore in disgust, my friend to pick and eat huckleberries, while I sat down and overhauled my fly-book; and from among the truck there, and some ravelings from a red flannel lining in a coat I had on, I constructed the fly above described; in fact, made two of them. About the time I had finished my lure the sky became slightly overcast and the trout began jumping, so we got into our boat and paddled over to a spot where they seemed to be particularly lively, and there we went to work. Well, to make a short story of it, I proved conclusively that my new fly was a sure " killer," for in about a hundred minutes I had taken sixty-five trout that weighed twenty-five pounds.

I had three flies on, the tail fly being a Brown Palmer, and the two new ones completing the whip. During the fishing I hooked and landed three at a time, four times. I knew that was our last chance, as we were to start for home the next morning, and we wanted some fish to take home with us; so I could not accuse myself of being a " butcher " or " swine " in this instance. I have named the successful fly the Parker, and I always have a number on hand.

I usually tie my own flies, and am very partial to a yellow, or yellow combination, particularly so for bass fishing. I always have on hand a number of " unknowns," and should take great pleasure in giving you the results of my experiments from time to time.

As to color of snells, I am inclined to favor the clear, uncolored gut; for these Western waters, my experience leads me to believe that it does not make much difference, if all the other conditions are right, the angler included; but for leaders I always favor and use an azure tint.

I prefer a Sproat hook to any other; think it the best for flies, either trout or bass. I tie the bodies " fat," according to Henshall. I find the bass fly tied with the concave side of the wing out to be best in work, according to my notion. I have never tried trout flies

so made. Use in all cases a single clear snell. I believe it sufficiently strong for almost any fish hereabouts that will rise to the
fly. I have here hooked, played for twenty minutes, and landed
bass that weighed 4¾ pounds, and used a No. 2 Sproat mounted on
a clear single snell of medium weight and size.

I have had moderate success with the following on Long Lake,
near Brainerd (in this State), in bass fishing. They are all of my
own designing and make.

|  | *Body.* | *Wings.* | *Hackles.* | *Tail.* |
|---|---|---|---|---|
| Black Duke. | Scarlet che-nille. | Black single feather, con-cave out. | White or gray. | Black os-trich herl. |
| Mikado. | Green chenille. A sure thing. | Yellow mallard, concave out. | Yellow. | Scarlet. |
| Teaser. | Bottle-green chenille. | Dark drab from pigeon, single feather. | Gray mal-lard. | Scarlet. |
| Dandy. | Scarlet chenille. This is an A1 fly. | Guinea hen, sin-gle feather. | White. | Peacock. |
| Yellow Betsy. | Orange chenille. | Wood duck breast. | Brown. | Wood duck bars. |

The above are all on No. 1 or No. 2 Sproat hooks.

| | | |
|---|---|---|
| *Wisconsin.* | Parmacheene Belle.<br>Brown Hackle.<br>Montreal.<br>Coachman.<br>Deer Fly. | Trout. |

JOHN L. STOCKTON,                    Chicago,                    Ill.

Last year, in June, I found the Parmacheene Belle, Brown Hackle, Montreal, Red Ibis, Deer Fly, and Coachman to take well where we fished in northern Wisconsin.

We usually fished from three o'clock in the afternoon until sundown, going up the river in a "dug out" canoe in the morning, and then dropping slowly down the stream, the guide holding or checking the boat as required. Fishing from the boat in this way enabled us to escape in a measure the flies, which were otherwise very troublesome.

---

| *Wisconsin.* | Brown Hackle. | Trout. |
|---|---|---|

A. GALPIN,                    Appleton,                    Wis.

My experience is limited, but I might say that I have found the Red and Brown Hackles more generally useful than any other flies. Should favor clear snells, long strands.

---

| *Wisconsin and Michigan.* | Leadwing Coachman.<br>Abbey.<br>Seth Green.<br>Professor.<br>Montreal.<br>Academy. | Trout. |
|---|---|---|

F. C. SHATTUCK,                    Neenah,                    Wis.

The following are the favorite flies that I have used during the past year or two: Leadwing Coachman, Abbey, Seth Green, and Professor.

I also use, in lakes and ponds where the trout are large, lake flies Academy, Abbey, Montreal, and occasionally the lighter colors.

My experience has been that in light, open pools the light-colored flies are better than the dark, and *vice versa;* and that, in taking large trout, they rise to a fly more readily in the afternoon, between three and six o'clock, than at any other time; however, I have made some excellent catches in the early morning and during the forenoon with flies.

The trout fishing in the northern part of Wisconsin and Michigan Upper Peninsula is as good as can be found anywhere. The headwaters (which abound in lakes and ponds) of the Oconto, Pensaukee, Brulé, Iron, Escanaba, and in fact all the streams are full of trout, and a person does not have to be an expert to fill his creel in an hour or two of fishing on a favorable day. A party of four, the writer being one of the number, drove with teams from Shawano, last June, to the headwaters of the North Branch of the Oconto, and took up their abode in a lumber-camp shanty, which is situated on the stream and near several lakes and ponds. Our catches could have been made enormous had we desired to kill the fish. The trout ranged from a quarter to two and a half pounds each, and were as fine in flavor as I ever took from New England waters. The last day before returning home, wishing to take some of the beauties to our friends, we arranged for a full day's fishing. The weather was fine, and the wind southwest. I never have had such sport before. Though we spent but a small portion of the day fishing, our catch was, in round numbers, four hundred and sixteen; total weight, one hundred and thirty-three pounds. The fish were weighed on Uppenham & Russell Co.'s scales at Shawano.

Of all the sports from my childhood days to the present time, nothing compares with fishing for brook trout. My annual two weeks' fishing trip has become an anniversary which I hope to maintain as long as I have activity.

---

| *Wisconsin.* | { Frank Gray Fly. | { Black Bass and<br>{ Wall-eyed Pike. |

C. L. VALENTINE,            Janesville,            Wis.

Inclosed I send a fly made by Mr. Frank Gray, of this city, the oldest fly-fisherman of this locality, and the one most successful.

Mr. Gray makes what flies he uses. That inclosed is the best I have ever seen for wall-eyed pike. Mr. Gray attaches to the hook, at times, a small strip of either white or red cloth, about half an inch long, and prefers the fly on a heavy single snell. For forty years past he has taken fish here, black bass and pike, with this fly, never using any other bait in fishing; it is good for early-morning fishing, but best from five to eight o'clock in the evening, from August to November.

The fly should be called after its maker, Frank Gray.[1]

[1] See plates for Frank Gray fly.

## PLATE X.

No. 240. Cleveland.  No. 243. Dark Flaggon.
No. 241. Cheney.  No. 244. Croppie.
No. 242. Chippy.  No. 245. Barnwell.

No. 240. The Cleveland. There was once a jolly club of three, who styled themselves the "Texas Club," saying that "their membership consisted of President, Secretary, and Treasurer." The club was a fishing-club, and met summers to rejoice in being together and in fishing "galore." The Secretary and Treasurer were rivals always; their joys would have been incomplete without the never-ceasing spirit of contest. What one had the other had, too, if money or skill could procure it, be it a big fish or a new hat. The Cheney fly was made and named in honor of the Secretary. A little later, the maker of the Cheney fly made a fly with a gallina wing and red and black body, somewhat similar to Dr. Henshall's Polka, and to it was given the title Cleveland, after the Treasurer. But alas for human hopes! One day the maker of these flies met the Treasurer, and this conversation ensued : —

*Treasurer.* I have wanted to meet you for a long time. I have a question to ask you. Now, honestly, don't you think you put just a *little* more color into the Cheney fly than you did into the Cleveland? Now answer me frankly.

*Maker.* I did not intend to do so, I assure you.

*Treasurer.* Well, but I think you did. Could n't it be dressed up a trifle, some way?

*Maker.* I am glad you spoke to me about it. I shall be pleased to try again, and make a fly more worthy the name.

*Treasurer.* Yes, do; and mind you put a little more gilt on it than is on Cheney's.

This new Cleveland fly is an earnest endeavor to construct a fly the embodiment of strength, modesty, brilliancy, and other sterling merits, traits that win and hold the friends of Mr. William D. Cleveland outside as well as within the Texas Club.

No. 241. There is probably no greater enthusiast in this country over matters piscatorial than Mr. A. N. Cheney, the present editor of the fishing department of "Shooting and Fishing." It would be a pleasure to quote from some of Mr. Cheney's letters regarding his interest in this subject, for his love for it has led him to gather an almost unlimited amount of information. His accuracy has come to be almost undoubted, and his theories are always respected, because practicable and reasonable, while his expression of them is clear, vigorous, and interesting, as well as graceful and original. Even before Dr. Henshall's "Book of the Black Bass," Mr. Cheney had written many papers of this then little-appreciated fish, calling attention to it and giving interesting accounts of its habits, and introducing to anglers the merits of this game fish that has now come to be so highly valued. One summer when Mr. Cheney was staying at Schroon Lake, a few flies, all of them new combinations, were sent to him to try. Among them was one with a body like that of the present Cheney fly, but with a black wing. Later in the season Mr. Cheney visited Manchester, when he said, " If that fly had a different wing, it would be just about my idea of a perfect fly for black bass." Feathers were therefore inspected to find a more suitable wing, and finally those of the mallard with a black bar decided upon. The fly was then made, under Mr. Cheney's supervision. When finished to his satisfaction he named it the Cheney, and his success with the fly in many different waters has proved the correctness of his theories and conclusions drawn from previous experiments.

We hope that Mr. Cheney will some day collect his writings and that they may be printed all together, and thus be more available, as they would be interesting to any reader, fisherman or otherwise, and sure to be warmly welcomed by the many who know and value his genial wit, courtesy, unfailing generosity, and true, loyal nature.

No. 242. Chippy. An account of this fly, invented by Colonel Park, of Columbus, Ohio, will be found in the letter from Mr. Hugh Hardy.

No. 243. Mr. Shields, who is the inventor of both the Flaggon and the Dark Flaggon, advises the latter for use on Lake Chateaugay.

No. 244. Mr. D. C. Estes, in a letter to the " American Angler," wrote as follows : " It took me many years to find a fly that ' croppies ' would take, but I now take them readily with a fly." Then followed the description of a fly like that in plate, to which he adds, " and a swan shot on the snell near the head of the fly."

No. 245. Barnwell. This fly was made from a description given by Mr. Robert B. Roosevelt in his book entitled " Game Fish of the North," wherein he writes of it as " a beautiful and effective fly for black bass." Mr. Roosevelt did not name the fly he recommends, but we have always called it " the Barnwell," Barnwell being the *nom de plume* of the author when " Game Fish of the North " was first published by Carleton in 1852.

Made by C.F.ORVIS, Manchester,Vt.

M.Bradley Co.Lith.

PLATE Y: DESCRIPTION PAGE 413

Made by **C.F. ORVIS**, Manchester, Vt.

M.Bradley Co.Lith.

PLATE Z: DESCRIPTION PAGE 427

M. Bradley Co. Lith.

Made by **C. F. ORVIS**, Manchester, Vt.

PLATE AA: DESCRIPTION PAGE 441

264
265
266
267
268
269

M. Bradley Co. Lith.

Made by C.F.ORVIS, Manchester,Vt.

PLATE BB: DESCRIPTION PAGE 457

Then came a day of absolute idleness, while the showers came and went, and the mountains appeared and disappeared in sun and storm, — that perfect physical enjoyment which consists in a feeling of strength without any inclination to use it, and in a delicious languor which is too enjoyable to be surrendered to sleep.

Charles Dudley Warner.

MARYLAND, TENNESSEE, KENTUCKY, GEORGIA, AND
MISSISSIPPI.

A. F. DRESEL . . . . . . . ⎰ Lord Baltimore.
⎹ Polka.
⎱ De Gem.
⎰ Seth Green, etc.

JAMES C. CHAMBERLIN.

WILLIAM A. OBENCHAIN . . . . { Trout Flies.

S. C. CLARKE.

J. H. STEWART . . . . . . . ⎰ North Carolina
⎱ Indian Flies.

|  |  |  |
|---|---|---|
| *Maryland.* | { Lord Baltimore.<br>Polka.<br>De Gem.<br>Toodle-bug.<br>Seth Green.<br>Professor.<br>Ferguson.<br>Silver Doctor.<br>Hackles. | } Black Bass. |

A. F. DRESEL,                          Baltimore,                          Md.

For the Potomac River and its tributaries, the Lord Baltimore has almost invariably taken the largest bass, while in numbers the Polka, De Gem, Seth Green, Black Hackle, and Professor have proved the more successful.

The Silver Doctor has been good, especially from September on, while a small Gray Hackle seemed to strike their fancy while " gnatting."

In 1885 I wanted a fly with certain colors in it, but knowing of none suited to my idea, had De Gem tied as an experiment. I have done very well with it, principally in shallow waters like the Great Capon Creek and the Potomac at Harper's Ferry.

The Lord Baltimore and other flies mentioned are good throughout the season.

---

*Tennessee.*

JAMES C. CHAMBERLAIN,                          Nashville,                          Tenn.

While I am an enthusiastic fisherman, and as fond of the sport as I was in my boyhood, thirty or forty years ago, when I angled for brook trout among the mountains of Pennsylvania and in Maine and New Hampshire, times and circumstances have greatly changed, and my surroundings are such that I have now but little use for the gaudy-colored fly ; and since my removal to Tennessee at the close of the late war, I have fallen in entirely with the customs of the natives, and for many years past have used a more natural and substantial lure than the artificial fly.

The rivers and streams of the South are not so clear as those of the North, and for game fish the minnow and spoon trolls are almost exclusively used.

We have no brook trout east of the mountains that divide this State from North Carolina, unless perhaps a few in the streams in the extreme eastern part of the State. Our only game fish are the black bass and jack-fish, which latter is nothing more nor less than the fresh-water salmon of the Susquehanna and other Eastern streams.

We also have the white perch, sun perch, and croppie, or a speckled perch ; but these are only semi-game, and will not strike at the artificial fly at all.

I sometimes amuse myself by fishing with an artificial fly for the purpose of experimenting ; but the best fisherman will have little returns for his efforts who will attempt to use them exclusively in the streams of this section.

They can be used to good purpose in the central and eastern portions of Kentucky and in east Tennessee, but west of the Cumberland Mountains they can hardly be regarded a success.

*Kentucky.*                         Trout Flies.

WILLIAM A. OBENCHAIN,          Bowling Green,                    **Ky.**

My favorite flies are as follows : —

| | |
|---|---|
| Coachman. | Brown Hackle. |
| Royal Coachman. | Black Hackle. |
| Professor. | March Brown. |
| Gray Drake. | Chantrey. |

I have been more successful with these flies, particularly in the Linville and its tributaries, in Mitchell County, North Carolina, in the months of July and August. I have found the first four very killing when used early in the morning or late in the evening. But in a large mill-pond in Grandmother Creek, the water of which is continually stained by the remains of the large hemlocks in and about it, I found the same flies excellent even during the middle of the day.

I prefer the Sproat hook, small size, say Nos. 7, 8, and 9, ordinarily ; that is, for fishing in cloudy weather or late in the evening. In very clear water, or bright days, a No. 10 or No. 11 is preferable ; but for general fishing a No. 8 gives me the best results. As to snells, give me bright single gut, stained, and from five to six inches long.

The following incident, perhaps the first of the kind, occurred several years ago in Mitchell County, North Carolina, while I was fishing in Webb's mill-pond, in Grandmother Creek, a few hundred yards from where it empties into Linville River.

This mill-pond, by the breaking of the dam, has since then almost entirely disappeared ; but at that time it was very large and deep, and much of the bottom was covered with moss, which, together with the numberless sunken logs, formed an excellent hiding-place for the trout, many of them very large, that were plentiful in the pond. A dense growth of laurel extended down to the water's edge nearly all the way round, so that a boat was necessary to enable me to reach the best fishing-places and to make a long cast. Even then one had to be careful to keep his flies clear of the many dead hemlock-trees that stood erect in the pond.

I had just taken several fine trout from the vicinity of a sunken log, when a very large one jumped out of the water a little to my right. Turning in that direction, I straightened out my line behind me, so as to cast my flies where the trout had disappeared. I had just given the forward spring to my rod, when, most unexpectedly, it struck against something, and my line fell limp behind me. I thought at first that my boat had drifted too near one of the old hemlock-trees, but, quickly ascertaining that this was not the case, I looked up at my rod, and, to my great surprise, saw a cedar-bird (*Bombycilla Carolinensis*), with outstretched wings, settling slowly down in front of me. These birds frequent that region in the summer season, and were numerous about the pond, flitting from tree to tree. It was evident that the little unfortunate had flown against my rod just as I had given it the forward motion, and struck it with sufficient force to stun it for a time.

I could easily have picked it up out of the water, so near did it fall to me, but I was too intent on securing the speckled prize which I was sure was near the same spot, waiting for another passing fly. Quickly recovering my line, I dropped my lures at the proper place, and in less time than it takes to tell it had a twelve-inch beauty securely hooked, and darting furiously through the tinted water. After having him safe in my landing-net, I looked to see what had become of the little cedar-bird. While I was playing my trout, it had floated slowly some thirty or forty yards down the pond, and just at this moment had recovered sufficiently to rise from the water and fly, with unsteady wing, to the nearest shore, where it disappeared from view among the laurels.

---

*Georgia.*

S. C. CLARKE,                                  Marietta,                                  Ga.

It may seem like rank heresy to the orthodox believer in many theories, but my experience with trout flies and trout fishing, extending over fifty years, and north, south, east, and west, leads me to the belief that trout, bass, and salmon will, when hungry, or, as we say, "on the feed," take almost any well-made fly, and when "off the feed" cannot easily be tempted by any combinations of fur or feathers.

Color and size in the artificial insect I think more important than form, and I would tend to Mr. Pennell's theory of three typical flies for a day's angling, as soon as a book filled with fifty varieties. As to the old theory of imitating the natural fly, and having one for every month and each separate water, it seems to me to be pedantry.

---

*Mississippi.*          North Carolina Indian Flies.

J. H. STEWART,                          Jackson,                          Miss., 1887

The two specimen flies which I inclose you will see are reversed hackles, made by cutting narrow strips of deerskin with the hair left on, wrapped around the hook a few times, and well tied at each end. The North Carolina Indians tie them to perfection, using some sort of cement or waterproof varnish over the thread, and for the bodies the various colors and length of hair from different skins, but usually rather stiff hair, preferring it from the deer's legs. They often cut the hair off and use it without the skin, but made in this way the flies are not as durable. They use feathers occasionally in the same way.

The effect of this reverse method, *i. e.* tying the hair to point from instead of towards the bend of the hook, is very perceptible in swift water. Every little move in drawing back, as the flies float down, gives them the appearance of a live worm trying to get out of the water. It does not amount to much with feathers, as they have no worm or caterpillar appearance.

In addition to the forms I send to you, they sometimes use three or more stiff hairs, running down over the curve of the hook half an inch or more, to represent the feelers on the caterpillar's head. The advantage of twisting the skin around the hook is to give it a sort of a whirling motion in the water as the current strikes it.

I send you specimens of hair on the skin. Trim the skin down thin, soak well in warm water, and then stretch it thoroughly, and cut it in strips to suit.

NOTE. — The flies sent were tied in exactly the method of the recently patented "fluttering fly," and it is claimed that these flies have been used by the North Carolina Indians for generations. — M. E. O. M.

## PLATE Y.

No. 246. Bob White.

No. 249. Gov. Alvord.

No. 247. Caddis, cork body.

No. 250. Ferguson.

No. 248. Epting.

No. 251. De Gem.

No. 246. The following letter from Mr. Dunlap gives an account of the Bob White : —

CEDARVILLE, GREENE CO., OHIO, *April* 6, 1891.

MR. CHAS. F. ORVIS:

*My dear Sir,* — I inclose you a specimen of the fly Bob White, designed by me in the year 1889, but not used until the season of 1890, when I gave it a thorough test in connection with the best flies known to me for the waters of this locality. My reasons for not trying it sooner were that the fly was made more to utilize what I considered a beautiful feather combining good colors, and to gratify a natural disposition to originate and construct, than with the hope of producing anything equal to my favorite fly, the Gov. Alvord, which for some time I had regarded unapproachable as a fly for the small-mouth black bass of our rocky streams. But last year I began to use it as an upper fly in connection with Grizzly King and Gov. Alvord, the latter as stretcher. In this rather disadvantageous position I found that it was sometimes taken in preference to either of the other flies, and I concluded to give it a fair trial by substituting it for Gov. Alvord as the tail fly, with the latter as first dropper. In this position it was almost invariably taken in preference to either of the other flies, or any flies used in connection with it during the season. It seemed to have the preference under all ordinary conditions of water and at all times of day. So I came to the unexpected but gratifying conclusion that in Bob White I had the best fly of all those known to me. I send it to you because I know that you are interested in these things, and because I have, perhaps, a pardonable pride not only in the merits of the fly, but also in its rather comely appearance. I also hope that some one may be induced to try it on trout, and I should be glad to hear with what result.

The feather from which Bob White is made is found in the wing of our quail, close to the body of the bird. There are a number of feathers there with the whitish-brown border and dark, velvety, mottled appearance which practically answer the same purpose; but I have selected the one in the fly as the handsomest and most desirable, and therefore the typical feather for the fly. I had at first thought of naming the fly Bob White, but did not decide to do so until I had hooked my first bass on it. While playing this fish, a quail near by was whistling "Bob White," and I decided, then and there, to name the fly accordingly.

Yours very truly,

JEP. G. DUNLAP.

No. 247. Caddis, cork body. Allusion has been made to the habits and form of the caddis flies in the opening chapter of this book, and from that the form of this fly will be seen to be more like that of the drakes than the caddis. But it is known to too many as a caddis fly to attempt to change the name; it would only result in confusion, misunderstanding, and failure. We do not know who first tied them in this manner. The first we ever saw was sent to us by some one living in Albany, N. Y., who said he could procure no more like it, but that they were "most taking flies." We tried them, and afterwards endeavored to improve upon them at the suggestion of General R. U. Sherman, making them with pale olive wings, and covering the cork body with a delicate shade of olive silk. General Sherman said that the fly then greatly resembled those found at Bisby Lake; and this imitation, made according to his suggestions, proved very successful for the Bisby Lake trout.

Mr. William J. Cassard reported remarkable success with the fly with gray wings, like that shown in the plate, for black bass at Lake Gogebec and in the St. Lawrence.

No. 248. Mr. Chas. W. Epting, of Philadelphia, has invented two flies bearing his name: one, a hackle, depicted in Plate A, which he advises for trout; and this larger fly, which he has found most useful for bass. Mr. Epting considers the correct tint of the furnace hackle used in making these flies of utmost importance. The body of the bass fly is wound with silkworm gut, which renders it hard and durable.

No. 249. This bass fly, of quiet aspect, named after the much-esteemed governor of New York, Governor Alvord, bears a strong resemblance to the Academy, and by frequent mention of it in the lists given by fishermen it will be seen how widely the fly is known and used for black bass.

No. 250. In the fly-lists of one dealer in fishing-tackle we find mention of four different Fergusons; indeed, the confusion had come to be so great concerning this fly that it almost seemed as though any fly with a yellow body and a green hackle might be called a Ferguson. A request was sent to Major T. B. Ferguson, Fish Commissioner of Maryland, asking him to give us a correct pattern of the fly indorsed by his name. Major Ferguson sent to us a fly exactly like that shown in the plate, and said that it was the " true and only " Ferguson. We therefore repudiated all others, and apply the name to this fly alone. The Ferguson proper is probably the most generally successful fly for black bass in the entire list.

No. 251. Mr. A. F. Dresel, of Baltimore, Maryland, made and named " De Gem," as related in his most entertaining letter.

O Florida, thou poem of the States,
   Thou coral garden where the warm sea sings,
'T is sweet in dreams to drift beyond thy gates,
   Like voyagers old who sought immortal spring,
'Neath golden skies impearled with ibis wings,
   Afar from crystal season's lines of blue,
And cloudy conifers of ice and snow,
   And with the double sense of beauty view
In things we feel the things we are to know,
   And almost hear the palpitating strings
Of life harps lost in answering numbers play.
   Would that my song could like thy bird songs flow
Like wingèd poets to the sun-land true !
   Sweet would I sing, O Rivière du Mai !

HEZEKIAH BUTTERWORTH.

## FLORIDA, LOUISIANA, TEXAS, ARIZONA, AND NEVADA.

GEORGE TROWBRIDGE . . . . . . . { The Cracker.

H. P. UFFORD . . . . . . . . { Fiery Dragon.

C. S. Wells . . . . . . . . .
{ Scarlet Ibis.
Cheney.
Montreal.
Professor, etc.

W. L. CARPENTER . . . . . . .
{ Brown Ant.
Yellow Sally.
Coachman.
Royal Coachman.

ERNEST HARRIS . . . . . . . .
{ Coachman.
Brown Hackle.
Professor.
Alder, etc.

| *Florida.* | { The Cracker. | { For Channel Bass and Sea Trout. |

GEORGE TROWBRIDGE,　　　　　New York,　　　　　N. Y.

I noticed your inclosure about Supplement to " Fishing with the Fly." Here is an account of one fly, " the Cracker," a comparatively new creation. It has been on the market now about eighteen months. I inclose sample.

In regard to its origin. While fishing in the Homosassa River, February 2, 1885, I caught a channel bass of six pounds on a home-made fly, which resembled, when new, the Blue Jay of the Orvis-Cheney collection.

This channel bass was the largest I had ever caught with the fly. I at once put the fly aside as a " record-breaker," and tied up some more like it.

On February 24, 1886, I tried another fly like this on the Mosquito Lagoon, at Oak Hill, Fla., and there caught in one afternoon one channel bass, 4 lbs. 8 oz., and one of 4 lbs. 6 oz. These were the first fish which had ever been caught in the Mosquito Lagoon with the fly.

On March 12, 1886, I had very good luck with a red-winged fly in the same waters, taking one channel bass, 3 lbs., one sea trout, and one channel bass of 7 lbs. This was the best record yet.

On January 12, 1887, in the Homosassa River, with a blue-bodied fly, I took three sea trout, six black bass (large mouth), one channel bass, 9 lbs. 4 oz. " Better and better," I thought.

Meantime I had been successful with flies having more of a variation of colors in wing and tail. These were not " record-breaking " flies, but very good for all-round work, and especially fascinating to the sea trout. The luckiest models always contained red, peacock sword feathers, blue and yellow in wing and tail. Blue was always attractive to channel bass.

Without going more into detail, I compared my lucky models, eliminated a color from one and added a feather to another. Thus I developed a new series of flies from the fundamental fortunate shapes and colors. Next I went out on the river and tried each new creation. This was the crucial test. If one was good, I kept its record and made more flies like it. The less successful I cast aside. Finally I settled on one model as being the most successful. This I called the Cracker.

As far as the origin of the name goes, it is appropriate for two reasons. First, it was "born and brought up" in Florida, and, being a native of that State, is entitled to the native's name, Cracker. Second, it is pronounced a "crackin' good fly" by those who have tried it. It is not in any sense a theoretical fly, but purely practical in its origin and its results. As to what the fly, as it now appears, has done, I think that its record cannot be beaten. It has caught every variety of fish which rises to the fly, when it has been cast over the waters that these fish inhabit. I do not think that black bass have been caught with it, because I never had any one tell me that he had tried it for black bass.

Here is a record of three Crackers which are on my table as I write : —

I. St. James City, Charlotte Harbor, Fla., January, 1888, 15 sea trout, 28 lbs. ; 2 channel bass, $7\frac{1}{4}$ and $3\frac{1}{2}$ lbs.

II. Sarasota, Fla., April 5 and 6, 1888, 3 channel bass, 17, $23\frac{3}{4}$, 22 lbs.

III. Sarasota, April 9, 1888, 3 channel bass, $12\frac{1}{4}$, $20\frac{1}{4}$, $18\frac{1}{2}$,— 51 lbs. April 10, 4 channel bass, 14, 18, 14, 14, — 60 lbs. Total,

Made by C.F. ORVIS, Manchester, Vt.

PLATE CC: DESCRIPTION PAGE 469

Made by **C.F. ORVIS**, Manchester, Vt.

M. Bradley Co. Lith.

PLATE DD: DESCRIPTION PAGE 479

Made by **C.F. ORVIS**, Manchester, Vt.

PLATE EE: DESCRIPTION PAGE 489

M. Bradley Co. Lith.

Made by C.F. ORVIS, Manchester, Vt.

PLATE FF: DESCRIPTION PAGE 503

111 lbs. on one fly in two days. All these fish were killed with single leader and 8½ oz. trout rod.

Now as to variety. This is an enumeration of the fish taken with this kind of fly in the salt water of Florida : —

Tarpon (weight, 1 lb. 3 oz., small, but it is the only one that has yet been taken with the fly in Florida).

Channel bass (largest, 24 lbs. 5 oz. In April, 1889, I saw Mr. John D. Wattles, of Philadelphia, while using a Cracker fly, hook, play, and land a 15 lb. channel bass, using a 5½ oz. Bethabara wood rod). Sea trout, cavaillè, rovaillè, bluefish, Spanish mackerel, grouper, mangrove snapper, skip-jack, sailor's choice ; also a nondescript, called a " tenpounder." I never could find any one who knew it intimately enough to give it a Latin nickname.

On April 8, 1889, while fishing New Pass Bar, I caught a sheepshead with this fly. Depth of water three feet, strong tide, grassy bottom.

In the North, this fly has taken trout in Maine, in the Adirondacks, and in Canada. It has caught, but not killed, one salmon. It is also good for sea trout.

In regard to size of hook and dressing. The smallest fly that I have ever used has been tied on No. 8 hook. This size is good for small brook trout in Maine, — " Kennebago size," as they say there. No. 3 is about right for trout from ¾ lb. to 1½ lb. No. 1 is what I use for the largest channel bass. It is a good size for trout from 1 to 3 lbs. in Canada. If trout are expected to run larger than that, I prefer a larger fly.

In one respect the Cracker belies its name, or rather its namesakes. It is purposely *overdressed*. The mohair of the body should be picked out to make it fluffy.

Friends who have used this fly report favorably of it from all quarters, but all of the statements made above are from my own experience, and I vouch for them.

---

| *Louisiana and Minnesota.* | Fiery Dragon. | Black Bass. |

H. P. Ufford,          Lake Charles,          La.

I regret very much my inability to be of any aid to you in your laudable undertaking. Of necessity, the great bulk of my fishing for the past many years has been for the black bass, and most of that with bait. The most successful flies I have used for bass have been those in which green and yellow predominate. One in especial, a monstrosity of my own making, with a yellow body, green hackle, and yellow wings, has proved very killing on the lakes of Minnesota. I am sorry I have no specimen of the Fiery Dragon, as a friend of mine named it, to send to you, but perhaps you can gather some idea of it as a work of art (?) when I tell you how I made it. On a 2/0 Sproat hook I wound half a yard, more or less, of yellow gimp, and in the last dozen turns or so wrapped in one or two feathers from the teal duck for tail and hackle; I then tied on a couple of canary-bird feathers for wings, and had a horrible-looking thing which ought, by rights, to have scared any fish into a state of gibbering idiocy, but which gave me seventeen bass, one June afternoon, in Detroit Lake, Minn., when they would n't touch a Cheney, Oriole, Coachman, Red Ibis, Seth Green, or anything I could offer them.

[Of later date.] Many thanks for the Fiery Dragon, which came duly to hand; the larger one is like my recollection of the nondescript I made, and I think it will prove a " killer."

---

|  |  |
|---|---|
| *Texas.* | { Scarlet Ibis.<br>Cheney.<br>Montreal.<br>Professor.<br>Royal Coachman.<br>White Miller. |

C. S. WELLS,                        Victoria,                        Texas.

Your idea of collecting information in regard to the use of flies in different sections is a good one, as, if the material thus received is compiled and published, it will be very interesting reading for anglers.   In this part of the country we have but one fish, the large-mouth bass, that takes a fly with anything like satisfaction to the angler.

With an experience that extends throughout the length and breadth of the United States, I consider the large-mouth bass of Southern waters the peer of any game fish to be found in the fresh water of our land, not excepting even the lordly *Fontinalis*.   After repeated trials of all the best known varieties, styles, and shapes of flies, I have settled on the Scarlet Ibis, Cheney, Montreal, Professor, Royal Coachman, and White Miller as comprising all the best varieties for our waters.   One curious fact that I have noticed in my fishing experience in this State I do not remember to have seen mentioned as occurring elsewhere ; and that is, the dropper is almost invariably the fly taken when one fish is hooked.   On account of the many obstructions, such as tules, brush, and lily-pads, that occur in the waters where our bass are found, I always use a six-foot leader with but two flies attached. In recovering the line after a cast, and just before the hooks are drawn from the water for the back cast, the dropper will skip along the surface three or four feet more out than in the water, and hanging perpendicularly. This appears to be an irresistible attraction for the bass, and I venture to assert that at least seventy-five per cent. of all I have caught with the fly in this vicinity have been hooked on the dropper fly. I have sometimes imagined that it was the fly, and not its position on the leader, that made the dropper most attractive, and changed their positions, but without any change in results.

I am not exclusively a fly-fisherman, but prefer the fly to all other methods, if the fish can be induced to take it. I favor mist-colored leaders for clear waters.

Have never found the bass in this State to prefer a natural to an artificial fly ; by this, I mean that whenever I find them breaking water after natural insects they will take the fly readily. Strange as it may appear in a fish of such exceeding voracity, the large-mouth bass is at times as capricious and as dainty in his likes and dislikes for the different lures as the most finicky and highly-educated trout.

One of my most pleasing angling experiences of recent date was the conversion of a friend from an indifferent bait fisherman to an enthusiastic and accomplished fly-fisher, by the loan of my copy of " Fishing with the Fly." " I have ordered an outfit," he wrote, " and am going in for the poetry of the art."

During the past season I watched closely the results from using particular patterns of flies in fishing for bass (large mouth), with the view of determining the comparative killing qualities of each. I used about a dozen different varieties, including the old standard favorites, and found that if there was any difference in their killing power it was so slight as to be not worth mentioning, with the exception of the White Miller, which, after sunset, appeared perfectly irresistible, and would be taken in preference to all others, while it was equally killing during the day. Next season, therefore, my book will be made up of about one half White Moth or Miller, and the balance distributed among a half dozen or so of the different standard sorts. Hackles are no good for our bass.

---

| *Arizona.* | Brown Ant.<br>Yellow Sally.<br>Coachman.<br>Royal Coachman. | Trout Flies. |
|---|---|---|

W. L. CARPENTER, Fort Whipple, Ariz.

I am only familiar with fishing west of the Missouri River, where I have had an experience of twenty-five years, which has convinced me that but three flies are needed for Western fishing, namely, Brown Ant, Yellow Sally, and Coachman or Royal Coachman.

The Brown Ant will be taken under all circumstances where the Brown Hackle and similar flies would be useful. It is probably mistaken by the trout for the Crane fly (*Tipulidæ*), which are very numerous in early spring throughout the Rocky Mountain region.

The Yellow Sally is taken by the fish for the yellow-bodied grasshopper, which forms the principal part of their food in August. I believe all flies with yellow bodies or wings prove effective for that reason, holding as I do the opinion that fish can distinguish colors.

The White Millers are very numerous in June and July, and the imitation is particularly taking late in the afternoon and until too dark to see it.

I think that flies are usually made with too small bodies. They are all made much smaller than the bodies of the insect they represent, and would prove more taking if made more in the style of the Reuben Wood and Seth Green.

Prefer the Sproat hook with heavy gut, stained.

---

| | | |
|---|---|---|
| *Nevada.* | Coachman.<br>Brown Hackle.<br>Black Hackle.<br>Professor.<br>Black Gnat.<br>Cow Dung.<br>Alder.<br>Abbey. | Trout. |

ERNEST HARRIS,                    Carson City,                    Nev.

My favorite flies are Professor, Black Gnat, and Cow Dung. Of course I use many others, but I find those mentioned good, morning, noon, and evening. The Coachman, Alder, Abbey, and Montreal are the ones the most of my fishing chums use. Brown Hackles and Black Hackles are also used a great deal here, but the Coachman is first choice for fishing in the pools.

All of our fishing here is for brook trout, as our river and lake trout seldom take a fly in this neighborhood.

I prefer the Sproat bend, but the sneck with the side bend is generally used.

Snells should be about four inches long, and of size to accord with the fly; No. 8 is my choice in size for hook.

Leaders should be light, and I rather think the unstained gut is the most durable.

## PLATE Z.

No. 252. Golden Dustman.

No. 253. Henshall.

No. 254. Knight Templar.

No. 255. Jungle Cock.

No. 256. Holberton.

No. 257. Holberton II.

**No. 252.** The Golden Dustman was designed by Dr. Henshall in 1883. In his book entitled "More about Black Bass," he writes: "I have been experimenting with a fly of my own designing, for several seasons, that is yet a puzzle to me. Sometimes it is the most killing fly I ever cast, the bass rising madly when they would notice no other fly; but on other occasions it is not at all successful, the bass refusing it altogether, always taking the other fly in the cast. I have not yet determined the most suitable conditions and occasions for using it, though I am inclined to think it best on cloudy days. It is constructed entirely of metallic colors."

We made a fly from the formula given by Dr. Henshall, sent it to him for criticism, and received the following reply : —

"Yours of the 20th inst. and the flies came this morning. The 'Golden Dustman' flies are *just right* in every way, but the smaller of the two is the proper size. I like even a smaller hook, and a Sproat instead of an O'Shaughnessy, though of course that is a mere matter of individual preference. Many anglers prefer the O'Shaughnessy hook. It is a most brilliant, beautiful fly, and at times the most successful I have ever used for black bass. You have hit the nail on the head, for I could not tell them apart from some that I tied a year ago last spring. The larger one is just right for Florida, and it is a very successful fly in these waters for all coast fishes that rise to the fly."

We imagine this fly would prove killing for salmon, owing to its iridescent effect, or as Dr. Henshall says of it: "The idea is to get the metallic reflections from the various shades of yellow and brown, without green."

**No. 253.** The Henshall was also made and named by Dr. Henshall, who reckons it among his favorite four flies for black bass.

Dr. Henshall has been placed in charge of the angling exhibit at the coming Columbian Exposition, and it is a pleasure to repeat what has been said of him in one of the journals of the day : —

" Dr Henshall is the best known angling expert in the United States in all kinds of angling, though he is better known, perhaps, as the ' apostle of the black bass,' and is the author of two works entirely devoted to this grand game fish : the ' Book of the Black Bass,' and ' More about Black Bass.' He has for many years been a valued contributor to various scientific and angling periodicals. He is president of the American Fisheries Society, president of the Ohio Fish and Game Commission, secretary of the Cincinnati Society of Natural History, and secretary-treasurer of the Cuvier Club of Cincinnati, the most prominent club of its kind in the United States, besides being an honorary member of the principal angling associations of America and England.

" Dr. Henshall is a native of Baltimore, Md., but removed to Cincinnati, Ohio, when a boy, where he graduated as a physician, and practiced his profession for many years at Cynthiana, Ky. Afterward he resided a few years at Oconomowoc, Wis., of which growing city he was the first mayor. He returned to Kentucky in 1878, and to Cincinnati in 1888, where he at present resides. His headquarters are at Washington, where he is special agent of the United States Fish Commission."

Our own knowledge of him is that of a most agreeable man, always thoughtful for the pleasure and comfort of all around him, gifted and accomplished beyond most men, but, above all, a man to trust and respect as one who would stand a faithful comrade in sunshine or storm.

No. 254. The Knight Templar is a combination suggested and named by Mr. William J. Cassard in 1885 or 1886.

No. 255. The Jungle Cock bass fly is named from the wing feathers taken from the jungle fowl described in the history of the trout flies. For the bass fly, the feathers are selected from those pendent on each side of the tail feathers ; the colors in the fly were chosen because believed to be those most generally captivating to black bass. The fly shown in the plate was first tied by C. F. Orvis in 1879 ; it has since ranked high among the favorites.

No. 256. Mr. Wakeman Holberton, of New York city, has designed a number of attractive flies, among them this bearing his name. Mr. Holberton has painted some very pleasing pictures of trout with flies grouped about them, and is an authority on matters connected with fly-fishing, writing frequently for the papers under the *nom de plume* of " Scarlet Ibis." The fly called the Holberton is known to some anglers as the Greenwood Lake.

No. 257. Holberton II. We have had some hesitation in deciding what to do in regard to this fly. It is widely known as the Holberton, and had been much used before the Holberton proper made its appearance; but Mr. Holberton affirms that he is not responsible for his name being applied to the fly, and we cannot find who is, yet the fact remains that it is called the Holberton by many, and is too successful a fly not to be mentioned with the other favorites. We have, therefore, designated it the Holberton II., in concession to the popular nomenclature.

Room ! Room to turn round in, to breathe and be free
And to grow to be giant, to sail as at sea
With the speed of the wind on a steed with his mane
To the wind, without pathway or route or a rein.
Room ! Room to be free where the white-bordered sea
Blows a kiss to a brother as boundless as he ;
And to east and to west, to the north and the sun,
Blue skies and brown grasses are welded as one ;
And the buffalo come like a cloud on the plain,
Pouring on like the tide of a storm-driven main ;
And the lodge of the hunter to friend or to foe
Offers rest ; and unquestioned you come or you go.
My plains of America ! Seas of wild lands !
From a land in the seas in a raiment of foam,
That has reached to a stranger the welcome of home,
I turn to you, lean to you, lift you my hands.

JOAQUIN MILLER.

*London*, 1871.

# COLORADO, WYOMING, UTAH, AND IDAHO.

E. C. WOODWARD . . . . . . . $\left\{\begin{array}{l}\text{Coachman.} \\ \text{Gray Drake.} \\ \text{Governor.} \\ \text{Willow, etc.}\end{array}\right.$

M. D. BYERLY.

L. Z. COMAN . . . . . . . . $\left\{\begin{array}{l}\text{Coachman.} \\ \text{White Miller.} \\ \text{New Fly, etc.}\end{array}\right.$

S. W. HATCH.

J. W. HUNT.

JOHN A. LEHREITTER . . . . . . $\left\{\begin{array}{l}\text{Brown Hackle.} \\ \text{Coachman.}\end{array}\right.$

J. S. LAWRENCE . . . . . . . $\left\{\begin{array}{l}\text{Coachman.} \\ \text{Leadwing Coachman.} \\ \text{Royal Coachman.}\end{array}\right.$

CHARLES P. HILL . . . . . . . $\left\{\begin{array}{l}\text{Scarlet Ibis.} \\ \text{Black Gnat.} \\ \text{Coachman.} \\ \text{White Miller.}\end{array}\right.$

COL. P. T. SWAINE.

C. S. FARREN . . . . . . . . $\left\{\begin{array}{l}\text{Royal Coachman.} \\ \text{Coachman.} \\ \text{Professor.} \\ \text{Imbrie, etc.}\end{array}\right.$

W. P. WEBSTER . . . . . . . $\left\{\begin{array}{l}\text{Dark Stone.} \\ \text{Professor.} \\ \text{Hackles.}\end{array}\right.$

L. C. EASTMAN . . . . . . . . $\left\{\text{Red Hackle.}\right.$

| | | |
|---|---|---|
| *Colorado.* | Coachman.<br>Gray Drake.<br>Governor.<br>Willow.<br>Black Gnat. | Trout. |

E. C. Woodward, Leadville, Colo.

The best fishermen in this part of Colorado use rather quiet-colored flies; in size, No. 8 is about the largest, No. 10 the average, and No. 12 the smallest. The Coachman is the fly most commonly used. Gray Drake, Governor, Willow fly, and Black Gnat I should select as those that I have had best success with.

The largest fish that I have known of being caught here with a fly (4½ lbs.) was caught with a very small black fly of Scotch make.

The custom here is to use a leader about eight feet long, colored a little to destroy its glitter. I color leaders by working them in tea, and then dropping them into a weak solution of green vitriol (sulphate of iron), and immediately after taking from the iron solution putting them into water till all the iron is washed out. The leaders can be colored faintly or almost black, according to the time they are left in the iron solution. I do not find that the leaders are weakened by this, as all of mine stand a five-pound pull on a spring balance. The largest fish have been caught here about the middle of the day. The streams here are so cold, being fed from melting snow, that the fish seem disinclined to rise before the sun has warmed them a little. Sunrise here is apt to be frosty even in midsummer, and insects are scarce till the sun thaws them out.

I think more fish are caught here in the fairly swift water than in the pools. We speak of the eddies in swift water as "riffles," and fish there.

*Colorado.*                    Trout Flies.

M. D. BYERLY,                          Alma,                          Colo.

The flies that are used in the mountains of this State are the Queen of the Water, King of the Water, Brown Caughlan, and Royal Coachman. I have fished with good success with those flies for nine years, and never fish with a hackle.

Trout will not rise here at the approach of a storm or in windy weather.

--------

|              |                                                        |          |
|--------------|--------------------------------------------------------|----------|
| *Colorado.*  | { Coachman. <br> White Miller. <br> Brown Hackle. <br> New Fly. | { Trout. |

L. Z. COMAN, M. D.,                    Boulder,                    Colo.

My favorite flies are Professor, yellow body, Brown Hackle, yellow body, Coachman, and the White Miller for evening fishing. There is, also, a fly that I have not been able to get lately, and do not know the name of; it has a slate wing and silver body. I have noticed all bright bodies seem to take well, especially those with a glimmer of metal.

I like a large hook, as the fish will take it, and it is more apt to fasten them. For the larger hooks I would have a doubled and twisted snell; the doubling makes them stronger, and the twisting prevents tangling.

I like hooks with a sharp angle just below the barb (like the old Limerick); the fish cannot throw themselves off as easily as from hooks of other shapes.

Would always have the snells stained; think they are not so easily seen by the fish.

*Colorado.*        Trout Flies.

S. W. HATCH,                Conejos,                Colo.

My favorite fly is one with a yellow body, light brown hackle, and darker brown wing. The Brown Hackle also proves a staple fly during all the fishing season. Very late in September the Coachman is a most killing fly, and during the high water in our streams, in May and June; yet it is hard to tell what the trout prefer during that time. I once used as a tail fly a dark brown winged fly with a light brown body, while my fellow-fisherman used as tail fly a Royal Coachman. There was no perceptible difference in our catch, the trout seeming to take one as greedily as the other. Late in the season, among the well-known flies, the Professor and Grizzly King are " taking " flies in our waters, but as a rule I always use a small dark fly as the tail fly. The Oak fly is a new one with me. I expect to prove it a favorite fly this coming season.

Fishermen on our streams prefer a small hook, not larger than No. 5, usually either No. 6 or 7. A few use as large as No. 3, but they are the exception.

I prefer a light leader and snell always, and cannot perceive that it makes any difference whether they are stained or clear.

---

*Colorado.*        Trout Flies.

J. W. HUNT,                Buena Vista,                Colo.

The favorite flies here are as follows : —

| | |
|---|---|
| Plain (or white wing) Coachman. | Black Gnat. |
| Lead (or dark wing) Coachman. | Gray Hackle, green body. |
| Jungle (or spotted) Coachman. | Brown Hackle, peacock body, etc. |

Use light flies for early season and day.

Use dark flies late in the season and in the evening.

No. 8 and 10 hook are mostly used here. Short heavy snells, say about four inches long. Hooks should be bent and sharp-pointed and well-tempered.

I have added the experience of others, and the above is the result.

---

| *Colorado.* | { Brown Hackle. <br> { Coachman. | { Trout. |

JOHN A. LEHREITTER,　　　　　　　Salida,　　　　　　　Colo.

I find, for general use and good results, that with a plentiful supply of Brown Hackles and Coachmen there is but little need of any other flies in our mountain streams.

I will mention that, as our streams are swift, a good stiff, well-made fly is desirable. I mean a fly with some body to it; none of those cheap flimsy excuses called trout flies.

One time on Taylor River, a friend fishing alongside of me, with more success than I, gave me a fly with a yellow body, the same kind that he was using. I hooked a few fish, and finally a larger one took the fly, when snap went the snell; after that I used my own stock, and did not break any more snells.

As the waters here are very clear, I prefer the uncolored snells and leaders.

---

| *Colorado.* | { Coachman. <br> { Leadwing Coachman. <br> { Royal Coachman. | { Trout. |

J. S. LAWRENCE,　　　　　　　Gunnison,　　　　　　　Colo.

The experiences of individual anglers are so varied that it would be quite difficult to say with any certainty what particular flies have been used with the greatest success.

My own experience has been that the three kinds of Coachman, viz., Common, Royal, and Leadwing, are superior to all the other flies in taking our mountain trout. About a No. 6 O'Shaughnessy hook is the one I would choose for a season's fishing. A six-foot single leader, with short loops at intervals, is to me the most desirable one. Of course it is taken for granted that a split bamboo rod is the only satisfactory one to use.

---

|  |  |  |
|---|---|---|
| *Wyoming.* | Scarlet Ibis.<br>Black Gnat.<br>Coachman.<br>White Moth. | Trout. |

CHARLES P. HILL, Rawlins, Wyo.

For my favorite fly I must be guided by the ones I have found the best in our Western waters, and therefore must concede the palm to the "Scarlet Ibis;" there are other very useful and killing flies, but the Ibis is always good. Black Gnat, Coachman, White Moth, and Professor have also always been killing flies with me, but my cast is incomplete without the Ibis, sometimes as a dropper, but more frequently the stretcher fly. Last season, in fact, on a two weeks' trip, when I first put my rod together at the Three Forks of Snake River, I made my cast as follows, Ibis (stretcher), Miller, and Black Gnat (they were good flies and were on a good leader, and I have the same leader bearing the same flies in my book now, and they seem good for another trip); and though I fished daily in Snake River, Slater Creek, and the Savory, and had most excellent success, I did not use anything else. I tried other casts just to see the effect, but while I caught some fish, I had the surest rises and killed more fish with the first mentioned.

Regarding size of hook, I find the small hook very much the best with us, No. 9 and 10 being my favorite sizes.

I think I like the quite light leaders and snells the best, and I don't find the difference in color of much importance.

I never was much of an angler until I learned to fish with the fly, and while my companions would talk enthusiastically of the pleasures of the rod, I preferred my gun ; but I have since learned (though not to be an expert, by any manner of means) to fish with the fly, and I consider it the most enjoyable sport in the world.

---

*Colorado.*                                    Trout Flies.

COL. P. T. SWAINE, U. S. A.,                Fort Keogh,                Mont.

My experience in fly-fishing has been confined to four seasons in the mountains of Colorado. Almost any fly named in the popular lists was used, resulting in a selection of the Coachman as a favorite, particularly for morning and evening fishing. In the middle of a bright day I found a Grizzly King a good substitute, and I always used a Brown or Black Hackle with each of these flies.

---

*Wyoming.*
$\left\{\begin{array}{l}\text{Royal Coachman.}\\\text{Coachman.}\\\text{Professor.}\\\text{Imbrie.}\\\text{Black Gnat.}\\\text{Dark Cow Dung.}\\\text{White Miller.}\\\text{Montreal, etc.}\end{array}\right.$ $\left\{\text{Trout.}\right.$

C. S. FARREN,                          Cokeville,                          Wyo.

The best flies for this section, that is, those that I use most frequently, are those named in the following list: Royal Coachman,

White Wing Coachman, Professor, Imbrie, Black Gnat, Dark Cow Dung, White Miller, Brown Hen, Dusty Miller, Abbey, Dark Montreal, Gray Drake, Brown Hackle, Ginger Hackle, and Black Hackle.

The two Coachmans are my standard flies. I use them at all times, no matter if it is a bright or a dark day, and I always catch trout on them when all others fail. I have fished all day with the plain Coachman for a tail fly, and have only changed it when I wanted to put on a new one. The Royal Coachman is not quite as good as the plain, but I would as soon think of going out after trout with no rod as to go without the two Coachman flies. I have caught the genuine mountain trout here, all I could carry, when other men were fishing beside me with other flies and could not get a rise, and the same thing has happened when fishing for salmon trout.

The reason I like the Coachman is that it is a combination of white and dark, and in the Royal Coachman you have the three different shades, light, dark, and red.

I use Nos. 1, 2, and 3 Sproat hooks.

-------

| | | |
|---|---|---|
| *Idaho and Utah.* | { Dark Stone.<br>Professor.<br>Hackles. | { Trout. |

W. P. WEBSTER, Salt Lake City, Utah.

My experience "fishing with the fly" has been mostly in the headwaters of the Snake River in eastern Idaho, and other streams between the Yellowstone Park and southern Utah. If confined to two patterns, I would choose the Dark Stone and Professor. They would cover all needs of season and time of day in this section. When fishing in the tributaries of the Gunnison River, in western Colorado, I found a small fly which, described as " pepper and salt " (don't know its name), took better than any other. It is not equal to the two kinds mentioned. In this locality, any fly, salmon-color in appearance, is good. Have found a grasshopper fly with large brown outside and yellow inside wings and blue body, to be very killing. Think a fly of similar description with a scarlet hackle would be a great success. The body to be dark, but rather pale. The wings might range from dark brown to cinnamon. Hook for large flies, Sproat; for small, sneck Kendall. Leaders and snells, single, light stained. Light gut is strong enough, and not nearly as liable to splinter as the heavy. Have never used short loops, but think they must be good for tail flies.

---

*Idaho.*          Red Hackle.

L. C. EASTMAN,          Soda Springs,          Idaho.

The trout take the fly here until late in November. It is not necessary to pattern after an insect for them. A good stiff wing would help most flies.

The Brown Hackle with a red body succeeds here at any time of the day. Hooks should be large No. 2 and No. 3, tied on short strands of mist-colored gut, double at hook.

PLATE AA.

No. 258. Matador.                     No. 261. Oriole.
No. 259. Ondawa.                      No. 262. Oconomowoc.
No. 260. La Belle.                    No. 263. Polka.

No. 258. Matador. This fly was designed by Mr. William J. Cassard, of New York city, and later named by C. F. Orvis the Matador; *i. e.*, the killer. Its gay, rich dress reminds one of the picturesque matador of the Spanish bull-fights, who is also the triumphant killer.

The fly is calculated to be effective for large trout in deep, strong waters, and ought to be taking for black bass.

Mr. Cassard has also invented two similar patterns that are excellent bass flies, which he calls the Romany Rye and Romany Ree, both having wings of the black barred feathers of the wood duck, like those of the Matador.

No. 259. The Ondawa is a bass fly, to which has been given an old Indian name belonging to a little river in a valley of the Green Mountains. It is an ideal trout stream which can be waded or fished from a boat. It winds and doubles upon itself in never-ending curves. Numberless mountain streams swell its waters, and contribute the fingerlings to grow to vigorous trout in the cool, fern-shaded pools. The river gradually widens and deepens until it joins the Hudson near Schuylers-ville, so famous in Revolutionary times.

Many anglers who read these lines will remember restful, dreamlike hours spent drifting down the Ondawa. " Hard's ripples," " the pent bridge," and other pools dear to memory, will once more glimmer and beckon. They will remember, too, the quiet smoke after luncheon, while resting under the shade of the meadow elms, where eyes could wander from mountain to mountain that circle and guard the quiet valley. Later came the ride home, the cool night air fanning our faces, and bringing to us the odor of the willows, balm-o'-Gilead, and roadside mint ; then the welcoming lights, greetings, supper, and a rehearsal of the day's doings.

A little girl of thirteen, who was permitted to go on one of these fishing-trips, in her delight wrote the following verses to

## THE LOVELY ONDAWA.

Down on the river,
The sunshiny river,
Down midst the eddies
And deep limpid pools,
There's where my heart lies,
There's where the trout rise:
I think that's the place
To go fishing, don't you?

As we float down the river,
The sunshiny river,
By willows and alders
That droop as we pass,
The fish are a-flashing,
The streamlet is dashing:
I think that's the place
To go fishing, don't you?

We reach the red bridge,
Find the horses in waiting;
We all hurry in,
And are off with a rush
Up the long road,
With the fireflies flashing:
I think that's the place
To go fishing, don't you?

No. 260.   La Belle.   This bass fly was the first made by C. F. Orvis in 1879, and when tried was found to be excellent in some waters for black bass.   For a long time the fly had no name, until one day somebody said it "reminded him of a pretty girl in a white muslin dress and a blue sash, it ought to be taking;" so then and there it was named La Belle.

No. 261.   The Oriole was invented in 1870, and we quote from Dr. Henshall's book his own description of the origin of the Oriole fly and its name : —

THE ONDAWA

"UP THE LONG ROAD"

" The Lord Baltimore fly originated with Professor Mayer, of the Stevens Institute of Technology, Hoboken, N. J. Its formula is as follows : Lord Baltimore: body, orange ; hackle, tail, and wings, black, with small upper wings of jungle-cock. Professor Mayer and I, being natives of Baltimore, and knowing that black and yellow formed a good and taking combination in an artificial fly, each designed, unknown to the other, a fly to embody these colors ; and as they are the heraldic colors of the State of Maryland, and were the heraldic colors of Lord Baltimore, Professor Mayer aptly named his trout fly Lord Baltimore, while I designated my black bass fly the Oriole, from the Baltimore oriole, or hanging-bird, which beautiful songster was named in honor of Lord Baltimore, as its colors were the same as his own, black and orange."

Since taking this account from his book, Dr. Henshall has visited Manchester, and one May day, while we were sitting under the old apple-trees, chatting and watching the shadows drift down the mountains and flicker over the sloping fields, a tiny oriole came fluttering by. When she stopped to swing on the currant bushes near us, I motioned to him to notice, and then said : " I could never understand why our Oriole fly should be made with the canary-yellow wings, as it is." He replied : " It should not be made so ; it was not originally." " And yet," I said, " it is now so generally made the other way that I doubt if the fly made with orange, like the color on that bird, would be accepted as the right fly. What can one do about it ? " " I do not know," was the answer ; and this is another illustration of the errors that creep into fly-making and add to the mysteries of fly-nomenclature. The fly depicted in the plate is the one with the yellow wings, being the one better known, and probably the one intended by the several writers who refer to it in their letters.

No. 262. The Oconomowoc bass fly was invented by Dr. Henshall in 1872. Its name was the one used by him as his *nom de plume*, he having adopted it from a lake near his former home in Wisconsin.

No. 263. The Polka. Dr. Henshall writes in his book entitled " More about Black Bass : " —

" Each angler will soon adopt a few flies for his own fishing, none of which I may have mentioned, but he will nevertheless continue to use them, and swear by them on all occasions ; and this is one of the glorious privileges of the art of angling.

" As a father naturally thinks his own children the best, smartest, and handsomest, I may be pardoned for placing in my list, and strongly recommending as general flies, my Polka, Oriole, Oconomowoc, and Henshall, leaving to others the p₁ ise or condemnation due them." — Dr. Henshall created the Polka in 1870, and it has been most popular ever since its appearance.

I sit beneath thee, mountain pine, —
I breathe thy balm, I drink thy wine, —
  Upon the lonely hill.
The world lies far beneath my feet ;
Again my life is strong and sweet,
  In regions high and still.

I listen to the longed-for hymn,
Chanted within thine arches dim,
  Far up the azure air.
Ye subtle murmurs, floating o'er
From some far spiritual shore,
  What messages ye bear !

What hints of high, immortal things
Come floating down on unseen wings,
  To thrill the heart of care, —
To reassure the fainting mind,
That saddens, lest it cannot find
  Worlds that are still more fair !

Ah, when the restless city street
Again receives my rested feet,
  I 'll lift my vested wine ;
I 'll listen, in my chamber dim,
The low chant of thy far-off hymn,
  O sacred mountain pine !

And when the springs of life run low,
Effort grows feeble, purpose slow,
  Fill, fill thy chalice up.
Again and yet again I 'll stand ;
Again and yet again thy hand
  Shall fill my empty cup.

MARY CLEMMER.

# MONTANA.

"TAMARACK" . . . . . . . $\left\{\begin{array}{l}\text{Coachman.}\\\text{Professor.}\\\text{Grasshopper.}\\\text{Cheney, etc.}\end{array}\right.$

J. R. HOFFLIN . . . . . . . $\left\{\text{Professor.}\right.$

J. V. NYE.

CAPT. HARRY READE.

WILLIAM H. DEWITT . . . . . $\left\{\begin{array}{l}\text{Coachman.}\\\text{Brown Hackle.}\end{array}\right.$

LIEUT. C. A. DEVOL . . . . . $\left\{\begin{array}{l}\text{Coachman.}\\\text{Brown Hackle.}\\\text{Black Gnat.}\\\text{Deer Fly.}\end{array}\right.$

W. W. ADAMS . . . . . . . $\left\{\begin{array}{l}\text{Coachman.}\\\text{Royal Coachman.}\\\text{Hackles.}\\\text{Jungle Cock, etc.}\end{array}\right.$

|  | Coachman. |  |
|---|---|---|
|  | Professor. |  |
|  | Grasshopper. |  |
| *Montana.* | Imbrie. | Trout. |
|  | Cheney. |  |
|  | Captain. |  |
|  | White Miller. |  |

"TAMARACK,"                    Missoula,                              Mont.

I have often been asked, "What kind of flies do you use?" or "What is the best fly to use?"

To answer these questions I must beg leave to spin a yarn, and to tell it in my own language. I have never cast a fly east of the Rocky Mountains, and can speak only of the waters of the Pacific slope.

During a residence of ten years in Montana, I had to learn the art of fly-casting, fly and rod making, and nearly all the other essentials to an angler's success. The first fly (?) I ever saw I made myself, and it came about in this way. In October, 1877, while accompanying an expedition to the far West, we marched overland from Corinne, Utah, to Missoula, Montana, a distance of six hundred miles. We were forty-one days on the road, and suffered some hardships, including a snow blockade of five days on the main divide of the Rockies, where the thermometer fell from forty above to twenty below zero in twelve hours. For the benefit of those who do not know, I will say that all marches are regulated by wood and water, especially the latter. Our fifth camp was on a beautiful little stream about twenty feet wide, which wound and twisted in nearly all directions in its efforts to reach the Snake River, and from there to the Pacific.

As soon as the tents were pitched we rushed to the stream, clear as crystal, for water; and oh! the beauty of the sight! Trout of all sizes, from the two-pounder down, were literally swarming in a pool. Immediately every one who had a hook and line hunted them up, picked up the first stick he could find for a "pole," and got ready for business; but there were neither flies nor hoppers to be had. When I was a little boy, I heard my father speak about catching trout with a piece of red flannel. My boyhood recollections stood me in good place. Running to my tent, I got a piece of flannel, tied it on the hook, and made my first cast. An eight-inch trout, spying such a curious object, rapidly slashed and jerked through the water, came to the surface to investigate, and, after following it for a while, made a rush, and the next moment he was high in the air and fell gasping several yards from his native element. By this time the banks of the stream were so crowded with fishermen using salt pork for bait that my "fly" was no longer a success. Casting fat pork was so vigorously carried on that even Idaho trout became shy. I took my trout in one hand, my "fly-rod" in the other, and started to seek quieter waters, where I would not be annoyed with vulgar fishermen and salt pork.

Going up stream about one hundred and fifty yards, I came to where a bunch of alders had been uprooted by a freshet and had fallen into the water, but still held by their roots to the bank. This made an eddy in the stream, and below the bushes it was smooth. I could see clearly to the bottom, and what a sight! At least two dozen large trout were quietly swimming about, eager for anything in the shape of food, except my red flannel, and no amount of skillful or scientific casting would induce a strike. My better half, having joined me, suggested cutting up my fish for bait. I did so, and in less than half an hour I had fourteen trout, ranging in weight from one to two pounds, strung on a forked willow, and we marched back to camp, where we soon became the centre of attraction and the envy of all the other fishermen, — we having caught three times the number that all the others had. The fish were soon dressed, and as the aroma of fried trout and bacon floated on the evening breeze I had many anxious looks cast towards my table (on the ground); but as my own mess numbered eight persons I did not issue any invitations.

Many were the pipes of navy plug that I quietly smoked that night before retiring, and why? I had suddenly tasted the joy of fishing with the fly.

After having learned to tie a fly, I turned my attention to rigging up a pole.

We arrived at our destination, Missoula, Montana, November 14, 1877. That country was then the sportsman's paradise, but winter had already set in, and I was interested in deer-hunting. During my tramps in the Bitter Root Mountains I found just what I wanted for a pole, already made, in the young fir and tamarack which grow in the coulees high up in the mountains as thick as cane grows in the South, and in size from an inch to an inch and a half in diameter at the ground, growing straight as an arrow, and with a beautiful taper, from twelve to twenty feet high. Here was my ideal pole, just what I wanted. I selected one about eighteen feet in length, and after smoothing it nicely I laid it up for the winter. When spring came I put on the mountings, which consisted of the smallest screw-eyes I could get, for guides. These I placed about eighteen inches apart, screwed into the pole. A twisted wire loop, firmly lashed on, served me well for a tip; and when the reel plate was attached with two screws on each side, and firmly wrapped with waxed thread, my pole was ready for work.

My first fly having proved a success only once, I began to study how to improve on it. When the snow melted in the spring, I found a great many wild-goose feathers scattered around, and these I took and made into flies. I sent to New York and got a box of long-shanked bass hooks, and soon had a dozen *beautiful* (?) flies tied and laid carefully away, ready to use as soon as the ice went out of the river.

For the benefit of the beginner I will briefly describe them : wings, gray goose ; body, blue steel (hook); head, yellow silk about the size of a pea, but the size depended upon the obstinacy of the feathers, which persisted in slipping up and down. The more they slipped, the more wrapping I applied. When the fly was completed it could be seen a hundred yards ; and why not ? Did n't I want the trout to see it, or how was I going to catch them ? Name and origin of this fly was never published.

The ice went out of the river at last, and with fifty yards of braided silk bass line (formerly used when bass fishing in Kentucky) and my Frankfort reel I went a-fishing. Talk about long casts ! With a pole of eighteen feet, and twenty-four feet of line reeled off, I would stand upon a sandbar, revolve my pole at arm's length over my head until my fly made a noise like a quail rising from a brier thicket, and launch forth. The fly would strike the water from forty to fifty feet away, with a splash and splutter equal to that made by a wounded duck. I labored with a zeal worthy of better success for two or three hours without a rise, and then went home firmly convinced that either there were no trout in the river, or else the season was too early and they were chilled too badly to rise.

It did not take me long, however, to find out that the fault lay in my flies. A local dealer having received a supply of flies (the first that I had ever seen) from San Francisco, I bought nearly all he had, choosing the gaudiest and most attractive, and from that time I had no trouble, but met with good success.

Now, a word about my eighteen-foot tamarack. I continued to use it nearly all summer, until it became very dry and brittle. It did me good service (at the expense of muscle), until one day in making an extra long cast the line caught in a bush; the pole was broken in three pieces, and fell a total wreck behind me.

This is no made-up tale, but a true story of my first fly-rod.

With it I caught more and larger trout than falls to the lot of a great many $4\frac{1}{2}$ and 5 ounce split-bamboo devotees ever to see. Yes, and I used it with a No. 3 Frankfort, Ky., reel. I used this reel for ten years in Montana and Dakota, and will never use any other. A jovial friend of mine calls it a " nail keg," but that is because he never used it; to do so would soon convince him (?) that for all purposes there are none better. Kid glove and $4\frac{1}{2}$ oz. ryestraw anglers I am not writing for, neither do I want them to agree with me. When a man is so effeminate as to use such light rods, and then worry the rod-maker for something lighter, he had better stay at home. The trout stream is unhealthy for him.

Having some idea of jointed rods, from seeing cuts of them in catalogues, I procured a few tools and started in to make a fly-rod. No more " poles " now. From the bottom of an old boiler I got a piece of sheet-copper, and from this, with the assistance of a blacksmith, I made two single ferrules, one four and the other three inches long, the larger three quarters, and the smaller half an inch in diameter. The next thing was to find suitable wood for my rod. It must be remembered that no hard wood of any kind grows in that country (Montana), and at the time I am writing about everything had to be freighted by wagon five hundred miles. Hickory wood was retailing at twenty cents per pound, but with the assistance of an ash-fork handle and two whipstocks I made a rod which I thought was quite a success; but I had not quite gotten over my idea as to length, and this rod was about sixteen feet long. It was not equal to my tamarack, and I soon found out that it was *not* a success. I made another, using the metal connecting parts of a jointed gun rod which screwed together in the place of ferrules. I soon tired of this; it was too limber.

By writing to dealers, I found out that I could purchase mountings of all kinds, which I did; and from that time on, I went into the rod business, using ash and hickory and with stronger ferrules of German silver. I worked down to as low as 12 ounces in weight and $10\frac{1}{2}$ feet in length. As I became educated in rod-making, I cast about for lighter material than hickory, but it proved a failure. I finally wanted something better than I could make, and sent East and got a very fine split bamboo. Oh! it was a beauty, but it had one fault: the reel seat was below the hand, and my " nail keg " would not work in that way. I sold it (the rod) and went to ash and hickory, which for rough use, in my estimation, stands at the head of all woods except pecan, and that is superior to hickory in not warping. I once struck and landed two three-pound trout at once, in a very strong current, where the banks were abrupt and bushy, and this without a landing-net. I could give many instances of this kind, and of others where large trout were hooked and had to be held until tired out, where the giving of as much as two feet of line would have been the loss of the fish, and my hickory rods, although not so beautiful in finish nor so elegant in taper, never once failed me. I never had a rod broken by a fish except once, and that rod was made for me by a very expert carpenter, and he put it together with dowels. So much for dowels. I would not accept a doweled rod as a gift.

As regards the kind of flies suited for the waters of the Pacific slope, my experience covers a long period, and all kinds of weather, light and shade, from daylight to dark, and no doubt differs from that of others. I have had some men advise dark flies, and have seen others have good success with them, but I always preferred those of a light color, and for the best of reasons, — success. They are more attractive in all kinds of weather and water, present more the appearance of the natural insects of the country, especially the grasshopper, which is the most killing bait that was ever cast on the Western water-shed. Of my favorite flies, and the only ones that nearly always proved successful (and I have tried them nearly all), I will mention Coachmans, Professors, Grasshopper, Imbrie, Cheney, Captain, and White Miller. Of course there are many others that I have used, and with good success, but for all purposes I prefer the Coachmans and Professors, with reversed wings. I once had a very large trout, in a swirl, quietly take my stretcher, and then my dropper, which was a Royal Coachman, was taken with a rush, and I landed him with both flies fast.

In regard to size of flies, experience also proves that both the very large or very small should be avoided. Very small flies will fill your creel with small fish, while very large ones will send you to camp with it empty. With medium-sized flies I have always caught my largest fish; and when flies failed, I was not beyond the use of hoppers, bugs, or other substitutes.

Casting on lines, or leaders and snells, are much better colored, but not too dark. Should be of good single gut. Leaders of six feet and snells six inches are about the proper lengths. A cast of two flies, rarely three, have always been my preference. Long snells, or too many of them, are apt to get snarled with the leader, or caught in the bush. Long snells caused the wreck of my tamarack.

Do not use double or twisted leaders for trout. Medium-sized gut is strong enough, and if you should happen to get fastened some time in a deep rapid current, better lose a part than your entire cast by having your line break instead of snell or leader.

----

*Montana.*          Professor.          Trout.

J. R. HOFFLIN,                    Minneapolis,                    Minn.

One year ago I had the pleasure of spending three weeks with an old Indian scout and trapper, Jack V. Nye, fishing and shooting along the Yellowstone, Rosebud, and Stillwater rivers, Yellowstone County, Montana. His success was so marked and great in catching handsome trout that when your letter came I forwarded the same to him. Inclosed find his reply.

----

J. V. NYE,                    Nye City,                    Mont.

Some of your questions will be very hard for me to answer, especially those regarding the size of the hook, although I know what kind of a hook I want for trout, but do not know the number of it; so I will send you some of my favorite flies, showing the sizes and kinds I use here in Montana. I believe they are all well known with the exception of one, — the Yellowstone trout fly ; it takes this name because it looks very much like a fly that we have here in June and July.[1]

I always use light-colored single snells. I never use gaudy flies. Of the six dozen flies in my fly-book, you will not find a red or a white fly. I use the light flies early in the morning and evening, and the dark flies when it is bright.

The fly inclosed was a Professor, tied on No. 7 hook.

## PLATE BB.

No. 264. Marston.  No. 267. Lake George.
No. 265. Manchester.  No. 268. Max Von Dem Borne.
No. 266. Horicon.  No. 269. Munro.

No. 264. The Marston bass fly was designed by C. F. Orvis, and named by Mr. A. N. Cheney after his friend, the editor of "The London Fishing Gazette," Mr. Robert B. Marston, in consequence of his interest in black bass fishing, and his endeavors to introduce these fish into the waters suited to them in Great Britain.

Mr. Marston deserves the gratitude of the entire angling fraternity on this side of the Atlantic for his unvarying kindness and courtesy extended to them. He has always shown a cheerful readiness to be of assistance or to welcome friendly advances, and has probably done more than any other to promote a cordial feeling of interest and friendship between the anglers of the two countries.

No. 265. Manchester.

"Only a little village street
Lying along a mountain's side.

.   .   .   .   .   .   .

I know not, then, why it should bring
Into my eyes such sudden tears.
But unto the mountain's sheltering
The little village seems to cling,
As child, all unaware of fears,
Unconscious that it is caressed,
In perfect peace and perfect rest,
Upon its mother's breast."

Back in the year 1761, Benning Wentworth, governor of the province of New Hampshire, granted a charter which read as follows : —

### Province of New Hampshire,

George the Third, By Grace of God, Great Britain, France, and Ireland, King, Defender of the Faith. To all whom these presents shall come : Greeting.

Know ye that we, of our special grace, certain knowledge, and mere motion, for the due encouragement of our truly well-beloved Benning Wentworth, Esq., our Governor and Commander-in-chief of our said province of New Hampshire, in New England, and of our council of our said province :

Have, upon the considerations and reservations here-in-after made, given and granted, and by these presents our heirs and successors do give and grant in equal shares, unto our other governments, and to their heirs and assigns forever, whose names are entered upon this grant, to be divided among them into seventy equal shares: all the tract and parcel of land situate, lying and being within the said province of New Hampshire, containing by admeasurement twenty-three thousand acres; which tract is to contain six square miles and no more, . . . butted and bounded as follows : At the northwest corner of Arlington, from thence due north by Sandgate, six miles; thence due east six miles; from thence due south six miles to the northwest corner of Sunderland; from thence due west by Sunderland aforesaid; being the bounds began at, — and that same to be, and hereby is incorporated into a township by the name of Manchester.

This stately document was the beginning of Manchester, destined to be famous in history, but as yet never more than "a little village street." A party of explorers on their way to Salem, N. Y., were attracted by old Equnnuck, — now metamorphosed from its Indian naming and modernized into Equinox, — and climbed to its summit from the New York side. Thence they looked down upon the quiet valley, and it was beautiful to their eyes ; so these men from Amenia sought possession of the "New Hampshire Grants," which had been so cheerfully conceded by Governor Wentworth, but their ownership was afterward disputed by claimants from the State of New York. Some of the owners from Amenia came with their families, and were soon after followed by the English Puritans from the Connecticut Valley, — sturdy farmers, strong in mind and body, and grave and courteous in demeanor. These people were disposed to pursue their own way peacefully, till the soil, and people the land ; for, as one old writer quaintly says of them, "they were wise, strong men, and very prolific." But the aggressions of the New York

MANCHESTER

" land-jobbers," as the New York contestants were called, compelled these settlers to organize means of defense, and the organization so created was known as " the Green Mountain Boys," of which Ethan Allen was colonel. The story of their early struggles is an interesting one, full of self-denial, determination, and bravery. In time the New Hampshire Grants were called Vermont, from *verd mont*, in reference to its rolling mountains of green. The news from Ticonderoga and other battle-grounds of the Revolution became alarming, and a " Council of Safety " was appointed to meet at Manchester. Ira Allen, the youngest member of the council, proposed the enlistment of a full regiment. The older members declared it impossible without funds, but gave him until the next day to perfect a plan for the same. He then solved the problem by suggesting that they seize and confiscate Tory estates for the general welfare. This measure was approved and executed. The Tories were not so numerous in Manchester as in some of the neighboring towns, but all were driven forth into Canada, and only the loyal allowed to remain.

Manchester village was the rendezvous for troops, and the meeting-place for the commissioners ; thence they went forth to the struggle that ended in establishing independence. The place has ever since been peculiarly American. There is no large industry to bring into Manchester foreign elements. To-day one will hear in the post-office and village store the same old names that occur in the original organization of the town ; and though he may have been for long years a wanderer from the ingleside he first knew, when he returns he will recognize the faces of the sons and daughters, though their fathers and mothers may be resting in beautiful Dellwood, that last earthly abiding-place of these homefolk.

It is a good place " to come back to." We all feel this, and, realizing that we shall find it ever the same, our hearts turn towards it amid changes, and in times of trouble or weariness, and we remember thankfully that the old trees will wave a welcome, the mountains will steadfastly guard this " fair countrie," and that where their shadows reach we may find a resting-place.

This little fly is only a reminder ; the yellow and the green only an emblem of the sunshine that is ever flickering through these peaceful shades.

No. 266.   Many years ago, Mr. A. N. Cheney gave to us a fly which he said was at one time believed to be the only fly that would take black bass in Lake George, N. Y., but that other patterns have since been found effective there. After this the fly was occasionally made and used, and to identify it we called it " the

Lake George fly ; " but having learned later that two other flies claim the name, we must relinquish it in connection with this fly. But Lake George has other and older names, and we feel at liberty to continue the connection by one of these. Lake St. Sacrament was the name given to it by the Pope and the French nation, but Horicon is the old Indian name, meaning " pure water." It is the name we like best, and it rightfully belongs to the lovely lake. Cooper, in his fascinating tales, has created for it a halo of romance, and so we will call this old fly of Lake George by the waters' old appellation, Horicon. Reference will be found to this fly in the letter from Mr. Jeptha Dunlap.

No. 267. This Lake George fly is one of the rightful claimants to the name, and has many of the merits of the Parmacheene Belle. It was designed and named by Mr. John Shields.

No. 268. Count Max von dem Borne, of Germany, author of the celebrated treatise on fish culture, entitled " Fischzucht," tied the original of this fly, and sent a copy of it to this country, saying that he had had with it much success. Mr. C. F. Orvis therefore placed it in the list of good bass flies, believing that black bass, by going abroad, are not likely to change their tastes and habits, as are some of the more vacillating members of the human race.

No. 269. Mr. Julius P. Bucke, the inventor of the Munro, recommends it in his letter on Canadian fishing.

| *Montana.* | Brown Hackle. | |
|---|---|---|
| CAPT. HARRY READE, | Fort Shaw, | Mont. |

During my very brief experience in trout fishing in the vicinity of Fort Missoula, Mont., I found the Brown Hackle to be the most effective.

---

| *Montana.* | { Coachman. { Brown Hackle. | { Trout. |
|---|---|---|
| WILLIAM H. DeWITT. | Helena, | Mont. |

It is a pleasure to reply to your letter, and give you some information upon fly-fishing in Montana waters, — information gleaned from a considerable experience in that most charming sport vouchsafed to office-tired mortals.

As to the favorite or effective flies, I have always held that there is a thousand per cent. more in the manipulation than in the construction. Make a long cast, drop the flies gently, do not let the trout know that you are in the same county, and your success is nine tenths secured. I will agree to give a " chump" every fly in the market, and I will beat him all day, casting, without change, a gang of three Brown Hackles, or Coachman, sixty or seventy feet, at any season or in any water. It is infinitely more important that the flies drop upon the water,

> "Softer
> Than petals from blown roses on the grass,"

than that colors or styles be observed. The notion of ascertaining the trout's taste for flies by dissecting his stomach, or of following the color of the natural flies in the atmosphere, is absolute nonsense. As an illustration, I have filled my creel in the winter, in a partly frozen stream, casting flies off an ice floe, when there was not a live fly nearer than Florida.

One is amply supplied in these waters if his book contains three Hackles, Black Gnat, Professor, Coachman, Royal Coachman, and Cow Dung; also the Jungle Cock attachment. I find that the shank of the hook covered with red or green wound with gilt thread is very effective. There are many flies brought out every season similar to the above, with slight variations and new names. They are good, and good because they resemble those mentioned.

The so-called " fluttering fly " is a thorough failure. I have cast the flutterer and straight fly in one gang, the latter doing all the execution, and the former as lonesome as Republicans in " Precinct 34," in the recent election. Its motion is jerky. Neither motion nor appearance resembles nature, and it always looks like the parrot after his historical interview with the monkey.

I as emphatically condemn the flies, recently placed upon the market, made in the verisimilitude of flies and insects. They are a thing of beauty upon the dealer's card, and attractive to an amateur buyer; but three or four casts make hotchpotch of them, and excite the ridicule of a crafty, four-year-old trout who has been snapping up grasshoppers for three seasons.

The only testimony I can give as to time of day and season is, that lighter flies should be used on dark days, and at early and late hours, and in cloudy water, and the darker ones in clear water and under bright skies. This distinction, however, I do not regard as of great importance. I go back to the principle of the motion, and not the color.

Another important matter is your day. It should be bright and sunny, the water clear, and the stream falling, or at least stationary. On a cloudy day, with rain falling or threatening, and the stream swollen, even though the water be clear, stay at home.

The selection of the season follows the same rules as that of the day. Some time in February the streams break up ; the snow in the valleys runs off and carries out the ice. The water soon falling, there is fine fly-fishing from the middle of March to the middle of May. At that date, or from then to the first of June, commences the " June rise." The warmer suns attack the heavy accumulations of snow in the mountains and in deep cañons and shaded gulches, and the country is flooded for a month or six weeks, and fly-fishing is a suspended art. By the first of July the conditions are favorable, and remain so until ice closes the streams. The dates are, of course, approximate. Seasons vary. But the fisherman cannot miss it if he comes in April, or any time after July 1st. The law does not limit the season. You may cast your flies in January or July.

I speak of these conditions, times, and seasons as to the mountain trout of Montana only. The requirements are quite different, I believe, with the speckled brook trout, the *Salmo fontinalis* of the Eastern waters.

And, in passing, I would thank some one to refer me to a classification of the Montana trout. I have never seen one. The *Salmo fontinalis*, found east of the Mississippi River, I do not believe lives in this State. I have landed thousands of trout, and have fished the waters of every county of Montana, and have never found the brook trout of the East. Nor does our trout answer the description given in the United States Fish Commissioner's reports of the *Salmo pupuratus* or the *Salmo irideus*. That is popularly and locally called the mountain trout, and to be ichthyological and Latin we will call him *Salmo montanus*. Even with this classification and name there are a half dozen varieties of the species, differing in proportions and markings. For instance, I have seen a trout as long as my forearm outweigh one the length of my whole arm. Last season I saw Hon. J. B. Clayberg, Attorney-General, land a salmon trout thirty inches long, weighing three and a half pounds. It was as thin as the fat woman's husband in a dime museum.

The mountain trout has not the brilliant carmine and blue spots of the brook trout. His spots are all black : sometimes irregular in shape, like sprinkled pepper, in large sizes; sometimes perfectly round. They are found on the fins and tail as well as on the body, and are generally distributed from gill to tail. Occasionally the sides are clear, and nearly all the spots are crowded into the space from anal fin to tip of tail. In the latter variety the meat is inclined to the salmon-pink color. Ordinarily it is white. Such are the general characteristics of, and variations in, the mountain trout. Both as a game fish and a table delicacy he is not the equal of his Adirondack brother.

You inquire as to leaders and snells. The necessary qualities of a leader are strength and invisibility. Its use is to prevent the trout from observing the connection between the fly and the fisherman. Answering your questions as you put them, the leader should be as light in weight as is consistent with holding your fish. One familiar with the water he is working on knows about the weight of the fish he will hook. Let him test his leader with his pocket scales. A mist leader is less visible than a clear one. The latter is too much of a reflector of the sun's rays. On the same ground of invisibility, select a single leader or snell in preference to one twisted or double, and also take the long strands to avoid the visibleness of frequent knots. Leaders made of the qualities I describe possess sufficient strength for all uses in our streams. A double leader is an abomination. Avoid them as the professional fly-flirter hates a bait-fishing chump.

I learned the "divine art" of fly-casting on Pennsylvania and New York waters, and for the *Salmo fontinalis,* the king of the *Salmonidœ.* The *Montanus* does not rank with his Eastern relative, but he is of a family of princes, and wears his purple royally in the dancing waters and pitching cataracts of his Rocky Mountain kingdom.

He who hath no fish lore in his mind and no fish love in his soul

> " Is fit for treasons, stratagems, and spoils ;
> The motions of his spirit are dull as night,
> And his affections dark as Erebus.
> Let no such man be trusted."

Fit out your friend, next season, with a seven-ounce bamboo and the accoutrements as I have indicated ; send him to the Blackfoot, Flathead, Thompson, Upper Yellowstone rivers, or any one of a hundred others in this Rocky Mountain region ; and he will go home a better, greater, and nobler man for all time.

---

|  |  |
|---|---|
| *Montana.* | ⎧ Coachman.<br>⎨ Brown Hackle.<br>⎩ Black Gnat.<br>  Deer Fly. |

LIEUT. C. A. DEVOL,                     Fort Missoula,                          Mont.

The best all-round flies for these streams are the Coachman and Brown Hackle.

In the Little Blackfoot, which has not been much fished, these two flies will kill all day, and nearly as fast as casts can be made.

I have caught fifty-five fish in about two hours, averaging nearly a pound each, without moving more than two or three rods down stream.

In the Bitter Root River, on whose banks the post is located, the fish are more wary, and a greater variety of flies is needed, the Black Gnat proving very good in the early season. Later on, and especially towards evening, when the fish are jumping at the small gray millers that hover over the water, I have taken many fine trout on a fly with a green body, name unknown to me. I have tried the White Miller and Gray Hackle under the same circumstances, but neither seems to tempt them as does the small fly I have referred to. The Professor I have found good occasionally, but not often. The Bee, too, has been a failure as far as my efforts are concerned. The use of a great variety of flies is apt to reduce the catch, in my opinion, instead of increasing it, as one is continually tempted to change flies after a short trial, whereas a little patience with the fly in use may be all that is needed, and every change and experiment uses up a good deal of time.

I think that a half dozen flies to resemble the species generally, if adopted, would be a good thing in the end. I have no theories about the shape of hooks; the ordinary hook, No. 6, has proven satisfactory. In regard to the snell, I think clear is good enough; don't think the fish ever notice it. I prefer it single.

I use the ordinary three-foot leader, single, with two droppers.

For all-round work the following are standard for this vicinity:

| | |
|---|---|
| Coachman. | Professor. |
| Royal Coachman. | Gray Alder. |
| Brown Hackle. | Queen of the Water. |
| Gray Hackle. | Black Gnat. |
| Jungle Cock. | |

A selection with various colored bodies, but always the spotted wing, Grizzly King.

With these in my book, I would be prepared to catch a good basket in any part of Montana or Idaho.

The past season, my most killing flies were the Queen of the Water and a Jungle Cock, spotted wing and yellow body. I had very fine luck with some flies made to represent the horse fly.

Trout are very plenty, game, and full of fight, and the care necessary in my Maine home to catch a few is not required here.

The hook in common use is the Sproat. It is my favorite, and although I have tried other shapes, have always got back to Sproat. I will now stay there.

Our streams are very rapid, and make the use of large-size gut absolutely necessary. Good fly-fishermen do not use double gut at all here, but heavy single gut. I speak of trout, not of salmon trout. A light stain, in my opinion, is a decided improvement.

As the trout run large, pounds are common. I use No. 6 Sproat.

Next spring, I intend to send you an insect we call here the salmon fly. It is a most killing bait, and it ought to make a very successful fly.

## PLATE CC.

No. 270. Lake Edward.　　No. 273. Mather.
No. 271. Massasaga.　　No. 274. Owner.
No. 272. Frank Gray.　　No. 275. McCloud.

Nos. 270 and 271. Mr. Walter Greaves, of Ottawa, in his clear and comprehensive letter regarding the best flies for Canadian waters, tells of two flies of his own invention, which he has named the Lake Edward and Massasaga, after the localities where they have been most successful.

No. 272. Mr. C. L. Valentine, of Wisconsin, writes of the origin and name of the Frank Gray, and its efficiency for wall-eyed pike.

No. 273. The Mather was made by C. F. Orvis, several years ago, and named by Mr. A. N. Cheney in compliment to his popular friend, Mr. Fred Mather. Some one, in speaking of Mr. Mather recently, said that he was "really one of the most accurate scientists we have in this country, for what he knew he had learned with his own eyes, and thought upon with a clear, strong mind." The only trouble is, that he will not write freely of all he knows, and benefit others by his knowledge and observations, though occasionally he gratifies his friends with lucid papers, abounding in a strong sense of the humorous. Mr. Mather is celebrated for his success in fish culture and transportation. He was for a long time editor of the fishing department of "The Forest and Stream," associated on that paper with Mr. Charles B. Reynolds, who is another careful student and delightful writer.

No. 274. Mr. J. S. Owner, of Hagerstown, Md., writes, giving description of the Owner, or Red Guinea, and adds: "It originated with me in 1885, and for two summers it was a very successful fly. Then it seemed to give way to the great variety, principally all black, like the Silver Black, or white, as the Parmacheene Belle or Coachman. In the years that the Owner was popular, I remember that the waters of the Potomac were very low and clear. Fishing, for that reason, was better early and late : at daylight to eight or nine A. M., and from four P. M. till dark ; even after dark, if there were a full moon, clear sky, and clear, *low* water. I, with a companion, fished one night until half past ten, not having caught a fish until it was dark. The position we occupied was on the walls of an old fish-pot, at the head of a long reach of deep water, the water within the fish-pot being about two feet deep, and with clear, pebbly or rocky bottom. The flies were hardly ever laid out, but they were taken by one and frequently two fish, all of good size, from one to three pounds. At 10.30 P. M. we had all we could carry, and stopped."

No. 275. The McCloud was made by C. F. Orvis, in 1879, and named by Mr. Horace D. Dunn, of San Francisco, who thought it would be successful on the Californian river of that name. The fly has sometimes been called the McLeod, but it should properly be spelled as is the name of the river.

The hills were brown, the heavens blue,
A woodpecker pounded a pine-top shell,
While a partridge whistled the whole day through
For a rabbit to dance in the chaparral,
And a gray grouse drumm'd, " All 's well, all 's well."

## WASHINGTON.

C. E. NEWTON . . . . . . . . $\left\{\begin{array}{l}\text{Professor.}\\\text{Coachman.}\\\text{Brown Hackle.}\end{array}\right.$

J. O. BINGHAM . . . . . . . $\left\{\begin{array}{l}\text{Coachman.}\\\text{Professor.}\\\text{Scarlet Ibis.}\\\text{Hackles, etc.}\end{array}\right.$

ROBERT FROST . . . . . . . . $\left\{\begin{array}{l}\text{Brown Hackle.}\\\text{Coachman.}\\\text{Professor.}\end{array}\right.$

JOHN P. TWEED.

COL. J. G. C. LEE . . . . . . . $\left\{\begin{array}{l}\text{Curtis.}\\\text{Lord Baltimore.}\\\text{Black Gnat.}\\\text{Professor, etc.}\end{array}\right.$

| *Washington.* | Professor.<br>Coachman.<br>Brown Hackle. | Trout. |
|---|---|---|

C. E. Newton,                     Spokane Falls,                     Wash.

My experience has been that the Professor, the Brown Hackle, and the Coachman are the best flies here at all seasons of the year. I find our trout bite all of them well. I would like to suggest a fly that would be taking in August and September. It is on about a No. 10 hook, with drab wings, with white lining and yellow body. I do not know what you would call it.

My experience has been that the fly makes very little difference. It is the way that it is thrown and handled that makes the successful fisherman. Many fishermen (so called) might try every fly known to the fraternity and would have no success. There is more in knowing the habits of the fish, and the most enticing way to handle the lure to induce a trout to take it, particularly if the fish be one of those wary fellows that is suspicious of everything. Any old hunter knows there are plenty of old suspicious bucks in the woods that no ordinary hunting will capture. You have got to invent new tricks to get them within gunshot. Just so with a trout. I have followed a stream a mile behind three or four other fishermen, and my basket at night would contain the most pounds, if not the most in number. I have very little faith in changing flies, but have a great deal in changing position and throwing a fly from the most natural point, and making it act as much like a natural fly as possible. A wild trout has a voracious nature, and unless he has been hooked or frightened, any moving object in the water attracts his attention, and he is just as liable to jump at a Black Gnat as he would at a salmon fly or any other fly. There is much more in throwing your fly than there is in the selection of it, and to be a successful fisherman a man needs to study the habits of the fish. There are hours of the day when you cannot induce a trout to jump at a fly. In this country, it is next to impossible to catch trout with any success in the light of the moon, as fish then feed at night. The most sport I have ever had fishing was catching trout by moonlight. When fish feed nights, which is quite common, you can do better in two hours than all day over the same ground by daylight. If you are skeptical, try it. My word for it, you will be pleased at your success. Use only a very light-colored fly. A Coachman is good. As to snells, make them as near the color of the water as possible. Hooks are optional with the fisherman. I like both the Limerick and the sneck hooks. I write this at your request, not because I wish to obtrude any opinions or theories of my own upon you. I have done a great deal of fishing, and what I have written you is my personal knowledge and my own success in the matter. If this is of any value to you, use it as you see fit.

---

| *Washington.* | Coachman.<br>Professor.<br>Brown Hackle.<br>Red Hackle.<br>Scarlet Ibis. | Trout. |

J. O. BINGHAM,　　　　　　　　Spokane Falls,　　　　　　　　Wash.

My favorite flies are, Coachman, Professor, Brown Hackle, Red Hackle, Scarlet Ibis, about in the order named; Coachman and Professor in the morning, and the others for evening fishing on the lakes; Scarlet Ibis and Red Hackle on the river any time during the day, morning or evening. The latter is always the best time for fishing in this country, say from six P. M. until quite dark. The most striking instance of the superiority of above flies that I can recall is a trip taken by eight of us on Lake Cœur d'Alene last summer, in July (late). Four took one bay with two boats, and the other four another, also with two boats. The other boys used some "mongrel" flies, with a few Coachmans and Professors among the lot, and in eight hours took something like fifty trout. We used the above flies almost exclusively, and caught in the same time something over four hundred and eighty trout, averaging at least one pound each, and probably much more. Some of them weighed six and seven pounds, and we kept none shorter than about eight inches.

---

| *Washington.* | { Hackles. <br> Coachman. <br> Professor. | { Trout. |

JOHN P. M. RICHARDS,          Spokane Falls,          Wash.

I would state, as the result of my own experience, as well as that of friends, that the flies which take the most trout here are Red and Brown Hackle, Coachman, and Professor. In the Spokane River and lakes in the vicinity, June and July are the best months, and after sunset the best time of the day.

On the large lakes, such as Pond d'Oreille and Cœur d'Alene, late in the season, the most killing bait is a small kidney spoon. I would remark that during all the season trout will take a natural grasshopper before any fly (artificial).

For snells, I find the best are smoke-colored, heavy and double.

*Washington.*    { Brown Hackle.
                   Coachman.        { Trout.
                   Professor.

ROBERT FROST,                     Olympia,                      Wash.

I seldom go out with more than four kinds of flies, viz., Brown Hackle, peacock body, Brown Hackle, red body, Coachman, and Professor; these are good all the year round in this State. If I were to add any to them, it would be the Governor, Royal Coachman, and Cow Dung fly. These may not suit the Eastern States, but I will guarantee they are good in all parts of the Northwest.

The sizes are No. 4 and No. 6.

-----

*Washington.*          Trout Flies.

JOHN P. TWEED,                    Olympia,                      Wash.

My favorite flies, among those best known, are the Coachman, Royal Coachman, Brown Hackle, red body, White Miller, Black Gnat, and a fly similar, but with a red silk winding and red tag in wing.

Dark flies should be used at the first of the season and on bright days; light colors on dark days and evenings.

Larger flies are used than in the East, about No. 5 or No. 6. Snells should be just tinged to destroy their glitter, and with strength just sufficient to give way before the leader will part.

*Washington.*    $\left\{\begin{array}{l}\text{Curtis.}\\ \text{Lord Baltimore.}\\ \text{Brown Hackle.}\\ \text{Black Gnat.}\\ \text{Professor.}\end{array}\right.$

Col. J. G. C. Lee, U. S. A.,      Vancouver Barracks,      Wash.

The foregoing list of flies comprises all my favorites. I have had great sport with the Curtis and Lord Baltimore flies. I always use small double hooks, with clear, light, strong single gut, and long loops.

## PLATE DD.

No. 276. Scarlet Ibis.          No. 279. Toodle-bug.
No. 277. Parker.                No. 280. Read.
No. 278. Raven.                 No. 281. Premier.

**No. 276.** There are many Scarlet Ibis flies, named after the bird supplying the feathers that form their chief feature. The Scarlet Ibis shown in the plate is a favorite of C. F. Orvis, and was first made by him in 1878.

The feathers of the ibis are of constant value to the fly-maker, and enter into the composition of nearly half the patterns. The peculiar red is the natural color of the feathers furnished by a bird whose entire plumage is of this brilliant hue, except the tips of the wings, which are a blue-black. The red ibis (*Ibis ruber*) is found in tropical America, chiefly Brazil, where it lives in the marshy districts in the vicinity of the estuaries. The young are at first covered with a blackish down, which gradually turns gray, and then becomes almost white; at this time they begin to fly. When about two years old, the red makes its appearance, the feathers becoming more and more brilliant as the birds grow older. When ready for the fly-maker's use, all trace of the gray or white has disappeared. There is a great choice in the skins imported; only those of the older, more brilliant birds being desirable. It is often erroneously supposed that the ibis from which these feathers are obtained is the bird known as the " sacred ibis " of the Egyptians, which was regarded by that people almost with adoration, and after death was reverently embalmed. Historians differ as to the origin of the respect felt for this bird; some attributing it to its devouring the serpents which would otherwise have multiplied to a distressing extent; others to a tradition ascribing some connection between its plumage and the moon's phases; but the generally received opinion is, that the appearance of the ibis announced the overflow of the Nile. To kill one of these birds, by accident or otherwise, was considered a capital offense, and the punishment was so severe that it would indicate a more cogent, deeper reason for their careful protection, and suggest that they were cherished because of some theory in connection with the Egyptian belief in the transmigration of souls.

The prettiest fancy connected with the ibis of the Nile was, that it is symbolic, because " it has the shape of a heart, and its feathers are black at the extremities, but white elsewhere, to indicate that truth is dark outwardly, but clear within."

The white ibis of Florida is similar to the Egyptian ibis, and its feathers are often used as a substitute for swan's feathers.

No. 277.   The origin and naming of the Parker is given by Mr. W. P. Andrus, in his letter in the Minnesota and Wisconsin division.

No. 278.   The Raven is a black bass fly much liked by the fishermen of La Crosse, Wis.   From its success in that vicinity, it is becoming known and used by fishermen in other localities.

No. 279.   The Toodle-bug, or Katoodle-bug, for it is known by either name, is the invention of Myron Whitney, formerly living in Upton, Maine.   One of his friends writes of him, " He was a guide for many years at the Rangeleys, and understood the cravings of the finny tribe, and could place a fly on the water in a long cast as well as any man I ever saw."   The same writer recommends highly the Katoodle-bug, saying that " at the Rangeleys it would often do the work when others would fail."   The fly is also much used for black bass.

No. 280.   The Read is another favorite for black bass fishing in Wisconsin, and is named after Mr. George Read, a resident of La Crosse.

No. 281.   The Premier is one of C. F. Orvis's patterns, named in 1878 by his brother, Mr. L. C. Orvis, because its colors were the same as those in the robes of state worn by the Prime Minister of England.   It has always been a most important fly for black bass.

Thou bring'st me back the halcyon days
  Of grateful rest, the week of leisure,
The journey lapped in autumn haze,
  The sweet fatigue that seemed a pleasure,
The morning ride, the noonday halt,
  The blazing slopes, the red dust rising,
And then the dim, brown-columned vault,
  With its cool, damp sepulchral spicing.

Once more I see the rocking masts
  That scrape the sky, their only tenant
The jay-bird, that in frolic casts
  From some high yard his broad blue pennant.
I see the Indian files that keep
  Their places in the dusty hether,
Their red trunks standing ankle-deep
  In moccasins of rusty leather.

BRET HARTE.

From *On a Cone of the Big Trees.*

## CALIFORNIA.

RAMON E. WILSON . . . . . .
{
Willard Gray.
Wilson Ant.
Bicknell Fly.
Beans Fly.
Shain Fly, etc.
}

E. F. PETTENGILL . . . . . .
{
Gray Drake.
Green Drake.
Royal Coachman.
White Miller.
}

G. E. DAVIS . . . . . . . .
{
Caddis.
Black Gnat.
White Miller.
Royal Coachman.
Professor, etc.
}

ST. CHARLES A. BIEDERMAN . . .
{
Brown Hen.
Yellow Bumble.
}

| | | |
|---|---|---|
| *California.* | Willard Gray.<br>Wilson Ant.<br>Bicknell Fly.<br>Beans Fly.<br>Shain Fly.<br>Spiders.<br>Governor.<br>Duns.<br>Cow Dung, A. P. Williams' pattern. | Trout. |

RAMON E. WILSON,　　　　　San Francisco,　　　　　Cal.

Owing to the large extent of territory in the State, and the climatic differences existing therein, I venture the suggestion that anglers from different sections will materially differ in their answers to the questions you propound.

We have but one fish which will take the fly, viz., the trout. Those in our Coast Range streams, on the west, differ considerably in their habits and food from those in the Sierras, on the east. All our Coast Range waters are supplied from rains, and the streams have an exit into the ocean, while the waters of the Sierras are supplied by melting snow, and the fish do not find their way to the sea. The fish in the latter depend in a large measure upon case worms for their food, while the fly is the common food of the fish in the former.

The fish in the Coast Range, as a rule, are small, while those in the Sierras are large. For example, in the Feather River, in Lassen County, brook trout of five and six pounds are not uncommon, while fish have been caught weighing nine and ten pounds. Of course I am writing of fly-fishing.

For the mountain fishing, as it is called in the Sierras, larger flies and tackle are used than on the Coast Range. I would say for the former, the flies well known and most commonly used are the Coachman, Stone flies of various patterns, and the Brown Hackle of different kinds; and in addition, some local flies like the Willard Gray, the Salmon fly, and the Williams Cow Dung.

Samples of the Willard Gray and the Williams Cow Dung I send inclosed. In size, the hooks range from 6 to 9, American numbers. The Salmon fly is patterned after the fly of the caddis-case worms, found in great abundance in all of the waters of the Sierras.

The Willard Gray and the Williams Cow Dung are modifications of well-known flies, and their names are derived from gentlemen who suggested the pattern, viz., Mr. William Willard and Senator A. P. Williams.

In the Coast Range, the tackle and flies in use are very small. The streams are so accessible and fished so much that the fish have become very wary, and it requires the combined skill of the fly-maker and angler to creel them.

Most of the flies in use are tied on Pennell sneck bend hooks, ranging in size from 1 to 5, as those hooks are numbered. The varieties most used, I think, are the Red Spinner, March Brown, Black Spider, Hen Pheasant Hackle, Governor, Red Ant, Red Spider, and Duns of various shades.

We have an old fly-tier by the name of J. S. Bean, who has lived here in San Francisco for many years. He is most ingenious and prolific in his devices for new flies; but few of them, however, are in general use. I will send you three devices, more or less novel in the combination of colors.

No. 1 is called the Bicknell fly. It is purely a fancy fly, and was named after a genial old angler here. The wing is taken from the bronze curlew or black ibis frequently found in our fresh-water marshes. It is a good fly in most waters.

No. 2, the Beans fly, is made after a pattern gotten up by Mr. T. Ellert Beans, a noted angler from San José. He uses it with astonishing success in waters about Lake Tahoe. He told me he took the pattern from an actual fly, but I have never seen the fly.

No. 3 is the Wilson Ant. You will notice the wing of this fly is entirely different from those in common use for any ant. I took the pattern from a natural winged ant found in our sand-hills. They come out in August and September in great numbers. I have used it with great success in our coast streams, and in the lakes and streams of the Sierras.

There is probably no section of the whole country where so great a diversity of opinion prevails in regard to fishing-tackle, especially as to the color of flies and the kind and size of hooks. You will find anglers of fair repute fishing in waters in the northern portion of the State with flies large enough to kill salmon, and with tackle in proportion.

In San Francisco, I think the modern tendency of anglers is to the use of small flies and small tackle. For some four years past I have been using the sneck bend hook; the largest No. 5, and from that down to 00. I find that I can kill more fish and get more pleasure with them than in the use of large tackle and flies.

Last season, I fished in the Sierras and in our coast streams considerably, and used exclusively small flies without any snell; that is, the down-eyed Pennell bronzed hook. I have proven to my entire satisfaction that the fly tied on the down-eyed hook is far superior to the fly tied on the snelled hook.

| | | |
|---|---|---|
| *California.* | Gray Drake.<br>Green Drake.<br>Royal Coachman.<br>Black Gnat.<br>White Miller.<br>Hackles. | Trout. |

E. F. PETTENGILL,                    Eureka,                    Cal.

Fly-fishing is in its infancy here as yet, but it is getting more popular every season. The mountain streams are very clear in this locality, so that dark flies are the best, such as the Brown Hackle and Black Gnat for June and July fishing; later in the season, the Red Ibis, Royal Coachman, and Golden Palmer. For evening fishing white flies are good. I use the Carlisle hook, No. 6 to 10, and a long strand of clear gut. The trout in these streams range from eight ounces to one and a half pounds. In the river and lake fishing the water is more or less colored, so that lighter flies are better, — the Coachman, Gray and Green Drake, White Miller, and a fly I don't know the name of. It has blue and white wings, with light drab body, and is very good on a bright day; so also is the Gray Hackle; in fact, we all carry a good supply of Hackles.

I use in the rivers and lakes a double leader, stained short loops, also stained No. 4 to 8 hooks, Carlisle.

The trout weigh from one pound to five, and quite often salmon weighs from eight to twelve pounds.

| | | |
|---|---|---|
| *California.* | Caddis.<br>Black Gnat.<br>White Miller.<br>Royal Coachman.<br>Coachman.<br>Professor.<br>Brown Hackle. | Trout. |

G. E. DAVIS, M. D.,        San Francisco,        Cal.

The best flies for the California waters I have found to be Brown and Black Hackles, with a gold or silver tag, dun, stone, or brown hen's wing, Professor, Coachman, Royal Coachman, Black Gnat, White Miller, and Caddis.

The Caddis is made to copy the natural fly found early in the summer months along our streams, and it is a most killing fly.

The Caddis and dark flies, such as the Brown Hackle (with gold tag and peacock herl body), Black Hackle, and Black Gnat, have been best early in the season; later on came the Duns, Professor, Coachman, Royal Coachman, and White Miller; in the evening I have found the fishing best from the time the shadows strike the water, although the warm mornings are also good.

The best months, in this State and on our streams, are April, May, and June, and September and October.

I have found the Sproat hook to serve my purpose best, in sizes running from No. 6 to No. 10, using frequently No. 7 or No. 8.

I generally use single leaders, and prefer those of medium size. On the McCloud River, where the water is very rapid and the fish larger, one is likely to fasten to two fish; therefore on that river I use the double leaders, and only two flies on my leader.

I am sure the reinforced snells on flies are a great improvement, as the flies are much less apt to break off at the end of the hook after being used any length of time.

| *California.* | { Brown Hen. <br> { Yellow Bumble. | { Trout. |

St. Charles A. Biederman,                    San Francisco,                    Cal.

For the last two seasons I have been most successful with the Brown Hen and Yellow Bumble, on No. 8 hook; the Brown Hen has often been successful when other flies have failed. I also made a fly myself, which I have used in Boulder Creek and the Big Basin in Santa Cruz County, and in two streams in Tahoe. I took a No. 9 hook, and in the construction of the fly used a gray hen's feather, a piece of brown satin, deer hair, and tinsel thread, tying the concave of wing outward; with that I have caught five fish to one with the flies now on sale.

I am quite positive regarding snells, feeling that they should be light, clear, and with short loops; have given up using the heavy long strands entirely.

I am curious to find out more about an eel that I caught in the San Lorenzo. It was a silvery gray, 3 ft. 2 in. long, 3 in. around in the thickest part, $1\frac{1}{4}$ in. around tail, and weighed $12\frac{3}{4}$ lbs. I had to use a net in landing him, after playing him two good long hours.

## PLATE EE.

No. 282. Yellow Miller.

No. 283. White Miller.

No. 284. W. H. Hammett.

No. 285. Triumph.

No. 286. Tipperlinn.

No. 287. "W. T."

**Nos. 282 and 283.** The Yellow Miller and the White Miller are flies made in imitation of the natural insects. Their effectiveness is proved by their frequency in the lists of the different anglers given in these pages.

**No. 284.** The W. H. Hammett was designed by Mr. W. H. Hammett, of Newport, R. I., and intended for black bass fishing in that State. The fly has proved of more extended service, and taking with trout as well as bass.

**No. 285.** The Triumph was an attempt to combine in a rather dark fly the colors thought alluring to black bass; the result was so satisfactory that it was called a triumph, and continued to be known as such. Invented by C. F. Orvis, 1882.

**No. 286.** The Tipperlinn. A long time ago, in the first of our fly-making, a dear friend was often beside the fly-table, embroidery in hand or reading aloud, while we busied ourselves with the flies. Much of her time had been spent in Scotland, and a house where many of her happiest days had been passed was called Tipperlinn. One day, as we were busy together, she said suddenly, "Now make a fly unlike anything you ever have made before, for I have a name I want to give it." The fly was made, and she called it Tipperlinn. Memory often brings visions of Mattie Williamson's bright face, winning manners, and gracious intelligence, and we cannot yet feel reconciled that she could not have been spared longer to us, she was so talented and so lovely, and loved and needed by so many.

**No. 287.** The "W. T." Mr. W. Thomson has written much of interest in the fishing papers, but of all his accounts we think we like best that of his departure from his home in Scotland, with twenty other young men, for Australia, to engage in sheep raising. Arriving there, they found gold had been discovered; then came their weary tramp through the sands to the gold-fields, and the halt on the way when they had a day of wonderful fishing. All this and more he relates in his quiet graphic language, until your interest is keen and lasting in this man of adventures. Later life found him settled in Canada, and now in Michigan. We shall ever hold in grateful remembrance a few letters of kindly encouragement once written to us by " W. T. ;" and although we see less of his writings in the papers than we did, we wish for him for whom this fly was named, peace and comfort in these his later years.

Let earth in gold be garmented,
And tented in her tent of blue ;
Let goodly rivers glide between
Their leaning willow walls of green ;
Let all things be fill'd of the sun,
And full of the warm winds of the sea,
And I beneath my vine and tree
Take rest, nor war with any one.

JOAQUIN MILLER.

# OREGON.

Gen. O. D. Green . . . . . .
{ Black Midge.
Royal Coachman.
Montreal.
Grizzly King, etc. }

Gen. J. H. Eaton . . . . . . .
{ Coachman.
Brown Hackle.
Jungle Cock.
Green Drake, etc. }

E. Shelley Morgan . . . . . .
{ Natural Flies
  for Bait. }

S. H. Green . . . . . . . .
{ Royal Coachman.
Professor.
White Miller.
Yellow May, etc. }

W. F. Burrell . . . . . . .
{ Coachman.
Deer-hair Flies. }

H. O. Wilkinson . . . . . . .
{ Brown Hackle.
Governor.
Coachman, etc. }

Dr. Jay Tuttle . . . . . . .
{ Brown Hackle.
Nicholson.
Professor. }

M. O. Lownsdale . . . . . . .
{ Silver Lady.
Maid of the Mist.
Humming Bird.
Coachman.
Jock Scott.
Donkey, etc. }

| *Oregon.* | { Black Midge. <br> Royal Coachman. <br> Grizzly King, etc. | { Trout. |

GEN. O. D. GREEN,     Fort Leavenworth,     Kansas.

My daily official duties are such that, after completing them, any more writing is a painful labor; but yet, in view of the fact that I take a deep interest in all legitimate matters connected with fly-fishing; that I have been a lifelong lover, and for very many years a keen follower, of the gentle sport; and further, that I am indebted to you personally for several nice suggestions or hints in your writings, I feel that it would be simply churlish in me not to give you a few words in reply to your courteous letter of inquiry. However, I shall ask you to give full credit to my statements as to lack of time, and consequently to make due allowance for haste, condition, and brevity.

I will consider your questions in the order you put them. First, name my favorites in the order of my preference: Black Midge, an imitation of a small green grasshopper, name unknown, Royal Coachman, Montreal, Grizzly King, Cow Dung, Coachman, Jungle Cock, and Brown Hackle. This is a small list in view of the almost infinite variations, but in my experience of nearly forty years, and extending from the Berkshire Hills to the Pacific coast, I have never struck a stream, pond, lake, nor a day where a cast could not be made from it that would do as good service as mortal man ought to ask. Of course I know there are restricted localities and seasons where some special fly is, or is supposed to be, possessed of universal attractions and ability; but I contend, nevertheless, that a cast made up from the given list, properly handled, is abundantly able for the sportsman's purpose on any waters.

To the second question my testimony is largely given above, but in connection therewith, and as the result of my experience, I should add, disregard very greatly the term " locality " and the sense in which you use it, and substitute therefor a consideration of the differing conditions between rapid-running and standing (lake or pond) waters, and between large and small waters.

In rapid-running waters my cast will be : for upper dropper, a Black Midge ; for lower dropper, either a small green grasshopper, Montreal, or a Cow Dung, according to fancy, but nine times out of ten it will be the grasshopper ; for stretcher, a Royal Coachman or a Grizzly King always.

For standing waters both droppers will be as above, either bright or dark days, but the stretcher will be varied between the lightest and darkest colored accordingly as the day may be dark or bright. In considering the difference between large and small waters, which practically means the difference between large and small fish in a general sense, I should use essentially the same casts as before indicated, only increasing the size of the flies commensurately with the size of the water to be fished.

A complete answer to your third and fourth questions involves information and time requisite to produce a treatise on the subject of fly-fishing. I have neither, and accordingly pass them over. In answer to the fifth : several years ago I saw a fly in use on the Williamson River, in southern Oregon, which was a world's wonder for large fish, and I have never heard of it since ; I presume it to be entirely new to you and all other Eastern fishermen. It was a very large fly, — as it should be, according to my theory of " large waters," Williamson River being a genuine river, and the home of the greatest number of the largest fish of any stream in the world, unquestionably. I do not remember all the distinguishing features of the fly, but the main one was the use of the small feathers from the neck of the loon (great American diver), each of which had a white dot about the size of and greatly resembling a fish's eye; whether or not its wonderful acceptability was due to those " fish eyes " I do not know, but at the time I so believed. In the river mentioned a two-pound fish was a small one, and I doubt if one of that size ever got a taste of this fly, for the reason that those of from 5 lbs. to 12 lbs. (the latter was the largest size caught while I was there, though they are caught as high as 16 lbs., or even heavier) were so greedy for it that the " small fry " had to take a back seat, as it were. I should not be surprised if this fly were " taking " on the Rangeley Lakes, or other large standing waters in Maine and Canada.

I understand the inventor was Surgeon Henry McEldery,[1] U. S. Army, and you can correspond with him, if you desire, at Fort Wayne, Detroit, Mich.

For ordinary fishing I want the smallest practicable hooks, and prefer the Sproat for kind and shape.

I use the very finest (lightest) leaders, mist-colored preferred, and of course want snells to correspond; for upper dropper a snell from five to seven inches in length, lower dropper about four inches, single strands.

[1] See Klamath, No. 67, Plate J.

Gen. J. H. Eaton,                    Portland,                              Oregon.

Favorite flies in the order here named : —

| | |
|---|---|
| Coachman. | Brown Hackle. |
| Brown Hackle, with Palmer body. | Romeyn. |
| Jungle Cock. | Soldier Palmer. |
| Green Drake. | Yellow Drake. |
| White Miller. | Professor. |

I prefer the Coachman (including Royal Coachman) and Brown Hackle. I use the Coachman on all occasions and in all waters. I like the Brown Hackle with palmer body, the hackles alternating with yellow or red in the spirals; when these are worn or ineffective, I then use the other flies named, as I may fancy; I am almost always successful with Coachman and Brown Hackle.

Kind of hooks: preferably always Sproat and O'Shaughnessy, Nos. 11 and 12 and 6. The steel wire of the O'Shaughnessy seems rather heavy for small flies; size of wire of the Sproat is better.

Snells about five inches long (as you make them); they should be reinforced (doubled) about three fourths inch near the hook, — so made by Mr. Bean, of San Francisco. It is unimportant whether they are stained or clear, but they should be of light, single gut. The same as to gut leaders; double or twisted leaders are not used for ordinary trout fishing on this Pacific slope; single, strong gut is sufficiently good.

In some of the creeks in Oregon, in May and June, there is a yellowish fly produced from a worm or caddis-like insect upon which the trout feed; when feeding on this they will touch no artificial fly unless strongly resembling it. I am not able to give a minute description of said fly, but it is known to my friend, Major J. P. Canby, U. S. A., stationed here in Portland.

*Oregon.*      Natural Flies for Bait.

E. SHELLEY MORGAN,      Portland,      Oregon.

Accompanying this, I send you three specimens of flies, two of them males, and one female. You will notice the males are much the larger.

I do not know whether I can give you a good description or history of these flies or not, but I will tell you all I know of them.

They are first found in August, on the bottom of flat rocks at the edge of the mountain streams.

I have often turned a stone over and found as many as twelve or thirteen shells on a stone. When in the water on those stones, they are in a shell of gravel and mud about an inch long. How long they stay in that state, or get so, I do not know, but when they get far enough along the shell bursts, and they crawl out on top of the rocks, where the sun seems to develop them, and then they fly on to the willow-trees along the banks; there they cling to the leaves until they fall, or the wind blows them off into the river.

Before the flies came out we used to gather these shells, break them open, and use the flies as they were for bait; but they are very soft and tender then, and will not remain on the hook long.

These flies always float down stream head first. When a large trout sees one, he gently rises to the surface, opens his mouth to let the fly float in, and then disappears. These large trout generally lie close to the banks, as most of the flies float near them when they fall from the branches that line the banks of the streams.

The fly usually floats with outspread wings, especially when attached to the hook. A very light hook should be used, the bend coming out at the head of the insect.

Some of the male flies are much larger than any I have sent to you.

These flies are most plentiful on the bushes in the middle or latter part of September. They are by far the best bait I have ever used.

The 3d of last September, two friends and I started from one ranch on the McKenzie River, and in two hours returned with thirty-eight pounds of trout: the largest one measured from tip to tip sixteen and three quarters inches; the smallest one, ten and one half inches. We had six that averaged thirteen and one half inches. Those we caught with these flies, most of them taken from the shells, as the others were very scarce at that time; that is, the fully developed ones.

NOTE. — This letter was most interesting to us, because accompanying it were three specimens of *stone flies*. Mr. Morgan's letter would imply that they were caddis flies, as he mentions taking the undeveloped flies from the cases formed in the bottom of the streams, but the flies sent were undoubtedly stone flies. These would naturally be found on the stones, as he first mentions in his letter, but it is questionable whether the same insect was found in the cases. We are inclined to think that both stone flies and caddis flies inhabited the stream, and in some way he confounded the larvæ of the two flies, either of which are valuable as bait, and not unlike in the larval and pupal stages, though the imago or perfect fly is dissimilar. (See mention of these in Part I.) The flies were sent to Professor Packard for identification, who also declared them to be stone flies, but was uncertain as to the species and genus. — M. E. O. M.

| *Oregon.* | Royal Coachman.<br>Professor.<br>Brown Hackle.<br>Soldier Palmer.<br>Yellow May.<br>White Miller. | Trout. |

S. H. GREEN,                    Portland,                              Oregon.

Permit me to say that, after a pretty thorough trial of many of the leading flies, in these waters, I have settled down to the following combination for all seasons of the year, in all kinds of weather, and at all times of day : stretcher fly, Royal Coachman ; lead fly, Professor ; with Brown Hackle for middle or second dropper.

I was in the Molalla country last summer, two weeks in June and two weeks the last of August, fishing for trout. The Molalla, with its tributaries, come from the Cascade Range, regular mountain streams. Myself and companion tested the matter thoroughly (to our own satisfaction) there. I have tested the fly-question at a dozen different places in Oregon and Washington, and at nearly all seasons, morning, noon, and evening, the above-described arrangement proved most satisfactory.

I would add that the Imbrie, the Reuben Wood, the Soldier Palmer, and in some streams, late in the evening, the Yellow May, were also excellent.

Mr. W. J. Newman, my companion in many of these trips, after fishing the waters of Idaho, Montana, Utah, Wyoming, Oregon, and Washington, determined that the above arrangement is about the most reliable, except that in Colorado and Montana he would at dusk use a White Miller in preference to a Hackle. The White Miller for Oregon waters is not good.

---

| *Oregon.* | { Coachman.<br>{ Deer-hair Flies. | { Trout. |

W. F. BURRELL, Portland, Oregon.

My favorite flies for the waters of the Northwest are Coachman and Deer-hair flies ; the latter are tied from the deer's hair when it is " in the red."

Salmon fishing with a fly, in the Clackamas River, a tributary of the Willamette, was a new experience with us last spring. My brother, Herman J. Burrell, now of Moscow, Idaho, was quite successful in fishing there, and if you ask him, he can perhaps give particulars about the kind of flies and tackle used. It was the first time salmon had been known to take the fly in Oregon or Washington fresh waters.

---

| | | |
|---|---|---|
| *Oregon.* | { Brown Hackle.<br>Governor.<br>Coachman.<br>Cow Dung.<br>Green Drake. | } Trout. |

H. O. WILKINSON, Fort Klamath, Oregon.

The favorite flies in this vicinity are Brown Hackle Palmers, Dark Coachman, Governor, Bee, Claret, Cow Dung, and Green Drake. The waters here are all from springs, and are perfectly clear; hence the use of dark flies. We fish entirely within a radius of fourteen miles, and have no less than ten fine trout streams, where we take the Rainbow and Dolly Varden trout in large numbers, and in sizes ranging from fingerlings to eight and ten pounds.

No hook smaller than No. 8 Sproat is of use, while the general sizes are Nos. 2, 1, and 1/0, with heavy stained snells. During the early day such flies as the Brown Palmer or Brown Hackle, Governor, and Coachman prove the most killing, while for evening work the Cow Dung and Green Drake are best.

Men who have fished the world over say that here they find the finest sport they have ever enjoyed, and although I am only an observing novice, I am sure no better could be obtained. I believe, however, there are better flies than we have been using for these waters, and some time I intend to take a greater assortment and experiment upon their respective merits. We are four hundred and fifty miles from the nearest tackle shops, Portland and San Francisco, so I have never carried in my book any but the well-known flies.

A recent article in the "Forest and Stream," by Captain Bendire, said the Ibis was the favorite fly for these waters, but this is not corroborated by those who have tried it; in fact in this country you can scarcely find any one using a Scarlet Ibis.

---

| *Oregon.* | { Brown Hackle. Nicholson. Professor. | } Trout. |
|---|---|---|

DR. JAY TUTTLE,        Astoria,        Oregon.

Among the well-known flies, the Brown Hackle, red body, catches more fish than any other. Next to this my favorite is the Nicholson, next the Professor.

I never enjoy catching anything less than a half-pound fish. I use a good-sized fly, and sometimes, late in the season, September or October, late in the afternoon, the fish will rise to an Ibis when nothing else will lure them. I have not paid particular attention to style of hook, but think they have generally been No. 1 Limerick. I like a long snell, and double of slender gut. I fish, or have fished, the waters of Coos Bay and tributaries, and of Tillamook Bay and tributaries, and the tributaries of Columbia River in western Oregon.

# PLATE FF.

No. 288. Fiery Dragon.      No. 290. Humming Bird.

No. 289. Maid of the Mill.      No. 291. Silver Lady.

No. 288.

> "To-day I saw the Dragon-fly
> Come from the wells where he did lie.
> An inner impulse rent the veil
> Of his old husk : from head to tail
> Came out clear plates of sapphire mail.
>
> "He dried his wings ; like gauze they grew.
> Through crofts and pastures wet with dew
> A living flash of light he flew."

A brief account of the Fiery Dragon fly will be found in the letter from Mr. H. P. Ufford, its originator. In connection with what he writes it may be well to mention that though trout are supposed to have an aversion to the natural dragon-fly, we have frequent testimony regarding them as a lure for grayling; also many statements of their being found in the stomachs of these fish. Very perfect imitations can be made of the several different species of dragon-flies, and though they are a little unwieldy to cast and retain a resemblance to a " living flash of light," yet with care they might be so manipulated as to be effective.

Nos. 289, 290, and 291. The Maid of the Mill, Humming Bird, and Silver Lady are the inventions of Mr. M. O. Lownsdale. In his letter written from Oregon he gives full details regarding these flies and their success in deep waters. They are certainly a revelation as trout flies, and will solve the difficulties to many who have been unsuccessful with the ordinary small trout flies, such as are used on the streams of the Eastern States.

Oregon.

{
Silver Lady.
Maid of the Mill.
Humming Bird.
Coachman.
Queen of the Water.
Reuben Wood.
Jock Scott.
Donkey.
}

M. O. Lownsdale,                 Portland,                    **Oregon.**

> " Just out of the swirl of the veering stream,
>     In niches and caverns 'neath moss-fringed shelves
> Like gossamer floating in idle dream,
>     In weirdest haunts hewn by the river-elves,
> In castles of crystal whose turrets old
>     And battlements rugged like outworks rise,
> In vestures of silver and azure and gold
>     The indolent king of the river lies."

Ever since the settlement of the country by the white people Oregon has been preeminently noted as a paradise for the trout fisherman. But of late years the encroachments of civilization have robbed many of the streams of their plethora of fish, and the angler must now seek the more inaccessible mountain streams for the sport which he might have enjoyed, a few years ago, in all the streams of the Willamette Valley. But in the brawling rivers that tear through our narrow mountain passes are still to be found those monsters whose tugging at the point of a six-ounce rod plays such havoc with the fisher's pulses.

We have no brook trout in Oregon, the *Salmo Irideus*, or Rainbow trout, being our only representative of the trout family. Specimens of these gamy fish have been taken weighing seven and eight pounds, and possibly heavier, but the average weight of " big fish " in our waters is about three pounds. The streams running from and through the Coast Range Mountains to the sea are probably the finest trout rivers in America. In appearance they are typical fishing rivers, and, as they traverse a very rugged country, are a succession of riffles and immense pools.

A party of three, of whom the writer was one, passed the summer of 1889 in these mountains, accompanied by a servingman, who was at once guide, muleteer, and cook. During the greater part of the summer we were continually moving our camp, thus securing new ground for each day's work. We were only moderately successful in the early part of the season, for, though there were myriads of small fish in the rivers, the big fellows did not come up from the ocean until about the middle of July. In many of the interior rivers these trout never visit salt water, but in all the coast streams they make an annual seaward pilgrimage after the salmon spawning season. In July our party was on the Doherty, a stream of great local celebrity, so that we were able to take advantage of the mid-summer run.

An experience of many years has taught us the efficacy of large flies for this class of fish. Large fish do not rise often, and a very substantial and toothsome morsel is needed to tempt them up through the clear deep pools they most affect. I will not say that small flies may not often receive as many strikes as large ones, but in rough water heavy fish will tear out the hold of a small hook. Our flies are constructed somewhat like bass flies, imitating no insect, but suggesting approximately the appearance of a nondescript moth. We have three varieties which have been found to be extremely satisfactory. No. 1 is the Silver Lady, tied with silver body, brown hackles, slate-colored wings, and often silver streamers for tails. The wings are solid feathers taken from a young robin's wing, with the under slate-colored side being turned outward. No. 2 is the Maid of the Mill, with rough canary-colored body bound with gold tinsel, yellow and brown hackles, and double wings, each of four gaudy feathers from the Mongolian pheasant, with streamers of golden pheasant plumes. No. 3 is the Humming Bird, a fly with either silver or lemon-colored body, orange, scarlet, and brown hackles, wings of the peacock-blue feathers from a mallard wing, with red and white streamers. All these flies are tied on Sproat hooks from No. 1 to 00 in size, and are from one and a half to two inches in length. Large and gaudy weapons indeed for a trout fisherman. However, they are the results of many experiments, and it is an almost unvarying rule to see large fish taken on them in pools where common flies were unsuccessful, or if successful had ceased to attract.

Of the well-known flies, our favorites for the large trout of this locality are the Coachman, Queen of the Water, and Reuben Wood; and among salmon flies, the Jock Scott and Donkey, the smallest of which should be on No. 2 Sproat hooks. One of these flies is always on my cast as a dropper.

The large trout in the Doherty River seldom notice a fly before nine o'clock in the morning, a habit of which I heartily approve; and, on our working-days, the sun has already burnished the overhanging maples before we put the "bugs" in motion. Our last day's sport on the Doherty will long be remembered by two of our party. We fished from Dry Stocking Camp, through the wilderness, past the Islands, and on to Gum-boot Bar, a distance of about three miles. This was a Silver Lady day, for the fastidious fellows would notice nothing else. At the entrance of the wilderness is the most magnificent pool on the river, and we had scarcely flecked its quiet surface with our casts when a four-pounder, bewitched by the charms of the Lady, came with such a rush from the limpid depths that he sprang sheer five feet in the air with his glittering prize. He struck the water heavily, and was off with such impetuous speed that the next moment an iridal flash in the air at the very foot of the pool told that he had discovered the treachery of his Lady. But, like all his tribe, he scorned surrender, and rushing to the riffle above he thrashed the surface of the swift current for an anxious moment, then was off again for the quiet water below, where, after a nervous half hour's battle, he was guided into the shallows and the net slipped under him. He was the king of the day, but on the two rods at work at least twenty fish were taken that weighed from two to three pounds each.

In these fishing jaunts, when the mountains are clothed in their most voluptuous dress, when the forest is redolent with the odors of swooning flowers, and the river gleams with a thousand silver lights, while everywhere are rivulets that drain what must be the springs of eternal youth, one may drink deep of an elixir of life more potent than that of Septimius Felton. In this sense, our last day on the Doherty was idyllic and prolific of thrilling scenes, while the victories we dramatically rehearsed about the camp-fire at Gum-boot Bar seemed heroic; and when we laid down at night, bathed in the amorous breath of the pines, we were fretted only by the " thrut " of a great trout striking in the pool below, and were lulled to rest by the witching song the siren of the river sings; and a crescent burning brightly in the eastern sky threw enchantment over all.

Here are cool mosses deep,
And thro' the moss the ivies creep,
And in the stream the long-leaved flowers weep,
And from the craggy ledge the poppy hangs in sleep.

Why are we weigh'd upon with heaviness,
And utterly consumed with sharp distress,
While all things else have rest from weariness?
All things have rest : why should we toil alone,
We only toil who are the first of things,
And make perpetual moan,
Still from one sorrow to another thrown ;
Nor ever fold our wings,
And cease from wanderings,
Nor steep our brows in slumber's holy balm,
Nor hearken what the inner Spirit sings,
"There is no joy but calm !"
Why should we only toil, the roof and crown of things ?

TENNYSON.

## "HIC HABITAT FELICITAS."

"Felicity. Enquire within.
 Truly, the goddess is at home ! "
 So read, so thought the rakes of Rome,
 Some frail one's lintel fain to win.

And now it blares thro' bronze and tin,
 Thro' clarion, organ, catcall, comb :
"Felicity. Enquire within.
 Truly, the goddess is at home ! "

For, tent or studio, bank or bin,
 Platonic porch, Petræan dome,
 Where'er our hobbies champ and foam,
 There o'r the brave old sign we pin :
"Felicity. Enquire within."                     HENLEY.

Oliver Wendell Holmes has said that "it's faith in something and enthusiasm for something that make life worth looking at." Frank, the fisherman of the picture, is one of those who, like "Fishin' Jimmy," "allers loved fishin', an' knowed 't was the best thing in the hull airth ; " but there are many of us who are never able to attain the felicity that bides under the tattered coat, or understand the restful joy in a temporary freedom from all ambitions, except, perhaps, a desire to capture a big trout that has long eluded us. A small boy of our acquaintance has ideas of his own which do not always accord with those of his guardians. One day his aunt gently reproved him for some breach of propriety, saying, "I would not do that, Teddy, dear," but Teddy promptly and cheerfully replied, "Teddy would ; " and although we might not

"HIC HABITAT FELICITAS"

find contentment in shabby garments and in wading the streams, Frank would, — and verily, is he not to be envied in it?

He has been guide, tutor, friend, to many a weary, brain-taxed citizen; his broad shoulders have taken many a burden from softer muscles, until now they are bent and weakened, but his voice is yet genial, and his cheerfulness contagious. By the camp-fire he has often sought to be " a fisher of men," and to convert his hearers to his doctrines of Jeffersonian democracy and Second Adventism. Few men have a better command of the Scriptures than he in support of the latter. After a long talk, one day, my father said to him, " Well, Frank, if it is to be as you say it will, and ' the righteous inherit the earth,' don't you think you would like your portion to be on the shores of Bourn Pond?" The sudden look of delight at the thought, and the earnest exclamation, " Well, Charley, I should!" was something to remember. Bourn Pond is a tiny lake away up on the mountain. The trees crowd to its very edge, and the trout that inhabit its deep waters are unlike those of the mountain streams, being shorter, plumper, and of salmon-hued flesh. There are many who will recognize Frank, and remember him as their guide to this favorite camping-ground in the Green Mountains.

Newspapers are tantalizing things, containing so much that you do not want to see, and so much that is too good to be lost. We have searched in vain for an old copy of the " Journal of Commerce," edited by Mr. William C. Prime. In one of his occasional letters to this paper Mr. Prime wrote charmingly and forcibly of Hobbies, their value and pleasure to mankind. We desired to quote from it his advice regarding true enjoyment and the vigor and happiness to be found in cultivating some special interest. We cannot attempt to repeat his words, but we wish we were qualified to urge, as he did, the advantage of some agreeable and absorbing pursuit as a recreation and change from the weary routine of the duties and responsibilities of life. It has been the aim to show in these pages how many there are who find in fishing just this restful occupation. As Mr. Prime has said elsewhere, "To you, my friend, who know nothing of the gentle and purifying associations of the angler's life, these may seem strange notions," and again, "I have gathered together the chapters of this book, if perchance it may serve as a companion to any who would go a-fishing if he could, but cannot, or help another who has gone a-fishing to enjoy the rest which he thus obtained," we shall be more than repaid.

We have purposely introduced the expressions, fancies, and opinions of many, that it may be realized what a goodly company there is who, as Walton says, find fishing "like the virtue of humility, which has a calmness of spirit and a world of other blessings attending upon it."

We are reluctant to lay aside this last sheet, there is so much more we fain would add. Our books have been around us in constant companionship, and we have wanted to call attention to so much more in them of value. These authors, and those whose letters are in this collection, are all "brothers of the angle," and we are sure they will find a keen pleasure in a thorough knowledge of one another. We owe a debt of deep gratitude to those whose names will be met over their letters, and to those whose writings, longer known, have furnished us words to confirm our more doubtful authority, or to enhance the interest of a fly by legend or tale of human nature, or a word picture of memorable beauty.

But there are others who believe that "angling is an art worthy the knowledge and practice of a wise man," who have not written, who nevertheless have shown a helpful interest. Among these are Mr. L. D. Alexander, of New York city, and Mr. Robert Clark, of Cincinnati, whose fine collections of angling-books will be displayed at the coming Exposition; Mr. James B. Baker, who first suggested and urged our keeping notes recording any facts of interest relative to artificial flies, that their history might be preserved in some tangible form, this book being the result of that suggestion; Mrs. M. E. Robbins, who made the drawings of insects; Mr. Thacher and Mr. Way, who loaned the photographs to be reproduced. Mr. W. C. Prime, Dr. Henshall, Mr. A. N. Cheney, Professor J. H. Gerould, the Rev. William B. Walker, and many other kind friends have been gratefully in mind as we have tried to unite the voices of many; and their faith and encouragement have made the arranging of this collection a pleasure, and the expression of our own opinions easier. The words of Omar Khayyám are with us : —

> " Yon rising Moon that looks for us again —
> How oft hereafter will she wax and wane ;
> How oft hereafter rising look for us
> Through this same Garden — and for *one* in vain !

> " And when like her, O Sáki, you shall pass
> Among the Guests Star-scatter'd on the Grass,
> And in your blissful errand reach the spot
> Where I made One — turn down an empty Glass."

# INDEX TO PLATES AND FLIES.

INDEX TO PLATES AND FLIES.

| | |
|---|---|
| 271. Massasaga . . . . . . . . CC | 281. Premier . . . . . . . . . DD |
| 258. Matador . . . . . . . . AA | 186. Prime Gnat . . . . . . . S |
| 273. Mather . . . . . . . . CC | 71. Prince Edward . . . . . . J |
| 176. Maurice . . . . . . . . S | 192. Professor . . . . . . . T |
| 268. Max von dem Borne . . . BB | 190. Puffer . . . . . . . T |
| 275. McCloud . . . . . . . CC | 197. Quack Doctor . . . . . . T |
| 21. Mitchell . . . . . . . B | 196. Quaker . . . . . . . T |
| 56. Moisic-Grub . . . . . . H | 195. Queen of the Water . . . . T |
| 179. Montreal, old pattern . . . . S | 278. Raven . . . . . . . DD |
| 54. Moose . . . . . . . H | 280. Reade . . . . . . . . DD |
| 57. Mooselucmaguntic . . . . H | 200. Red Ant . . . . . . . T |
| 177. Morrison . . . . . . . S | 202. Red Ash . . . . . . . T |
| 269. Munro . . . . . . . BB | 198. Red Fox . . . . . . . T |
| 62. Nameless . . . . . . . I | 1. Red Hackle . . . . . . A |
| 180. Neversink . . . . . . . S | 201. Red Head . . . . . . T |
| 69. New Lake . . . . . . . J | 230. Red Quill . . . . . . V |
| 61. Nicholson . . . . . . . I | 203. Reuben Wood . . . . . . T |
| 68. No Name . . . . . . . J | 199. Romeyn . . . . . . . T |
| 24. Notion . . . . . . . . C | 40. Royal Coachman . . . . . E |
| 181. Oak Fly . . . . . . . . S | 146. Royal Governor . . . . . Q |
| 262. Oconomowoc . . . . . . AA | 223. Saltoun . . . . . . . V |
| 182. Olive Gnat . . . . . . . S | 79. Saranac . . . . . . . L |
| 259. Ondawa . . . . . . . AA | 6. Scarlet Hackle . . . . . . A |
| 66. Oquossoc . . . . . . J | 276. Scarlet Ibis, Bass . . . . . DD |
| 184. Orange Black . . . . . . S | 205. Scarlet Ibis, Trout . . . . U |
| 116. Orange Coachman . . . . . O | 76. Seth Green . . . . . . K |
| 183. Orange Dun . . . . . . S | 209. Shad Fly . . . . . . . U |
| 65. Orange Miller . . . . . . I | 206. Shain Fly . . . . . . . U |
| 261. Oriole . . . . . . . AA | 81. Sheenan . . . . . . . L |
| 274. Owner . . . . . . . CC | 18. Silver Doctor . . . . . . B |
| 185. Pale Evening Dun . . . . . S | 72. Silver Doctor, H. P. Wells's pat- |
| 191. Parker . . . . . . . . T | tern . . . . . . . . K |
| 277. —— . . . . . . . . . DD | 73. Silver Doctor, J. G. Shearer's pat- |
| 60. Parmacheene Belle . . . . . I | tern . . . . . . . . K |
| 188. Peacock Fly . . . . . . S | 74. Silver Doctor, C. F. Orvis's pat- |
| 189. Pheasant . . . . . . . . T | tern . . . . . . . . K |
| 59. Plymouth Rock . . . . . . H | 207. Silver Horns . . . . . . U |
| 263. Polka . . . . . . . . . AA | 77. Silver Ibis . . . . . . . J |
| 194. Poor Man's Fly . . . . . T | 291. Silver Lady . . . . . . . FF |
| 33. Popham . . . . . . . . D | 219. Silver Sedge . . . . . . V |
| 187. Portland . . . . . . . S | 216. Soldier Gnat . . . . . . U |

# CORRESPONDENTS.